HAWTHORNE AND WOMEN

HAWTHORNE

AND WOMEN

Engendering and Expanding the Hawthorne Tradition

Edited by

JOHN L. IDOL JR. and
MELINDA M. PONDER

UNIVERSITY OF MASSACHUSETTS PRESS Amherst

Copyright © 1999 by the University of Massachusetts Press

All rights reserved

Printed in the United States of America

LC 98-28167

ISBN 1-55849-174-0 (cloth); 178-3 (pbk.)

Designed by Milenda Nan Ok Lee

Printed and bound by BookCrafters, Inc.

Library of Congress Cataloging-in-Publication Data

Hawthorne and women : engendering and expanding the Hawthorne
tradition / edited by John L. Idol Jr., and Melinda M. Ponder.
p.   cm.
Includes bibliographical references and index.
ISBN 1-55849-174-0 (cloth : alk. paper). — ISBN 1-55849-178-3
(pbk. : alk. paper)
1. Hawthorne, Nathaniel, 1804–1864—Characters—Women.
2. American literature—Women authors—History and criticism.
3. Hawthorne, Nathaniel, 1804–1864—Knowledge—Literature.
4. English fiction—Women authors—History and criticism.
5. Hawthorne, Nathaniel, 1804–1864—Influence. 6. Influence
(Literary, artistic, etc.) 7. Women—Books and reading. 8. Sex
role in literature. 9. Women and literature. 10. Women in
literature. I. Idol, John L. II. Ponder, Melinda M.
PS1892.W6H39   1999
813'.3—dc21   98-28167
CIP

British Library Cataloguing in Publication data are available.

This book is published with the support and cooperation of the
University of Massachusetts Boston.

For Nina Baym, Rita Gollin, David Kesterson, and Thomas Woodson,
whose pioneering scholarship and criticism inspired us to do this book

CONTENTS

MELINDA M. PONDER AND JOHN L. IDOL JR.

ACKNOWLEDGMENTS

The authors and publisher gratefully acknowledge permission to use the following materials: John Gatta's essay entitled "*The Scarlet Letter* as Pre-text for Flannery O'Connor's 'Good Country People,'" by permission of the *Nathaniel Hawthorne Review;* John Idol's essay entitled "Mary Russell Mitford: Hawthorne as the Best Living Writer of Prose Fiction," a portion of a longer essay on Mitford as a champion of American authors, which appeared in *Studies in the American Renaissance* (1983), by permission of the editor, Joel Myerson; a condensed version of Patricia Dunlavy Valenti's "Memories of Hawthorne," which originally appeared in *a/b: Auto/Biography Studies* (Spring 1983). Quotations from the correspondence of Sophia Peabody Hawthorne by permission of Henry W. and Albert A. Berg Collection, The New York Public Library, Astor, Lenox, and Tilden Foundations.

INTRODUCTION

Melinda M. Ponder and John L. Idol Jr.

Nathaniel Hawthorne's chagrin that women authors were besting him and his male contemporaries in the marketplace prompted him to call these creators of popular fiction "scribbling women," a demeaning label that he might not have tried to pin on all women writers. In more judicious moments, he realized how important women writers were in building the kind of national readership that would help him sustain his writing career. Although he knew that women critics such as Margaret Fuller and his sister-in-law Elizabeth Palmer Peabody boosted his work in important literary reviews, he lived too short a life to have more than just an inkling of how revered he would become among women writers as they sought to establish their careers. How women as readers, critics, and writers responded to him led us to propose a session on Hawthorne and women at a meeting of the Philological Association of the Carolinas.

When we asked Rita Gollin and David Kesterson to join us for a panel at a gathering of that group at Clemson University, a collection of essays on the topic had not entered our minds. But gatherings of scholars at conferences often stir interest and generate ideas for further study. Such was the case when we began discussing the role of women in launching, supporting, and sustaining Hawthorne's literary reputation. That exchange of ideas led us to identify one group of women whose primary goal was to empower Hawthorne. But what of those women who turned to Hawthorne as a mentor when they studied and practiced the craft of writing? Here was another group, much larger than the other. Had they not also attended the so-called School of Hawthorne? Shouldn't they be considered alongside the men who helped to engender the Hawthorne tradition in American letters? Such questions led us to invite other Hawthorneans to help us weigh Hawthorne's impact as a mentor.

When Richard Brodhead visited the School of Hawthorne, he paused to examine the work of selected male authors, although he knew full well that many women and samples of their writing could be found in the classroom. As he notes in passing in *The School of Hawthorne,* aspiring women writers showed up early and stayed late to learn what they could about the craft of writing and the ways of gaining a publisher. Brodhead's purpose was not to discuss all the promising students who heard the summoning bell but to demonstrate how forces at work in the American literary tradition—including Hawthorne's towering genius—combined to create a powerful institution, one that busily and effectively established a canon of American fiction in the later half of the nineteenth century.

Hawthorne, Brodhead insists, was central to the creation of the traditions of American prose fiction. "It is scarcely too much to say—with some exceptions that are partly significant *as* exceptions—Hawthorne presides over the writing of prose fiction in America in the later half of the nineteenth century. When the writers of this generation look back to an American literary past, it is above all Hawthorne that they look to" (51).

We share Brodhead's conviction and wish in these pages to examine a few more selected samples of work done by students in the Hawthorne school. We also want to bring into sharper focus the work of critics who helped to empower Hawthorne by writing reviews and notices of his work. Those two purposes gave the impetus for this book, an impetus made all the more interesting, we think, because Hawthorne felt decidedly ambivalent about the role of women in literary affairs. He could both defame women writers and declare that women were greatly responsible for what- ever success he enjoyed. Dismissing women writers as "scribblers" no doubt owes more to his jealousy of the financial success of certain women authors than to his regret that they were not artistically accomplished. He was quick to see that women writers were serious (and successful) competitors in the marketplace. He should not have been surprised, however, to discover that women would honor his achievement by acknowledging his mastery of the writer's craft. His successful bid to match or surpass the scribbling sons of England placed him in the forefront of American letters, lifting him to be headmaster of his own school. Whether his pupils sat at his feet, or learned from him in the privacy of their own rooms, Hawthorne provided lessons on subject matters, themes, style, modes of characterization and description, use of local settings, and, above all, patterns to follow during the psychological probing of human nature.

Brodhead has shown us how male students, a few of them battling the anxiety of influence doggedly, put the headmaster's lessons to good use. How female writers, some of them knowing that the headmaster sometimes heatedly scorned writings by members of their sex, put those lessons to use, how they found in Hawthorne's work an engendering force, how they dealt with their own anxieties of influence, and how they ultimately followed the dictates of their own genius all seemed worthy of study. Given the fact that Hawthorne, in certain moods, would have closed the door to practically every aspiring woman student—at his or any other writer's school—we thought it would be particularly interesting to see how selected women writers looked back to Hawthorne for guidance and inspiration and tried to make the cultural and institutional forces that helped him succeed also work for them.

As we worked to pull this project together, we discovered that someone else was exploring how Hawthorne had guided and inspired women writers. We happily welcomed the publication of Emily Miller Budick's *Engendering Romance: Women Writers and the Hawthorne Tradition, 1850–1990* since, to our way of thinking, Budick's rich study was additional proof that Brodhead's pioneering examination deservedly stirred further investigation and commentary.

The essays collected here push that investigation along, but we make no claim that every important writer whose life and work Hawthorne touched in some significant way has been discussed in these pages. With few exceptions, the pieces appearing here represent choices made by invited Hawthorne critics and scholars from a master list of women writers whom we considered to be Hawthorne's pupils. Our ultimate hope is that, one day, all of Hawthorne's pupils will get their due.

Our gathering of essays differs, however, in one important aspect from the studies of Brodhead and Budick: we include pieces concerning women writers whose reviews, notices, and endorsements of Hawthorne's work helped to lift it to the pinnacle of American letters. Before our project developed into a book that far exceeded the contracted number of pages, we intended to reprint more than twenty reviews and notices of Hawthorne's stories and romances by women critics. Except for the four selections surviving in the appendix to this volume, those pieces had to be dropped. Many of them can, however, be found in J. Donald Crowley's *Hawthorne: The Critical Heritage* (1970) or John L. Idol Jr. and Buford Jones's *Nathaniel Hawthorne: The Contemporary Reviews* (1994). Professor Jones is preparing a comprehensive collection of reviews by women. A brief overview of reviews and notices of Hawthorne's work appears below in the third section of our introduction.

Women in Hawthorne's Creative Life

Throughout his literary career, Hawthorne involved women in his writing by seeking their responses to his writing, their help with its preparation and marketing, their emotional and financial support, and their ideas. He began this lifelong pattern of writing for women as his first and most important readers when he was thirteen years old. While being prepared for college by a tutor in Salem, Massachusetts, Hawthorne wrote to his widowed mother, an intelligent and sensitive woman then living in Maine, asking her for her response to his real ambition:

> What do you think of my becoming an Author, and relying for support upon my
> pen. Indeed I think the illegibility of my handwriting is very authorlike. How proud
> you would feel to see my works praised by the reviewers, as equal to proudest produc-
> tions of the scribbling sons of John Bull [England]. (13 Mar. 1821; *CE* 15: 139)[1]

Hawthorne also made use of women for his subject matter and then turned to them as his colleagues, competitors, and disciples. Not surprisingly, Hawthorne's tales and sketches of ordinary scenes in New England and of the domestic stories inside local history appealed originally to women readers because of both his subject matter and his clear but elegant style. Millicent Bell calls such restricted literary subject matter and tone "a feminine vision" (13), a side of Hawthorne noted alike by female and male reviewers (14). Such congruence with his female readers boded well for Hawthorne's future popularity since publishers assumed that the majority of their readers were women (Coultrap-McQuin 46–47).

Cathy Davidson has argued that fictional narratives have been participants in a culture's fictions and have thus empowered their readers (45). In fiction, a woman reader found "a version of her world existing for her sake, and . . . women characters whose opinions mattered" (Davidson 12). In addition, as Wai-Chee Dimock has shown, by creating a gap between what the "female reader is and what she might become," the text becomes an agent of change for its female readers (614). Such domestic fiction is powerful because, according to Jane Tompkins, it asks "what is power, and where is it located?" (160). Sentimental novels "teach the reader how to live without power while waging a protracted struggle in which the strategies of the weak will finally inherit the earth" (165), a theme taken up by Hawthorne as well in his longer works.

Hawthorne's works appealed to women readers partly because he knew about and respected the complexity of women's lives; he had been writing for women readers all his life, shaping his work for their eyes, and he had been surrounded by unusually gifted, literate women whose creative talents had helped him shape his own work.

Because his father had died when Hawthorne was four years old, he grew up living with his two sisters, Elizabeth ("Ebe") and Maria Louisa, his mother (Elizabeth Manning Hawthorne), his mother's sisters—Mary, who was the first relative to suggest that all his aunts and uncles pool their resources to help pay for Hawthorne's college education, Maria, and Priscilla—and his grandmothers Manning and Hawthorne. As recent commentators such as Emily Budick and Walter Herbert have noted, such a childhood in the midst of a variety of girls and women gave Hawthorne an antipatriarchal, feminist perspective on life.[2] He knew firsthand about the cruel impoverishment of single women like his widowed mother and unmarried aunts and, later, his own sisters. His relationships with these women were positive, on the whole. He learned of their abilities and respected their strengths. Although he was separated from his mother during most of his adolescent and college years, he had a tender and loving relationship with her, and his mother's death no doubt influenced his creation of Hester Prynne, his strongest female character.

Forced by the geographical distance between his grandmother's home in Salem, Massachusetts, and his mother's home in Raymond, Maine, Hawthorne learned early to communicate with paper and pen, usually weekly with his mother and, often, with his imaginative and literate sisters. He became proud of his narrative skills, later writing to his sister Louisa that, though his letter was only for her, "it is truly a pity that the public should lose it" (*CE* 15: 214). Soon he went beyond epistolary creations to a journalistic work. With Louisa in Salem, he turned out a handwritten miniature newspaper, *The Spectator,* a facsimile imitation of the Salem *Gazette* full of timely family news and original poetry and essays which he sent to his mother and other relatives in Maine.

In addition to writing from his childhood for female readers, Hawthorne also included them from the beginning in his literary interests and activities. He shared his reading excitement over the novels of Scott, Radcliffe, and Smollett with Louisa (*CE* 15: 114), enthusiastically recommended Scott's *Lord of the Isles,* Hogg's *Tales,* Godwin's *Caleb Williams, St. Leon,* and *Mandeville* to his sister "Ebe" (15: 132), and noted that he had read "all most all the Books which have been published for the last hundred Years," including *Melmoth, Tom Jones, Amelia, Eloisa, The Abbot,* R. L. Edgeworth's *Memoirs,* and M. G. Lewis's *Romantick Tales* (15: 134). Shortly after Hawthorne arrived at Bowdoin College to begin his first year as a college student, he wrote to Ebe that, to his surprise, it was a "much more civilized place than one would expect to find in this wilderness," with the 1,200 and 600 volumes in the libraries of the two student societies "generally well chosen, and they have many of the best English Authors" (15: 159–60). The next year he continued to describe all the books he could procure, apparently to explain why he hadn't read the two novels Ebe had mentioned in her letters (15: 174).

His sisters were also Hawthorne's colleagues and collaborators in his early efforts to develop his voice and become a writer. He requests that his Uncle Robert bring Ebe home to Salem with him because he wants her to talk to (*CE* 15: 112). On his sixteenth birthday in 1820, Louisa wrote to her mother that "Nathaniel delivered a most excellent Oration this morning to no other hearers but me" (15: 125; MSS, Bowdoin College). Ebe was also his competitor, no doubt spurring him on to his early publishing attempts. He wrote to Louisa, "Tell Ebe she's not the only one of the family whose works have appeared in the papers" (15: 115), apparently written after Ebe had sent poems to a "Boston Newspaper" (J. Hawthorne 1: 102, qtd. in *CE* 15: 116). He and Ebe evidently traded their writing samples, and when he was angry at Ebe for not sending him some of her poetry, he promised to withhold his from her (*CE* 15: 131–32).

While Hawthorne was still at Bowdoin College, he continued to share his writing life with her. He wrote Ebe about making "progress" on a novel (J. Hawthorne 1:

5

124), and after his graduation, in the summer of 1825, he showed some of his "Seven Tales of My Native Land" to Ebe, who "read them and liked them" (J. Hawthorne 1: 124). Turning to his sister for mutually satisfying intellectual companionship and stimulation, he discussed with her his plans to write *Fanshawe* before publishing his tales, and he often spent his evenings discussing political affairs with her. She recalled that after reading novels Hawthorne made an artistic study of them (J. Hawthorne 1: 125), a study which Ebe must have seen as well.

Because Hawthorne's days before his marriage were spent in writing, walking, and chatting with his sister, she played a central role in his development as a writer, with her own interest in the imagination, psychology, and aesthetics expanding his. She was an intelligent and sophisticated reader, as attested to by the books she chose for herself and Hawthorne from the Salem Athenaeum (Kesselring). Ebe provided him with a colleague and intellectual peer, helping him develop his own aesthetics strongly grounded in Anglo-Scottish theories of a visual and associative imagination. She said later that she would have liked to have been a librarian. To Hawthorne, Ebe was his superior in "general talent and . . . fine cultivation. . . . She has both a physical and intellectual love of books, a born book worm" (*CE* 18: 456).[3] (Even after his marriage to Sophia Peabody, he consulted Ebe for her opinion of his writing (see *CE* 16: 403n5), who thought he never wrote as well after his marriage when she was no longer his first reader and critic.[4] He later continued to encourage Ebe with her writing, particularly her translation of Cervantes' tales (16: 402).

In his first paid job as an editor, from January to August of 1836, he again turned to a sister as collaborator, this time to Ebe. For his *American Magazine of Useful and Entertaining Knowledge* he requested that she copy for him by extracting "whatever she [thought] suitable" from her reading (*CE* 15: 228–29). He urged her to adopt his methods: "I make nothing of writing a history or biography before dinner. Do you the same. . . . Concoct—concoct—concoct" (15: 230). He exhorted her to abstract— "you can't think how easy it is" (15: 235)—and to concoct by putting "other people's thoughts into your own words, and amalgamate the whole into a mass" (15: 243). To Louisa he gave the job of critic, asking her to read "this infernal Magazine and send me your criticisms" (15: 240), wanting her feedback to his opinion that it appeared "very dull and respectable" (15: 240).

In his next job, writing *Peter Parley's Universal History on the Basis of Geography, for the Use of Families,* again Ebe was his collaborator, probably doing the bulk of the work since he gave her his pay for the job. That he thought of her as his coauthor is clear from his letter to her on 12 May 1836: "Our pay, as Historians of the Universe, will be 100 dollars the whole of which you may have. It is poor compensation; yet better than the *Token;* because the kind of writing is so much less difficult" (*CE* 15: 247). He thus considered her his business partner as well. His assessment of the relative value of the pay, when compared with that from the *Token,* which had published some of his early tales and sketches, suggests that she was well acquainted with the *Token* pieces, at least as a helpful reader and possibly as a participant in their conception, composition, and revision for publication.

He excitedly wrote to her of his fame in London after the 7 November 1835 British *Athenaeum* "noticed all my articles in the last *Token,* with long extracts" (*CE* 15: 230–31). "The Minister's Black Veil," "The Wedding Knell," and many of these early tales such as "The Hollow of the Three Hills" focus on a woman's experience. With her formidable intellect and acerbic wit, Ebe provided Hawthorne with an ideal female reader whose real life consisted of ideas, good literature, and deep thinking, however cloaked in domesticity she might appear. In June of 1837, he acknowledged the essential psychological support he had received all along from the women in his family, his mother, two sisters, and aunt Mary Manning, who would think Longfellow "the most sagacious critic on earth" for his praise of Hawthorne's *Twice-told Tales* (*CE* 15: 255).

Four years later, Hawthorne again envisioned his writing as a joint venture with his sister. On 3 August 1841, he wrote to Louisa from Brook Farm that he had contracted to write and edit "a series of juvenile books . . . to be adapted to our market. . . . I wish Elizabeth [Ebe] would write a book for the series. She surely knows as much about children as I do, and ought to succeed as well. I do hope she will think of a subject—whether historical, scientific, moral, religious, or fanciful—and set to work. It will be a good amusement to her, and profitable to us all." He even adds in a postscript, "Cannot your mother write a book?" (*CE* 15: 555).

That Hawthorne found the women in his family a ready audience, capable assistants, and staunch supporters cannot be overemphasized. He was later to find additional intelligent, able backers among the Peabody women in Salem: Mrs. Elizabeth Peabody and her daughters Elizabeth, Mary, and Sophia, who eventually became his wife. The Peabody women were just as interested in Hawthorne's literary career as the women in his own family, and they were active in the intellectual community of Boston, introducing the more aristocratically reserved Hawthorne into important publishing networks and the artistic and philosophical communities in which Hawthorne needed to become known if he were to succeed as a writer. Mrs. Peabody set the tone for her daughters, reading Herodotus for recreation (Lathrop 7). As Hawthorne's daughter Rose later wrote, "Literature, art, and intercourse were the three gracious deities of the Peabody home" (Lathrop 3). An educator, Mrs. Peabody had published a catechism and children's version in prose of the first book of Spenser's *Faerie Queene* (*CE* 15: 24–25). The second Peabody daughter, Mary, was also an intellectual woman interested in education and abolition who early encouraged Hawthorne to base a novel about slavery in Cuba on her experiences there and who requested that he keep a journal of his experiences in western Massachusetts in the summer of 1838 (*CE* 15: 25–26).

However, it was the third Peabody daughter, Sophia, whom Hawthorne courted, and her artistic talents, both visual and literary, were no doubt part of her great appeal for him. As he had done in his boyhood, he once more shaped his writing for his female reader, using his epistolary talents to woo her during his long court-ship, persuading her of his devotion and creating the "married" personae they would come to live out (see Herbert). After their marriage, he stopped keeping pri-vate notebooks strictly for his own use and shaped his entries as responses and missives to Sophia.

Repeating the collaborative pattern he had established with his sisters, Haw-thorne continued to see the talented woman who loved him as a potential literary colleague and collaborator. He first learned of Sophia's talents as a writer when he read her "Cuba Journal" (Lathrop 20), which had been circulated among Boston literati, and was impressed enough with her writing to transcribe several passages into his notebook (*CE* 15: 30).[5] As editor Thomas Woodson notes, Hawthorne "intended, or at least promised, to use her letters as sources for his fiction," telling Sophia "that he could make a great many stories from my works" (*CE* 15: 28, quoting from Sophia to Elizabeth Palmer Peabody, 14 May 1838, Berg Collection, New York Public Library). He appreciated her power of description, both in language and in visual art, which he thought would be useful to him, just as Ebe's writing had been. He wrote to Sophia on 29 May 1840 that he wished she could be with him on board the ships he inspected in Boston Harbor

> because there are many things of which thou mightst make such pretty descriptions; and in future years, when thy husband is again busy at the loom of fiction, he would weave in these little pictures. My fancy is rendered so torpid by my ungenial way of life, that I cannot sketch off the scenes and portraits that interest me. (*CE* 15: 466)

A month later, he again praised her writing talent, asking her how she could say that he had ever written anything beautiful, "being thyself so potent to reproduce whatever is loveliest" (*CE* 15: 475). Unfortunately, since Hawthorne burned Sophia's letters to him in 1853 before their move to England, it is difficult to judge her talent accurately. Throughout his life, Hawthorne would continue to praise her skills, writing to William Ticknor that she excelled him as a writer of travels and to her sister Elizabeth of Sophia's superiority in "fullness and accuracy of description" (Lathrop 336) and to James Fields of her "narrative and descriptive epistles" (*CE* 15: 31n54).

After reading her beautiful prose letters for another year, Hawthorne came to see her role in his work a little differently, envisioning her in Ebe's former role of assistant, albeit in a more romantic setting:

> When we dwell together, I intend that my Dove shall do all the reading that may be necessary, in the concoction of my various histories; and she shall repeat the substance of her researches to me, when our heads are on the pillow. Thus will knowledge fall upon me like heavenly dew. (*CE* 15: 566)

Having been consigned to the role of a research assistant, Sophia instead took on the role of critic, and she must have been a little harsh in her comments about tales Hawthorne gave her to read before revising them for a publisher, as Hawthorne's apologies suggest:

> Sweetest, thou dost please me much by criticizing thy husband's stories, and finding fault with them. I do not very well recollect Monsieur du Miroir; but as to Mrs. Bullfrog [the story of a newlywed husband who is horrified to discover his wife's true appearance after their wedding], I give her up to thy severest reprehension. The story was written as a mere experiment in that style; it did not come from any depth within me—neither my heart nor mind had anything to do with it. (*CE* 15: 572)

And Hawthorne did change his tales as Sophia had suggested (15: 574n1).

Sophia, like his sisters, shared Hawthorne's love of reading. Along with trading titles of books read, Sophia became Hawthorne's audience, listening to him read aloud works by such authors as Spenser, Shakespeare, Milton, and, of course, himself. In the early days of their marriage, she wrote to her sister Mary that they were learning German together: "So we teach each other in the most charming manner, and I call it the royal road to knowledge, finally discovered by us" (Lathrop 56).

After his marriage, he continued to seek Sophia's help with his writing, consulting her even on his friend Horatio Bridge's manuscript of the *Journal of an African Cruiser* for which Hawthorne wrote the introduction (*CE* 15: 686). He consulted her about the quality of Epes Sargent's *Songs of the Sea* (*CE* 16: 208), about the title of *Mosses from an Old Manse* (16: 146), and he appointed her the "umpire" to decide the title of the volume to contain *The Scarlet Letter* (16: 306). He read her his manuscripts before he sent them off to be published, with the notable exception of his campaign biography of Franklin Pierce, whose politics no doubt might have troubled her. Hawthorne used Sophia's intensely emotional reaction to *The Scarlet Letter* ("It broke her heart and sent her to bed with a grievous headache—which I look upon as triumphant success!" [16: 311]) as a bellwether for his future readers. He wrote his publisher, James T. Fields, that he even needed to hear Sophia's response to *The House of the Seven Gables* before he could judge his own work ("Then I must read it to my wife;—and after going over it in that way, I shall know better what to think of it" [16: 382]). He happily reported to Fields that it had met with "extraordinary success" (16: 386). Later Sophia helped him revise *The Marble Faun* (*CE* 4: lxx), and as Herbert notes, Hawthorne explained that only Sophia is best able to comprehend *The Marble Faun* "precisely as I meant it," because she "speaks so near me that I cannot tell her voice from my own" (*CE* 18: 256).

Sophia's steadfast support, like that of his mother and sisters previously, encouraged and enabled Hawthorne to confidently pursue his writing career. He wrote to Evert A. Duyckinck, on hearing of Melville's praise of his books, of Sophia's important role: "I have all along had one staunch admirer; and with her to back me, I really believe I should do very well without any other" (*CE* 16: 362).

Hawthorne apparently felt quite positively about women in general, writing his old college friend Horatio Bridge about the birth of his first child, his daughter Una: "I think I prefer a daughter to a son; there is something so especially piquant in having helped to create a future woman" (*CE* 16: 25). And to Duyckinck he wrote, "there is a delightful awe in being the father of a future woman; it is more of a miracle than the other [fathering a boy]" (16: 87).

His idealistic romantic courtship and marriage as well as his interest in his children—both subjects he constantly wrote about in his notebooks—meant that he was able to treat in depth women's domestic and psychological lives as some of his most effective subject matter. Drawing on such knowledge for details of setting, characterization, and plot, Hawthorne was perfectly prepared to write successfully for women interested in recognizing something of their worlds in their reading, where, as Baym has observed, they could "reconstitute" themselves (*Woman's* xlii). As many critics have noted, complex women and gender concerns are at the center of Hawthorne's works. Hawthorne's positive view of women may have contributed to his casting them as potential social saviors: As Baym notes, "Cautiously, Hawthorne advances the notion that if society is to be changed for the better, such change will be initiated by women. . . . Although in his later works Hawthorne was to answer this question negatively, in *The Scarlet Letter,* the possibility, though faint, is there" (*Woman's* 73).[6]

As Joel Pfister has noted, "Hawthorne's fiction intermittently launches a critique of the sentimental construction of 'masculine' and 'feminine' roles upon which the economic and cultural ascendancy of his class relied" (8). " 'The Birth-mark,' then, is about the urge to control, not just a female body, but a female role, and this discursive management of the way women envisioned their womanhood was crucial to the ideological production of middle-class identity in uncertain times" (58).

Hawthorne's complex female characters, drawn partly from his depth of understanding and partly from literary conventions, set his fiction apart from that of his contemporaries. He had a variety of "female character types in antebellum popular culture" from which he could choose and "recombine" artistically into a complex heroine such as Hester Prynne of *The Scarlet Letter* (Reynolds 368). This "quintessential American heroine, reflecting virtually every facet of the antebellum woman's experience . . . was a heroine who could act out several of these roles simultaneously" (Reynolds 373).

Hawthorne's Hester, even today, appears to Emily Budick "as the heroic skeptic of [*The Scarlet Letter*]" (29). And such a character still empowers its female readers, as Budick explains:

> By incorporating the female letter, Hawthorne acknowledges his own origins within the female body; he graphically demonstrates (in her language) that his story is the extension of hers, that he (and perhaps all men or, for that matter, all women) only

edit and retell the stories their mothers tell to them. . . . When Hawthorne puts himself in his mother's line of inheritance and declares himself her heir, he accepts and explicitly acknowledges that his power derives from hers, that he is empowered, even as he is engendered, by his mother. (72–73)

While his opinion of women in general may have been positive, his ambivalence about women writers was more complex, as Nina Baym's essay in this volume shows. Since the more sensational adventure fiction garnered 57 percent of the literary market in the 1774–1860 period, Hawthorne was competing in a market full of women writers that appealed to only 22 percent of the readers (Reynolds 338). However, as Baym points out, many of the "formula blockbusters" that actually dominated the market were woman's fiction (*Woman's* xi).

Using the women in his family as his professional literary colleagues, coauthors, and collaborators, Hawthorne had reached and created a wide audience. As Brodhead points out,

> We can now see that the literary market expanded so rapidly after 1840 not out of an innate tendency to grow, but because of its conjunction, at this time, with a social development that provided new encouragement for reading: the new organization of work, family life, gender-roles, and moral structures of insurgent middle-class domesticity. As it removed women from the sphere of productive labor and made them custodians of nonmaterial values, the cult of domesticity created both a new domestic leisure reading could help fill and a new ethic to support that pastime. . . . In consequence, after 1840 and critically so around 1850, fiction writing took on the power to reach very large audiences in America, on the condition that it align itself with the values the new domesticity was constituted around. (19)

But Hawthorne's success with his women readers may have come at a high cost to his pride in his work as a writer: "Whether or not his convictions were wholeheartedly feminist, his authorial mode was that of the feminized male author who knows he has entered a female world in becoming a writer rather than a businessman or politician" (Bell 15).[7] Some of his dilemma was apparent in his decision to print the title page of *The Scarlet Letter* in red ink: "In soliciting buyers of questionable taste, Hawthorne bottled up an inward distress whose dimensions the novel itself explores, the dilemmas of a gender system requiring men to form and maintain a public identity, while women cultivate in retirement a sensitivity to the moral mysteries of the human heart" (Herbert 164).

As Hawthorne became more discouraged about his ability to support his growing family by his writing, his remarks about his female competitors in the literary marketplace of gift annuals, juvenile literature, and especially novels became more testy. He wrote to James Fields, one of his publishers, on 11 December 1852, "All women, as authors, are feeble and tiresome. I wish they were forbidden to write, on pain of having their faces deeply scarified with an oyster-shell" (*CE* 16: 624). A year later he wrote to William Ticknor, his other publisher, "ink-stained women are, without a single exception, detestable" (*CE* 17: 161). When he made his famous comment about "scribbling women," he was using a term to describe them that he used to describe himself as a professional writer. He had always used "scribbler" to describe himself, an interesting characterization.[8]

However, Hawthorne's reputation grew especially strong in England and continued to grow after his death. As Brodhead says, Hawthorne established the "coherence and continuity of American literature" and then began to function as an "agent who admits new authors inside that line" (9). As early as 1850, "other writers began to incorporate him into their writing, and reformulate him into their plans" (11). "Hawthorne presides over the writing of prose fiction in America in the later half of the nineteenth century" (51). Post–Civil War authors saw Hawthorne as a "founder: he who established the work they now seek to continue. . . . Hawthorne had a kind of hold over the whole literary enterprise of the generation that followed him that no other figure in the history of American fiction has exerted" (51).

While his subject matter was partly the domestic scene and women's lives, his aesthetics had been shaped by sophisticated theories of the imagination and psyche—and it began to be his complexity as a writer that appealed to the women who read him, particularly if they were interested in what he could teach them about their own writing.

An Overview of Reviews and Notices by Women

In both his native land and in the United Kingdom, women weighed Hawthorne's writings and, when time and space allowed, wrote perceptively about his work and him. Like their male counterparts, women critics often had deadlines to beat, limited column space available to them, and a tendency to judge works on the basis of their ethical, moral, or religious content. Where ample space was available, again like male reviewers, they offered samplings of Hawthorne's art, sometimes filling several pages with extracts from his tales or romances. But sometimes they, too, had to settle for a mere notice. Whether their pieces were long or brief, most of them agreed in finding Hawthorne an important writer. Although their ranks were comparatively thin, women reviewers helped to establish, promote, and preserve Hawthorne's literary fame.

With some exceptions, their reviews did not appear in obscure magazines or newspapers but in many of the leading publications of the day: Elizabeth Palmer Peabody's in *New-Yorker* and *Atlantic Monthly,* Anne Abbott's in *North American Review,* Margaret Fuller's in *Dial* and *New-York Daily Tribune,* Margaret Oliphant's in *Blackwood's Edinburgh Review,* Martha Tyler Gale's in *New-Englander,* Ada Clare's in *New York Saturday Press,* and (with some remaining uncertainty as to her authorship) George Eliot's in *Westminster Review.* The chief point to consider here is that their reviews and commentaries found outlets in places where their words could help build up, or tear down, a literary reputation.

Nearly all their reviews differ little from those written by men. In subjects treated, style, and perceptions of Hawthorne's genius and character, women reviewers generally responded to Hawthorne's fiction as if they were integral members of the New England (or national) clerisy. That they were writing for publications edited by men, as was usually the case, could have been a factor in how women shaped their reviews. Since most early reviews, whether done by men or women, were published anonymously, only readers with privileged information would have known for certain the gender of the reviewer. Possessing that information would not have meant much to anyone seeking to detect differences in gender-based assessments of Hawthorne's achievement. Men and women alike welcomed Hawthorne's short fiction, spoke admiringly of his range of subject matter, perceived him to be gentle and quiet of spirit, and granted him a stature equal to, or above, Washington Irving's. (Irving not only held the highest rank among American authors but also enjoyed an international following, especially in Great Britain.) Like Irving's, Hawthorne's work was such as would make a nation proud, an opinion most pronounced in Elizabeth Palmer Peabody, one day to become Hawthorne's sister-in-law, and Mary Russell Mitford, the staunchest of British women who championed Hawthorne's writings.

Regardless of sex, reviewers voiced similar complaints about Hawthorne's slight knowledge of everyday life, the real world. His reclusiveness left his writing without "real beef," a fault he could correct if only he would become more a man of the world. Appealing as he was morally and philosophically, he tended toward emblematic and allegoric presentation of characters and settings. Although Hawthorne would have liked to write as realistically as Anthony Trollope, his models continued to be Edmund Spenser, John Bunyan, and Sir Walter Scott. Had his reviewers, women or men, been able to peruse his notebooks, especially those he kept in England and Italy, they might have insisted that he was Trollope-like in his daily journalizing and surmised, with Hawthorne's ready agreement, that his allegorical tendencies hurt his artistry. In moments of sincere artistic self-assessment, Hawthorne knew that he paid dearly for his shy and private nature. No reviewer, woman or man, could, however, "bring him out."

While both men and women acknowledged Hawthorne's gifts as an allegorist (and its cost to his literary standing as well), women rather than men ventured full-fledged allegorical readings. In what may be accurately described as the first scholarly essay on the romance, Martha Tyler Gale, both daughter and wife of New England clergymen, published a moralistic allegorical reading of *The Marble Faun* in *New-Englander* (Oct. 1861). Several years later, Elizabeth Palmer Peabody used an allegorical reading of the same work to undergird her reading of Italian revolutionary politics (*Atlantic Monthly* Sept. 1868). Hope Reed's belated essay on *The Marble Faun* insisted that Hawthorne's allegory, while richly suggestive, nonetheless numbed the reader's mind (*Western* ns 5 May 1879). As is true with most allegorical readings of Hawthorne's fiction, these analyses reveal more about the interpreters than about Hawthorne's mind and art. Gale, Peabody, and Reed saw what they wanted, or were prepared, to see. And their preparation was largely Christian doctrine and Western moral and ethical philosophy, and much more of the former than the latter. Theirs are the readings of the American branch of the Victorian clerisy and could have readily come from the pens of men interested in allegory, although a male critic might have stopped short of presenting Miriam as symbolic of the political sufferings of Italy, as Peabody saw her.

Allegorical readings were, however, just one of the ways women enjoyed Hawthorne's work. Confessing that she liked "The Custom-House" better than the tale, Anne Abbott relished the tartness of Hawthorne's satire and praised his ability to draw deft portraits of Salem Custom House employees (*North American Review* July 1850). His description of nature and his efforts to raise the level of writings for children earned high marks as did also his probing look at human nature and profound understanding of human psychology. But the plaudits were not universal. Sure that his method of ending Zenobia's unhappy life was psychologically false, Margaret Oliphant, a Scottish critic, asserted: "We do not believe in Zenobia drowning herself. It is a piece of sham entirely, and never impresses us with the slightest idea of reality" (*Blackwood's Edinburgh Magazine* May 1855).

It is on the issue of fidelity to human nature and psychology that women reviewers and critics become most outspoken. If the aging British playwright, poet, essayist, anthologist, and tireless letter writer, Mary Russell Mitford, can instantly recognize part of herself in Hepzibah Pyncheon because, like the New England spinster of Hawthorne's creation, she had to fend for herself, we have the word of a leading professional writer that Hawthorne could render a character who struck a sympathetic chord: "Ah, I have a strong fellow-feeling for that poor Hepzibah—a decayed gentlewoman, elderly, ugly, awkward, near-sighted, cross!" (*Recollections of a Literary Life; or, Books, Places, and People*). Another woman of letters, Ada Clare, heard only a sour note when she considered Hawthorne's depiction of Hilda: "O fie! they slander us heartily, these men. This is no woman; 'tis a piece of pale Italian marble, that cheats us with the semblance of life" (*New York Saturday Press* 10 Mar. 1860). Clare did, however, find Miriam womanly and lovable. If Hilda proved to Clare, and many readers since her time, a moral monster, Hester, deemed immoral by her peers, stood as a moral giant for Jane Swisshelm, a professional journalist and publisher from Pittsburgh: "Hester Prynne stands morally, as Saul did physically amongst his contemporaries, the head and shoulder taller than the tallest. She is the most glorious creation of fiction that has ever crossed our path" (*Saturday Visiter* 28 Sept. 1850).

Clare's and Swisshelm's admiration of Hawthorne's strong-minded and strong-willed women undoubtedly reflects their protofeminist leanings. Not every woman critic was prepared to accept the moral and philosophical examination of the woman question inherent or explicit in Hawthorne's fiction. For example, Gertrude Mason, reacting to an excerpt in *Home Journal* (10 Oct. 1853) from Hawthorne's *Blithe-*

dale Romance, including Hollingsworth's denigration of the struggle of women for equality—

> Her place is at man's side. . . . All the separate action of woman is, and ever has been, and always shall be, false, foolish, vain, destructive of her own best and holiest qualities, void of every good effect, and productive of intolerable mischiefs! (*CE* 3: 122)

—revealed her antifeminist stance by asserting that Hawthorne played into the hands of the feminist camp by putting denigrating remarks in Hollingsworth's mouth. Through this speech, Mason claimed, Hawthorne "only gives the poor, miserable, abortive creatures he speaks of, another argument in support of their false and wicked theories" (*Home Journal* 12 Nov. 1853). On aesthetic rather than political grounds, Esther B. Carpenter, writing for *Women's Journal* (27 Aug. 1881), complained that Hawthorne "lost some of his fine insight when he turned from evolution to speculation, and analyzed woman as the philosopher and moralist, instead of the romancer. His mood at once became tinged with the conventional hues." Her unhappiness stemmed from Hawthorne's characterization of Sybil Dacy in *Septimius Felton,* among the last of the works that Hawthorne was attempting to complete before his death.

No work of fiction, however, stirred controversy as rapidly as did an extract from Hawthorne's *French and Italian Notebooks* on Margaret Fuller. Published in Julian Hawthorne's *Nathaniel Hawthorne and His Wife* (1884), this mean-spirited, unflattering, and gossipy assessment of her character (see *CE* 14: 155–57) provoked defenses of Fuller from both men and women. Sarah Freeman Clarke, a friend of both the Hawthornes and Fuller, expressed her disappointment in Hawthorne by insisting that his opinion of Fuller was "discreditable to his judgment of character." She blamed the son for making this journal entry public, for she believed that Hawthorne would never have allowed something so crude and cruel to see print (*Boston Transcript* 12 Dec. 1884). Pointing out that Mrs. Hawthorne had deleted the material on Fuller when she published *Passages from the French and Italian Note-Books of Nathaniel Hawthorne,* Caroline Dell sensed potential damage to Hawthorne's reputation as a result of Julian's indiscretion. She found the extract "revolting" and possibly demeaning to Hawthorne's memory (*Springfield Republican* 15 Dec. 1884). Julian's indiscretion aroused his aging aunt Elizabeth Palmer Peabody to deplore her nephew's tacky behavior and to defend his father by asserting that he would not have printed so private an assessment of Fuller's life and achievement (*Letters of Elizabeth Palmer Peabody* 428).

The Essays

Our arrangement of essays reflects, first, our conviction that Hawthorne wrote within a developing tradition of American letters; that, secondly, he profited from the help of women who understood his ambition and talent; that, thirdly his goal of recording New England life as he knew it presented both a model and a challenge for women writers in his region who followed him; and, finally that his thematic and aesthetic choices proved germinal resources for women writers from his age to ours. That conviction underlies the arrangement of the following essays into five groups, with the lead essay, by Nina Baym, serving to place Hawthorne within an energetic cluster of women writers working to help create and shape a tradition of American letters. Of course, as in most arbitrarily designed taxonomic schemes, a few essays might be justly moved from one of our groupings to another. To better underscore Hawthorne's continuing appeal to modern readers, we have formed a subset of our fourth group in order to present together five essays treating the theme of sexuality and sexual behavior.

The first group explores how three members of his immediate family actively involved themselves in promoting or sustaining his career and reputation. These are Elizabeth Palmer Peabody, Sophia Peabody Hawthorne, and Rose Hawthorne Lathrop. Their efforts in behalf of Hawthorne are treated, respectively, in essays by John L. Idol, Luanne Jenkins Hurst, and Patricia Dunlavy Valenti.

The second group considers five women whose New England background afforded them opportunities to see life with something of the same New England slant that Hawthorne brought to his work. In this group we might have placed Sarah Orne Jewett, Mary Wilkins Freeman, and Katharine Lee Bates. For what we see as ample reasons, essays about them appear with the group exploring thematic or aesthetic ties to Hawthorne. Within this group, then, are Margaret Fuller, Harriet Beecher Stowe, Louisa May Alcott, Elizabeth Barstow Stoddard, and Annie Fields. Fuller receives attention by David B. Kesterson for her importantly placed reviews of Hawthorne's early work and appears as a candidate to help resolve the "Beatrice riddle" in Thomas R. Mitchell's provocative essay entitled "Rappaccini's Garden and Emerson's Concord: Translating the Voice of Margaret Fuller." Stowe's presentation of New England village life reveals her to be an attentive student of New England ways of seeing and behaving, as James D. Wallace finds in his study of her story "The Mourning Veil." Claudia Durst Johnson incisively examines the roots of discord between the Alcotts and Hawthornes and relates them to national politics and Louisa May Alcott's efforts to launch her own literary career. Margaret B. Moore reveals how Stoddard situated her work on Hawthorne's literary turf and earned from him words of praise for her first novel. This group concludes with Rita K. Gollin's concise account of how Annie Fields sought both to take the measure of Hawthorne as one of his early biographers and to assist in keeping Hawthorne's work in the public eye.

The next group of essays demonstrates the importance of Hawthorne to three English women, Mary Russell Mitford, George Eliot, and Mary Ward. John L. Idol's piece on Mitford traces her discovery of Hawthorne's work and the energetic steps she took to make sure that Hawthorne enjoyed an English following. Patricia Marks argues that George Eliot's *Middlemarch* represents an effort to recast the character of Hilda while, at the same time, offering a revision of Hawthorne's romance aesthetic. In her wittily insightful essay on Mary Ward's reading of *The Scarlet Letter,* Carol M. Bensick examines how the romance struck the head and heart of a future novelist.

The fourth group brings together six essays on women writers whose fiction draws upon thematic and/or aesthetic elements in the Hawthorne tradition. Janice Milner Lasseter finds an aesthetic wellspring for Rebecca Harding Davis's realism in Hawthorne's concrete descriptive passages. It is Hawthorne's pictorialism and its kinship to luminist painting that ties the art of Sarah Orne Jewett to Hawthorne, says Gayle L. Smith in an essay treating *The Country of the Pointed Firs* and other Jewett pieces. While finding that Mary Wilkins Freeman and Hawthorne offer recognizably similar pictures of New England, Melissa McFarland Pennell suggests a thematic connection stemming from their common interest in the Puritan tempera-ment and the "role of class status and expectations . . . in the process of self-definition." Melinda M. Ponder reveals Katharine Lee Bates's credentials as a mem-ber of the Hawthorne school and places her in his service as an editor (an edition of Hawthorne for Crowell) and as teacher of American literature at Wellesley before focusing on how Bates's feminist principles and purposes enabled her to rework Hawthorne's *Our Old Home* into her best-known piece of travel writing, *From Gretna Green to Land's End.*

Willa Cather's novels about the upper Midwest and the Southwest indeed seem a far remove from the New England world of Hawthorne, Jewett, Freeman, and Stowe. Yet, an aesthetic and a thematic link tie the writings of Cather and Haw-thorne together. Such runs the argument of John J. Murphy in his essay, which focuses on links between *The Marble Faun* and *Death Comes for the Archbishop.*

Neither Hawthorne's American landscape nor his revelations about Puritan so-ciety satisfied Virginia Woolf's creative needs. Rather, she discovered in Hawthorne someone who had penetratingly read the behavior of children and had committed his observations to print. Elizabeth N. Goodenough explores the presentation of children in the works of Hawthorne and Woolf and discovers their mutual respect for what Hawthorne called the "unestimated sensibility" of the child.

The fifth group, taxonomically a subset of the preceding group, explores a topic, sexuality and sexual behavior, that does more than its part to keep Hawthorne and his work from being cast aside as irrelevant to present-day interests and concerns. Five essays have been placed together in this group, beginning with that of Karen Kilcup, who finds sexual resonances between Hawthorne's Hester and Pearl and erotic elements in certain Emily Dickinson poems. Denise D. Knight contends in her essay on Charlotte Perkins Gilman that social reform stood foremost in Gilman's approach to writing, that she was not content to look forward, as Hester Prynne did, to a brighter day when men and women would have a new truth revealed and find themselves on a better footing for "mutual happiness." Gilman would have that brighter day come today. In contrast to Gilman's hope for a better future stands

Edith Wharton's simultaneously Gothic and realistic reworking of a tale of seduction, *Summer,* which Monika M. Elbert reads in the context of *The Scarlet Letter.* It is this same romance that John Gatta finds central to his comments on Flannery O'Connor's "Good Country People." O'Connor openly declared herself to be both a student and a literary descendant of Hawthorne. Gatta's essay "*The Scarlet Letter* as Pre-text for Flannery O'Connor's 'Good Country People'" discusses how the themes of guilt, obsession, and the drama of salvation attest to the depth of O'Connor's study in the School of Hawthorne. A final testimonial to Hawthorne's relevance, problematic though it may be, to contemporary writers appears in Toni Morrison's *Beloved.* Franny Nudelman sees elements of gothicism in Morrison's novel about sexual behavior and links it to Hawthorne's manner of presenting characters. As evidence of Hawthorne's early emergence as a model for aspiring women and as a subject for discussion, in the appendix we present interesting comments by women writers who were contemporaries of Hawthorne.

Notes

1. Quotations from Nathaniel Hawthorne's works, letters, and notebooks are from the *Centenary Edition of the Works of Nathaniel Hawthorne,* ed. William Charvat et al. (Columbus: Ohio State UP, 1962–), hereafter cited as *CE* with volume and page numbers.

2. Budick 13, 19, 25, 29; Herbert 258, 265.

3. See Moore for a description of Ebe.

4. See Moore 3 and n. 14 on p. 8.

5. See Herbert 37–58 for his analysis of Sophia's talents and aspirations before her marriage.

6. See also Baym, "Thwarted Nature": "the question of women is the determining motive in H's works, driving them as it drives Hawthorne's male characters" (62), and his stories make statements "about the way in which men imagine them" (65). And Herbert: "Hawthorne takes up a complex debate about the 'natural' essence of gender that Sophia had invoked when she said that Rose—aged fifteen months—had an 'idea' of 'woman's rights' yet was also tenderly solicitous toward her brother" (9). "Yet Sophia did not believe, nor did Nathaniel, that nature had provided such an arrangement: the Hawthornes embraced a tradition that set the nurturing qualities of women at odds with the claim to political equality" (9). "Despite his ambivalence and androgynous sense of self and the sympathy he extends toward strong women in his works, he never retracted his early condemnation of 'a false liberality, which mistakes the strong division-lines of Nature for mere arbitrary distinctions.' The woman who feels compelled to seek a career at odds with her 'natural' destiny must do so, he argued, 'with sorrowing reluctance' because she is 'relinquishing part of the loveliness of her sex' ('Mrs. Hutchinson,' 168–69)" (Herbert 11).

7. See also Person; Davidson 32.

8. There are about twenty examples in early letters, eighteen in *CE,* vol. 15, three in vol. 16; e.g., he refers to himself as "a scribbler by profession" (*CE* 15: 270), and in his letter to Bridge, 3 May 1843, he says that "nobody's scribblings seem to be more acceptable to the public than

mine; and yet I shall find it a tough match to gain a respectable support by my pen" (*CE* 15: 688). For discussions of Hawthorne's comment, in addition to Baym's essay herein, see Wallace, and the sources listed in n. 5 of *CE* 17: 305 and Hawthorne's letter, *CE* 17: 307–8.

Works Cited

Baym, Nina. "Thwarted Nature: Nathaniel Hawthorne as Feminist." *American Novelists Revisited: Essays in Feminist Criticism.* Ed. Fritz Fleischmann. Boston: Hall, 1982. 58–77.

——. *Woman's Fiction: A Guide to Novels by and about Women in America, 1820–70.* 2nd ed. Urbana: U of Illinois P, 1993.

Bell, Millicent, ed. *New Essays on Hawthorne's Major Tales.* Cambridge: Cambridge UP, 1993.

Brodhead, Richard. *The School of Hawthorne.* New York: Oxford UP, 1986.

Budick, Emily Miller. *Engendering Romance: Women Writers and the Hawthorne Tradition, 1850–1990.* New Haven: Yale UP, 1994.

Coultrap-McQuin, Susan. *Doing Literary Business: American Women Writers in the Nineteenth Century.* Chapel Hill: U of North Carolina P, 1990.

Davidson, Cathy. *Revolution and the Word: The Rise of the Novel in America.* New York: Oxford UP, 1986.

Dimock, Wai-Chee. "Feminism, New Historicism, and the Reader." *American Literature* 63.4 (1991): 601–22.

Hawthorne, Julian. *Nathaniel Hawthorne and His Wife.* 2nd ed. 2 vols. Boston: Osgood, 1885.

Herbert, T. Walter. *Dearest Beloved: The Hawthornes and the Making of the Middle-Class Family.* Berkeley: U of California P, 1993.

Kesselring, Marion L. "Hawthorne's Reading, 1828–1850." *Bulletin of the New York Public Library* 53 (1949): 55–71, 173–94.

Lathrop, Rose Hawthorne. *Memories of Hawthorne.* Boston: Houghton Mifflin, 1923.

Moore, Margaret B. "Elizabeth Manning Hawthorne: Nathaniel's Enigmatic Sister." *Nathaniel Hawthorne Review* 20.1 (1994): 1–9.

Peabody, Elizabeth Palmer. *The Letters of Elizabeth Palmer Peabody: American Renaissance Woman.* Ed. Bruce A. Rorda. Middletown: Wesleyan UP, 1984.

Person, Leland S., Jr. *Aesthetic Headaches: Women and a Masculine Poetics in Poe, Melville, and Hawthorne.* Athens: U of Georgia P, 1988.

Pfister, Joel. *The Production of Personal Life: Class, Gender, and the Psychological in Hawthorne's Fiction.* Stanford: Stanford UP, 1991.

Renker, Elizabeth. "Herman Melville, Wife Beating, and the Written Page." *American Literature* 66.1 (1994): 123–50.

Reynolds, David S. *Beneath the American Renaissance: The Subversive Imagination in the Age of Emerson and Melville.* Cambridge: Harvard UP, 1988.

Tompkins, Jane. *Sensational Designs: The Cultural Work of American Fiction, 1790–1860.* New York: Oxford UP, 1985.

Wallace, James D. "Hawthorne and the Scribbling Women Reconsidered." *American Literature* 62.2 (1990): 201–22.

AGAIN AND AGAIN,
THE SCRIBBLING WOMEN

Nina Baym

I approach Nathaniel Hawthorne's famous remark about the "damnd mob of scribbling women" obliquely by reminding readers that since Hawthorne's letters to his publisher and counselor William Ticknor were first published in 1910 the phrase has taken on a powerful life of its own. For many years it has functioned to describe a literary scene and judge it at the same time, simultaneously invoking and deploring an antebellum culture of letters dominated by foolish females. Among uncountable examples of its deployment, I note the appearance of the phrase in two books of extreme significance for the study of American letters, Fred Lewis Pattee's *The Feminine Fifties* and F. O. Matthiessen's *American Renaissance,* both published shortly before the United States entered World War II. It isn't exaggerating much to claim that together these two books delineated the boundaries of nineteenth-century American literary study for decades thereafter. *The Feminine Fifties* depicted and satirized an antebellum literary world dominated by popular women writers and their feminized hangers-on; *American Renaissance* presented five refugees from this frivolous world as culture heroes battling for democracy.

It seems mean-spirited of these distinguished academics to have elevated some writers by the cheap trick of dragging others in the dust, and one might think in any event that when a great war looms critics would have had better things to do than pick on dead women—all the more since according to convention men fight wars to protect their cherished womenfolk. But, in fact, attempts to banish women from the precincts of literature are regularly part of attempts to make those precincts sacred, and they tend to acquire particular energy in militaristic moments. Laboring in the shadow of the war to come, Pattee and Matthiessen were trying to make something that mattered greatly to them—American literature—useful for the war effort by remasculinizing it (Susan Jefford's word), insisting that literature, too, is men's holy work, a form of soldiering that confirms one's manhood and bonds men to each other in life-sacrificing homosocial (Eve Sedgwick's word) situations. *Moby-Dick,* then, is a book worth dying for; indeed, Herman Melville virtually sacrificed his own life to write it. Not so *The Lamplighter* and Maria Susanna Cummins.

Nathaniel Hawthorne's well-turned epistolary phrase supplied Matthiessen and Pattee with crucial rhetorical ammunition. Pattee made the phrase into a chapter title: "A D——d Mob of Scribbling women." He says Hawthorne wrote Ticknor "that he was inclined to abandon fiction writing because of literary conditions in America," and then quotes: "America is now wholly given over to a d——d mob of scribbling women," and so on (110). Matthiessen observes in his preface: "Reflecting on the triumphant vogue of Susan Warner's *The Wide, Wide World* (1850), Maria Cummins's *The Lamplighter* (1854), the ceaseless flux of Mrs. E.D.E.N. Southworth's sixty novels, [Hawthorne] wrote to Ticknor in 1855: 'America is now wholly given over to a damned mob of scribbling women,' " and so on (x).

The independent career of this phrase, circulating in a range of critical discourses from scholarly monographs to *Time* magazine, cannot possibly be derailed by any attempt to resituate it in Hawthorne's career at the moment of original utterance. But, since such an attempt may help us to understand Hawthorne and his literary moment better, I will make it here. My argument must be speculative at some important junctures, but I will start on firm textual ground by noting that both Pattee and Matthiessen—in fact most people who use the phrase, even when they quote segments of the larger passage in which it is embedded—make one syntactically minor yet substantively major decision about how to frame it. The decision is major because it sunders the extract from what precedes it.

To demonstrate this as well as remind readers of the passage, I quote Matthiessen quoting Hawthorne:

> America is now wholly given over to a damned mob of scribbling women, and I should have no chance of success while the public taste is occupied with their trash— and should be ashamed of myself if I did succeed. What is the mystery of these innumerable editions of the Lamplighter, and other books neither better nor worse?— worse they could not be, and better they need not be, when they sell by the 100,000. (Matthiessen x–xi; *CE* 17: 304)[1]

The segment is accurate as far as it goes, but a word is missing from the first sentence: Hawthorne wrote "Besides, America is now wholly given over to a damned mob of scribbling women, and I should have no chance of success while the public taste is occupied with their trash—and should be ashamed of myself if I did succeed. What is the mystery of these innumerable editions," and so on. Besides. What is the mystery of that "besides"?

The passage figures in an epistolary discussion of Hawthorne's two careers as author and professional Democrat (thanks to Scott Casper for reminding us that he had two careers), which in turn is part of a conversation drawn out over more than two years in almost all the letters to Ticknor. When he wrote the passage—19 January 1855—Hawthorne was consul at Liverpool. His friend Franklin Pierce had rewarded him with this fairly lucrative appointment for writing a widely circulated campaign biography that may have significantly influenced an electorate to whom Hawthorne's name was better known than Pierce's. Hawthorne took the job, indeed he sought the job, because he wanted the money. His dream of a great popular and hence pecuniary success had not materialized. He had a big critical reputation but small sales.

Then, starting in April 1854—a mere nine months after arriving in Liverpool— Hawthorne faced first the likelihood and then the reality that Congress would enact legislation significantly reducing consular incomes. In some twenty letters to Ticknor, and another ten to his longtime friend and fellow Democrat Horatio Bridge, Hawthorne debated what to do. He sketched out such possibilities as: resigning at once, staying in the job six more months, staying in the job twelve more months, keeping the job but living more cheaply, resigning and remaining for a while in England, resigning and going to the Continent, resigning and returning to the United States. Each possibility was provided with a rationale, and each rationale, inevitably, conflicted to some extent with the others. Hawthorne asked Bridge and Ticknor to use their political influence, first to keep the bill from passing, then to delay its implementation. As Thomas Woodson's superb annotations to the full run of letters show (*CE*), what Hawthorne really wanted (and what, eventually, he got, since the bill passed but was never implemented) was the consulship on its original terms.

On the other side of the correspondence, Bridge and Ticknor apparently tried to console Hawthorne by suggesting that perhaps the consulship was not an ideal job for him; they may have taken this line in part because Hawthorne's letters continually complained about the position: the job is boring, the job is onerous, their living quarters are unsuitable, the weather is horrible, the English are dreadful people, the whole family is sick—on and on.

You're a writer, Bridge and Ticknor seem to have said. Come home and write. Ticknor especially would have found this line appealing. Having successfully hyped Hawthorne as the nation's leading man of letters, persuaded him out of his normal compositional habits into writing two big novels in as many years, republished his early books, made new books out of his uncollected materials, Ticknor and his firm had a substantial stake in Hawthorne's continued productivity. Hawthorne's letters respond to this; a letter of 12 October 1854, for example, says:

> You speak of another book for me. There is no prospect of that, so long as I continue in office; but if the Consular bill should pass at the next session, I shall soon be an author again. . . . No Consul can live as a gentleman in English society, and carry on the official business, on [the bill's] terms. But it would not cost me many pangs to resign. I hardly think, however, that the bill can pass during the short session. (*CE* 17: 264–65)

The letter coyly invites Ticknor to hope that the bill will pass so that Hawthorne will have no choice but to become an author again; its qualifying buts and howevers simultaneously convey the author's hope of escaping this fate.

The "scribbling women" letter, written three months later, is part of this conversation. It takes a different tack. Here Hawthorne is not outlining his options if the bill should pass; rather, he is justifying his decision to stay on the job now that it seems clear the bill will *not* pass, even though he had earlier described himself as willing, even eager, to resign. The beginning of the relevant passage is:

> It seems to be a general opinion that the consular bill will not pass. I had rather hold this office two years longer; for I have not seen half enough of England, and there is the germ of a new Romance in my mind, which will be all the better for ripening slowly. Besides, America is now wholly given over . . .

The scribbling women, then, come up among several reasons Hawthorne offers for deferring a return to authorship. Did the "besides" suggest a last-minute thought? Did he mean it? Did he mean any of his reasons? There is, after all, no corroborative evidence that he had the germ of any romance in his head at that time; this rationale was apparently cooked up to placate a publisher. Putting aside the vexed philosophical dilemma of sincerity, ignoring the fact that whether or not letters are reliable depth-psychology reports they are always rhetorical performances, one can still ask if Hawthorne meant what he said—or what he seemed to be saying—about women authors.

For Hawthorne quite ostentatiously revised his objection to women writers in his very next letter to Ticknor (2 Feb. 1855), implying that he had really meant to refer to just a certain class of women writers, not all of them. But had he really meant only a subset of women authors, there could be no logical connection between scribbling women *en masse* and his own career based on what they write, since by his own admission they write in various ways.

"In my last," the letter goes, "I recollect, I bestowed some vituperation on female authors. I have since been reading 'Ruth Hall'; and I must say I enjoyed it a good deal" (*CE* 17: 307–8). This letter then contrasts *Ruth Hall* to the generality of works by women, in ways that seem—but only seem—to explain and justify his earlier letter's complaint about *The Lamplighter:*

> The woman writes as if the devil was in her; and that is the only condition under which a woman ever writes anything worth reading. Generally, women write like emasculated men, and are only to be distinguished from male authors by greater feebleness and folly; but when they throw off the restraints of decency, and come before the public stark naked, as it were—then their books are sure to possess character and value. (*CE* 17: 308)

Feminists and others, I fear (myself certainly included, before I did the work that has produced this essay), have used all this hocus-pocus as a true guide, if not to real differences between *The Lamplighter* and *Ruth Hall,* at least to the way that Hawthorne really read them. When Hawthorne advances the metaphor of nakedness to praise the author of *Ruth Hall*—how admirable that she comes before the public naked as it were—he seems to define himself as a feminist sympathizer. But in a later letter to his wife, Sophia (18 Mar. 1856), Hawthorne uses this same metaphor to attack his friend and colleague Grace Greenwood:

> My dearest, I cannot enough thank God, that with a higher and deeper intellect than any other woman, thou hast never—forgive me the bare idea!—never prostituted thyself to the public, as that woman has, and as a thousand others do. It does seem to me to deprive women of all delicacy; it has pretty much an effect on them as it would to walk abroad through the streets, physically stark naked. Women are too good for authorship, and that is the reason it spoils them so. (*CE* 17: 456–57)

Certainly this rhetoric was performing for Sophia, who had given up whatever public ambition she might have had in exchange for drawing her life's meaning from Hawthorne's life, and who disliked Greenwood as a writer and person. Sophia had written to her sister Elizabeth Peabody on 8 February 1955, "I think her paper is miserable, & that she fails in truthfulness, essential truthfulness of mind & I do not like her," and then went on to criticize both the magazine that Greenwood edited for children, the *Little Pilgrim;* and her book of historical sketches for children, *Merrie England.* [2] Hawthorne certainly knew Sophia's likes and dislikes. But as a performance, his letter's coincidence of phrasing and incompatibility of meaning with the letter about *Ruth Hall* is striking. It is admirable, it is detestable, when women come before the public stark naked as it were.

To be sure, there is no reason to doubt that Hawthorne was jealous of the women's success and pleased to account for it as a function of debased public taste. "I should have no chance of success," he says—and then: "and should be ashamed of myself if I did succeed." What wouldn't he have given for the chance to feel that shame! Where Greenwood is concerned, a vein of hostile and demeaning commentary runs through Hawthorne's letters and his English journals. Perhaps his felt rivalry with women writers became particularly acute in the case of another Ticknor author who was more productive and much more successful than he. He wrote to Ticknor on

6 January 1854, "I am getting sick of Grace. Her 'Little Pilgrim' is a humbug. . . . Ink-stained women are, without a single exception, detestable" (*CE* 17: 161). He wrote James Fields on 20 January 1854 that her travel book (*Haps and Mishaps of a Tour in Europe in 1853*) was "miserable stuff—nothing genuine in the volume—I don't care a button for it" (*CE* 17: 166). But Hawthorne's letters to Greenwood herself praised her work lavishly. So the scribbling women remark, while functioning uniquely to stitch Hawthorne's self-contradictory discourse about his own authorial career to his self-contradictory discourse on women authors, multiplies contradictions rather than resolves them.

Matthiessen did not mention Hawthorne's differentiation of *Ruth Hall* from *The Lamplighter* in the two successive letters dealing with women writers. Pattee struggled to mesh the contrast with his own thesis about a monologic feminine voice in the 1850s and finally gave up: where *Ruth Hall* is concerned, he says, Hawthorne simply made a mistake (120). Several feminist critics have observed that Pattee doesn't seem to have read either novel. Some defend Hawthorne from other feminists' charges by making the contrast signify a liberated appreciation of robustly forthright writing by women along with a protomodernist distance for the treacly sentimentality, tearful narcissism, and Christian piety of the typical domestic novel. This line of argument assumes, of course, that Hawthorne had read not only *Ruth Hall* but also *The Lamplighter* and that he saw in *The Lamplighter* then what these critics see now.

Note, however, that while Hawthorne praises the author of *Ruth Hall* for throwing aside the restraints of decency and writing as though the devil was in her he contrasts this performance to women who write like "emasculated men." Whatever that phrase might mean, it is difficult to see it referring to an expressly feminine domestic novel that offers itself as emerging from a specifically female sensibility. It rather suggests women trying to write the kind of work that men wrote and, of course, failing, producing as Hawthorne says a book like a man's, except more foolish and feeble, or producing perhaps a book like a foolish and feeble man's book. Now, nobody who has read the *The Lamplighter* believes that it is anything like a failed man's book. Academics in the pro- and antisentimentalist camp alike agree that it is driven by a feminine domestic ideology which, whether conniving with or overridden by dominant masculine values at some subtextual level, nevertheless thinks it is an alternative to them.

And actually, Hawthorne's characterization—or rather, noncharacterization—of *The Lamplighter* (for what, actually, does he say about the book?) does not imply a sentimental domestic fiction. All he says is that it and others "neither better nor worse" are successful trash. Critics have filled the vacuum of this rhetoric with novels of their own making. They deplore domestic fiction; hence, so did Hawthorne. But I think it most unlikely that Hawthorne would have called *The Lamplighter* trash if he had recognized it as a domestic fiction. The example of his own *The House of the Seven Gables,* which he persisted in calling his best and favorite novel, makes absolutely clear that he had a considerable stake in domestic ideology himself.[3] In fact, I think that he was attacking *The Lamplighter* because he thought it was *not* a domestic novel, and I think he made this mistake because he had not read it.

To repeat this point: it seems to me virtually certain that Hawthorne had not read *The Lamplighter* when he penned his comment to Ticknor. I find only one other reference to the novel in his writings; this is in an entry in *The English Notebooks* dated 24 August 1854 and written at Chester. Here, as in the letter to Ticknor, *The Lamplighter* is yoked invidiously to his own books:

> At the Railroad Station, Sophia saw a small edition of Twice-told Tales, forming a volume of the Cottage Library. . . . The shilling editions of the Scarlet Letter and Seven Gables are at all the bookstalls and shop-windows;—but so is the "Lamplighter" and still more trashy books. (*CE* 16: 75)

Although the conjunction of his own work with *The Lamplighter* produces an irascible spasm which the scribbling women remark five months later reenacts, here it is not connected with women authors, and it does not demonstrate knowledge of the book's contents. He sees it; he recognizes it for trash; and he irritably dissociates his finer book from the trash that surrounds it. Hawthorne is not the first (or the last, as Pattee and Matthiessen both show) to dismiss trash as such without reading it.

But if Hawthorne would likely not have dismissed domesticity as trash, and if he identified *The Lamplighter* as a trashy book, then what did he think it was? I think he was using the term "trash" to invoke the genre of sensational underclass literature that had emerged in western Europe and the United States in tandem with the growth of urban and industrial culture. The great progenitor of this type was Eugene Sue's *Mysteries of Paris,* originally serialized in 1842 and 1843 and circulated in the United States in a number of different translations. The immense popularity of the book in this country is widely attested in reviews which praised or deplored it according to whether the critic approved or deplored the quasi-socialistic program frankly advocated in its pages. For the conservative *Southern Literary Messenger,* reviewing the work in December 1843, it "must produce something of the evil, that would flow from keeping company with the characters described"; the novel's moral tendency implied that as a matter of principle "the young, the pure and the virtuous" should be introduced "into all the haunts of vice, debauchery and infamy with which the world abounds." But for Horace Greeley's *Tribune,* reviewing the book in the same month, "No work of the age has made a more vivid impression than this, and though its exhibition of human depravity and villainy are horrible, almost beyond belief and endurance, yet we believe more good than evil will result from its publication."[4] The book inspired a host of American imitations: by the 1850s, urban exposés, at once sensationally exploitive and more or less politically radical, had become a staple of popular literature in the United States. Among better-known titles are George Lippard's *Quaker City,* George Foster's *New York by*

Gaslight, Elizabeth Oakes Smith's *The Newsboy,* Anne Sophia Stephens's *Fashion and Famine* and *The Old Homestead.*

All these books combined sensational spectacles of urban violence with demonstrations of redemptive goodness in the downtrodden poor. This vision told against the great American fantasy that in our republic, whose lack of hereditary aristocracy threw open the prospect of social advancement to all, nobody was poor who hadn't chosen to be so. These books were also especially fascinated with the prostitute figure (Sue's heroine was a pure-souled woman of noble birth who, forced into prostitution, retained a virginal heart and mind). From a domestic standpoint, the figure of the virtuous prostitute was particularly galling, since domestic ideology required the monogamous middle-class home as its precondition and fulfillment.

To make their genealogy clear, many of these urban novels echo Sue's title. Wright's bibliography of American fiction for 1774–1850 lists *Mysteries and Miseries of New York, Mysteries of Boston, Mysteries of City Life, Mysteries of Fitchburg, Mysteries of Haverhill, Mysteries of Lowell, Mysteries of Manchester, Mysteries of Nashua, Mysteries of New York, Mysteries of Papermill Village, Mysteries of Philadelphia, Mysteries of Rochester, Mysteries of Springfield, Mysteries of Troy,* and *Mysteries of Worcester,* all dating from 1844 and after, the majority published in 1844 and 1845. Wright's bibliography for 1851–75 adds *Mysteries and Miseries of New Orleans, Mysteries and Miseries of San Francisco,* and *Mysteries of St. Louis,* all published in the early 1850s. The very phrasing of Hawthorne's question—"What is the mystery of these innumerable editions of the Lamplighter"—echoes the titles of the many books about the lower strata. How could he *not* have had this tradition in mind when he asked about the "mystery" of *The Lamplighter?*

In *Beneath the American Renaissance,* David Reynolds has argued that our "major"—namely, Matthiessenian—authors worked by appropriating and transforming just this kind of "trash" into pure gold. Though Reynolds puts it differently, one might argue that the transmutation consists in bourgeoisifying these disruptive images, which, in fact, is exactly what *The Lamplighter* does. When Gerty, the abused and homeless child heroine, is rescued early on in the novel by the greathearted lamplighter Trueman Flint, a vision of domestic order, neatness, and contentedness overrides the opening scenes of urban squalor and brutality. Rescuing the urban genre from its radical sensationalism, reclaiming it for property, social hierarchy, and the work ethic, were precisely Cummins's projects in *The Lamplighter.* And this was recognized in its own day; indeed, it was better recognized in its own day than in afteryears, when Cummins and her work were "feminized."

But one had to read the book to know its values. The title alone, like *The Newsboy,* or *Old Haun, the Pawnbroker,* conveys only that the book is about the urban poor. Indeed, Susan Williams, who has studied the reception and publicity surrounding *The Lamplighter,* has turned up a review conceding, exactly, that the title might lead one, erroneously, "to class it among the works with which the press swarms in illustrations of the lower strata" (*New York Tribune* 28 Mar. 1854). I suppose, then, that if Hawthorne had recognized what *The Lamplighter* was about and how it worked he would not have targeted it for his wrath; and I conclude, therefore, that he had not read it, and instead excoriated the book on the basis of the one thing he knew about it—its title. I surmise also that, when he perceived his own work tumbled together promiscuously with *The Lamplighter* and other, unnamed, still more trashy books (some of which may indeed have been sensation novels), he feared that the bourgeois face-saving lesson of *The Scarlet Letter*—that fallen once is fallen forever—and the redemptive example of the pastoral Phoebe in *The House of the Seven Gables* would be buried in a heap of books showing the fallen as unfallen and situating virtue in city slums.

Although Hawthorne had not scrupled to complain about Grace Greenwood to their joint publisher, he may have felt especially free to attack *The Lamplighter* because it had been published by Ticknor's Boston rival, John P. Jewett. If Ticknor was even mildly jealous of Jewett's enormous success with the book—it seems that in the 1850s only *Uncle Tom's Cabin* surpassed it in sales, and that book too had been published by Jewett—he might enjoy hearing from his highest-toned author that the competition was just trash. And both these best-sellers were written by women! Whether Hawthorne knew in August 1854 that the author of *The Lamplighter* was a woman, he obviously knew it when he wrote the scribbling women remark to Ticknor five months later. If trash was bad in and of itself, woman-authored trash would perhaps be worse. Hawthorne's linking of literary women and prostitutes—which comes out with particular force in letters to his wife, as though to compensate her for whatever public ambitions she had sacrificed when she became Mrs. Hawthorne—would be all the more cogent if the women authors were writing to praise or exculpate fallen women.

Yet, even if *The Lamplighter* had been the book that Hawthorne apparently thought it was—which it was not—in 1855 he certainly knew much better than to think that this, or the domestic sentimentalism that was its supposed opposite, comprised the sum of female literary endeavor. He was acquainted with many literary women, friends with a few, related by marriage to two, and aware of the work of numerous others. If he could not have avoided the knowledge of a literary marketplace in which work by women circulated widely, neither could he have avoided knowing that much women's writing was neither sensational nor domestic. Among women publishing politically and historically informed writing directed toward contemporary public issues whom Hawthorne knew to some extent were these twelve at least: Jane Cazneau, Lydia Maria Child, Margaret Fuller, Sarah Hale, Julia Ward Howe, Eliza Buckminster Lee, Mary Peabody Mann, Anna Cora Mowatt, Elizabeth Peabody, Catharine Maria Sedgwick, Harriet Beecher Stowe, and of course Grace Greenwood.

It would take a great deal more space than I have here to detail the accomplishments of each of these women and consider the extent to which Hawthorne knew about them. It seems clear that a man whose sister-in-law was Elizabeth Peabody, a man who had been a friend of Margaret Fuller, must have known that literary women wrote much more than domestic and sensation fiction. No man who had read Eliza Buckminster Lee's 1848 novel *Naomi; or, Boston Two Hundred Years Ago*—which is far more obviously engaged with Puritan history and the contemporaneous debates over its legacy than *The Scarlet Letter,* and which contained all the historical background that Hawthorne would have needed to write his own work—could reasonably think that literary women were indifferent to public affairs. "C. Montgomery"—whose bellicose journalism about Mexico appeared among other places in the *Democratic Review* at the very time when Hawthorne was publishing in that journal, and who may well have inspired John L. O'Sullivan to coin the phrase "Manifest Destiny"—was in reality a woman named Jane Cazneau; if Hawthorne was aware of this fact, he would have known of at least one woman whose public journalism was trying to shape United States foreign policy. As for Harriet Beecher Stowe, about whose work Hawthorne is oddly silent, nobody could escape knowledge of her novel and the cultural furor surrounding it. The two seem elaborately to have missed meeting each other in England when Stowe was traveling and Hawthorne was consul; when they sailed on the same ship from England to the United States in 1859, Hawthorne remained sequestered in his cabin, ostensibly on account of seasickness. Given Stowe's enormous English reputation, her achievement would have confronted him repeatedly during his Liverpool years. If he contrasted their reputations and the grounds on which they were based, he could hardly have avoided recognizing the contrast in their engagements with the public sphere.

Grace Greenwood's work may be of particular interest here, however, because, as we have seen, Hawthorne's letters and journals single her out as the paradigmatic woman author. Greenwood, whose "real" name was Sara Jane Clarke, later Lippincott, is one of those many nineteenth-century literary women whose accomplishments have been concealed from us by their sylvan pen names.[5] Born in 1823, she began to publish professionally in the 1840s and remained active until a few months before her death in 1904. To be sure, she wrote pietistic, domestic, and sentimental sketches; but in the course of her long career she earned a much wider reputation for journalistic letters on public topics. These appeared at first in Nathaniel Willis's *Home Journal;* but when she began to voice strong antislavery sentiments she transferred her work to the *National Era* and the *Saturday Evening Post.* Two collections of her magazine work, both called *Greenwood Leaves* (and why, by the way, is "Greenwood Leaves" a feminine title and "Leaves of Grass" masculine?), were published by Ticknor and Fields in 1850 and 1851. The collections include letters showing that she was an antiexpansionist Whig opposed to the Mexican War; a supporter of the European revolutions of 1848 despite being a pacifist; an opponent of slavery, colonization, and capital punishment; an advocate of women's rights (in the first collection she called George Sand "the female Prometheus of the age" [362]), of female dress reform, of cheap postage, and of international copyright.

It is less important for my argument what Greenwood's views on this or that public matter were than that she felt free to reveal them, indeed clearly took her journalist's job to include having many opinions on political issues of the day and expressing them. This material entwines entirely unself-consciously with much more stereotypically sentimental material, suggesting or figuring a seamless web of female discourse in which the woman writer moves from the home fires to the public sphere without apology, registering absolutely no sense of impropriety.

The second series of *Greenwood Leaves,* for example, includes seven letters of reportage from Washington on the Senate debates over the Compromise of 1850. That this should have been her topic at all, quite apart from what she wrote about it, says a great deal about what it could mean to be a literary woman in the antebellum era. Much of her commentary describes the legislators' arguments and assesses the rhetorical effectiveness of their speeches: "Mr. Clay was suffering from recent indisposition, but he spoke with great energy and with keen flashings of his wonderful eye. It cannot be denied, however, that he oftener parried the attacks of his opponents with wit, than met them in argument" (302). One could interpret this approach as evading the political content in favor of the aesthetic, but it is no small matter for a lady journalist to opine on the success or failure of great statesmen to make their points effectively. Greenwood herself called attention to her temerity in characteristically humorous fashion (yes, she also wrote humor and satire, including some perceptive parodies of leading male writers of the day):

> I know I am, in these letters, taking unusual liberties with this august body— making very free with their worships—and as I bent over from the gallery, with eye and ear on the *qui vive* for absurdities, incongruities, and all sorts of comicalities, it is to be feared that the great actors below must regard me as the reverse of "the sweet little cherub that sits up aloft."
>
> But why should one be restrained by awe or reverence from having one's own, independent, careless, merry say, here as elsewhere? Are they not our servants, after all, these mighty men of the nation—these Senatorial demi-gods? (308)

But Greenwood's commentary was not limited to rhetorical criticism. At times her discourse merged the rhetorical and the political (as perhaps it merged in the minds of her contemporary readers):

> Thursday we listened to a long and most peculiar speech from the lately appointed successor to Mr. Calhoun. This was a powerful dose of the extremest South Carolina ultra-ism. The honorable Senator arose under the shadow of the greatness of his predecessor, feeling on his shoulders more the burden of his nullification, than the mantle of his inspiration. (310)

And elsewhere Greenwood's political views come unabashedly to the fore, as in this:

> Mr. Soulé addressed the Senate at length, on his amendment to the Compromise Bill. The exordium of his speech was, I should say, unfortunate. He indulged rather freely in censures and sarcasms on certain principles and sentiments prevailing throughout a large portion of his adopted country, and honestly and firmly advocated by some of the ablest and most honorable members of that Senate to which he has been exalted through the very spirit of liberty and toleration which he seems himself to disregard. (309)

And this:

> I have incurred the disapprobation of my Southern readers by simply doing justice to some of the prominent exponents of the principles and policy of the North. Ah, my friends, could you know how often I have refrained from speaking their praise, out of consideration for your delicate sensibilities! (321)

On 17 April 1852, Hawthorne wrote Greenwood praising this very book and its letters in particular. These, he said, "are the best that any woman writes—of course, better than any man's" (*CE* 16: 532). What could he have meant here? Perhaps, as I have argued was the case for his remarks about *The Lamplighter,* Hawthorne simply had not read the letters when he wrote something about them. His tribute could then be interpreted as a chivalric hypocrisy based on a set of assumptions about women versus men as letter writers. These assumptions might involve ideas about the letter as a private form and about women as custodians of the private sphere. But if Hawthorne was thinking of the letter as a private form associated with women, then it would seem to be appropriate for Greenwood to write letters but not to publish them, since an act of publication makes the private into something public. Of course, by the 1850s the public epistle was a venerable literary form; letters need not have been classed automatically as private documents (see Zboray). Perhaps Hawthorne supposed that women were better at writing public letters precisely because, in general, they handled a family correspondence that was meant to be shared and circulated among a wide audience of kin and acquaintances—that was, in some sense, already public. But at the least, he does not seem to be objecting to the publication of letters by women. Just the reverse.

If Hawthorne actually read the letters for which he praises Greenwood, however, then his praise of Greenwood for writing political letters that are "of course, better than any man's" goes beyond granting the propriety of women publishing letters, beyond even the propriety of their publishing on political topics, to suggest that women are superior political commentators to men, at least when they write in the epistolary form. Perhaps he meant that women were more adept at connecting their politics—when they had a politics—to their personalities than men, or more forthright about the connections between politics and other domains of sensibility. But whatever he meant, if he had looked at Greenwood's letters with any care at all, he could not possibly have escaped awareness of their openly political and fundamentally public nature. So, if to be public and political is to be a man, Greenwood was a man; then, for Hawthorne to say that because she was a woman she was "of course" better at what she was doing than any man would be to imply that, at least in the literary arena, women were ultimately better at being men than men were themselves. Here are certainly grounds for considerable anxiety.

In an interesting essay on Hawthorne and the scribbling women, James D. Wallace has argued that Hawthorne's reaction to women writers originates in his identification with them, because he recognized himself in their marginalized relation to the public sphere. My quite different, indeed opposite, point is that texts like Greenwood's are not at all marginal to that sphere but on the contrary are right in the middle of it. Grace Greenwood's popular antislavery letters were much more obviously, and actively, and perhaps effectively, doing public work than Hawthorne's ruminative and speculative fictions, which were presented in their own day (not least by the author himself in his prefaces) as issuing from the wayside, from, quite literally, the margins. Always excepting the campaign biography, little in Hawthorne's writing before the date of the scribbling women letter approaches Greenwood's outright political expressiveness. If self-recognition is the issue, women writing like Greenwood would force Hawthorne to realize that he was marginalized and they were not.

In his own day, too, Hawthorne was publicized emphatically as a nonpolitical writer. The friends who tried to save Hawthorne's job in the Custom House for him insisted he had never written a political line, and they assumed that the public would agree. As Richard Brodhead has amply demonstrated in *The School of Hawthorne,* Hawthorne's writing was connected by his friends, his reviewers, his audience, and by the author himself with a sphere that was supposedly neither public nor private but transcended both to constitute the realm of high art. The critics Hawthorne liked best—Edwin Whipple, Henry Tuckerman—touted his romances in just this way. To be sure, this rhetoric might have been a smoke screen, but it was advanced with Hawthorne's consent and connivance, which suggests that he chose to put himself forward as an author whose work declined engagement with issues of public moment. However one may agree with this or that academic political reading of Hawthorne's fictions, one has to wonder what cultural work they could have done, really and truly, in their own time if the culture itself was unaware that such meanings existed—if, in fact, the culture was being tutored to approach Hawthorne's fiction contrariwise as sites with nothing whatever to say about public affairs.[6]

To the extent that choosing the profession of authorship involved the biographical Hawthorne in questions about his class and masculinity, to the extent that he liked to imagine authorship as a gentlemen's fraternity, women writing in public modes would arguably threaten him more than women writing in domestic genres. But rather than taking the biographical approach, I prefer to think about the challenge and threat that this writing posed to the gender of his authorial persona. He was making a name for himself with fictions that seemed to be characterized by ethereality and a rejection of the actual world, at the very moment when women writers were laying literary claim to the real world he was rejecting. Was Hawthorne, then, taking on the persona of an obsolete, or even an imaginary, woman author? Or was he writing beyond sexual personae altogether to present himself as a suprasexual, or asexual, veritably angelic or ghostly authorial self? In Harriet Beecher Stowe's *Sunny Memories of Foreign Lands,* her travel narrative of 1854 based on her European voyage of 1853, the author placed Hawthorne early on with every expectation that her view of him was conventional. The party toured Speke Hall, "the first really old thing we had seen since our arrival in England."

> We heard that there was a haunted chamber, which was not to be opened, where a white lady appeared and walked at all approved hours.
>
> Now, only think what a foundation for a story is here. If our Hawthorne could conjure up such a thing as the Seven Gables in one of our prosaic country towns, what would he have done if he had lived here? Now he is obliged to get his ghostly images by looking through smoked glass at our square, cold realities; but one such old place as this is a standing romance. (1: 35–36)

A contrast between Hawthorne's supposedly disembodied—might one say politically irrelevant?—authorial project and her own cogent materiality is not merely implicit, for Stowe notes within a few sentences that the housekeeper who showed them around the romantic Speke Hall also showed them her down-to-earth kitchen, and then "presented her copy of Uncle Tom, and begged the favor of my autograph" (1: 36). Indeed, the cultural work of *Uncle Tom's Cabin* and its author are featured throughout Stowe's account of her travels in Scotland and England, an unsurprising and by no means immodest emphasis, given that she toured the British Isles in part as guest of antislavery societies. No similar recognition would ever be part of Hawthorne's lot; but it would be impossible to argue on the basis of his writing that he worked toward any such end.

Given these and numerous other possibilities for understanding the interrelations of sexual identity and the profession of authorship at a moment when concepts of gender roles, sexuality, and authorship were all in flux, it seems to me finally that the culturally and biographically most significant point about Hawthorne's famous epistolary phrase is probably not his writing it in the first place but his speedy retraction. The very next book by a woman he happened to read became an occasion to withdraw the slur. I take the retraction, in fact, to signify this much larger and immensely practical reversal: from "I should have no chance of success while the public taste is occupied with their trash" to "Whatever success I have is part of theirs; the rising tide floating their boats, is also floating mine; without them, I should have no chance of success at all."

Notes

1. Quotations from Nathaniel Hawthorne's *Letters* are from the *Centenary Edition,* hereafter cited as *CE* with volume and page numbers.

2. Sophia quoted in a footnote to Hawthorne's *Letters* (*CE* 17: 309). For a subtle discussion of the psychodynamics of the relationship between Sophia and Nathaniel, see Herbert.

3. For an influential discussion of the imbrication of *The House of the Seven Gables* in domestic ideology, see Brown.

4. Reviews quoted in my *Novels, Readers, and Reviewers* 180, 213.

5. Hawthorne always addressed her, and spoke of her, as Grace.

6. For suggestive although opposed readings of the politics of *The Scarlet Letter,* see Bercovitch and Berlant. I would never deny that cultural and political values and meanings are necessarily part of the constitution of all literary works, including those that present themselves to their publics as nonpolitical. Nor would I want to denigrate attempts to recover such values and meanings. But I find that usually, when critics insist that the meanings they have found actually affected the author's reading public—that is, actually did cultural work—they go beyond the evidence at hand.

Works Cited

Baym, Nina. *Novels, Readers, and Reviewers: Responses to Fiction in Antebellum America.* Ithaca: Cornell UP, 1984.

Bercovitch, Sacvan. *The Office of "The Scarlet Letter."* Baltimore: Johns Hopkins UP, 1991.

Berlant, Lauren. *The Anatomy of National Fantasy: Hawthorne, Utopia, and Everyday Life.* Chicago: U of Chicago P, 1991.

Brodhead, Richard. *The School of Hawthorne.* New York: Oxford UP, 1986.

Brown, Gillian. *Domestic Individualism: Imagining Self in Nineteenth-Century America.* Berkeley: U of California P, 1990.

Casper, Scott. "The Two Lives of Franklin Pierce: Hawthorne, Political Culture, and the Literary Market." *American Literary History* 5 (1993): 203–30.

Greenwood, Grace. *Greenwood Leaves: A Collection of Sketches and Letters.* Boston: Ticknor, Reed and Fields, 1850.

——. *Greenwood Leaves: A Collection of Sketches and Letters, Second Series.* Boston: Ticknor, Reed and Fields, 1851.

——. *Haps and Mishaps of a Tour in Europe in 1853.* Boston: Ticknor and Fields, 1855.

Hawthorne, Nathaniel. *The English Notebooks.* New York: Russell and Russell, 1962.

——. *The Letters, 1843–1853.* Ed. Thomas Woodson. Vol. 16 of the *Centenary Edition of the Works of Nathaniel Hawthorne.* Columbus: Ohio State UP, 1985.

——. *The Letters, 1853–1856.* Ed. Thomas Woodson. Vol. 17 of the *Centenary Edition of the Works of Nathaniel Hawthorne.* Columbus: Ohio State UP, 1987.

Herbert, T. Walter. *Dearest Beloved: The Hawthornes and the Making of the Middle-Class Family.* Berkeley: U of California P, 1993.

Jeffords, Susan. *The Remasculinization of America: Gender and the Vietnam War.* Bloomington: Indiana UP, 1989.

Matthiessen, F. O. *American Renaissance: Art and Expression in the Age of Emerson and Whitman.* 1941. Galaxy ed. New York: Oxford UP, 1968.

Pattee, Fred Lewis. *The Feminine Fifties.* New York: Appleton-Century, 1940.

Reynolds. David S. *Beneath the American Renaissance: The Subversive Imagination in the Age of Emerson and Melville.* New York: Knopf, 1988.

Sedgwick, Eve Kosovsky. *Between Men: English Literature and Male Homosocial Desire.* New York: Columbia UP, 1985.

Stowe, Harriet Beecher. *Sunny Memories of Foreign Lands.* 2 vols. Boston: Phillips, Sampson, 1854.

Wallace, James D. "Hawthorne and the Scribbling Women Reconsidered." *American Literature* 62 (1990): 201–22.

Williams, Susan S. " 'Promoting an Extensive Sale': The Production and Reception of *The Lamplighter.*" *New England Quarterly* 69 (1996): 179–200.

Wright, Lyle H. *American Fiction, 1774–1850: A Contribution Toward a Bibliography.* San Marino: Huntington Library, 1969.

Wright, Lyle H. *American Fiction, 1851–1875: A Contribution toward a Bibliography.* San Marino: Huntington Library, 1965.

Zboray, Ronald J. *A Fictive People: Antebellum Economic Development and the American Reading Public.* New York: Oxford UP, 1993.

ELIZABETH PALMER PEABODY

John L. Idol Jr.

Among the many additional subjects worthy of further study are Hawthorne's rumored engagement to Elizabeth Palmer Peabody and her comparison of Hawthorne's writing to that of his son, Julian. For the first subject, a good starting point is Norman Holmes Pearson's *Hawthorne's Two Engagements* (Northampton, Mass.: Smith College, 1963) and James R. Mellow's *Nathaniel Hawthorne in His Times* (Boston: Houghton Mifflin, 1980). For the second, see Peabody's "The Two Hawthornes," *Western Journal* ns 1.6 (1885): 352–58.

Writing to his wife (27 June 1848) during her visit with her sister Mary in West Newton, Massachusetts, Nathaniel Hawthorne recounted a recent dream:

The other night, I dreamt that I was at Newton, in a room with thee, and with several other people; and thou tookst occasion to announce, that thou hadst now ceased to be my wife, and hadst taken another husband. Thou madst this intelligence known with such perfect composure and *sang froid*—not particularly addressing me, but the company generally—that it benumbed my thoughts and feelings, so that I had nothing to say. Thou wast perfectly decided, and I had only to submit without a word. But, hereupon, thy sister Elizabeth, who was likewise present, informed the company, that, in this state of affairs, having ceased to be thy husband, I of course became her's; and turning to me, very coolly inquired whether she or I should write to inform my mother of the new arrangement![1]

This dream occurred nearly six years after Hawthorne had married Sophia and more than eleven after Elizabeth Palmer Peabody, Sophia's older sister, had discovered Hawthorne. From the outset of her discovery, Elizabeth had undertaken to arrange things for Hawthorne, to boost him and his writing whenever she could. In time she published, sold, remaindered, and reviewed his books; she invited him to contribute to her attempt to launch a literary publication; she actively sought an appointment for him as a civil servant; she provided much information about Hawthorne to his early biographers; she stepped in as business adviser to Sophia when Hawthorne's widow lost confidence in his publishers, Ticknor and Fields; she watched newspapers and periodicals to see that errors or false impressions about Hawthorne were corrected; she eagerly supported an effort to make the Wayside a Hawthorne memorial, and suggested that a statue of Hawthorne be carved and placed on the grounds of Hawthorne's Concord home. She became, in short, a tireless champion, working energetically to make Hawthorne's literary and personal life as much a bed of roses as she possibly could, but, as we shall see, Hawthorne sometimes found her ministrations prickly.

Once Louisa Hawthorne set Elizabeth Peabody straight that certain anonymous stories appearing in S. G. Goodrich's *New England Magazine* were the work of her brother, Nathaniel, and not, as Peabody had guessed, the admirable creation of her sister, Elizabeth, Peabody instantly conceived a cause for his genius and soon began to promote his work. Having discovered him in a household that seemed to her a hermitage of recluses, Peabody said to Louisa: "If your brother wrote those stories, he has no right to be idle." Such talent as he showed in the widely appreciated "The Gentle Boy" could be brought to bear in Peabody's favorite goals: to educate children, to win adults to the spiritual values she espoused, and to announce to the literary world that an American writer could stand comparison with English and European artists. Soon after the publication of *Twice-told Tales,* she wrote Horace Mann, her brother-in-law, about her discovery, giving a few facts about Hawthorne but primarily attempting to persuade Mann that Hawthorne should be enlisted to write books for schoolchildren:

> If you have leisure—I think that a suggestion from you to *Capen*—who thinks everything of you—to endeavour to enlist Hawthorne by good offers to write for the young—would perhaps secure him to this work—But it should be done soon. (Peabody, *Letters* 200–201)

Though she found Hawthorne interested in "such things as interest my mind" (Peabody, *Letters* 200), Mann considered that Hawthorne's tales put too little emphasis on duty and devotion and, consequently, did not approach Capen in Hawthorne's behalf.

Such things as interested her mind were being expressed in letters to friends, among them William Wordsworth, and in a review of *Twice-told Tales* a few weeks after her letter to Mann. On 24 March 1838, the *New-Yorker* carried a transcendentalized appreciation by Peabody. She reported that Hawthorne was a recluse who nonetheless studied profitably where Wordsworth had studied, in nature and in the human heart.

> There is throughout the volume a kindliness and even heartiness of human sym-
> pathy—a healthy equilibrium of spirits, and above all, a humor, so exquisitely com-
> bined of airy wit and the "sad, sweet music of humanity," that it contradicts the notion
> of misanthropical or whimsical seclusion. (30)[2]

She declared his philosophic outlook to be Wordsworthian but refused to assert that
he took it from Wordsworth. Since both were scholars in the School of Nature, they
both knew that "ideal beauty may be seen and felt most profoundly in the common
incidents of actual life" (30).

She chose to illustrate Hawthorne's treatment of incidents from actual life by
looking closely at "Sunday at Home" and "Little Annie's Ramble." The first was
"worth a thousand sermons on the duty of going to church. It quickens the reader's
love of religion; it shows the adaptation of Christianity to our nature, by adding to
the common phenomena of the sacred day the pathos and grace which are to be
drawn up from the wells of sympathy" (Idol and Jones 31).

Though drawn to such sentimental, morally satisfying, and spiritually uplifting
sketches and tales as "Sunday at Home," "Little Annie's Ramble," "The Vision of
the Fountain," "David Swan," and "A Rill from the Town Pump," she recognized
the depth and power of "The Gentle Boy," "The Prophetic Pictures," "Fancy's
Showbox," and "Wakefield." The closing observation of "Wakefield" she deemed
"terror-striking" (Idol and Jones 32).

Much as she wanted her readers to admire and learn from Hawthorne's pictures of
life and his probing of the laws of human nature, she desired even more to win them
to her belief that America had at last produced a writer capable of meeting the
nation's spiritual needs. For her, art was "the highest interest of our state . . . a beauty
which at once delights the eye, touches the heart, and projects the spirit into the
world to come" (Idol and Jones 34). Hawthorne, if given the opportunity to write
and the support of his countrymen, could create that art and perform his office
worthily. To win their livelihood, artists should not have to be yoked to the "dray-
cart of utility" (34).

Meanwhile, she made sure that influential people in her circle read Hawthorne.
She was delighted to learn that Washington Allston, a mentor to her sister Sophia,
was already reading *Twice-told Tales* but was disappointed that Emerson had not yet
read Hawthorne's work. "[Emerson] is in a good mood to do so, however, and I
intend," she told Sophia, "to bring him to his knees in a day or two, so that he will
read the book, and all that Hawthorne has written" (Peabody, *Letters* 226). She must
have been disappointed ultimately that Emerson found little to enjoy or admire in
Hawthorne's writing.

As she sought support for Hawthorne and outlets for his work, Hawthorne
returned favors, asking his friend John O'Sullivan to consider her essay entitled
"Claims of the Beautiful Arts" for publication in *Democratic Review,* a journal in
which Hawthorne's work often appeared (*CE* 15: 272).

Having grown accustomed to her promotion of his work, Hawthorne accepted her proposal that she become the publisher of a series of books for children when she established her book shop on West Street in Boston. Eventually, three books bearing her imprint appeared: *Grandfather's Chair* (1840—but dated 1841), *Famous Old People* (Jan. 1841), and *Liberty Tree* (Mar. 1841). Although she sold copies of these books in her book shop and attempted to place copies in other bookstores, the venture was not successful, leaving her the job of trying to find someone to take the books off her hands, even at half price, when she moved her book shop. When it appeared that another publisher might buy remaining copies in 1842, Hawthorne wrote a letter, expressed in the third person, insisting that Peabody take "to herself the publisher's share of the profits" (*CE* 15: 609). The deal fell through, and she had to cart the books to her new shop on Washington Street.

Among the works cluttering up the Washington Street shop was *Aesthetic Papers,* a publishing venture that Elizabeth had hoped would become a periodical. She had invited Hawthorne to contribute a tale to it. He offered her "Ethan Brand," but she wanted something lighter, accepting "Main Street" instead.

Even if most of her efforts to become a publisher failed, she gained knowledge of the business end of the trade and could, much later, step in as business adviser when Sophia lost confidence in Hawthorne's publishers, Ticknor and Fields. Writing to Moncure Conway, she reported that "People say that Ticknor & Fields have grown rich on Hawthorne's books. This is probably an exaggeration" (Peabody, *Letters* 345). Therefore, she tried to mediate between Sophia and the firm when Hawthorne's widow expressed a belief that Hawthorne "had been cheated all his literary life by his publishers—& kept unnecessarily anxious by their never giving him an account—so that he never knew what he had a right to spend" (Peabody, *Letters* 454).

Despite her idealistic promotion of Hawthorne as this country's best hope of becoming its first first-class literary artist, Peabody undertook practical steps to help Sophia and Hawthorne enjoy married life. It was she who went to Concord to oversee arrangements to rent the Old Manse. She perhaps encouraged the Emersons to send Thoreau to put in a garden for the bridal pair at the Old Manse. When Hawthorne suffered from "brain fever" following the death of his mother and Sophia had to spend all her time nursing him, Peabody came to Salem to babysit Una and Julian. Had she been allowed to assume all the nursing duty she wanted to give, she would have traveled to Europe to care for Sophia, but Hawthorne put his foot down firmly even as he sought to agree with Sophia that Peabody might appropriately be described as " 'divinely benevolent.' " He added, "As you yourself feel," he wrote to Peabody, "it is more than you deserve; and yet you deserve it as much as any human being I ever knew; for, intermixed with gravel, and granite, and flint, and clay, and all sorts of rubbish, there really does exist in you the rich vein of gold, out of which (purifying it by the action of her own mind) Sophia shaped that golden crown and put it upon your head. Divine Benevolence! Perhaps, not; but a deep and warm humanity you have; nor is it inconsistent with all the errors we have accused you of, and a great many more" (*CE* 18: 6). Among those indelible errors surely was an earlier Peabody suggestion that Una, not yet eight years old, had the potential to be an ideal spiritual medium (Peabody, *Letters* 274). But more bothersome was Peabody's attempts to place her abolitionist writings in the Hawthorne household. When Hawthorne bluntly told her to stop sending her tract to Sophia, Peabody singled out Una for indoctrination, an act evidently growing out of Peabody's conviction that Hawthorne failed to understand the condition of slaves. She said that he had not seen slaves or fugitive slaves and lacked patience to read abolitionist literature (Peabody, *Letters* 445).[3] Hawthorne refused to pass her letter on to Sophia. His patience having worn thin, Hawthorne replied that he "did not mean to close all correspondence forever, but only on that particular subject. I hope, in whatever years we may have left, to exchange many letters, and see you many times; for there are few people whose society is so pleasant to me. I never in my life was angry with you; and if you will only allow me to think of you as I please (or rather, just as I cannot help) I really think we shall find great comfort in one another. Upon my honor, I consider myself the one person in the world who does justice to your character!—an assertion at which you will probably laugh outright" (*CE* 17: 330).

Staunch abolitionist that she was, Peabody found Hawthorne's views untenable, declaring to Hawthorne's close friend Horatio Bridge that Hawthorne, by his own admission, "knew nothing about contemporaneous history" and "could not understand it until it was at least a *hundred* years old!" (Peabody, *Letters* 445). Fearing that she would carry on her fight publicly by exposing his views, Hawthorne said, "I do not write (if you will please observe) for my letter to be read by others" (*CE* 18: 591). When, more than two decades later, his letter did appear in Boston and New York papers, Peabody was "amazed" to see it in print. "I never showed it to *any body but* Ellery Channing" (Peabody, *Letters* 445). Her regret seems genuine, and she surely lamented that she breached a promise that the two had earlier made to burn each other's letters. But she would not have regretted the crusader's zeal that led her to tell Hawthorne that dedicating *Our Old Home* to his friend and patron Franklin Pierce was unthinkable and more than a little galling, for she concluded that Hawthorne had "written to antagonise what he was zaney enough to call my fanaticism."[4]

Political and philosophical differences aside, Peabody had a crusader's zeal to keep Hawthorne's name in the forefront of American letters. To that end, she succeeded in placing a belated review of *The Marble Faun* in the *Atlantic Monthly* (Sept. 1868) under the title of "The Genius of Hawthorne." She would later include the essay in *Last Evening with Washington Allston, and Other Papers* (1886) with the title "Hawthorne's Marble Faun." Ranging widely across the body of Hawthorne's work, Peabody sought to show traits of Hawthorne's genius as she argued her thesis that the romance was to be understood in the context of "the atmosphere of Rome," which she deemed "immoral" (Peabody, *Last Evening* 293). In a letter to her nephew Horace Mann Jr., written while she was doing her review for the *Atlantic,* she spelled out her charges against Roman Catholicism: many cardinals and many young monks are "excessively licentious" and the Church at Rome, though there are individuals in it who are good, is guilty of "corruption & shamminess." She then added,

> I have been reading the Marble Faun. . . . It is a very gentle & lightly touched picture of the dirt and wickedness—but it is full of the deepest truth. I think it is really a most profound book upon Rome in a theological, political, & moral point of view,—with the most delicate humanity & the most *tender*—its fine ironies & sarcasms could only come from a most humane soul—& the genius—which has strewed every page with so much beauty is transcendant. (Personal letter to Horace Mann Jr., 26 Feb. 1868, Mann Collection, Antioch College)

That genius could express "what he *felt with his mind,* and *thought with his heart*" and therefore waken to consciousness "shades of feelings" and "delicacies of thought" that, though experienced by all, "were never embodied in words before" (Peabody, *Last Evening* 293). In his ability to create "understanding within those whom he addresses," Hawthorne "takes rank with the highest order of artists." He did so through "the elevation and fineness of truth his work communicates" (Peabody, *Last Evening* 294). As a great moral teacher, Peabody placed Hawthorne in the company of Aeschylus. Like the greatest writers, Hawthorne did not see a literary work "as merely an instrument for giving pleasure, but as a means to discover truth, or, rather, to put his readers on the track of discovering it in company with himself" (Peabody, *Last Evening* 294).

Peabody found Hawthorne's interest in crime and sin to be a characteristic of his mind. She saw a line of development from "Endicott and the Red Cross" through *The Scarlet Letter* to *The Marble Faun.* Thus, she considered his focus on Miriam and Donatello and his use of the portrait and history of Beatrice Cenci as central to his purpose of exploring crime and sin in a context beyond the Puritan world of New England. But Peabody convinced herself that Hawthorne was doing something more than universalizing his theme. He was exposing, however gently and delicately, the "corruption & shamminess" of Rome: "Only in Rome does natural innocence and virtue kneel in helplessness before personified vice, clad in sacramental garments, and armed with the name and prestige of Father!" (Peabody, *Last Evening* 297). Peabody takes as a Hawthornean master stroke his move to make Miriam "the symbol of Italy" (Peabody, *Last Evening* 306).

That dark shadow that falls upon Miriam, the model who takes the brown frock and cowl of a Capuchin, symbolizes the Roman Catholic Church. What she sees as "fine sarcasm" in Hawthorne Peabody turns into diatribe as she reflects on Roman Catholic monastic orders, especially the Capuchins and the Franciscans, the former denounced as filthy in their "loathsome dresses" and the latter for their idleness and begging (Peabody, *Last Evening* 306–7).

This daughter of New England certainly was in no mood to doff Puritanical armor and settle into ecumenical dialogue with representatives of the Roman Catholic church. She supposes that Hawthorne still donned similar Puritanical garb when he wrote *The Marble Faun:*

> It was in this mockery of a Church and State that Hawthorne seized the idea of his *chef-d'oeuvre;* and the more we shall see into his multifarious meanings, the more we shall acknowledge that he has uttered no idle word from the beginning to the end. (Peabody, *Last Evening* 314)

As a kind of transcendental Puritan of Puritans, Hawthorne went behind corrupt, showy, immoral Rome and looked at original Italy, to an "age of the world before this sin-shadowed human experience began" (Peabody, *Last Evening* 314). If the model was present-day corrupt Rome, Donatello was natural innocence.

Peabody's review of *The Marble Faun* is not wholly a pretext for another Protestant assault on the Roman Catholic church. While acknowledging that she has not made "an exhaustive analysis of the Romance," she points out that "the mere drama of it is wonderfully knit together, all its incidents growing directly out of the characters, and their interactions with universal laws" (Peabody, *Last Evening* 328). Readers would also find "delicate criticisms on pictures and statues, ancient and modern, with original thoughts on nearly every subject of moral, intellectual, and aesthetic interest" (Peabody, *Last Evening* 329). Having declared as much, she returned to her transcendental pulpit for the peroration:

> "The Marble Faun" takes a high place in that library of sacred literature of the modern time which is the prophetic intimation of the Free Catholic Christian Church, "whose 'far-off coming' shines,"—a Church whose *credo* is not abstract dogma, but the love of wisdom and the wisdom of love; whose cathedral is universal nature, and whose ritual is nothing short of virtue, truth, and charity, the organs of piety. (Peabody, *Last Evening* 330)

Like critics before or after her, Peabody cut and shaped the cloth she found in Hawthorne's romance to fit the sails of the boat she launched upon her own literary, moral, theologic, and philosophic seas. In giving *The Marble Faun* a belated boost, she commandeered it for her own fleet.

Though she might force his work to serve her own agenda, she zealously watched to see that misinformation was corrected. For example, when she learned that Ada Shepard, a sort of nanny-companion to the Hawthorne children during the Italian sojourn, had been suggested as a model for Hilda, Peabody wrote a letter to *The Commonwealth* (7 Feb. 1874) to say, "I know from personal conversation with my brother-in-law on the subject that neither of the women in 'Marble Faun' were portraits" (Peabody, *Letters* 372). She also rushed to defend Hawthorne when Julian made his father's opinion of Margaret Fuller public in his biography of his father and mother. Peabody explained, in a letter to the *Critic* (17 Sept. 1887), that the elder

Hawthorne never meant his journal entries to be published, at least not in the form in which he recorded them (Peabody, *Letters* 428). She had long before wanted to stand as Hawthorne's champion when his first publisher, Samuel Goodrich, had used an unflattering description of Hawthorne ("his brow thick, his mouth sarcastic, his complexion stony, his whole aspect cold, moody, distrustful") in his *Recollections of a Lifetime* (New York and London, 1856). Hawthorne acknowledged that Goodrich drew "no very lovely picture," but he begged Peabody not "to take up the cudgels on my behalf," especially since Peabody's recollection about who actually cut up the group of tales Hawthorne called the "Storyteller" was, Hawthorne wrote, "rather inaccurate" (*CE* 18: 89–90).

Among the most delicate tasks Peabody had to undertake to keep misinformation from harming Hawthorne or his circle was keeping Julian from mishandling or falsifying materials about Hawthorne and his family. Although Julian had come to her for information (and used much of it accurately), she expressed disappointment that he had not asked for more. From as early as 1838 or 1839, she had considered herself the best authority on Hawthorne's "true psychological biography," since, as she told Horatio Bridge, Hawthorne gave me "his own account . . . of the growth of his mind" (Peabody, *Letters* 445). Had she completed her contemplated "Reminiscences of My Contemporaries," no doubt she would have given that account as well as she could a half century or more after hearing it. In any event, she proved to be a primary source of information for several Hawthorne biographers other than Julian. She supplied details to Moncure Conway, Thomas Wentworth Higginson, Amelia Boelte, and Horatio Bridge. Her recollections helped color—and still do—our impression of the Hawthorne family as largely dysfunctional, for Peabody presented them as cooped-up recluses as well as isolates within their own home.

She considered Hawthorne as essentially a poet, a writer more symbolic than realistic, one more to be admired for his moral and intellectual dignity than for his ability to make characters live upon the page. In this judgment she joined such critics as Mary Russell Mitford, Melville, and Henry Fothergill Chorley, Hawthorne's most ardent English admirer. Whether he was symbolic or realistic, Peabody remained Hawthorne's champion. She never tired of the role, from her early discovery of *Twice-told Tales* to her watchdog phase of seeing that biographers, including her nephew Julian, got Hawthorne's story right. Despite her political and philosophic disagreements with him, she insistently considered him to be the nation's first literary heavyweight. She worked energetically to engender and empower Hawthorne, having, in a sense, rung the bell that summoned others to the School of Hawthorne.

Notes

1. Hawthorne, *Centenary Edition* 16: 228; hereafter cited as *CE* with volume and page numbers.

2. Elizabeth Palmer Peabody, rev. of *Twice-told Tales, New-Yorker* 5.1/105 (24 Mar. 1838): 1–2; rpt. in *Nathaniel Hawthorne: The Contemporary Reviews,* ed. John L. Idol Jr. and Buford Jones (New York: Cambridge UP, 1994) 28–34. Page references in text are to Idol and Jones.

3. Peabody's zealous support of abolitionist causes troubled Hawthorne. Responding to yet another of her pieces on the subject in a letter to her dated 8 October 1857, Hawthorne wrote: "The good of others, like our own happiness, is not to be attained by direct effort, but incidentally. All history and observation confirm this. I am really too humble to think of doing good" (18: 116). In a sentence in the Bowdoin College copy of this letter not included in the letter as published in the *Centenary Edition,* Hawthorne pursued the matter further, underlining a point he had made resoundingly in *The Blithedale Romance.* "If I have been impertinent enough to aim at it, I am ashamed what wretched things men perpetrate under the notion of doing good!" Sentence from Nathaniel Hawthorne Collection at Bowdoin College published by permission.

4. Letter to Mrs. Harriet M. Lothrop, Sept. 1887. Published in *Nathaniel Hawthorne Journal* 2 (1972): 7.

Works Cited

Hawthorne, Nathaniel. *The Centenary Edition of the Works of Nathaniel Hawthorne.* Ed. William Charvat et al. Columbus: Ohio State UP, 1962–.

Idol, John L., Jr., and Buford Jones. *Nathaniel Hawthorne: The Contemporary Reviews.* New York: Cambridge UP, 1994.

Peabody, Elizabeth Palmer. *Last Evening with Allston, and Other Papers.* Boston: Lothrop, 1886.

——. *The Letters of Elizabeth Palmer Peabody: American Renaissance Woman.* Ed. Bruce A. Ronda. Middletown, Conn.: Wesleyan UP, 1984.

Sophia Peabody Hawthorne's
Contribution to Her Husband's Career

THE CHIEF EMPLOY OF HER LIFE

Luanne Jenkins Hurst

Though few of the over 1,500 extant letters by Sophia Hawthorne have been published in their entirety, some have been included in *The Centenary Edition of the Works of Nathaniel Hawthorne*, ed. William Charvat et al. (Columbus: Ohio State UP, 1962–), vols. 15–18. Many of these letters, like the works treated herein, show Sophia's fostering of Nathaniel's career, as does her 1870 preface to *Passages from the English Note-books*.

Sophia Hawthorne once wrote to her sister Mary Mann: "If I could help my husband in his labors, I feel that that would be the chief employ of my life. But all I can do for him *externally* is to mend his shirts & socks—spiritually, it is another thing" (6 Apr. 1845, ms., Berg Collection).[1] Ironically, she seems not to have realized how much she did do to help Nathaniel Hawthorne "in his labors." Sophia was always Nathaniel's most devoted admirer, and in her letters she consistently promoted him as the greatest and most creative artist alive. These letters also reveal her reactions to his stories and romances as he finished them and read them to her (her reactions being clearly important to him), and they reveal her fierce loyalty to him—sometimes leading to a strong rebuke of a beloved sister who dared to criticize her husband's social aloofness or leading her to chastise her mother for failing to send books for Nathaniel to read. Perhaps her greatest contribution to her husband's literary career was her concern for the sanctity of his study. When they moved to a new home, one of her first occupations was making Nathaniel's study as physically comfortable and visually pleasing as possible. She also established a pattern in the early years of their marriage of never interrupting him when he was writing and did her best to keep the children and even visitors from intruding. Her letters reveal the Hawthornes' daily life, and the person who made everything run smoothly was clearly Sophia Hawthorne. She shielded her husband from social contacts he would have found trying, including contact with the "busy & confused" Peabody household (13 Apr. 1843), defended him against criticisms made by professional reviewers or family and friends, and insulated him from the children's noise as much as she could. Though she did not recognize it, Sophia Hawthorne made a major contribution to the success of her husband's career as one of America's great men of letters.

For Sophia Amelia Peabody, who grew up in a very sociable family, marriage to Nathaniel Hawthorne must have required some adjustment in her expectations about the social interaction she would have with others. She not only adapted but did her best to shield her husband from others when he wished to avoid them, and she defended him vigorously when she perceived a need. She made many obligatory social calls on her own and did her best to account innocuously for her husband's obvious avoidance of her parents' noisy, crowded, and matriarchal household. When she had to write her mother (three months after her marriage) to change the date of a proposed visit, she was careful to explain that it had been *her* mistaken assumption that she and Nathaniel would come at the earlier time; "for my husband says he never thought of going as soon as I had planned" (9 Oct. 1842). She also emphasized his mother's being "in an ecstacy of impatience" to see him as the reason for his leaving her in Boston and going right on to Salem. Already she had begun to smooth the way for him socially and to shield him from contacts that he would find unpleasant.

Her sister Mary's criticism of Nathaniel caused Sophia to write: "His abomination of visiting also still holds strong, be it to see no matter what angel—I do not care to perplex him with entreaties for this end." Later in the same letter, she continued:

> I wish my darling May would not express surprise or displeasure any more for his not doing this & that with regard to visits— It does not good, & only makes me feel uncomfortable that she should not let this point go, & think of him in other regards. Of what moment will it be a thousand years hence whether he saw this or that person? Whereas, it is of great account that he should not be constantly disturbed by the presentment of this question. If he had the gift of speech like some others, Mr Emerson & Wm Greene, for instance, it would be different, but he evidently was not born for mixing in general society. His vocation is to observe & not to be observed. (9 Oct. 1842)

Here, her tone was kinder and more conciliatory than it would be almost a year later when Mary raised the issue again:

> Mary Mann has not the smallest notion of him. What she regards as weakness in him is but a very *strong* resolution & an Idea. I have myself hardly come near the depth & riches of his intellect & its laws after six years of intimate communion—& then how can any one judge him who has seen him hardly six times & then never intimately? But I spoil my subject by trying to write about it. (3 Sept. 1843, to Mrs. Elizabeth Peabody)

In both letters Sophia emphasized Nathaniel's hospitality when others visited him and said it was his calling to observe: "His vocation is that of a poet, of the highest grade—who must stand apart & observe, & not be mingled up with the petty, though often genial & graceful little ceremonies & etiquettes of life" (3 Sept. 1843, to Mrs. Peabody). Though her husband could make himself "approach other persons," she asked indignantly,

> But why should he? Why, in the name of common sense & reason should he? Are not there enough persons to pass their days or a portion of them in social intercourse with men & women? Does it not take all sorts of people to make a world—? & why should not each one fulfill his calling? He has not the gift of tongues—he is not a talker like Mr Emerson— He was not born to chat nor converse. Words with him are not 'airy nothings' nor even of little weight as with most people— Words with him are worlds— suns & systems—& cannot move easily & rapidly— (3 Sept. 1843, to Mrs. Peabody)

Sophia Hawthorne soon became so accustomed to living in the "retirement" that Nathaniel found necessary that she was overwhelmed by a visit back to her parents' home and requested:

> Tell my sistreen that I do not want them to make another beautiful party for me. I have promised my husband to go to bed at ten o'clk while I am in Boston, & I had rather see each person separately. It is much more satisfactory, for I am like a bewildered bee among choice flowers when so many rare people are all present, attracting me. (22 Feb. 1843, to Mrs. Peabody)

In a later letter she referred to how "busy & confused" everything was during her visit (13 Apr. 1843, to Mrs. Peabody). These requests and reactions show how completely Sophia had adjusted to and come to understand her husband's disposition. This understanding also led her to treat his study as the most important room in their home, no matter where they lived.

When they were newlyweds, Sophia carefully decorated Nathaniel's study at the Old Manse and learned not to interrupt him when he was writing. In addition to hanging her own paintings of Lake Como, she adorned the study with reproductions of famous works by European masters and gave an honored place to a bust of Apollo. After she had a miscarriage in February 1843, she made a special point of having Nathaniel's study cleaned so that it would not remind him of the "sad Scenes enacted there," and Nathaniel deviated from his usual practice to have her sit with him while he wrote (22 Feb. 1843, to Mrs. Peabody). Generally, however, Sophia did not interrupt Nathaniel while he was writing. One of the few times when she did, she described to her mother what happened: "I went into the orchard & found my dear husband's window was open, so I called to him, on the strength of the loveliness [of the spring day], though against rules. His noble head appeared at once & a new sun & dearer shone out of his eyes on me, but he could not come then because the Muse had him entrapped in a gold net—so I was obliged to be content with Mary [the maid]" (20 Apr. 1843).

Though her description was poetic, Sophia made it clear that she knew better than to argue with the Muse. She respected Nathaniel's privacy as an artist so much that she never asked him what he was working on. She once explained to her mother, "I can comprehend the delicacy & tricksiness of his mood when he is evolving a work of art by a small degree of the same in my own case— And his must be far greater, because he is so much greater, & his thoughts go far out of sight" (9 Jan. 1844). She waited for him to discuss his creations in his own time. He often read them to her before sending them to the publisher, but occasionally she did not see them until they were in print (as was the case with his *Life of Franklin Pierce*).

When they left the Old Manse and moved in with Nathaniel's mother and sisters, Sophia feared that their family of three would not be able to stay together and prayed earnestly about their new situation. Even at that time of inner turmoil, one of her main concerns was that Nathaniel have a study: "He & Una are my perpetual Paradise, & I besieged Heaven with prayers that we might not find it our duty to separate, whatever privations we must outwardly suffer in consequence of remaining together. All I asked for was for them, & for a quiet spot in which he might write. Heaven has answered my prayers most bounteously—" (7 Sept. 1845, to Mrs. Peabody).

In later accommodations, Sophia continued her preoccupation with Nathaniel's study. When they lived at 18 Chestnut Street in Salem (1847), she lamented the fact that her husband had no separate place for writing. While visiting her parents, Sophia wrote to Nathaniel:

> Thou, beloved, oughtst not to be obliged to undergo the wear & tear of the nursery— It is contrary to thy nature & to thy mood— Thou wast born to muse & to be silent & through undisturbed dreams, to enlighten the world— I have suffered only for thee in my babydom— When I can once shut thee away in thy study, & shew thee our jewels only when they are shining—then it will be unalloyed delight day by day— (16? July 1847)

Not surprisingly, when they moved to 14 Mall Street two months later, Nathaniel's study was on the third floor with his mother's and sisters' living quarters located on the second floor to insulate him from the noise of the children on the first floor. Sophia did spend most of her time with the children, and as they grew, she conducted her own school for them. (Being from a family of educators, she was better qualified than many who taught in more formal situations.) In the Mall Street house, Sophia made it possible for Nathaniel to have the seclusion he needed to write *The Scarlet Letter*.

After the Hawthornes moved to Lenox in May 1850, Nathaniel, as was his custom, took the summer off from writing. This summer he especially needed to recover from the strain of the previous year when he had been dismissed from the Salem Custom House, his mother had died, and he had written *The Scarlet Letter* in a few intense months. When the autumn arrived, however, Sophia's letters once more reflected her concern that Nathaniel have an appropriate retreat for writing. They had arranged a study for him in the summer, but she was concerned that it would not be warm enough in the winter. She wrote to her mother for advice on a special way of heating a small room with hot water in a tin container. She also mentioned the possibility of his "taking the guest-chamber for his study. It will be the most quiet room unless the wind blow all its trumpets louder on that side of the house than upon any other. But he would not have the sun there" (29 Sept. 1850). What he did have was the situation he needed to write *The House of the Seven Gables* that winter and *A Wonder Book for Girls and Boys* in the following months.

When the Hawthornes rented the Manns' home in West Newton (Nov. 1851 to May 1852), Sophia made special arrangements for "Mr Hawthorne's house-comfort," requesting that her father, who lived nearby, "make his visits to me . . . in the morning while Mr Hawthorne is writing, so that our afternoons & evenings may be en famille." She added, "I want my time to teach the children, . . . & we do not want any body at all but our five selves—" (2 Oct. 1851, to Miss Elizabeth Peabody). During this time of what Sophia called "*complete* retirement," Nathaniel wrote *The Blithedale Romance.*

After they bought the Wayside in Concord, Sophia seems to have paid even more special attention to Nathaniel's study—his first in his own house. She wrote to his sister Louisa: "The study is very pleasant & quite high studded & I purpose to have it the best adorned of any room in the house. Apollo reigns there, & the Transfiguration & Endymion & the Comos hang on the walls— And there are to be two book cases—one already is up" (17 July 1852). In a letter to her mother, she described the new carpet on the study floor, noting that it "looks like rich velvet" (6 June 1852). Sophia may have had in mind a remark that Nathaniel had made almost two years earlier when they were arranging his study in Lenox. He described his ideal study, and she resolved to help him have it one day:

> Mr Hawthorne said this morning that he should like to have a study with a soft, thick Turkey carpet upon the floor & hung round with full crimson curtains, so as to hide all rectangles. I hope to see the day when he shall have such a study. But it will not be while it would demand the smallest extravagance, because he is as severe as a stoic about all personal comforts, & never in his life allowed himself a luxury. It is exactly upon him therefore that I would like to shower luxuries—because he has such a spiritual taste for beauty. It is both wonderful & admirable to see how his taste for splendor & profusion is not the slightest temptation to him—how wholly independent he is of what he would like, all things being equal— (29 Sept. 1850), to Mrs. Peabody)

Nathaniel had recently published his third major novel (*The Blithedale Romance*) when he purchased the Wayside. He must finally have felt secure enough financially to permit himself a little bit of luxury in his new study, for he would have had to approve the expenditures, though it was Sophia who chose the carpet, paint, wall-paper, and other supplies and supervised the improvements to the whole house. She went to the house a day or two ahead of Nathaniel and was pleased to have many of the carpets down before he and Julian arrived—"So that he had quite a civilized impression of the house at first glance. & was delighted with it, not having seen it since his first visit in snow-time, when it was desecrated . . . with all sorts of abominations, & it seemed fit only for a menagerie of cattle" (6 June 1852, to Mrs. Peabody). In the study at the Wayside, Nathaniel wrote his biography of Pierce as well as *Tanglewood Tales* before leaving for England. When the Hawthornes re-turned to the Wayside seven years later, they added the famous tower to house Nathaniel's study. Perhaps because of her experience as an artist in her own studio in the years before her marriage, Sophia always recognized the importance of her husband's having a sanctuary for his work, and she made it possible for him to withdraw from ordinary life to produce extraordinary art.

Before the Hawthornes had been married a year, they had established what was to be a lifelong pattern (interrupted only by the times when Nathaniel held public office) of Nathaniel's writing in the mornings without interruption and coming out of his study by afternoon (or sometimes evening) for time with his family. When Nathaniel was working on a romance or other long work, he would sometimes write all day. At such times Sophia would not interrupt him even to get needed supplies from his study. While he was writing *The Scarlet Letter,* she wrote her mother,

> Will you ask Father to buy half a ream of good letter paper for us as cheap as possible. I have no paper. And I want some yellow envelopes[.] I have no ink down stairs & cannot disturb Mr Hawthorne. He writes immensely— I am almost frightened about it— But he is well now & looks very shining— (27 Sept. 1849)

When he was working on *The House of the Seven Gables,* Sophia apologized for not writing often to her sister Mary Mann and explained: "I have very little time to write at all—because the children are always about me, you know. I have no Antonia [Mary's maid], & Mr Hawthorne is writing & I do not like to put them into his care even in the afternoon, because he still is mentally engaged when out of his study" (9 Sept. 1850). Clearly, she was making sure the children were well cared for, but she was also giving Nathaniel the necessary time and space for his writing. After he finished the romance, she wrote to her mother, "Papa now descends from his study at noon, instead of at night, & this causes a great rejoicing throughout his king-dom—" (12 Feb. 1851).

When Nathaniel had finished a story or romance, he often read it to Sophia, and she often passed on her reactions to his works in her letters to her mother and sisters. She wrote to her sister Elizabeth in February 1850:

> Mr Hawthorne read to me the close of the Scarlet Letter last evening. If I may compare the effect of the Moral Sublime of the Great Stone Face to the distilling of the dew of Hermon—(for such seemed my tears) I must liken that of the Scarlet Letter to a Thunder Storm of Rain—& forked lightning leaping from the black cloud to write with its finger of fire on the darkness. . . . The omnipotence of the Moral Sentiment here triumphs over the world— The human being is rent in twain to give egress to this irresistible Power— Earth dwindles before it—all the ceremonies & pomps of common life pale at its Sovereign urgency— I really thought an ocean was trying to pour out of my heart & eyes—but I had the magnetic power upon me of Mr Hawthorne's voice also—swaying me like a mighty wind—(spirit means wind) tremulous with the pathos of GOD's Word speaking through him. ([4 Feb. 1850])

After he read the end of *The House of the Seven Gables* to her, Sophia wrote to her mother:

> There is unspeakable grace & beauty in the conclusion, throwing back upon the sterner trajedy of the commencement an etherial light & a dear home-loveliness & satisfaction— How you will enjoy the book,—its depth of wisdom, its high tone, the flowers of Paradise scattered over all the dark places, the sweet wall-flower scent of Phoebe's character, the wonderful pathos & charm of old Uncle Venner. I only wish you could have heard the Poet sing his own Song as I did; but yet the book needs no adventitious aid— It makes it[s] own music, for I read it all over again to myself yesterday, except the last three chapters. (27 Jan. 1851)

Three weeks later she wrote a more extensive critique to her sister Elizabeth:

> "The House of the Seven Gables" is a totally different book from the "Scarlet Letter". I might quote the words which Little Bun used to the mountain.
> "Talents differ: all is well & wisely put." It is, I think, a great book. While I listened I was in enchantment from the wisdom, the depth of insight, the penetration into the reality of things, the tragic power, the pathos, the delicate grace, the jewels of rarest beauty scattered throughout, like flowers over broad prairies— And you know his wonderful reading! . . . I always feel, when my husband is reading his own works that it is impossible they can ever seem just so when any one else reads them. Yet I find they bear the test, & so I found with this. For I read it all over to myself before it went to the Publishers. The Rosebud Phoebe blooms on the darker picture as Juliet shone on the night, like a jewel in an Ethiop's ear. And Alice's pale, stately head bends like a regal white lily before a rough gale. I am charmed by the simplicity of the plot. It is as simple

as a Greek tragedy, & certainly the diamond purity, the marble severity & perfection of the style never has been, never can be surpassed. A foolish book written in such a style would have a worth—but when it is but the setting of a rich jewel of Truth, how must it be? (16 Feb. 1851)

In this same letter Sophia gave some insight into Nathaniel's feeling about a work after it was published as well as her awareness that he was likely to discount her praise as coming from someone who loved him and was not objective. As positive reviews vindicated her opinion, she indulged in the luxury of saying, "I told you so." She also gave a perceptive explanation for why her husband's works might not appeal to the broadest segment of the public and predicted a greater fame for him in the future than in his own time:

> For himself, he is tired to death of the book. It seems to him at present perfectly inane; but so it is, I think, every time— I am rather shy of commendation—because it is too much like striking the same note— I am too near— But I venture roundly to assert my impression & then wait humbly till there be a reverberation from remoter spheres. Then I triumphantly say "So *I* said." The absolute freedom from caricature, even from the most airy, tricksy caricature in all he writes perhaps is one reason why the popular ear may not be as quickly arrested as by a writer of far less truth & power,—just as the common eye would prefer a striking painting a little exaggerated to a pure marble statue that is more beautiful & true at the end of a thousand years to the one who contemplates it aright than when first it appears among men. . . . And he who rises to such a lofty point of view as to see unclouded emanations from the source of Light, & then is so simple as most simply to record his visions, Such an one is not often recognized in his day & generation as the Seer he will afterwards prove. (16 Feb. 1851)

A more controversial work than his romances was Nathaniel Hawthorne's campaign biography of Franklin Pierce. The defensive tone of Sophia's reaction to it reflected her awareness that even her own family might respond negatively to what her husband had done:

> I have just now finished reading the little Biography which I did not see in manuscript. It is as serene & peaceful as a dream by a green river, & such another lily of testimony to the character of a Presidential candidate, was, I suspect, never before thrown upon the fierce arena of political warfare. Many a foot & hoof may trample on it, but many also will preserve it for its beauty. Its perfect truth & sincerity are evident within it, to say nothing of the moral impossibility of Mr Hawthorne uttering any but words of truth & good faith. As no instrument could wrench out of him a word he did not know to be veracious in spirit & letter—so also no fear of whatsoever the world may attribute to him as motive would weigh a feather in his estimation. He does the thing

he finds right, & lets the consequences fly— They are nothing to him— (10 Sept. 1852, to Mrs. Peabody)

As this quotation shows, Sophia often idealized Nathaniel's character. She also could not resist defending him and his writings against various critics. One especially telling passage occurs in a letter to her sister Elizabeth in reference to *The Scarlet Letter:*

> Mr Hawthorne does not know why Mr Channing should think his book the using up of "stormy gasses." He is not conscious of it— Mr Bellows seems to have also an idea that he has purified himself by casting out a legion of devils into imaginary beings. But it was a work of the imagination wholly & no personal experience, as you know very well. Mr Channing has a wonderful comprehension of Mr Hawthorne, but he is mistaken in supposing him to be gloomy in his nature. Not Ariel is more pervaded with light & airy joy for himself; but he sees men & he sees passions & crimes & sorrows by the intuition of genius, & all the better for the calm, cool, serene height from which he looks. Doubtless all the tendencies of powerful, great natures lie deep in his soul; but they have not been waked, & sleep fixedly, because the noblest only have been called into action— In no person have I ever known the spiritual practically so predominant—& the Right so supreme over the wrong, the intellectual—over the physical. Mr Bellows is singularly obtuse about the tone & aim of the "Scarlet-Letter". This questioning of its morality is of all criticisms the funniest—especially this notion some short sighted persons have about the author's opinion of the crime! when the whole book is one great tragic chorus of condemnation—when such terrible retribution follows—when even the retribution lives & breathes in Pearl from beginning to end. It is curious, is it not? I think ministers are peculiarly exercised by the book— They have some singular fear of it. (21 June 1850)

Sophia insisted again in a later letter that Nathaniel was *not* gloomy. She was referring to Cornelius Mathews's calling her husband "Mr. Noble Melancholy" in his account of a famous picnic of literary men in the Berkshires (published in the *Literary World* on 31 Aug. 1850). She admitted, "He is pensive, perhaps—as all contemplative persons must be . . . because he sees & sympathizes with all human suffering—" Then she continued (and once more showed her idealized view of him): "He has always seemed to me, in his remote moods, like a stray Seraph, who had experienced in his own life no evil, but by the intuition of a divine Intellect saw & sorrowed over all evil— As his life has literally been so pure from the smallest taint of earthliness—it can only be because he is a Seer, that he knows of crime" (4 Sept. 1850, to Mrs. Peabody).

Being married to a woman who thought so highly of him and was so clearly happy to be his wife and to do whatever she could to make his life comfortable and his circumstances conducive to his chosen career had to be a major factor in the success of Nathaniel Hawthorne as an author. The fact that she was clearly an intelligent and thoughtful admirer must have also been encouraging to her husband. Before her marriage Sophia Peabody was recognized in Salem and in Boston as a gifted artist, and modern scholars are not the first to wonder if she ever regretted giving up her art to become Mrs. Nathaniel Hawthorne. When a visiting friend raised a similar question in 1850, asking why Sophia "did not paint & draw & hire people to take care of the children," her private response (which she later reported to her sister Elizabeth) was that her children were "the best pictures I ever painted, the finest poetry I ever could write, better poetry than I ever can write" (16 Feb. 1851). Though this declaration does not address her relationship with Nathaniel, it reflects her happiness in her domestic situation in general and harmonizes with other, more direct remarks about her joy in being his wife. She wrote to him in 1847: "*I* do not need to stand apart from our daily life to see how fair & blest is our lot. . . . Every mother is not like me—because indeed no other mother has such a father of her children, & such a husband to herself— . . . This I tell thee all the time, but thou canst not believe it." Later in the same letter, she continued:

> The beauty & loveliness & nobleness & grace which possess me in the shape of these fairest children which enchant all peoples—these lay hold on the basis of being—these are permanent & immortal—my mind & heart dwell on them— Above all, beyond them is thyself—who art my everlasting satisfaction—my ever present felicity—my pride & glory & support—my sufficiency— I ask no more— GOD has poured out his horn of beneficence upon my head—into my cup— I am the happiest of women— (16? July 1847)

Note

1. All of the original manuscripts of Sophia Peabody Hawthorne's letters that are cited in this essay are located in the Henry W. and Albert A. Berg Collection of English and American Literature of the New York Public Library, Astor, Lenox and Tilden Foundations, and are quoted by permission.

MEMORIES OF HAWTHORNE

Patricia Dunlavy Valenti

In addition to the biographical works discussed herein, Rose Hawthorne Lathrop produced a substantial body of fiction and poetry. For a full treatment of these imaginative works, which, though frequently characterized by ambiguity and Gothic elements, demonstrate little of her father's influence, see chapter 5 of Patricia Dunlavy Valenti's *To Myself a Stranger: A Biography of Rose Hawthorne Lathrop* (Baton Rouge: Louisiana State UP, 1991). The legacy of the Brook Farm experiment and American transcendentalism upon Lathrop's religious evolution is suggested in Diana Culbertson's introduction to *Rose Hawthorne Lathrop: Selected Writings* (1993) in the Paulist Press series on Sources in American Spirituality. This volume also presents a representative sampling of Lathrop's essays and letters on religion and issues of social justice.

B etween 1894 and 1897, Rose Hawthorne Lathrop published a number of articles and one book about her father, Nathaniel Hawthorne. Rose's focus upon her father as a literary topic occurred during a period of radical change for her. Having converted to Roman Catholicism in 1891, she abandoned her twenty-four-year marriage to George Parsons Lathrop early in 1895 in order to forge an entirely new identity as a nun caring for the homeless who were dying of cancer. Why—some thirty years after Nathaniel's death, at this moment of tumult and change—did Rose "most signally set aside" her father's "command" against writing about his life, a command which she had "respected for a number of years" (*Memories* 477)?[1] Perhaps the answer to this question lies in the fact that she was setting aside not a paternal prohibition against biography but a more profound, cultural prohibition—that against female autobiography.

In the spring of 1894, the *Ladies Home Journal* had asked Rose to contribute a piece entitled "My Father's Literary Methods." Acutely in need of money, Rose welcomed a marketable topic. This article was extremely well received and led to her publishing "The Hawthornes in Lenox" in the November 1894 *Century Magazine,* "Some Memories Of Hawthorne" in the *Atlantic Monthly* in four installments from

February through May of 1896, and "Hawthorne as Worker" in the *Cambridge Magazine* for June of 1896. Much of this material was collected and expanded in *Memories of Hawthorne,* published by Houghton Mifflin in February of 1897. The success of "My Father's Literary Methods" also prompted numerous lucrative lecture opportunities for Rose on the topic of her father and his Concord cohorts.

A more significant motivation to undertake these lectures than financial gain, however, was Rose's perception that they would be "useful," for "to do something that is *of use* to good ends," she wrote about these talks to a friend, Bessie Hunt, "is my longing" (4 Oct. [1894?], Sophia Smith Collection). In February of 1895, when Rose left George permanently, she wrote to another friend, Charlotte Holloway, explaining that, as a Catholic convert, she had a "sense of duty toward *usefulness.* This idea and longing have been so constantly the object of my prayers, that I have no doubt they are the greatest love of my heart." Elsewhere in this letter, Rose noted that "for one of my temper and associations and talents" convent life was highly suited (22 Apr. 1895, Berg Collection; emphasis added).[2]

A Story of Courage: Annals of the Georgetown Convent of the Visitation of the Blessed Mary,[3] published by Houghton Mifflin in December of 1894—just two months before Rose left George—vividly demonstrates her values after her conversion. Ostensibly a history (albeit an inaccurate one) of the French order of Visitation nuns in America, the book is replete with anecdotes and biographical sketches through which Rose considers the themes of useful work, communal life, and individual obligation to a larger community than the family. Rose compares Visitation nuns (and religious sisterhoods generally) to secular experiments in forming "community associations" (the transcendentalists' experiment at Brook Farm, for example), and she concludes that nuns "have solved the question of community life on a great scale" (v). Asserting that "the private family, essential though it is, . . . is only a type of the whole human family" (373), Rose pointed to the life of the widowed foundress of the order, Jane de Chantel, who, Rose claimed, "was considered . . . almost inhuman for daring to propose to leave her four children and her father and her aged father-in-law to take some care of themselves" so that she might care for the poor and homeless (134). Writing specifically about the duty to care for a larger community than the family, Rose wrote: "To the nun, this mother's love, brother's love, love of friend, is the mere A B C, or beginning of the language of spiritual works; the instrument of the poetry of higher action, which must be brought into play, towards all human creatures alike" (48).

Rose concludes *A Story of Courage* with similar ideas cast in polemical tones:

> We ought really, all of us, to regard the great human family with the same tenderness we have been in the habit of bestowing upon the single, private family. Christ taught us that we should not restrict our love and interest to the narrow limits of the threshold of the home. (37)

Indeed, while the desire to be useful and of use was emerging as a dominant theme in Rose's life, the words "useful" and "of use" began to constitute Rose's "discourse," that is, her "way of putting things—a vocabulary, a rhetoric, a pattern of argument—that is connected to [her] identity." As Clifford Geertz has noted in *Works and Lives,* the "author-function" (referring to Foucault) is made manifest through a "signature" or "writerly identity" which, particularly in Rose's writing at this time, can be recognized in her "author-saturated texts" (8–9). *A Story of Courage* establishes Rose's vocabulary and rhetoric—her argument for a woman's usefulness to a community beyond the immediate family—and by the summer of 1896 Rose had acted upon the conclusions of this argument. She acquired nursing skills at New York Memorial Hospital and then moved to an apartment in a tenement district of Manhattan, where she immediately began caring for homeless women who were terminally ill with cancer.

Notwithstanding the rigors of this newly established life, Rose accepted H. O. Houghton's offer to publish her articles about her father in a book form. *Memories of Hawthorne* incorporates, with very few and insignificant deletions, the texts of all four previously published articles about her father. What she added beyond these early articles reflects[4] not only Rose's signature in biography but her own autobiography, for as Heilbrun has noted, "until recently, confronting the relation to the father was the only way to female self-realization" (65). Expounding further on this pattern of development frequently evinced in female autobiography, Heilbrun's comments point out with uncanny precision the function of Rose's *Memories of Hawthorne:*

> [F]athers, as representatives of the patriarchy, are the pivot on which, usually in memory, the new awareness turns. Mothers have no obvious role in this change, but some other female mentor or figure, often not even known personally, most often dead [in Rose's case, Jane de Chantel], operates in the new female plot to enhance the reaction from the father and encourage or inspire new awakening. (64)

The first seven chapters, which constitute better than a third of Rose's book, might suggest that *Memories of Hawthorne* is a misnomer, for these chapters are not Rose's memories nor are the chapters strictly speaking about her father. Rose opens the book with a preface acknowledging "that this volume is really written by Sophia Hawthorne; whose letters from earliest girlhood are so expressed, and so profound in thought and loveliness, that some will of sterner quality than a daughter's must cast them aside." Rose then introduces chapter 1 with a brief statement of her intention to "preserve, as well as I can by selections, the effect produced *upon me* by the many packages of letters which I opened some years ago" (2; emphasis added). Thus she quickly establishes that, although much of the book will not, in fact, be composed of her memories, much of the book will be about the effect of events upon her.

In the first three chapters, composed of entirely new material, Rose inserts an occasional note to clarify facts or create a transitional sentence or two between letters. Chapters 4 through 7 incorporate and greatly expand "The Hawthornes in Lenox," but again Rose's comments are confined—as they must be for one who could have no memory of the events—to explanations of an editorial nature.

Although obviously using those letters in her possession to flesh out her book, Rose's choice of beginnings, additions, and inclusions indicates her writerly identity by suggesting a gender-inflected biographical method. If, as Susan Stanford Friedman points out, *auto*biography for a woman is possible only when "the individual does not feel herself to exist outside of others, but very much with others in an interdependent existence that asserts its rhythms everywhere in the community" (38), the woman writer of *bio*graphy may likewise present the life of her subject in a contextual framework. This would be particularly so for a female biographer whose own "identity theme," to use Lichtenstein's term (Holland 454),[5] resonated with the communal aspects of another's life. And Rose indicates her deliberate choice of this contextual biographical method when she asserts that her departures from chronology are intended to capture "the atmosphere which surrounded Hawthorne and the aspect of typical personalities which he enjoyed" (*Memories* 234).

In chapter 7, Rose's "memories of Hawthorne" actually begin with her family's move from Concord to Liverpool when she was two and a half. Rose announces that she will be "prefacing [family letters] and interpolating a few girlish memories of my father." But the first memories she presents are not of her father but of her own juvenile feelings of displacement: "I was . . . much younger than the others [her sister, Una, and her brother, Julian], and was never allowed to grow, as I wished, out of the appellations of Rosebud, Baby, and Bab. . . . I grew into [a] girlhood [that] made me seem to myself a stranger who had come too late" (212–13). Chapters 7 through 11, which absorbed the first two installments of "Some Memories of Hawthorne," continue to present the Hawthorne family's life in England between 1853 and 1856 through the charming lens of Rose's childhood sensations and recollections of "her first remembered home" (291). Rose's specific memories of her father, however, create a portrait of Nathaniel vastly different from the man portrayed by biographers such as Randall Stewart, James Mellow, Robert Cantwell, and most recently, E. Haviland Miller. A man who from young adulthood fretted over his apparent lack of energy and occupation, Nathaniel was comfortable only with very few close friends and his wife, who observed tellingly that he despised "to be touched more than any one I ever knew" (qtd. in Miller 43). Even the Edenic quality of the first years of his married life was marred by Hawthorne's fears that he was an "idler," a characterization of himself that was undoubtedly corroborated by neighbors, one of whom, observing Hawthorne standing for hours, his eyes riveted on the ground, remarked: "Poor fellow, . . . he does look as if he might be daft" (qtd. in Miller 246). His perceived idleness and his feeling that the first decade of his adult life had been wasted fed his anxiety about being able to support his family and contributed to a recurring fear that he would end up in an almshouse.

Therefore, in 1853 when he was offered the post of United States consul to Liverpool with its promise of financial security, he accepted. But the public nature and constant activity of that position wore him down physically and psychologically. Adding to his frustrations was the fact that his remuneration as consul was far less than he had expected. Hence, he returned to New England in 1860, a weary, broken man who was plagued more than ever by the specter of his own failures and fear of the almshouse.

Rose, however, remembers her father as an industrious, active man who was committed to useful work, sympathetic to the value of communal life, and aware of his duties to a community larger than the private family. One recollection of him during their stay in England illustrates her vision of her father's energetic response, even in trivial matters:

> I remember his standing once by the fire, leaning upon the mantelpiece, when a vase on the shelf toppled over in some way. It was a cheap, lodging-house article, and yet my father tried to save it from falling to the floor as earnestly as he did anything which he set out to do. His hand almost seized the vase, but it rebounded; and three times he half caught it. The fourth time he rescued it as it was near the floor, having become flushed and sparkling with the effort of will and deftness. For years that moment came back to me, because his determination had been so valiantly intense, and I was led to carry out determinations of all sorts from witnessing his self-respect and his success in so small a matter. People of power care all the time. (*Memories* 301–2)

Rose had drawn a similar picture in "Hawthorne as Worker" in the *Cambridge Magazine,* a periodical "devoted to education, co-operation, brotherhood." In this article, which she combined with "My Father's Literary Methods" to form "The Artist at Work," chapter 15 of *Memories of Hawthorne,* Rose claims that "Nature turns at the sight of a man who will not work. . . . In reading the histories of great men we find their biographers breathless with surprise at the amount of labor these heroes could perform" (70). Associating Nathaniel with François Millet, "the peasant's prophet," Rose asserts that "Hawthorne worked hard and nobly" (71). He "was not selfish. His abstemious method of existence, his constant labor, his unwavering response to people who came to confess their sins and for help in their destitution— these facts show that the beauty of his art developed from the beauty of his ascetic, diligent brotherhood" (75).

Attributing to her father a habit of diligent work, not unlike the unremitting labor in which Rose herself was engaged while she put together *Memories of Hawthorne,* she ascribed to her childish self-awareness a sense of guilt—inspired by her father—over normal childhood play. In recounting her acquaintanceship with

Hannah, the only playmate Rose seems to have had before her return to the United States, she describes the effect her father's presence had upon their make-believe games: "He would look askance at my utterly useless, time-frittering amusement, which I already knew was withering my brain and soul" (351).

At the moment in her life when Rose had abandoned the private family to respond to the incessant demands of impoverished and diseased women, she claimed similar virtue for her father: "Poverty, trouble, sin, fraudulent begging, stupidity, conceit,—nothing forced him absolutely to turn away his observation of all these usual rebuffs to sympathy, if his inconvenience could be made another's gain" (450–51). Rose's assessment of her father's response to the demands of the human community differs markedly from Nathaniel's reaction to the obligations of his office as consul which he recorded in *The English Note-Books*:

> I am sick to death of my office,—brutal captains and brutal sailors; continual complaints of mutual wrong, which I have no power to set right, and which, indeed, seem to have no right on either side; calls of idleness or ceremony from my travelling countrymen . . . ; beggars, cheats, simpletons, unfortunates so mixed up that it is impossible to distinguish one from another, and so, in self-defense, the Consul distrusts them all. (8: 68–69)

For a person with Nathaniel's reclusive nature, the interpersonal demands of the consulate were taxing in ways Rose could not fathom. For a man who, by his wife's account, could not bear to be touched, his experience with a sickly child in an almshouse must have been almost unbearable. Veiling this incident in third-person anonymity when Nathaniel recounted it in *Our Old Home* (thereby placing himself at an even greater distance from its reality), he described a man of more than "customary reserve, shy of actual contact with human beings, afflicted with a particular distaste for whatever was ugly, and accustomed to that habit of observation from an insulated stand-point." Suddenly a "sickly, wretched, humor-eaten infant . . . prowled about him like a pet kitten" until he "took up the loathsome child and caressed it as tenderly as if he had been its father." This repugnant embrace became the sign "that he was responsible, in his degree, for all the sufferings and misdemeanors of the world in which he lived, and was not entitled to look upon a particle of its dark calamity as if it were none of his concern" (300–301).

Rose does not refer to this incident in any of the articles about her father or in the 1897 edition of *Memories of Hawthorne*. Later in her life, however, she associated with this incident her inspiration to establish charity work. In fact, when the Riverside Press printed a second edition of the book in 1923, Rose added the following in a preface:

> The patients of the Servants of Relief for Incurable Cancer, as we call ourselves, are of the class to which belonged the child whom my father found in an English hospital

which he visited and of whom he wrote in *Our Old Home.* His words in regard to this little child made a great impression upon me when I read them as a girl; and I was glad to have the latter years of my life devoted to the field of diseased poverty. (vi)

Rose drew from this incident with the child a meaning far beyond any Nathaniel could have conceived. His momentary and uncharacteristic embrace of this orphan could never have been transmuted into a thirty-year commitment as it was for his daughter. Rose physically and symbolically "embraced" her dying charges, forbidding the use of rubber gloves or masks in their care and insisting that caregivers share everything, even tableware, with them (Valenti 174, 144). Rose's interpretation of events recorded in *Our Old Home* again reveals her writerly identity as a biographer.

In the concluding chapters of *Memories of Hawthorne,* however, Rose's additions to previous publications are more than the reflection of her signature. This additional, purely autobiographical material demonstrates the evolution of her adult identity and an apologia not only for her conversion to Roman Catholicism but for her adoption of religious sisterhood. Chapters 12, "Italian Days: I," and 13, "Italian Days: II," of *Memories of Hawthorne* utilize all the third installment of "Some Memories of Hawthorne" and significantly add approximately thirty pages of Rose's reminiscences of her childhood experience in Rome and Florence along with her adult notions of Roman Catholicism.

Alternating between past-tense childhood recollection and present-tense adult commentary, Rose notes that her initial observation of Catholicism was influenced by her "party, which for some reason seemed inclined to impute the most death to the faith which has the most form." Consequently, Rose did not "read the signs of the subterranean churches aright, any more than the uncultivated Yankee reads aright an Egyptian portrait" (376). Her first impression of monks was similarly conditioned by her mother and sister: "Through the streets of Rome trotted in brown garb and great unloveliness a frequent monk, brave and true; and each of these, I was led by the feminine members of my family, to regard as a probable demon, eager for my intellectual blood" (376). Rose thought the monks' chanting in the street to be "child's play," which she imitated to the entertainment of her family; but their chant in churches created quite another impression: "Who does not feel," asks the adult Rose, the convert to the Church of Rome, "without a word to reveal the fact, the wondrous virtue of Catholic religious observance?" (377). Realizing her autobiographical digression, Rose concludes chapter 12 with an attempt to adjust her remarks to the memory of her father: "Upon all these things I delighted to think and afterwards to ponder, because I realized that they were of vital interest to the intelligence which was to me greatest and dearest" (380).

If that statement is something of a non sequitur, Rose's attributing to her mother positive judgments about the monastic life in the following chapter seems similarly fallacious, for it contradicts her earlier assertions about her mother's distrust of monks. Rose quotes portions of a letter where Sophia notes the "wonderful picture" of monks in procession, "their sweeping black robes upon the marble pavement" (390–91), and comments that her mother "still clung to the Puritanical idea that in religion itself, 'What looks so wondrous, wondrous fair, His providence has taught us to fear. . . . Angels only are fit to live as monks pretend to live' " (391). But, Rose insists, her mother "contradicts this theory. No one was more adapted to perceive the godliness of monastic sacrifice, when she realized the object of it" (391). Both parents, she claimed, "felt the physical weight of Catholicity, or the Cross, and half guessed its spiritual spring" (392). Interpreting her mother's positive response to the burial of a child in the church of San Spirito—Sophia had written that "it seemed as if angels were welcoming the young child to heaven" (390)—Rose yokes past memories and present judgments in one sentence: "Glorious scenes were constantly soothing this sense of human sorrow, scenes such as cannot be found in regions outside the Church" (389).

The last page of *Memories of Hawthorne* contains a moving description of Rose's final memory of her father: "The last time I saw him, he was leaving the house to take the journey for his health which led suddenly to the next world. . . . Like a snow image of an unbending but old, old man, he stood for a moment gazing at me. . . . We have missed him in the sunshine, in the storm, in the twilight, ever since" (480). But the poignancy of these concluding words is dissipated by the chapter which precedes it—a rambling, disjointed chapter filled with letters and reminiscences of her father's friends and family which seem to conclude the work neither chronologically nor emotionally.

Once again, however, an autobiographical statement emerges through narrative discontinuities. Rose opens the chapter with a lengthy and detailed account of a conversation she had with Oliver Wendell Holmes over dinner in the early 1880s, a conversation which she claims she "dashed down . . . verbatim" (457) later that night. Holmes did not recognize Rose at first:

> "And you don't know who I am, yet?"
> He smiled, gazed . . . , and leaned towards me hesitatingly. "And what was your name?" he ventured.
> "Rose Hawthorne."
> He started, and beamed. "There! I thought—but you understand how—if I had made a mistake—Could anything have been worse if you had not been? I was looking, you know, for the resemblance, but"—
> "The complexion," I helped him by interrupting, "is entirely different." (457–58)

Holmes's stammering identification of Rose mirrors her own halting movement toward self-awareness. Look though Holmes might, he saw no resemblance to her father. The girl who had been "a stranger who had come too late" was Rose Hawthorne. The author of *Memories of Hawthorne,* Rose Hawthorne Lathrop, would within a year of that book's publication become Sister Mary Alphonsa. In her biographical sketches of her father, Rose reflected her own life of active industry on behalf of a community composed of all humankind. Her recollections of the Hawthorne family's experience in Italy, however, gave her the opportunity to write her own life as a child and to present her beliefs as they had evolved three decades after her father's death.

Although Nathaniel was the apparent catalyst for this auto/biography, Rose's work parallels that of later nineteenth-century daughters of famous writers, whose methods—subversive or otherwise—enabled them, as Marilyn Yalom tells us, "to make [their] presence felt in a work consecrated to a male protagonist" (53–54). Indeed, *Memories of Hawthorne,* like Adèle Hugo's *Victor Hugo raconté par un témoin de sa vie,* gave a female author the pretext for writing her own life. Just as Adèle imaginatively embellished incidents of her father's life with elements of the "feminine sensibility that privileges the domestic sphere and the nurturing of children" (Yalom 57), so Rose associated with both her father and mother the traits of character and sentiments which she privileged.

Carol Hanbery MacKay makes similar observations about Anne Thackeray Ritchie's memoirs of her father. Indeed, Ritchie's *Chapters from Some Memoirs,* published in 1894 from a series of essays which originally appeared in *Macmillan's Magazine,* provides detailed points of comparison with *Memories of Hawthorne.* Like Nathaniel Hawthorne, William Makepeace Thackeray had forbidden the writing of his life. Like Rose Hawthorne Lathrop, Anne Thackeray Ritchie undertook her father's biography thirty years after his death. And as I have noticed Rose's signature in *Memories of Hawthorne,* MacKay observes that Ritchie's discourse constructs *Chapters from Some Memoirs* through "metaphors which constitute a 'personal myth' . . . develop[ed] through a sequential narrative" (67). Thus we may read, MacKay points out, "Ritchie's extended 'memoirs,' namely her biographical endeavors, as a rich nexus of autobiographical writing" (67). Indeed, Rose must be lauded for the same reason Marilyn Yalom praises Adèle Hugo and other women in the past who "used whatever means were available to them, masquerading as biographers when necessary, so as to leave behind a textual manifestation of their will to be heard and remembered" (63).

Notes

A fuller version of this essay appeared in *A/B: Auto/Biography Studies* 8.1 (Spring 1993): 1–15.

1. Throughout this essay, I shall refer to the 1897 edition of *Memories of Hawthorne* unless otherwise noted. I will retain original punctuation.

2. Sophia Smith Collection, Neilson Library, Smith College, Northampton, Mass.; Henry W. and Albert A. Berg Collection, New York Public Library, Astor, Lenox and Tilden Foundations.

3. Although George Parson Lathrop's name appears along with Rose's on the title page of *A*

Story of Courage, Rose's journal entries for the winter and spring of 1894 demonstrate that she researched and wrote most of the book while she tended to George, who was convalescing from a chronic illness at the time.

4. I am deliberating using the word "reflects," for Rose is, as Myerhoff and Ruby put it, thinking about herself but without "explicit awareness of the implication of [her] display" (3).

5. I am borrowing Norman Holland's use of Heinz Lichtenstein's term to describe "a second person's hypothesis for searching out a persistent style in what the first has done. . . . Any such formulation of an 'identity theme,' will, of course, be a function of the you I see and my way of seeing—my identity as well as yours" (454).

Works Cited

Friedman, Susan Stanford. "Women's Autobiographical Selves: Theory and Practice." *The Private Self: Theory and Practice of Women's Autobiographical Writings.* Ed. Shari Benstock. Chapel Hill: U of North Carolina P, 1988. 34–62.

Geertz, Clifford. *Works and Lives: The Anthropologist as Author.* Stanford: Stanford UP, 1988.

Hawthorne, Nathaniel. *The English Note-Books.* Vol. 8 of *The Works of Nathaniel Hawthorne.* 15 vols. Boston: Riverside, 1883–84.

——. *Our Old Home.* Vol. 5 of the *Centenary Edition of the Works of Nathaniel Hawthorne* (Columbus: Ohio State UP, 1970).

Heilbrun, Carolyn. *Writing a Woman's Life.* New York: Norton, 1988.

Holland, Norman. "Human Identity." *Critical Inquiry* 4 (1978): 451–69.

Lathrop, Rose Hawthorne. "Hawthorne as Worker." *Cambridge Magazine* 2.2 (1896): 69–79.

——. "The Hawthornes in Lenox." *Century Magazine* 27 (Nov. 1894): 86–98.

——. *Memories of Hawthorne.* Boston: Houghton Mifflin, 1897; rev. ed. Riverside, 1923.

——. "My Father's Literary Methods." *Ladies Home Journal* 11 (Mar. 1894): 370–74.

——. "Some Memories of Hawthorne." *Atlantic Monthly* 77 (Feb., Mar., Apr., and May 1896): 173–86, 373–87, 492–507, 649–60.

——. *A Story of Courage: Annals of the Georgetown Convent of the Visitation of the Blessed Mary.* Boston: Houghton Mifflin, 1894.

MacKay, Carol Hanbery. "Biography as Reflected Autobiography: The Self-Creation of Anne Thackeray Ritchie." *Revealing Lives: Autobiography, Biography, and Gender.* Ed. Susan Groag Bell and Marilyn Yalom. Albany: State U of New York P, 1990. 65–79.

Miller, E. Haviland. *Salem Is My Dwelling Place.* Iowa City: U of Iowa P, 1991.

Myerhoff, Barbara, and Jay Ruby. "Introduction to Reflexivity and Its Relatives." *A Crack in the Mirror: Reflexive Perspectives in Anthropology.* Philadelphia: U of Pennsylvania P, 1982. 2–35.

Valenti, Patricia Dunlavy. *To Myself a Stranger: A Biography of Rose Hawthorne Lathrop.* Baton Rouge: Louisiana State UP, 1991.

Yalom, Marilyn. "Biography as Autobiography." *Revealing Lives: Autobiography, Biography, and Gender.* Ed. Susan Groag Bell and Marilyn Yalom. Albany: State U of New York P, 1990.

Formative Views by a Woman
of the Nineteenth Century

MARGARET FULLER ON

HAWTHORNE

David B. Kesterson

We do not know exactly when Sarah Margaret Fuller and Nathaniel Hawthorne met, but it was probably in 1840 or early 1841, before their encounter at Brook Farm in the spring and summer of 1841. Much has been written about the relationship of Fuller and Hawthorne,[1] a puzzling friendship that emits mixed signals. From the written record it is evident that the warm feelings of friendship often expressed by both individuals were more ardent on Fuller's side than Hawthorne's.[2]

Many passages in Fuller's journals and letters speak to her great admiration of Hawthorne and feeling of friendship with him and his wife Sophia as well. As early in their relationship as June 1842, when she had learned from Sophia Peabody of her impending marriage to Hawthorne, Fuller responded to Sophia that she would find herself very happy, "for if ever I saw a man who combined delicate tenderness to understand the heart of a woman, with quiet depth and manliness enough to satisfy her, it is Mr. Hawthorne" (Hudspeth 3: 66). In the same month, writing to Emerson about the Hawthornes' imminent move to Concord, she assured the Concord sage that "I think you must take pleasure in Hawthorne when yo[u] know him. you will find him more mellow than most fruits at your board, and of distinct flavor too" (3: 70). And we know that Fuller visited the Hawthornes extensively during their first two years in Concord at the Old Manse (from 1842 until late 1844), always commenting on the pleasantness of those visits and the exhilaration she found in them. On 19 August 1842, she confided to her journal:

> Went to see the Hawthornes: it was very pleasant. The poplars whisper so suddenly in the avenue their pleasant tale, and every where the view is so peaceful. The house within I like, all their things are so expressive of themselves and mix in so gracefully with the old furniture. H. walked home with me: we stopped some time to look at the moon[;] she was struggling with clouds. H said he should be much more willing to die than two months ago, for he had had some real possession in life, but still he never wished to leave this earth: it was beautiful enough. He expressed, as he always does, many fine perceptions. I like to hear the lightest thing he says[.] (Myerson 324–25)

From several passages such as this, it appears that Fuller's feelings toward Hawthorne were warm, enthusiastic, and open. No reserve is indicated.

Hawthorne's part in the friendship was reciprocal to a degree, but certainly he was not so wholly forthcoming as Fuller. We know that he devoted some time to the friendship while he lived at the Old Manse, walking with Fuller in the nearby woods, taking her canoeing on the Concord River, and inviting her to visit him and Sophia whenever she was in town. He apparently felt he could confide in her. Responding by letter to her bold request that he and Sophia, only one month wed, take in Fuller's sister Ellen and brother-in-law Ellery Channing as boarders at the Manse, Hawthorne politely demurred, gave his reasons, then assured her, "There is nobody to whom I would more willingly speak my mind, because I can be certain of being thoroughly understood" (Hawthorne, *Letters,* in *CE* 15: 648).[3] And when, a year later, Fuller tried again to get the Hawthornes to open their home—this time to friend Charles Newcomb—Hawthorne again refused, but wrote that he found it easier to give her a "negative" than to other people "because you do not peep at matters through a narrow chink, but can take my view as perfectly as your own" (15: 670). In the same letter he confides in Fuller about his personal activity that winter, sharing with her his joys of ice skating and of his and Sophia's close companionship (670–72).

There are, however, those other puzzling remarks Hawthorne made about Fuller that are equivocal, uncomplimentary, or occasionally outright condemnatory. He commented about her garrulousness, for example. Writing to Sophia, before their marriage when she was planning to attend one of Fuller's conversations in Boston, he quipped, "Would that Miss Margaret Fuller might lose her tongue!—or my Dove her ears, and so be left wholly to her husband's golden silence!" (*CE* 15: 511). Oblique references to Fuller appear in Hawthorne's Brook Farm account of a certain "Transcendental heifer" which belonged to her. Hawthorne writes that the cow is "fractious" and "hooks the other cows, and has made herself ruler of the herd, and behaves in a very tyrannical manner" (15: 527, 528). Then there is the ambivalent portraiture of the character Zenobia in *The Blithedale Romance,* who is partially derived from Fuller. Most damaging, of course, is the inexplicable negative passage in Hawthorne's *Italian Notebooks,* written a number of years after Fuller's death, in which Hawthorne writes of her:

> she was a woman anxious to try all things, and fill up her experience in all directions; she had a strong and coarse nature, too, which she had done utmost to refine, with infinite pains, but which of course could only be superficially changed. . . . She was a great humbug; of course with much talent, and much moral reality, or else she could not have been so great a humbug. But she had stuck herself full of borrowed qualities, which she chose to provide herself with, but which had no root in her. (*CE* 14: 155–56)

He goes on to speak of her "strong, heavy, unpliable, and, in many respect, defective and evil nature," which she adorned "with a mosaic of admirable qualities" (156). Why Hawthorne penned this damning commentary—which became infamous when Julian Hawthorne published it in his biography, *Nathaniel Hawthorne and His Wife* (1884)—is unclear. There are several explanations, including Katherine Anthony's improbable thesis that Hawthorne treated Fuller as he did because he got the same emotional satisfaction from attacking her verbally as did his Salem ancestors from punishing witches (93). Paula Blanchard believes that Hawthorne was no longer in full possession of his mind by the time the passage was written and that it thus may not reflect his full feelings toward Fuller (or perhaps, she writes, the "irrational hatred which was present all along was now no longer controlled by his kinder, younger self" [194]). Whatever the reasons, we are left with an uncertain and inconsistent accounting, on Hawthorne's part, of his friendship with Fuller.

Although the Hawthorne/Fuller personal relationship is an interesting, if somewhat disquieting one and deserves more attention, my purpose here is to focus on their literary relationship, specifically on Fuller's critical reaction to Hawthorne's works. Her commentary is limited to only four of Hawthorne's collections of tales and sketches prior to 1850. Fuller, we recall, died in 1850, only a few months after Hawthorne's first major novel, *The Scarlet Letter,* was published.

Fuller's reviews, all in the 1840s, result from her editing the *Dial* and reviewing for the *New-York Daily Tribune.* The first of the four reviews was in 1841. But curiously enough, her earliest reaction on record to Hawthorne's writing was some seven years earlier, in a letter to an unidentified recipient to whom she wrote:

> I took a two or three year old "Token," and chanced on a story, called the "Gentle Boy," which I remembered to have heard was written by somebody in Salem. It is marked by so much grace and delicacy of feeling, that I am very desirous to know the author, whom I take to be a lady. (Hudspeth 1: 198)

Though obviously mistaken as to the author's gender, she was already perceptive of the compelling talents and merits of the anonymous writer.

Three of the four pieces appeared in the *Dial.* Fuller, of course, was the first editor of that periodical, serving from July 1840 until March 1842, when the editor's chair became occupied by Emerson. Fuller's references to American authors in the *Dial* are very few; the fact that she reviewed three of Hawthorne's works there attests to the high esteem in which she held his writings. As Vivian C. Hopkins has pointed out, in "Margaret Fuller: American Nationalist Critic," Fuller envisioned a time in America's growth and maturity when its literature would be truly national, with all sections of the country contributing. Until that time arrived, however, she believed that the nation would have to draw inspiration and cultural value from Old World writers, a position which accounts for the majority of her criticism in the *Dial* being focused on English and Continental authors. But Hawthorne was one of the true jewels of America's fledgling national literature, the "best writer of the day," she would say in 1846, and thus he elicited her close critical attention.

Fuller's first review of Hawthorne to appear in the *Dial* was of *Grandfather's Chair: A History for Youth,* appearing in the January 1841 issue. Though brief—only a paragraph in length—it is highly praiseful. Fuller is glad to see this "gifted author" using his pen "to raise the tone of children's literature" (405). For, if children read, they should be exposed to those minds that can "raise themselves to the height of childhood's innocence, and to the airy home of their free fancy." No writer but Hawthorne among all America's imaginative writers "has indicated a genius at once so fine and rich, and especially with a power so peculiar in making present the past scenes of our own history." She praises Hawthorne for changing his tone in *Grandfather's Chair* from the "delicate satire that characterizes his writings for the old" to the "simpler and more venerable tone" appropriate to children. His so doing is a sign of the success he will enjoy in this "new direction of his powers." Fuller is glad to hear that Hawthorne will write other works for children, yet demands that he not forget his adult audience: he must "write again to the older and sadder, and steep them in the deep well of his sweet, humorsome musings" (405).

It is in keeping with Fuller's own personal as well as her literary interests that she would write this review—and another addressed below—on a children's work. She was exceedingly fond of children, frequently mentioning them in her letters and journals. And among the children who caught her eye, none did so more completely than the Hawthornes' first child, Una, whom Fuller adored and believed to be one of the most beautiful children she had ever seen (see Hudspeth, *passim*). Una completely won her heart.

A year and a half later, in July 1842, two additional Fuller reviews of Hawthorne appeared in the *Dial.* One was a brief two-sentence notice of *Biographical Stories for Children,* the book that contained portraits of Benjamin West, Isaac Newton, Samuel Johnson, Oliver Cromwell, Benjamin Franklin, and Queen Christina. Fuller is grateful for what she calls the "manly and gentle spirit" that has appropriated stories which have "wet the eyes or expanded the breasts" of fathers and reworked them in "so pleasing a form" to their children that the fathers "must needs glisten and sigh over them again" (131). The other review in the July 1842 *Dial* is a much longer piece, well over a page, devoted to the second edition of *Twice-told Tales,* published in that year. Fuller begins by pointing out that, ever since the publication of "The Gentle Boy," Hawthorne has been "growing more and more dear to his readers," who now can enjoy the advantage of having all his previously published stories in these two volumes. The review is largely positive, though Fuller has some reservations about the work. While delighting in "the soft grace, the playfulness, and genial human sense for the traits of individual character" (130) that Hawthorne displays in the stories, Fuller dwells on the "great reserve of thought and strength" in them. Hawthorne, she feels, remains partially distant and undisclosed to the reader because of this reserve:

> Like gleams of light on a noble tree which stands untouched and self-sufficing in its fulness of foliage on a distant hill-slope,—like slight ripples wrinkling the smooth surface, but never stirring the quiet depths of a wood-embosomed lake, these tales distantly indicate the bent of the author's mind, and the very frankness with which they impart to us slight outward details and habits shows how little yet is told. (130)

She points out again that he is a "favorite writer for children, with whom he feels at home, as true manliness always does," but senses that *Twice-told Tales* "scarce call him out more than the little books" for his juvenile audience. His tales are pleasing, "but they seem to promise more" than they give, which will be the case until their author should "hear a voice that truly calls upon his solitude to ope his study door" (130).

Fuller singles out with pleasure three new sketches in this second edition of *Twice-told Tales,* "The Village Uncle," "The Lily's Quest," and "Chippings with a Chisel," and again admires the "sweet grace" of "Footprints on the Seashore." The most successful tales, she feels, are the more realistic sketches, ones that she terms the "studies of familiar life." There is a vagueness about the other more "imaginative pieces" that she finds disturbing: "the invention is not clearly woven, far from being all compact, and seems a phantom or shadow, rather than a real growth" (130). Even the characters in these more imaginative pieces "flicker large and unsubstantial, like 'shadows from the evening firelight,' seen 'upon the parlor wall'" (131). Fuller believes this vagueness would be overcome if Hawthorne's genius were "fully roused to its work, and initiated into its own life, so as to paint with blood-warm colors." She wonders, indeed, whether Hawthorne is lacking in life's "deeper experiences, for which no talent at observation, no sympathies, however ready and delicate, can compensate." Nonetheless, despite the reservations, Fuller concludes the review by calling for more "new missives from the same hand" (131).

There was a lapse of four years before Fuller wrote again about Hawthorne. Much had changed in her life by then. She had been lured away from Boston to New York in late 1844 by Horace Greeley, editor of the *New-York Daily Tribune,* to write review articles for his newspaper. It appeared that Fuller had found the slot for which she was best suited, up to this point in her life, because her literary accomplishment during the nearly two years she was in New York was remarkable. She published two books—*Woman in the Nineteenth Century* (Feb. 1845) and *Papers on Literature and*

Art (Aug. 1846)—and some 250 essays for the *Tribune.* Her articles for Greeley's paper covered a broad range of subjects, but most were essentially literary, focusing on French, German, English, and American authors. She produced several columns a week, which usually appeared on page 1. Although Fuller did not consider the *Tribune* pieces her best work (according to Greeley she felt too "exhausted by previous over-work" and the work "hindered her free action to aim at popular effect" (Ossoli 2: 163). Horace Greeley felt that the *Tribune* pieces, as compared with the perhaps "more elaborate and ambitious" articles in the *Dial,* were "far better adapted to win the favor and sway the judgment of the great majority of readers" (Ossoli 2: 158). Greeley appraised her columns as being "characterized by a directness, terseness, and practicality, which are wanting in some of her earlier productions" (157–58). He commends her for "absolute truthfulness" and courage of conviction: If something were the truth she uttered it, "no matter what turmoil it might excite, nor what odium it might draw down on her own head." Greeley emphasized that "perfect conscientiousness was an unfailing characteristic of her literary efforts" (158).

Fuller's only review of Hawthorne in the *Tribune* was of *Mosses from an Old Manse,* prominently displayed in its entirety on the front page of the 22 June 1846 issue. It is her longest and most detailed review of a work by Hawthorne. She begins by hoping that what she has to say about *Mosses* will be neither "superfluous or impertinent"—superfluous because all "who possess the common sympathies of men" would naturally appreciate Hawthorne, and impertinent since there is so little worth saying about the quieting influence of Hawthorne's mind that hasn't been "so fitly and pleasantly said." Yet the critic would be remiss not to honor Hawthorne with a review, and perhaps the notice will attract the attention of those who might not be familiar with the volume.

She is glad to see the book published by Wiley and Putnam because a main reason for Hawthorne's not having been widely read, in her view, is that his books were not being "published in the way to insure extensive circulation in this new, hurrying world of ours." To be read, a book must be "trumpeted and placarded," as she is convinced this one will be. She applauds a wider range of subjects in *Mosses* than appears in his earlier volumes but detects the same charms as found in the earlier tales:

> There is the same gentle and sincere companionship with Nature, the same delicate but fearless scrutiny of the secrets of the heart, the same serene independence of petty and artificial restrictions, whether on opinions or conduct, the same familiar, yet pensive sense of the spiritual or demoniacal influences that haunt the palpable life and common walks of men, not by many apprehended except in results.

However, Fuller again regrets that Hawthorne is too mysterious, suggestive, and exclusive: "Still, still brood over his page the genius of revery and the nonchalance of Nature, rather than the ardent earnestness of the human soul." Hawthorne "intimates and suggests, but he does not lay bare the mysteries of our being."

Focusing on some of the specific pieces in *Mosses,* she finds in his introductory sketch "The Old Manse" "even more than his usual charm of placid grace and many strokes of his admirable good sense." "The Birth-Mark" and "Rappaccini's Daughter" "embody truths of profound importance in shapes of aerial elegance"; in these stories "shines the loveliest ideal of love and the beauty of feminine purity." "The Celestial Railroad" contains "wit" and "wisdom," and the natural and material objects are interwoven with the allegory with "graceful adroitness." "Fire Worship" is charming "for its domestic sweetness and thoughtful life." "Mrs. Bullfrog" is "an excellent humorous picture of what is called to be 'content at last with substantial realities!!,'" while "The Artist of the Beautiful" "presents the opposite view as to what *are* the substantial realities of life. Let each man choose between them according to his kind." Of "Roger Malvin's Burial," Fuller surmises that had it been the only thing Hawthorne had ever written "we should be pervaded with the sense of the poetry and religion of his soul."

"Young Goodman Brown," however, is the tale from *Mosses* that draws most of Fuller's commentary in the *Tribune* review. It is a story that discloses the "secret of the breast." Reading it as depicting a universal experience, Fuller wonders who has not had the dismaying jolt so forcefully portrayed in the story: the "hour of anguish, when the old familiar faces grow dark and dim in the lurid light—when the gods of the hearth, honored in childhood, adored in youth, crumble, and nothing, nothing is left which the daily earthly feelings can embrace—can cherish with unbroken Faith!" Some people, however, survive this shock of recognition "more happily" than Goodman Brown; those who "have not sought it—have never of their own accord walked forth with the Temptor into the dim shades of Doubt."

Hawthorne's style, Fuller observes, is "faithful to his mind, shows repose, a great reserve of strength, a slow secure movement." He is a "refined" and "clear" writer, "showing . . . a placid grace, and an indolent command of language." Concluding this, her longest piece of Hawthorne, Fuller says we will rest by the "full, calm yet romantic stream of his mind":

> It [*Mosses*] has refreshment for the weary, islets of fascination no less than dark recesses and shadows for the imaginative, pure reflections for the pure of heart and eye, and, like the Concord he so well describes, many exquisite lilies for him who knows how to get at them.

Fuller had one further prime opportunity to write on Hawthorne, in her 1846 essay entitled "American Literature: Its Position in the Present Time, and Prospects for the Future," but chose not to, though she refers to Hawthorne in the essay as "the best writer of the day, in a similar range with Irving, only touching many more points and discerning far more deeply" (399). Instead, she appended a reprint of the *Mosses* review from the *Tribune,* along with reviews of Charles Brockden Brown's *Wieland* and *Ormond* and Longfellow's *Poems.* Why the omission of Hawthorne is unclear, though Fuller explains near the close of the piece that the subject of the status of American literature present and future "lies as a volume in our mind, and cannot be unrolled in completeness unless time and space were more abundant" (399).

As mentioned above, Margaret Fuller did not live to read and review Hawthorne's major works of the 1850s: *The Scarlet Letter, The House of the Seven Gables, The Blithedale Romance* (we cannot help but wonder what her response would have been to the portrait of Zenobia!), and *The Marble Faun* in 1860. The ship bearing her, her husband Count Giovanni Ossoli, and their young son wrecked and sank on 19 July 1850 off Fire Island, New York, as Fuller was returning to America from Italy, where she had lived for three years. All three of the Ossolis were drowned. In *The Italian Notebooks* Hawthorne wrote of Fuller and that shipwreck with a strange mixture of censure and empathy:

> there appears to have been a total collapse in poor Margaret, morally and intellec-
> tually; and tragic as her catastrophe was, Providence was, after all, kind in putting her
> and her clownish husband, and their child, on board that fated ship. There never was
> such a tragedy as her whole story; the sadder and sterner, because so much of the
> ridiculous was mixed up with it, and because she could bear anything better than to be
> ridiculous. (*CE* 14: 156)

Hawthorne's personal relationship with Margaret Fuller remains a puzzle never to be completely solved. But as literary friends and acquaintances the record is clear that there was mutual respect and admiration between them (Hawthorne and Sophia even wrote Fuller a letter of congratulations in 1845 on the publication of *Woman in the Nineteenth Century*). As for her literary criticism of Hawthorne, Margaret Fuller's keen mind fastened on those traits that are so legendarily Haw-thornesque—from his "soft grace" and ease of style to his "genial human sense," to his quietude and repose, to a "great reserve of thought and strength," to the deep, probing portraits that conceal as much as they reveal. We recall that Hawthorne's *Twice-told Tales* left Fuller wanting more, despite her reservations with the work: "new missives from the same hand," she admonished. Would that history had allowed more critical "missives" on Hawthorne from the hand of Margaret Fuller. This forthright, perceptive woman of the nineteenth century would assuredly have brought her invaluable insight to bear on Hawthorne's novels and other works of the major decade of his career, thus providing a significant critique on the Hawthorne canon. It is an unfortunate lacuna in nineteenth-century appraisal of Hawthorne's major works.

Notes

1. For example, see Julian Hawthorne, *Nathaniel Hawthorne and His Wife* (Boston: Houghton, Mifflin, 1884); Oscar Cargill, "Nemesis and Nathaniel Hawthorne," *PMLA* 52

(1937): 848–62; William Peirce Randel, "Hawthorne, Channing, and Margaret Fuller," *American Literature* 10 (1939): 472–46; Austin Warren, "Hawthorne, Margaret Fuller, and 'Nemesis,'" *PMLA* 54 (1939): 615–18; Vivian C. Hopkins, "Margaret Fuller: American Nationalist Critic"; Darrel Abel, "Hawthorne on the Strong Dividing Lines of Nature," *American Transcendental Quarterly* 14 (1972): 23–31; John Paul Eakin, "Margaret Fuller, Hawthorne, James, and Sexual Politics," *South Atlantic Quarterly* 75 (1976): 323–38; Paula Blanchard, "Hawthorne and Margaret Fuller" in *Margaret Fuller: From Transcendentalism to Revolution;* Margaret Vanderhaar Allen, *The Achievement of Margaret Fuller* (University Park and London: Pennsylvania State UP, 1979); Joel Myerson, ed. *The Transcendentalists: A Review of Research and Criticism* (New York: The Modern Language Association of America, 1984); Thomas R. Mitchell, "Julian Hawthorne and the 'Scandal' of Margaret Fuller," *American Literary History* 7 (1995): 210–33; Scott Ash, "Rereading Antagonism as Sibling Rivalry: The Hawthorne/Fuller Dynamic," *American Transcendental Quarterly,* n.s., 9 (December 1995): 313–31.

2. As Joel Myerson points out, the Hawthorne-Fuller relationship was a "complex one." Hawthorne was "uneasy about . . . [Fuller's] aggressiveness but tended to treat it lightly." Fuller, in turn, liked Hawthorne, but found him "too reserved" ("Nathaniel Hawthorne," in *The Transcendentalists: A Review of Research and Criticism,* 333). Despite negative views of the Hawthorne-Fuller relationship by Julian Hawthorne (*Nathaniel Hawthorne and His Wife,* 1884) and early twentieth-century critics such as Oscar Cargill, William Peirce Randel, and Austin Warren (see n. 1), more recent critics such as Darrel Abel and Paul John Eakin (see n. 1) "have looked more positively on Hawthorne's relationship with Fuller," as Myerson states (334).

3. Quotations from Nathaniel Hawthorne's letters and notebooks are from the *Centenary Edition,* hereafter cited as *CE* with volume and page numbers.

Works Cited

Anthony, Katherine. *Margaret Fuller: A Psychological Biography.* New York: Harcourt, Brace and Howe, 1920.

Blanchard, Paula. *Margaret Fuller: From Transcendentalism to Revolution.* New York: Delacorte (Seymour Lawrence), 1978.

Fuller, Margaret. "American Literature: Its Position in the Present Time, and Prospects for the Future." *Papers on Literature and Art.* New York: Wiley and Putnam, 1946. 2: 122–43. Rpt. in Joel Myerson, *Margaret Fuller: Essays on American Life and Letters.* New Haven: College and UP, 1978. 381–400.

——. Rev. of *Biographical Stories for Children,* by Nathaniel Hawthorne. *Dial* 3 (July 1842): 131.

——. Rev. of *Grandfather's Chair: A History for Youth,* by Nathaniel Hawthorne. *Dial* 1 (Jan. 1841): 405.

——. Rev. of *Mosses from an Old Manse,* by Nathaniel Hawthorne—In Two Parts. *New-York Daily Tribune* 22 June 1846: 1.

——. Rev. of *Twice-told Tales,* by Nathaniel Hawthorne. *Dial* 3 (July 1842): 130–31.

Hawthorne, Nathaniel. *The French and Italian Notebooks.* Ed. Thomas Woodson. Vol. 14 of the *Centenary Edition of the Works of Nathaniel Hawthorne.* Columbus: Ohio State UP, 1980.

——. *The Letters of Nathaniel Hawthorne, 1813–1843.* Ed. Thomas Woodson. Vol. 15 of the *Centenary Edition.* Columbus: Ohio State UP, 1984.

Hopkins, Vivian C. "Margaret Fuller: American Nationalist Critic." *Emerson Society Quarterly* 55 (1969): 24–41.

Hudspeth, Robert N., ed. *The Letters of Margaret Fuller.* 6 vols. Ithaca: Cornell UP, 1983–95.

Myerson, Joel. "Margaret Fuller's 1842 Journal: At Concord with the Emersons." *Harvard Library Bulletin* 21 (July 1973): 320–40.

——. "Nathaniel Hawthorne." *The Transcendentalists: A Review of Research and Criticism.* Ed. Joel Myerson. New York: MLA, 1984. 328–35.

Ossoli, Margaret Fuller. *Memoirs.* Ed. R. W. Emerson, W. H. Channing, and J. F. Clarke. 2 vols. Boston: Roberts Brothers, 1884.

RAPPACCINI'S GARDEN AND EMERSON'S CONCORD

Thomas R. Mitchell

Readers interested in Fuller's life, writings, and relationships with contemporaries should begin with Bell Gale Chevigny's *The Woman and the Myth: Margaret Fuller's Life and Writings,* rev. ed. (Boston: Northeastern UP, 1993), and *The Letters of Margaret Fuller,* ed. Robert Hudspeth, 6 vols. (Ithaca: Cornell UP, 1983–95). The most complete anthology of Fuller's writings is Jeffrey Steele's *The Essential Margaret Fuller* (New Brunswick, N.J.: Rutgers UP, 1992).

I will compare the attempt to escape him to the hopeless race that men sometimes run with memory, or their own hearts, or their moral selves. . . . I will be self-contemplative, as Nature bids me, and make him the picture or visible type of what I muse upon, that my mind may not wander so vaguely as heretofore, chasing its own shadow through a chaos and catching only the monsters that abide there.

"Monsieur du Miroir"

Any entrance into Rappaccini's garden is clearly fraught with the humbling suspicion that we are following perilously in Giovanni's footsteps, carrying with us our own vial of interpretative poison. This is as Hawthorne would have it. Struggling to complete the tale that he had begun sometime in mid-October of 1844, Hawthorne read the unfinished manuscript to Sophia: "But how is it to end?" she asked him. "Is Beatrice to be a demon or an angel?" "I have no idea!" Hawthorne replied with emotion.[1] Hawthorne, in fact, ended the tale by condemning the very desire to conclude it, to fix himself to an "idea" that, by the falsity of a reductive certainty, would unravel the "riddle" of Beatrice. But then he began the tale for that very purpose, for the riddle of Beatrice had become for Hawthorne inseparably bound, as he writes of Giovanni, with the "mystery which he deemed the riddle of his own existence" (*CE* 10: 110).[2] The sources of the legendary complexity of the tale, I would contend, originate in the very complexity of the "lurid intermixture" (*CE*

10: 105) of emotions that Margaret Fuller had aroused in Hawthorne by October of 1844, emotions that would erupt most explicitly and disturbingly in 1858, eight years after her death, when gossip about her handsome but "clownish husband" would ignite Hawthorne into seeking, as he called it, the "solution of the riddle" of Fuller's character (and perhaps of his longtime fascination with her) in her inability to forever suppress or refine the "rude old potency" of her sexuality (*CE* 14: 156–57).

Because of that infamous notebook passage, Hawthorne's intimate friendship with Fuller between 1839 and 1844 has been either undervalued or misinterpreted. It is beyond the scope of this essay to present a reevaluation of that friendship, but I would contend that when Hawthorne confessed in his notebooks in 1858 to having been able to converse intimately with only "half a dozen persons in my life, men or women," he would have counted Fuller among that select number (*CE* 14: 178). Fuller's recently published journal accounts of her visits with Hawthorne at Concord in 1842 and especially in the summer of 1844 describe many private and quite personal conversations with Hawthorne as they walked through the moonlit woods of Sleepy Hollow or boated alone at evening for hours on the Concord.[3] For his part, Hawthorne described in a 21 August 1842 notebook entry the most private and intimate conversation he would ever record having with a woman other than his wife (*CE* 8: 342–43), wrote to Fuller the longest and most personal accounts he would ever write of his married life (*CE* 15: 647–48, 670–71), boasted to Sophia that Fuller had expressed "the fulness of her sympathy with him in a most satisfactory way,"[4] and, similarly, praised Fuller directly in letters for being what he would never avow so explicitly of or to another friend—one "to whom I would more willingly speak my mind, because I can be certain of being thoroughly understood," one who "can take my view as perfectly as your own" (*CE* 15: 648, 670).

Beginning the tale within weeks of his last of many evening walks with Fuller before she moved to New York and out of his life, Hawthorne seems to have "translated" his troubling triangle of friendship with both Fuller and Emerson into the "picture[s] or visible type[s]" of the tale—attempting through art, as his narrator in "Monsieur du Miroir" proclaims, to contain the "chaos" of his "musings" and through the concealed confessions of allegory to confront the "monsters that abide there."

The tale performs its subject; it is a riddle of a riddle, a translation that requires translation. The prefatory "Writings of Aubépine" suggests as much. Hawthorne invites us with self-deprecatory humor to read through the thin fiction of his self-representation, to "translate" it; for "Aubépine," we read "Hawthorne," for "translator," we read "author." In another sense, however, Hawthorne chose this transparent veil of translator because in transmuting life into art he had attempted in a very real sense to translate the language of his experience into the language of art. Compelled to read the riddle of Fuller's character and of his troublingly ambivalent relationship with her, detesting his very need to do so, and compelled also to conceal the very confession that is the tale, Hawthorne images in the mirror of Giovanni not only his reflection but ours. The tale performs his agony. We read the secondary language of the translator's tale, but in taking seriously Hawthorne's playful invitation to become translators ourselves, we are challenged to have the depth that Giovanni lacked, the faith to believe that we hear another, truer language, the first language of the tale's primary source.

The preface introduces both the public and the private texts and provides for the "individual" whom he claims as his audience an interpretative entrance into Rappaccini's garden. The "individual, or possibly an isolated clique" (*CE* 10: 91) capable of reading the tale is and is not a self-deprecatory appeal to his readers' aesthetic and class vanities; beneath the public text of Hawthorne's apology for his art may be read his solicitude of, literally, at least one individual reader who could take his view as perfectly as her own, for the private text of the preface seems to be a response to the challenges issued by Fuller in her July 1842 review of *Twice-told Tales*. Of his "imaginative pieces," Fuller had written:

> It is not merely the soft grace, the playfulness, and genial human sense . . . that have pleased, but the perception of . . . a great reserve of thought and strength never yet at all brought forward. . . . these tales distantly indicate the bent of the author's mind, and the very frankness with which they impart to us slight outward details and habits shows how little yet is told. . . . they seem to promise more, should their author ever hear a voice that truly calls upon his solitude to ope his study door.
>
> The invention is not clearly woven, far from being all compact, and seems a phantom or shadow, rather than a real growth. The men and women, too, flicker large and unsubstantial, like "shadows from the evening firelight," seen "upon the parlor wall." But this would be otherwise, probably, were the genius fully roused to its work, and initiated into its own life, so as to paint with blood-warm colors. This frigidity and thinness of design usually bespeaks a want of deeper experiences, for which no talent at observation, no sympathies, however ready and delicate, can compensate. We wait new missives from the same hand.[5]

Hawthorne's review of Aubépine's work not only acknowledges most of the same points of criticism but employs similar phrasing (*CE* 10: 91–92). Hawthorne will implicitly address Aubépine's "want of deeper experiences" in his treatment of Giovanni, but, here, he seems explicitly to address Fuller's criticism of his failure to "paint with blood-warm colors"—of his shadowy characters' "frigidity and thinness"—by instead blaming "an inveterate love of allegory" for making Aubépine "apt to invest his plots and characters with the aspect of scenery and people in the clouds and steal away the human warmth out of his conceptions." In phrases that parallel Fuller's challenge to his contentment with imparting but "slight outward details and habits" which suggest "how little yet is told" and with providing an "invention" that "is not clearly woven" or a "real growth," Hawthorne writes that Aubépine "contents himself with a very slight embroidery of outward manners,—the faintest possible counterfeit of real life." Occasionally Aubépine provides just enough "pathos and tenderness" to "make us feel as if . . . we were yet within the limits of our native earth," but these compensations of mere "observation" and "sympathy," no matter how "ready and delicate," Fuller argued, were not enough. Hawthorne must live more deeply and create a passionate art out of a passionate life. To do that, as Fuller rather provocatively urged him in her review, he must abandon his solitude and risk listening to "a voice that truly calls" upon him.

As Fuller was the "author" of the critique of Hawthorne's art that he seems to translate into his own critique of Aubépine's, so she will be, with Hawthorne, the original "coauthor" of the experience that he presents as translation. Performing its subject, this passionate tale indeed "paint[s] with blood-warm colors" the passionate response of a man to a "voice" that calls upon him to forsake his wary solitude for "deeper experiences." As often noted, the notorious shift in point of view in the tale (the sudden emergence of the narrative voice condemning Giovanni) is largely responsible for the complexity of the tale, but this complexity, I hope to demonstrate, originates in Hawthorne's own extraordinarily complex conversation with those voices within him that spoke most clearly in his dialogue with Fuller and Emerson. As Larry J. Reynolds has demonstrated of "The Old Manse," less than two years later Hawthorne would continue that dialogue with Emerson, attempting there, as he does here in "Rappaccini's Daughter," to interrupt the monologue of the self-reliant masculine individualist, who reads all nature as self, by engaging in an intimate dialogue with a feminine "Other" who promises release from the self, freedom from the walls of Rappaccini's garden. It is an Other whose voice Hawthorne recognizes in Fuller's, whose voice Hawthorne makes his own.[6]

Hawthorne's debt to both Milton and Dante in "Rappaccini's Daughter" is impossible to miss. But "Rappaccini's Daughter" is much more than simply Hawthorne's own Rappaccini-like "conmixture" of Milton's Adam meeting Dante's Beatrice in Hawthorne's re-creation of "the new Eden of the present world" (*CE* 10: 96). His narrator raises that possibility perhaps because he would prefer that we keep our interpretative eyes fixed there, focused on the distant, on the tale's intertextual negotiations between those classic texts. "New" and "present," however, should hold our attention, for the tale seems far more autobiographical, more concerned with the contemporary than the tale's transparent debt to its literary ancestors would lead us to believe.

The new Eden for Hawthorne was Emerson's Concord, and the feminine voice that spoke most alluringly in that garden was the voice of his protégé Fuller.[7] Much of the narrative form and thematic tensions of Hawthorne's tale seem to respond to Fuller's voice and echo her own figurative language. Determining the precise degree of intertextual appropriation of course is difficult, for both Hawthorne and Fuller drew upon a romantic discourse in which nature imagery commonly melded with biblical and Miltonic allusions. Nevertheless, the parallels are striking. In Fuller's

4 June 1842 letter to Sophia, for instance, Fuller reacts to Sophia's announcement of her impending marriage to Hawthorne by praising profusely Hawthorne's rare balance of the masculine and feminine ("If ever I saw a man who combined delicate tenderness to understand the heart of a woman, with quiet depth and manliness enough to satisfy her, it is Mr Hawthorne"). She then expressed her belief that marriage to this man offered the unique opportunity for love to develop into its rarest of forms, "intellectual friendship." To defend her belief that a man so under-standing of the heart of a woman is capable of forming such a relationship, Fuller employs an Edenic metaphor that has striking parallels within Hawthorne's tale, as we shall see:

> I do not *demand* the earnest of a future happiness to all believing souls. I wish to temper the mind to believe, without prematurely craving *sight*, but it is sweet when here and there some little spots of garden ground reveal the flowers that deck our natural Eden,—sweet when some characters can bear fruit without the aid of the knife, and the first scene of that age-long drama in which each child of God must act to find himself is plainly to be deciphered, and its cadences harmonious to the ear.[8]

Hawthorne could not have easily forgotten the provocative praise of Fuller's letter. "Rappaccini's Daughter," in fact, may be read on one level as Hawthorne's transfor-mation of Fuller's sensory, organic, and biblical figures for her affirmation of faith in Hawthorne's ability to form a union of "intellectual friendship" with a woman into the narrative and thematic figures of his betrayal of that faith. Entering the "un-natural" Eden of the new Adam whose intervention through the "aid of" the cold intellect's "knife" has transformed the "sweet" flowers of nature into "poisonous" plants intended to heal but capable of harm, Giovanni re-presents, as a "visible type," Hawthorne's own anxious entrance into the seductively influential and un-natural Eden of Emerson's transcendentalized Nature—into, that is, as he says in "The Old Manse," the "wonderful magnetism" of Emerson's Concord, where "the light revealed objects unseen before," where "uncertain, troubled, earnest wan-derers" sought his truth but too often saw its opposite in their own delusions, "night birds" envisioned as "fowls of angelic feather" (*CE* 10: 30–31). As Hawthorne in "The Old Manse" realigns Emerson's protégé Fuller with best friends Franklin Pierce and Horatio Bridge under the opposing influence of Hawthorne's own "magic circle" in Concord, where he heals (rather than deludes) their spirits through the "spell" of his own "tranquil spirit" (*CE* 10: 29), so Giovanni would save Beatrice from Rappaccini's poison by having her imbibe his antidote. Giovanni thus engages himself in the "age-long drama" of male rivalry for possession of a woman that he both loves and loathes. It is a drama that he says holds the "riddle of his existence" because he hopes that the torment of his confused but obsessive desire for her will end when he possesses the ability to define, with certainty, her mystery. Hermeneu-tically and biblically, he must "know" her to have her. However, because Giovanni, in Fuller's words, *does* "demand the earnest of a future happiness" by "prematurely craving *sight,*" because, in other words, he fails to be a "believing soul" and to accept from her lips the truth that she has to offer to him, nothing is "plainly to be deciphered." Nothing, that is, except that in failing to heed Beatrice's voice he "finds" not her but himself and the poison within his own "thwarted nature."

So close are several of the significant details in Hawthorne's tale to Fuller's own statements in her personal papers that it is possible that Fuller repeated many of these observations to Hawthorne during their numerous private conversations. Hawthorne's representation of those under Emerson's influence as plants cultivated in Rappaccini's garden parallels Fuller's own image of Emerson. In a 23 June 1842 letter to Emerson, she writes: "The new colonists will be with you soon. Your community seems to grow. I think you must take pleasure in Hawthorne when you know him. You will find him more *mellow* than most fruits at your board, and of distinct flavor too."⁹ Hawthorne's allegorical use of the insidious fragrances emanating from Rappaccini's garden closely parallels Fuller's metaphor for the powerful and potentially destructive nature of Emerson's influence on her; concluding a stay at Emerson's in September of 1842, Fuller observes in her journal: "I ought to go away now these last days I have been fairly intoxicated with his mind. I am not in full possession of my own. I feel faint in the presence of too strong a fragrance."¹⁰ In a later echo of Fuller's line, Hawthorne describes in "The Old Manse" Emerson's influence thus: "But it was impossible to dwell in his vicinity, without inhaling . . . the mountain-atmosphere of his lofty thought, which, in the brains of some people, wrought a singular giddiness—new truth being as heady as new wine" (*CE* 10: 31). The "magic circle" of his influence into which Hawthorne says in "The Old Manse" he drew his friends was also claimed by Fuller as "some magic about me which draws other spirits into my circle whether I will or they will or no."¹¹ Giovanni, of course, assigns a similar metaphoric power to Beatrice when he describes being drawn "irrevocably within her sphere" and compelled to "obey the law that whirled him onward, in ever-lessening circles" toward her (*CE* 10: 109). And, finally, Giovanni's initial description of his surprising ease in conversing with Beatrice as making him feel "like a brother" (*CE* 10: 113) to her is parallel to the characterization that Fuller, sister to five brothers and intimate friend of many men, assigned to her relationship with Hawthorne during the final days of their summer together in 1844; he had become, she wrote, "more . . . a brother" to her "than ever . . . any man before."¹²

More generally, but importantly, Fuller's unpublished "Autobiographical Romance," and her exploration of a feminist symbolism in her flower sketches for the *Dial,* "The Magnolia of Lake Pontchartrain" (1841) and "Yuca Filamentosa" (1842), suggested to Hawthorne an allegorical figure for Fuller of Fuller's own choosing. Noted for wearing a flower in her hair, Fuller had long associated the feminine side of her nature with flowers and her mother's garden.¹³ Her 1840 autobiographical sketch of her youth significantly allies the masculine influence of her father's harsh insistence on her intellectual development with the stern rational virtues of heroic, imperial Rome but counters that influence with the artistic world of Greece and the feminine world of her mother, linked figuratively with the beauty of her mother's garden and the nurturing love she bestowed on it.[14] While the sketch was not published in her lifetime, Fuller in talks with Hawthorne may have employed this figurative opposition to locate the continuing influence of her childhood on her life, which was, in fact, the most personal subject which Hawthorne himself identified as having discussed with Fuller during their long afternoon alone in Sleepy Hollow on 21 August 1842 (*CE* 8: 342–43). The influence of Fuller's father and, quite possibly, the influence of Emerson, who replaced her father as the intellectual mentor of her adulthood, seem clearly on Hawthorne's mind when, of all the possible descriptive statements he could have made to identify Fuller in "The Old Manse," he thinks of her as one "on whose feminine nature had been *imposed* the heavy gift of intellectual *power,* such as a strong man might have staggered under" (*CE* 10: 29; my emphasis). As Joel Pfister has noted, Hawthorne's tale appropriates the oppositions of the father's oppressive intellectual cultivation of his daughter against the mother's cultivation of her flowers.[15] "I kissed them," Fuller says of her mother's flowers. "I pressed them to my bosom with passionate emotions, such as I have never dared to express to any human being," and "an ambition swelled my heart to be as beautiful, as perfect as they."[16] Compare Fuller's statement with Hawthorne's description of Beatrice: "she bent towards the magnificent plant, and opened her arms as if to embrace it. 'Yes, my sister, my splendor, it shall be Beatrice's task to nurse and serve thee; and thou shalt reward her with thy kisses and perfumed breath, which to her is as the breath of life!'" (*CE* 10: 97). But for Fuller, as for Beatrice, her father's intervention in her natural development caused "much of life" to be "devoured in the bud." Unlike her beloved flowers, Fuller says that she cannot be "as perfect as they," for "living and blooming" in their "unchecked law," her mother's flowers can never know "the blights, the distortions, which beset the human being and which . . . no glories of free agency could ever repay!"[17] Hawthorne certainly had access to Fuller's more positive account of her father's influence on her extraordinary intellectual development in Fuller's thinly veiled autobiographical account of Miranda in "The Great Lawsuit." With "a strong electric nature, which repelled those who did not belong to her, and attracted those who did," Miranda, much like Hawthorne's Beatrice, was educated—given "the keys to the wonders of the universe"—by a father who believed "in the equality of the sexes" and held "no sentimental reverse for woman."[18] As Hawthorne would do of Beatrice, Fuller does not even mention Miranda's mother or the influence of her absence.

Had Hawthorne not seen Fuller often with flowers in her hair and heard her discourse on the special symbolism of flowers, "The Magnolia of Lake Pontchartrain" and "Yuca Filamentosa" alone would have been sufficient to establish for Hawthorne Fuller's identification of the feminine with the flower. In Jeffrey Steele's insightful analysis of Fuller's attempts at "psychological mythmaking," Fuller's flower sketches figure prominently in her search for myths and symbols that explore "the psychological dimensions of a female being forced to withdraw from heterosexual society and to rely upon her own resources," a search in which Fuller specifically sought to free herself from the domination of Emerson.[19] In both sketches, Fuller endows the flower with the mythic beauty and creative force of the feminine, powers which the male featured in each sketch fails to comprehend and thus rejects. Failing to find himself "in other forms of nature," the Emerson-like male narrator of "The Magnolia of Lake Pontchartrain" admits to having retreated into the "centre of [his] being" where he "found all being"; that is man's problem, Fuller's feminine voice, the magnolia, proclaims.[20] Imprisoned within the masculine self and imprisoning all with him, man can only "recombine the lines and colors of his own existence" and re-create the feminine, as Fuller says, as "a fairy—like them, only lesser and more exquisite than they, a goddess, larger and of statelier proportion, an angel,—like still, only with an added power." To transcend the self, to be truly creative, man must experience the feminine power of "the queen and guardian of the flowers," but that power cannot be known, she tells him, "till thou art it . . . till thou has passed through it."[21] In "Yuca Filamentosa," Fuller's identification with the yuca flower is clearly personal. Fond of reminding herself and others—including Hawthorne— that "Margaret" means "pearl," Fuller praises the pearl and the opal as the moon's "gems" and proclaims the night-blooming yuca as the moon's flower.[22] Engendering the calm, lonely moon as a feminine power bestowing a loving beauty on earth, Ful- ler clearly identifies herself with the mystery of the yuca, which blooms by brooding "on her own heart" and by allowing the moon to fill "her urn" but which withers under the "unsparing scrutiny" of the masculine sun. Inspired by the beauty of the moon-blooming yuca, the female speaker solicits the appreciation of a male friend, who proves to be as unresponsive to the moon's influence as the yuca is to the sun's.[23]

"Rappaccini's Daughter" seems to acknowledge the challenge of Fuller's feminist claim to a separate realm of knowledge by employing in parallel fashion Fuller's appropriation of the flower and the moon as symbols for woman's access to a beauty and a power—a knowledge—that transcends reliance on the "stern scrutiny" of the rational light of the masculine "sun." Giovanni, it should be noted, first observes Beatrice in twilight; as "night was already closing in," Beatrice and flower seem one as Beatrice proclaims sisterhood with the purple blossoms that she passionately embraces as her source of "the breath of life" (*CE* 10: 96–97). Under the influence of the moon, Giovanni is drawn to the power of the feminine, receptive enough to recognize its symbolism—"flower and maiden were different, and yet the same"— but too fearful to embrace its meaning—rejecting flower and girl as "fraught with some strange peril in either shape" (*CE* 10: 98). Under the complete influence of the "stern scrutiny" of the masculine sun, which, as the tale puts it, brings "every thing within the limits of ordinary experience," Giovanni finds that by taking "a most rational view of the whole matter" he can no longer recognize, much less embrace or repel, the "mysteries" that had been so "fertile" in his night dreams (*CE* 10: 98).

Though Hawthorne seems to parallel Fuller's symbolism, he does so, of course, with a twist. Both the purple blossoms and Beatrice herself have been transformed by the rational, "scientific" mind of Dr. Rappaccini into creations of extraordinary beauty and possible peril. The natural, creative forces that Fuller's symbolism celebrated are redefined through male consciousness, contained and transformed—by Rappaccini in his garden and by Giovanni in his mind—into the unnatural and destructive. Fearing these creative forces in nature and woman, Rappaccini imposes an artificial hybridization of the natural and unnatural on flower and daughter, imprisoning them within the walls of a private Eden where he can scrutinize but never touch. In Rappaccini's garden, the "secret powers" of the "Mothers," as Fuller called feminine creative force, have been so suppressed by the father's intervention that, in the absence of the mother, in the very absence of any mention of her absence, Beatrice becomes literally her father's creation.[24] Giovanni re-creates Beatrice in his own image. He projects his "lurid intermixture of emotions" onto a "hybridized" Beatrice—angel and demon, both being the feminine made unnatural by man's imposition of a meaning to contain the mysteries he cannot confront without first naming. Though not one of Nina Auerbach's examples, "Rappaccini's Daughter" illustrates Auerbach's thesis (which parallels Fuller's insights) that the nineteenth-century male's preoccupation with mythic representations of women as angels or demons arose in an age of religious doubt as vehicles for spiritual transfiguration, celebrating "the secrecy and spiritual ambiguity of woman's ascribed powers" even as they sought to suppress them: "The social restrictions that crippled women's lives, the physical weaknesses wished on them," she argues, "were fearful attempts to exorcise a mysterious power."[25]

Another Fuller sketch for the *Dial,* "Leila," celebrates this mysterious feminine creative power and condemns the frantic attempts of men to contain it. Selecting a name that she identified herself with and said meant "night," Fuller represents in Leila "all the elemental powers of nature," the creative force that when embraced "showers down . . . balm and blessing," instantly creates flowers and "rivers of bliss," and (in an inversion of the symbolic narrative Hawthorne would use) transforms "prison walls" into "Edens." When rejected by men, she can seem demonic. Confronting her, men "shrink from the overflow of the infinite," become "baffled" and "angry" in their inability to reduce her to "a form" to "clasp to the living breast." In the end, they proclaim her "mad, because they felt she made them so."[26] As Fuller's sketch and Auerbach's cultural mythography suggest, "Rappaccini's Daughter" may be read as a self-reflective narrative of the contemporary cultural process by which man is attracted to and appalled by a feminine power whose mystery and energy he compels himself to contain, whose "Eden" he must enclose in the "prison walls" of a home-restricted, artificially Edenic garden or of a rigid, knowable category—angel or demon. Feeling himself "within the influence of an unintelligible power by the communication which he had opened with Beatrice," Giovanni finds "her rich beauty" a "madness to him," a "wild offspring of both love and horror" (*CE* 10: 105). Unwilling or unable to escape her attraction, Giovanni attempts to rid himself of the "fierce and subtle poison within him" by redefining her "extraordinary being" within a "familiar and daylight view" which would bring her "rigidly and systematically within the limits of ordinary experience" (*CE* 10: 105). The angelic or the demonic—the Beatrice of Dante who redeems man or the Beatrice Cenci who avenges man's brutal dominion—both serve as rigid categories to subordinate the threatening power of the feminine.

Hawthorne's dialogue with Fuller's texts is narratively inscribed within the tale. Hawthorne enacts this "blood-warm" tale of his anxiety over Emerson's influence and over his own ambivalent feelings for Fuller through the complex tension of hermeneutical and, I would add, gender allegiances demanded by conflicting senses— Emerson's vision and Fuller's voice.

As Hawthorne said in "The Old Manse" of those "hobgoblins of flesh and blood" under the influence of Emerson's "light," those who gaze into, much less enter, Rappaccini's garden are apt to see "objects unseen before" (*CE* 10: 30–31). Like Emerson, an idealist with noble intentions, Rappaccini creates and cultivates unnaturally beautiful and possibly poisonous plants (and a protégé-daughter) in a garden which is oddly described as being "*peopled* with plants and herbs" that have "unearthly *face*[s]" just as Emerson cultivated brilliant but possibly deluded insights and followers (*CE* 10: 95, 110; my emphasis). If the "transparent eyeball" of Emerson was able to read through the symbols of the seen to the unseen, to "translate" Nature, so Rappaccini studies "every shrub . . . as if he was looking into their inmost nature" to discover the source of "their creative energy" (*CE* 10: 95). Human nature, however, is the real interest of Rappaccini's experimental studies, as Giovanni suspects of him and Hawthorne fears of Emerson. As he reads his plants, so he attempts to read Giovanni, fixing "his eyes upon Giovanni with an intentness that seemed to bring out whatever was within him worthy of notice" (*CE* 10: 106–7). His desire to penetrate and cultivate the essence of a person's individual virtues, however, serves a coldly intellectual and spiritual, rather than human, love, for he has "a look as deep as Nature, but without Nature's warmth of love" (*CE* 10: 107). Just as Emerson claimed to see the divine within the individual and to claim in "Self-Reliance" that the individual's obligations to the truth and to his own spiritual integrity took precedence over all other relations, including those of family, so Rappaccini is said to be willing to "sacrifice human life, his own among the rest, or whatever else was dearest to him, for the sake of adding so much as a grain of mustard seed to the great heap of his accumulated knowledge" (*CE* 10: 99–100).

The conflict between vision and voice is most succinctly stated when Giovanni asks Beatrice if he can trust what he has seen of her with his own eyes (*CE* 10: 111). Not trusting what he has seen, he quickly renegotiates the basis on which he will define Beatrice's nature by urging her, with vague sexual suggestiveness, to have him "believe nothing save what comes from your own lips" (*CE* 10: 111–12). Beatrice counters by demanding that Giovanni "forget whatever" he "may have fancied" regarding her and, pointedly, restates Giovanni's request to limit his contact to the truth of her lips' voice, not touch: "If true to the outward senses, still it may be false in its essence, but the *words* of Beatrice Rappaccini's lips are true from the depths of the heart outward. Those you may believe" (*CE* 10: 112; my emphasis). Giovanni does not, of course, believe. Like Rappaccini himself, he is wedded not merely to "sight" but to "vision," the idealist vision that reads nature as symbol and, as this tale demonstrates, sees not deep realities but shallow delusions. Appropriating Emerson's language as well as thought, Giovanni announces early on that Rappaccini's garden "would serve . . . as a symbolic language to keep him in communion with Nature" (*CE* 10: 98). Deeper than the irony of his misreading of the symbolism of Beatrice's nature, of course, is his very desire to read her nature as symbolic, for, as this tale suggests, the desire to read the physical for the symbolic arises from the desire to gain power over a nature that one actually fears having communion with. The symbol-making language of the eye imposes meaning through an interpretative monologue, but the language of the voice converses in the unending dialogue of a human communion.

Our own eyes, like Giovanni's, are apt to deceive us. For all of the critical commentary on Beatrice's beauty, we seldom notice that it is her voice and her voice alone that Hawthorne locates as the source of her beauty and her truth. Warning Giovanni against the deceptions of vision, Beatrice offers, as we have seen, the truths of the heart's voice. Though Giovanni will eventually ignore her advice, he is attracted to her first by her voice, not her physical beauty. He hears before he sees her, and her voice to him is "as rich as a tropical sunset," making him "think of deep hues of purple or crimson and of perfume heavily delectable" (*CE* 10: 96–97). Like the fountain in the heart of the garden, this "rich voice" is later described as coming "forth . . . like a gush of music" (*CE* 10: 104). Rich, purple, crimson, perfumed, musical—again and again the tale's descriptions of Beatrice's voice suggest that the essence of her beauty, her passion, and her truth resides in "the words" that come "from the depths of . . . [her] heart." Having initially characterized her physical beauty as coming from the effect of her spirit on her appearance—her "life, health, and energy" (*CE* 10: 97)— and having later characterized her, based on the impression left by their conversations, as being, surprisingly, "human" and "endowed with all gentle and feminine qualities," Giovanni finds that "whatever had looked ugly" in "her physical and moral system" had come to seem "beautiful" (*CE* 10: 114). Through conversing with Beatrice, Giovanni gains this temporary confidence in Beatrice, as the narrator observes, because he "founded" it on "something truer and more real than what we can see with the eyes and touch with the finger" (*CE* 10: 120).

In the power of Beatrice's voice to enchant Giovanni with the beauty of her spirit, Fuller's physical presence, never itself characterized by contemporaries as being conventionally beautiful, is translated into the tale. Famous for her series of organized intellectual discussions for the women of Boston, the "Conversations," and praised by all contemporaries for the brilliance of her talk, Fuller, in opposition to

Emerson's rhetoric of vision, employed and advocated a rhetoric of conversation as the way to truth. When Fuller warned Hawthorne that no mere "talent of observation" can compensate for the "deeper experiences" that would come from listening "to a voice that truly calls upon his solitude to ope his study door," she prescribed to Hawthorne the communion of dialogue rather than the solitude of the observer's eye and the monologue of its pronouncements. Similarly, she would condemn Emerson for being chilled by his attempt to read the "symbolic language of Nature" rather than "lie along the ground long enough to hear the secret whispers of our parent life."[27] Hawthorne's tale allegorizes these opposing rhetorics, endorsing Fuller's as it condemns Emerson's. In self-imposed isolation from the academy, Rappaccini listens only to his own voice and follows his monomaniacal vision to its unnatural end. The power of the uncompromising will of the individualist who has forsaken the subordinations of self that dialogue requires is employed, ironically and perhaps inevitably, to exert power over others. Desiring to give his daughter the power of the perfectly invulnerable individualist, he must subordinate her entirely to his will so that she may subordinate others. By repelling all human contact, he makes her immune from such violations of the self as Giovanni inflicts upon her in the first and only social relationship she is allowed to have. Literally and figuratively, however, Beatrice prefers Giovanni's poison to her father's. Before his coming, her need for human contact and dialogue had been expressed in her personification of the flowers as sisterly companions. Once Giovanni establishes a dialogue with her, her need for him is fulfilled in speech, not touch, and Giovanni's happiest moments are those in which he listens to her voice rather than to the interior voices which torment him with what he imagines he has seen and with what he desires and fears—her touch (see *CE* 10: 115–16).

Surely one of the happiest and most intimate moments that Hawthorne ever spent conversing with a woman is recorded in his notebook description of his 21 August 1842 conversation alone with Fuller in the woods of Sleepy Hollow. That description has interesting parallels within the tale. Written less than two months after Hawthorne's entry into Concord, the passage faintly suggests the dangers Hawthorne may have imagined in any movement toward Emerson's powerful influence. Journeying through the woods toward Emerson's house to look for Fuller, Hawthorne "misses" the "nearest way," "wanders," becomes entangled in the underbrush, and is consumed by his own "rage and despair" (*CE* 8: 340–41). As Hawthorne "could scarcely force a passage through" the bushes "which cross and interwine themselves about his legs," so Giovanni's first step into Rappaccini's garden to look for Beatrice requires "forcing himself through the entanglement of a shrub that wreathed its tendrils over the hidden entrance" (*CE* 8: 340–41, 10: 109). Hawthorne found Fuller—not in Emerson's house but in Emerson's "garden," Sleepy Hollow:

> I returned through the woods, and entering Sleepy Hollow, I perceived a lady reclining near the path which bends along its verge. It was Margaret herself. She had been there

the whole afternoon, meditating or reading. . . . She said that nobody had broken her solitude, and was just giving utterance to a theory that no inhabitant of Concord ever visited Sleepy Hollow, when we saw a whole group of people entering the sacred precincts. Most of them followed a path that led them remote from us; but an old man passed near us, and smiled to see Margaret lying on the ground, and me sitting by her side. He made some remark about the beauty of the afternoon, and withdrew himself into the shadow of the wood. (*CE* 8: 342–43)

Hawthorne's desire to be alone with Fuller and his perception of the romantic tableau presented by the positions of their bodies are evident in his emphasis on Fuller's reassurance of their solitude, the immediate threats to it, and the attribution of his own anxious self-consciousness to the intrusive old man. Safely alone, they began a conversation, and Hawthorne describes with an almost breathless excitement the seemingly endless grounds of their sympathetic interests:

Then we talked about Autumn—and about the pleasures of getting lost in the woods— and about the crows, whose voices Margaret had heard—and about the experience of early childhood after the recollection of them has passed away—and about the sight of mountains from a distance, and the view from their summits—and about other matters of high and low philosophy. (*CE* 8: 342–43)

As Fuller and Hawthorne talked of nature, family life, and "high and low philosophy," so Hawthorne describes Beatrice and Giovanni as talking of "matters as simple as the daylight or summer clouds," then of his "distant home, his friends, his mother, and his sisters," and, finally, "thoughts, too, from a deep source, and fantasies of a gemlike brilliancy" (*CE* 10: 113). Just as Hawthorne describes Emerson as an "intruder" whom they had first heard stalking the bank above them "hidden among the trees" as they talked, so Giovanni discovers that Rappaccini had been lurking "within the shadow of the entrance" and "watching the scene, he knew not how long" (*CE* 8: 343, 10: 114).

As the subtle narrative framing and tone of his account of that afternoon alone with Fuller suggest—and as his characterization of Giovanni's desire to violate "the physical barrier" that Beatrice's relationship "marked" between them more strongly intimates (*CE* 10: 116)—Hawthorne may have recognized within himself a sexual tension in his relationship with Fuller that threatened the "brotherly" nature on which their relationship was founded and depended. If so, Fuller's body would indeed have been poisonous—to Hawthorne's relationship with her and, of course, with Sophia. For Beatrice, the only love possible between her and Giovanni is the union of his "image in mine heart," a love of two hearts in dialogue "as unreserved as if they had been playmates from early infancy" (*CE* 10: 125, 115). Such a love is intimate friendship, but Giovanni's "shallowness of feeling and insincerity of character" make him incapable of sustaining the uniqueness of such a relationship with a woman without bringing it "within the limits of ordinary experience," those limits of course being a man's customary sexualization of his relationship with a woman. Giovanni may indeed hear her heart's truth, but he reads her body as the symbol of his own revulsion at the "monstrosity" of an obsession whose self-generated origins he cannot claim.[28]

Hawthorne, of course, cannot claim them either. But he does. By engaging in the kind of dialogue with Fuller that Giovanni silences with Beatrice, by translating Fuller into his own voice, Hawthorne with self-conscious irony attempts to reassert control over the troubling ambiguities of Fuller's character and of his relationship with her by allegorizing his condemnation of his Aubépine-like compulsion to allegorize her. "Is Beatrice to be a demon or an angel?" Hawthorne might as well have answered Sophia by saying that Beatrice was neither and that he was both.

Nina Baym, in her influential essay "Thwarted Nature," complained that both antifeminist and feminist readings of Hawthorne shared the same assumptions and drew the same conclusions, one to praise and the other to condemn. Identifying hers as a minority voice, Baym argued that Hawthorne's tales indict the very masculine prejudices that they dramatize. My reading of "Rappaccini's Daughter," obviously, is allied with Baym's vision of Hawthorne's purposes. Most cultural readings of mid-nineteenth-century texts make much of the power of the domestic ideal in shaping literary and lived representations of women. What is often underestimated, however, is the cultural power of those resistant to that ideology. That Hawthorne was to some degree allied with those engaged in that resistance is supported by an examination of the specific audience for which "Rappaccini's Daughter" was written and the context in which it was published.

Known for its politics—literary and national—*The United States Magazine and Democratic Review* was firmly committed to giving women a voice both in society and in its own pages. Six months before the publication of "Rappaccini's Daughter," for instance, the magazine ran an unsigned essay entitled "The Legal Wrongs of Women," which called for a complete revision of a legal and social system that sanctioned the virtual slavery of all women. Lest there be any doubt about the position of the magazine, an editorial note is printed at the foot of the first page of the essay asserting explicitly the magazine's "full approval and adoption of its views."[29] In that same issue, in an article entitled "Female Novelists," W. A. Jones, after reviewing major women writers, asserts that "there is a race of masculine writers, with feminine delicacy of mind, who ought to be added to the list of novelists for a lady's reading." Jones names Hawthorne and gives him his strongest endorsement.[30] The *Democratic Review,* in fact, lived up to its commitment to women's issues and to its solicitude for women readers by granting an extraordinary amount of space to women writers. The September issue of that year, for example, featured five signed pieces written by women, including works by Elizabeth Barrett and Lydia Maria Child. Hawthorne's audience for "Rappaccini's Daughter," we may assume, would have been more alert than many a twentieth-century scholar to the gender values being endorsed by the tale.

When Hawthorne included "Rappaccini's Daughter" in *Mosses from an Old Manse,* he carefully selected its first readers—his critical audience. As copies rolled off the press, Hawthorne wrote Evert Duyckinck a letter listing ten names to whom he wished copies sent (*CE* 16: 158–59). Fuller's name topped the list! As the critic for the *Dial,* Fuller had embraced Hawthorne's career early on and had helped secure his status within the literary community centered in Boston/Concord. He now looked to her to help do the same for him in New York. And she did. In her lengthy front-page *New-York Daily Tribune* review of *Mosses* on 22 June 1846, she characterizes Hawthorne's genius as so obvious to the discerning reader that anything she or any other critic could say would be either "superfluous or impertinent."[31] In that same year, after her comprehensive, highly critical assessment of American writers in "American Literature: Its Position in the Present," the essay that she wrote especially for *Papers on Literature and Art,* Fuller crowns Hawthorne, simply and authoritatively, as "the best writer of the day."[32]

Notes

1. Julian Hawthorne, *Nathaniel Hawthorne and His Wife* (Boston: Osgood, 1884) 1: 360.

2. Quotations from the letters, works, and notebooks of Nathaniel Hawthorne are from the *Centenary Edition of the Works of Nathaniel Hawthorne,* ed. William Charvat et al. (Columbus: Ohio State UP, 1962–), hereafter cited as *CE* with the volume and page numbers.

3. See Joel Myerson, ed., "Margaret Fuller's 1842 Journal: At Concord with the Emersons," *Harvard Library Bulletin* 21 (1973): 320–40; and Martha L. Berg and Alice De V. Perry, eds., " 'The Impulses of Human Nature': Margaret Fuller's Journal from June through October 1844," *Massachusetts Historical Society Proceedings* 102 (1990): 38–126.

4. Sophia Hawthorne to her mother, 22 Aug. 1842; ms. in Henry W. and Albert A. Berg Collection of English and American Literature, New York Public Library, Astor, Lenox and Tilden Foundations.

5. Rev. of *Twice-told Tales, Dial* 3 (July 1842): 130–31.

6. Larry J. Reynolds, "Hawthorne and Emerson in 'The Old Manse,' " *Studies in the Novel* 23 (1991): 60–81.

7. For an opposing view, see Julie E. Hall, " 'Tracing the Original Design': The Hawthornes in Rappaccini's Garden," *Nathaniel Hawthorne Review* 21 (Spring 1995): 26–35.

8. Robert Hudspeth, ed., *The Letters of Margaret Fuller,* 6 vols. (Ithaca: Cornell UP, 1983–95) 3: 66.

9. *Letters* 3: 70.

10. Myerson, "Margaret Fuller's 1842 Journal" 340.

11. *Letters* 1: 175.

12. Berg and Perry, " 'The Impulses of Human Nature' " 108.

13. Edwin Haviland Miller, *Salem Is My Dwelling Place: A Life of Nathaniel Hawthorne*

(Iowa City: U of Iowa P, 1991), in a note suggests that "perhaps the portrait of Beatrice . . . was influenced by Fuller's involvement with flowers" (548n21).

14. Margaret Fuller, "Autobiographical Romance," *The Essential Margaret Fuller,* ed. Jeffrey Steele (New Brunswick, N.J.: Rutgers UP, 1992) 24–43.

15. *The Production of Personal Life: Class, Gender, and the Psychological in Hawthorne's Fiction* (Stanford: Stanford UP, 1991) 67–70. See especially Pfister's general discussion of flower imagery in the "feminine culture industry" as a cultural context for "Rappaccini's Daughter" (65–66). Pfister too sees Fuller as an influence on Hawthorne's conception of Beatrice, but his assumption that Hawthorne merely recoiled from Fuller's "monstrosity" of masculine and feminine traits limits his recognition of Hawthorne's equally powerful attraction to her.

16. "Autobiographical Romance" 32.

17. "Autobiographical Romance" 37, 32.

18. "The Great Lawsuit: Man *versus* Men, Woman *versus* women," *Dial* 4 (July 1843): 1–47, 15–16.

19. *Representations of the Self in the American Renaissance* (Chapel Hill: U of North Carolina P, 1987) 100–33, 105, 109.

20. "The Magnolia of Lake Pontchartrain," *Dial* 1 (Jan. 1841): 299–305. Rpt. in Steele, *Essential Margaret Fuller* 44–49, 47.

21. "Magnolia" in Steele, *Essential* 48.

22. "Yuca Filamentosa," *Dial* 2 (Jan. 1842): 286–88. Rpt. in Steele, *Essential* 50–52, 51.

23. "Yuca" in Steele, *Essential* 52.

24. "Magnolia" in Steele, *Essential* 48. In her "Autobiographical Romance," Fuller blames her unnatural, lonely childhood on her father's overwhelming influence, her mother's absence ("My mother was in delicate health, and much absorbed in the care of her younger children" [27]), and her infant sister's death ("I was left alone. This has made a vast difference in my lot" [25–26]). For Fuller, as for Beatrice, flowers substitute for the absent mother and sister.

25. *The Woman and the Demon: The Life of a Victorian Myth* (Cambridge: Harvard UP, 1982) 8–9.

26. "Leila," *Dial* 1 (Apr. 1841): 462–67. Rpt. in Steele, *Essential* 53–58, 53, 56–57, 53–54. For Fuller's identification with the name Leila, see Ralph Waldo Emerson, William Henry Channing, and James Freeman Clarke, eds., *The Memoirs of Margaret Fuller Ossoli,* 2 vols. (Boston, 1852): 1: 219.

27. Rev. of *Essays: Second Series,* by Ralph Waldo Emerson, *New-York Daily Tribune,* 7 Dec. 1844: 1. Rpt. as "Emerson's Essays" in *Margaret Fuller: Essays on American Life and Letters,* ed. Joel Myerson (Albany: College and Univ. P, 1978) 240–47, 245.

28. My reading of the tale owes an obvious debt to Nina Baym, "Thwarted Nature: Nathaniel Hawthorne as Feminist," *American Novelists Revisited: Essays in Feminist Criticism,* ed. Fritz Fleischmann (Boston: Hall, 1982) 58–77. The "thwarted nature" of Hawthorne's male characters, Baym claims, is Hawthorne's indictment of the unnaturalness of that "part of the [male] psyche that repudiates human sexuality," that mutilates, in order to deny,

woman's sexuality (55–56). Though I accept much of Baym's argument, I would contend that in this tale Hawthorne seems equally troubled by man's inability to relate to woman in any other way than a sexualized one.

29. *United States Magazine and Democratic Review* 14 (May 1844): 477–82, 477.

30. *United States Magazine and Democratic Review* 14 (May 1844): 484–89, 488–89.

31. Rpt. in Myerson, *Margaret Fuller: Essays* 371–74. 371.

32. *Papers on Literature and Art,* 2: 122–43. Rpt. in Myerson *Margaret Fuller: Essays* 381–400, 399.

STOWE AND HAWTHORNE

James D. Wallace

In addition to the New England novels discussed below, interested readers will want to sample Harriet Beecher Stowe's New York society novels: *Pink and White Tyranny* (1871), *My Wife and I* (1871), and *We and Our Neighbors* (1875). Ranging still farther is *Palmetto Leaves* (1873), a novel which, according to Edward Wagenknecht, in *Harriet Beecher Stowe: The Known and the Unknown* (18), "virtually began the Florida boom" (New York: Oxford UP, 1965).

In the fall of 1863, during the middle of the Civil War she had helped to bring about, Harriet Beecher Stowe began a series of sketches about domestic life that would appear in the *Atlantic Monthly* all through 1864. When she collected these sketches in book form, as *House and Home Papers* and *The Chimney Corner,* she chose a masculine persona—Christopher Crowfield—as her narrative voice, although their subject and tone belonged decidedly to "woman's sphere." Some titles: "What Is a Home?" "Bodily Religion: A Sermon on Good Health," "Servants," "Cookery," "Home Religion," "Dress; or, Who Makes the Fashions." In fact, many of these same subjects are covered in much the same spirit in *The American Woman's Home,* the guidebook for wives and mothers that Stowe and her sister, Catharine Beecher, would issue in 1869. Stowe's gestures at creating a convincing male narrative voice in the *House and Home Papers* are few and feeble and, for that very reason, arresting. One such gesture occurs at the beginning of "The Lady Who Does Her Own Work," when she represents the man at leisure:

> I was lying back in my study-chair, with my heels luxuriously propped on an ottoman, reading for the two-hundredth time Hawthorne's "Mosses from an Old Manse," or his "Twice-Told Tales," I forget which,—I only know that these books constitute my cloud-land, where I love to sail away in dreamy quietude, forgetting the war, the price of coal and flour, the rates of exchange, and the rise and fall of gold. What do all these

things matter, as seen from those enchanted gardens in Padua where the weird Rappaccini tends his enchanted plants, and his gorgeous daughter fills us with the light and magic of her presence, and saddens us with the shadowy allegoric mystery of her preternatural destiny?[1]

This moment is arresting for several reasons. First, it suggests something about the "use" of Hawthorne's fiction by at least some nineteenth-century readers. Clearly he is a "much-loved" author. *Twice-told Tales* had first appeared in 1837, *Mosses from an Old Manse* in 1846, and already they have the status of old favorites, reread in preference to any more recent fiction. Second, Hawthorne takes the reader out of everyday life, away from the "business" of the masculine sphere—news, markets, money, the public arena—into "dreamy quietude" and solitary detachment, the world of imagination. Third, there is an "oriental" strangeness about Hawthorne's fiction, a quality that evokes words like "weird," "enchanted," "light and magic," "shadowy allegoric mystery," and "preternatural." Fourth, although the specific story in question, "Rappaccini's Daughter," is a kind of protofeminist fantasy in which a young man's attraction to and fastidious revulsion at the female body is analyzed and punished, the pleasure "Crowfield" takes and the escape he achieves are somehow specifically *masculine;* it may be an escape from the world of business, but it is not an entry into the domestic. Crowfield's wife takes care of that: she calls him out of the reverie of his reading by reminding him of his duty to write another article for the *Atlantic Monthly:* "my wife represents the positive forces of time, place, and number in our family, and, having also a chronological head, she knows the day of the month, and therefore gently reminded me that by inevitable dates the time drew near for preparing my—which is it, now, May or June number?"[2] Fifth, the selection of this particular author to represent Crowfield's indulgence in his imaginative life constitutes a form of "canonization": that is, it suggests that the authors Harriet Beecher Stowe read herself and considered important were male.

As Joan Hedrick has pointed out, earlier in the *House and Home Papers* Crowfield's daughter has planned to fill her house with uniform editions of Scott, Thackeray, Macaulay, Prescott, Irving, Longfellow, Lowell, Hawthorne, Holmes, and others, a list that elevates American authors to equality with British but does not include a single woman: "They represented the very best cultural authorities, the same kinds of white, male authorities—like Sir Walter Scott—whom Tom Sawyer invoked whenever he planned a foolhardy adventure. . . . she made no mention of Rebecca Harding Davis, whose *Life in the Iron Mills* had appeared in the *Atlantic* in 1861; or of Harriet Prescott or Rose Terry or Julia Ward Howe or Celia Thaxter. Her canon was male."[3] So is the canon of most nineteenth- and twentieth-century critics, except that many would include Stowe herself on the list. Writing in the 1930s, Van Wyck Brooks noted that the publishing house of Ticknor and Fields, by juxtaposing famous English writers with Americans, had established a canon for the American Renaissance, the tradition of writing (mostly by white males) that blossomed in the middle of the nineteenth century: "From this press the English writers and the New England writers came together, and each drew something from the general glamour. Browning and Longfellow, Emerson, Tennyson, Hawthorne, Holmes, De Quincey, Mrs. Stowe presented a common front as standard authors."[4]

All this suggests that for Stowe as for her persona, Christopher Crowfield, Hawthorne's influence was especially important. Curiously, their careers had similar trajectories. Both had written a first novel of the flight-and-pursuit type, involving high adventure, captivities, and a supernaturally self-sacrificing protagonist: Hawthorne's *Fanshawe* appeared in 1828 at his own expense, and Stowe's *Uncle Tom's Cabin* was issued in 1852 by John P. Jewett, a religious publisher who had worked with other members of the Beecher family. There, of course, this early similarity ends. Hawthorne immediately repented, collected all the copies of *Fanshawe* he could find, and burned them. He never mentioned the book again, and it was only republished after his death. *Uncle Tom's Cabin* sold 10,000 copies within the first week and 300,000 by the end of the first year. It made its author rich, famous, and, in literary and abolitionist circles, powerful.

In one other way, too, these first novels are alike: both are utterly uncharacteristic of their authors' body of work—are, indeed, essentially antithetical to their personalities. For both Hawthorne and Stowe, New England supplied a lifetime of inspiration. The history of the region, the character of its people, the spiritual legacy of Puritanism, the rigors and muted beauty of its climate, the narrow but deep vein of its cultural life—all this became the material both authors explored for their best and most personal work. Virtually all of Hawthorne's tales and sketches, *Grandfather's Chair* (1841), *The Scarlet Letter* (1850), *The House of the Seven Gables* (1851), and *The Blithedale Romance* (1852), owe a major portion of their special qualities to their New England setting, while Stowe's *The Minister's Wooing* (1859), *The Pearl of Orr's Island* (1862), *Oldtown Folks* (1869), and *Poganuc People* (1878) are the books about which Van Wyck Brooks wrote, "Mrs. Stowe's New England Novels, written with the same rude strength [as *Uncle Tom's Cabin*], established a school and a method. It was her New England, not Hawthorne's, that gave later writers their point of departure. She set the stage for Sarah Orne Jewett."[5]

Brooks's comment suggests a second important element to Stowe's body of work: she belongs not only to the "American Renaissance" but to what Jane Tompkins calls "The Other American Renaissance," the tradition of women's writing that developed over the course of the nineteenth century in the United States, a tradition that runs from the popularity of the novel of seduction in the late eighteenth century through the turn to naturalism at the beginning of the twentieth.[6] The ideological struggle that marks Stowe's forays into "woman's fiction" are, however, played out in a New England context that closely resembles Hawthorne's.[7] Lawrence Buell has summarized the ways both Hawthorne and Stowe represent a nineteenth-century response to "the parent strain of Puritan culture and its Edwardsean filiation," a response marked by ambivalence toward Puritan repression and relief at its decline:

Both writers are preoccupied with anatomizing the features of an age of consolidation that followed the key inaugural events of the epoch: with appraising, both sympathetically and satirically, the social rituals that sustained community and constrained individual deviance yet at the same time provoked it; and such consequences of institutionalization within a holy commonwealth as hypocrisy, secularization of piety, isolation of the clergy into a priestly caste, and the tensions arising from the conflict between the feeling that the younger generation is unworthy of its forebears and the desire to liberate it from the dead hand of the past.[8]

In *The Minister's Wooing,* the Reverend Samuel Hopkins, like Hawthorne's Arthur Dimmesdale, represents both the greatest achievements and the dreary ossification of Puritan theology. He is a master of doctrine, yet precisely because of his mastery, he lacks some basic human sympathy that Stowe considers fundamental to Christian love, and though he is certainly a worthy man, he is a very poor match for the novel's heroine, Mary Scudder. In a brilliant embodiment of the dilemma of the Puritan tradition, Stowe has her minister triumph over his lack of human warmth by renouncing his claim on the woman he loves: Hopkins attains his human dimension by forgoing the one real human contact he has ever felt. It is a plot twist worthy of Hawthorne.

But of course there are also major differences between the two writers. Buell summarizes these, as well:

> Stowe . . . treats the heart's interior perfunctorily and schematically, as contrasted with Hawthorne's anatomy of Dimmesdale—abstract and putative as it is. In these differing emphases, Hawthorne comes closer to capturing the nuances of such psychological records as the agonized diaries of Thomas Shepard and Michael Wigglesworth, whereas Stowe looks forward to recent historiographical emphasis on the social structures and external lives of the Puritans. Stowe thus became a model of later realistic portrayals in regional fiction, of the textures of daily New England life, rituals, and folkways, whereas Hawthorne, for whom Puritan attitudes had greater reality than their institutional correlatives, became the key transmitter to posterity of Puritanism's psychological and semiological aspects.[9]

Stowe's focus is outward, on the world of social relations, on village customs, on activity, whereas Hawthorne's is inward, on what he repeatedly called "the truth of the human heart." Moreover, Hawthorne's general view of human nature was pessimistic while Stowe's was optimistic, Hawthorne assumed a Calvinist view of human depravity and sin while Stowe took a more ceremonial, Episcopalian view, and Stowe believed in the possibility of social and political reform whereas Hawthorne found the very idea absurd.[10]

A comparison of two closely related stories will show how the important differences between Hawthorne and Stowe manifest themselves. In her biography of

Stowe, Joan Hedrick remarks: "Her short story 'The Mourning Veil,' published in the first issue of the *Atlantic* [1857], drew so obviously on Hawthorne's 'The Minister's Black Veil' that a writer of a later generation might have been inclined to sue for breach of copyright."[11] Both stories are concerned with the effect a veil has on its wearer and the wearer's associates, and Stowe may well have been stimulated (like Christopher Crowfield) by "reading for the two-hundredth time" "The Minister's Black Veil" in *Twice-told Tales*. But the resemblance ends there. Hawthorne's story, we recall, involves the Reverend Mr. Hooper, who appears at the meetinghouse one Sunday morning wearing a black veil. No one knows why, and lack of obvious motive is one of the reasons his parishioners and friends find the veil so ominous, oppressive, and, in the long run, unendurable:

> "I don't like it," muttered an old woman, as she hobbled into the meeting-house. "He has changed himself into something awful, only by hiding his face."
>
> "Our parson has gone mad!" cried Goodman Gray, following him across the threshold.[12]

Among the villagers, Hooper becomes a figure of dread, and they speculate endlessly about why he has donned the veil, what it feels like to wear the veil, what the world looks like from behind the veil. The local physician observes that "the strangest part of the affair is the effect of this vagary, even on a sober-minded man like myself. The black veil, though it covers only our pastor's face, throws its influence over his whole person, and makes him ghost-like from head to foot" (374). Even the woman who loves Hooper is affected. She sits down with him to clarify the meaning of his behavior but is no more able to understand it than anyone else: What "grievous affliction," she asks, has moved him to put on the veil? " 'If it be a sign of mourning,' replied Mr. Hooper, 'I, perhaps, like most other mortals, have sorrows dark enough to be typified by a black veil.'" When she urges him to give a reason so that no one will suspect him of scandal, he only will say, "If I hide my face for sorrow, there is cause enough . . . and if I cover it for secret sin, what mortal might not do the same?" (378–79). And when he refuses to show even her his face once more, she breaks off with him, though he pleads, "Oh! you know not how lonely I am, and how frightened to be alone behind my black veil" (379). Hooper becomes a man apart, a person who, like Hester Prynne in *The Scarlet Letter,* serves the community even while he is shunned like a leper.

For Hawthorne, the veil is the mark of alienation, a kind of parable about the ultimate loneliness of every human. But the story has another effect as well: every reader is drawn, like the people of Hooper's village, into the swirl of speculation about the meaning of the veil. True, readers and critics are less likely than Hawthorne's villagers to cast the veil in moralistic terms; instead, we tend to interpret it as a literary allegory about meaning and its representation. The most extreme example of this, surely, is J. Hillis Miller's deconstructive monograph on the story, *Hawthorne and History: Defacing It,* where he argues paradoxically that "the story is the unveil-ing of the possibility of the impossibility of unveiling."[13] However we care to summarize it, the meaning of the story remains tantalizingly out of reach, one of Hawthorne's finest and most characteristic ambiguities.

Stowe's veil belongs to a different universe of discourse. "The Mourning-Veil" begins in a luminist intensity of light that promises a Transcendentalist experience:

> The evening light colored huge bouquets of petunias, which stood with their white or crimson faces looking westward, as if they were thinking creatures. It illumined flame-colored verbenas, and tall columns of pink and snowy phloxes, and hedges of August roses, making them radiant as the flowers of a dream.[14]

In this light Albert and Olivia and their four children, a family "of the wealthiest class" that has recently moved to "the quiet little village of Q——" (205), are opening a package of items shipped from the city: muslin, lace, ribbon, buttons, a bracelet. Among these items, mysteriously, is a black veil. The family call it a "mistake of the clerk": "what should we mourn for?" But Father Payson, the minister of the village, is passing by and overhears them. His comment is, "And yet till one has seen the world through a veil like that, one has never truly lived" (207). Rose, the oldest daughter, asks Payson what he meant, and he readily explains that "It was a parable, my daughter":

> "Sorrow is God's school," said the old man. "Even God's own Son was not made perfect without it; though a son, yet learned he obedience by the things that he suffered. . . . Take all sorrow out of life, and you take away all richness and depth and tenderness. Sorrow is the furnace that melts selfish hearts together in love." (208–9)

The rest of the story flows inevitably from this core parable, with its perfect trans-parency of meaning. That night a fire starts in the baby's room, and Rose is fatally injured while saving her sister. Olivia puts on the veil, but at first it reflects only her own bitterness and despair. For the first time, she sees the disappointment and misery of other people's lives:

> I was trusting in God as an indulgent Father; life seemed beautiful to me in the light of His goodness; now I see only His inflexible severity. I never knew before how much mourning and sorrow there had been even in this little village. There is scarcely a house where something dreadful has not at some time happened. . . . Ah, this mourning-veil has indeed opened my eyes; but it has taught me to add all the sorrows of the world to my own; and can I believe in God's love? (214)

Her minister, however, knows very well "all the ways of mourning" (213), and he explains to Olivia that every human sorrow eventually becomes a human joy. Seven of his own children have died, but with "every one some perversity or sin has been subdued, some chain unbound, some good purpose perfected. God has taken my loved ones, but he has give me love. He has given me the power of submission and of consolation; and I have blessed him many times in my ministry for all I have suffered, for by it I have stayed up many that were ready to perish" (215). So it proves for Olivia. At length, a "deeper power of love sprung up within her; and love, though born of sorrow, ever brings peace with it" (216), and she ends by counting the veil "among her most sacred treasures" (217).

Equally revealing is a comparison of the way each writer portrays traditional rituals of community, the activities that serve to bind individuals into groups and to shape a group's personality. In *The Blithedale Romance,* the transcendentalist visionaries who are living communally in the country gather for an evening of entertainment—at first, *tableaux vivants,* and then Zenobia, the Margaret Fuller figure who dominates Blithedale, offers to "trump up a wild, spectral legend, on the spur of the moment."[15] Among her listeners is Priscilla, a slight, pale girl who adores Zenobia but whom Zenobia, for unknown reasons, seems to resent. The story she tells is "The Silvery Veil," a legend that simultaneously allegorizes relationships among the communards and demonstrates the difference between putting a man or a woman in the mysterious position "behind the veil." The legend concerns the Veiled Lady, a clairvoyant or medium who performs covered by a veil: "all the arts of mysterious arrangement, of picturesque disposition and artistically contrasted light and shade, were made available in order to set the apparent miracle in the strongest attitude of opposition to ordinary facts" (635). Theodore, a young man who has seen her performance, sneaks backstage and hides in order to "find out the mystery of the Veiled Lady" (728). When she comes floating into the room, she immediately calls him out and asks what he wants. " 'Mysterious creature,' replied Theodore, 'I would know who and what you are!' " (730). The Veiled Lady counters with a bargain. If Theodore will kiss her *before* he lifts her veil, "thou shalt be mine, and I thine, with never more a veil between us! And all the felicity of earth and of the future world shall be thine and mine together" (731). The prudent Theodore, who apparently has never read Chaucer's story of the Loathly Hag, prefers to see the Lady first and to kiss, if he likes, afterward. But as soon as he lifts the veil and sees a pale, lovely face, the Lady vanishes, and Theodore pines, "forever and ever, for another sight of that dim, mournful face—which might have been his life-long, household, fireside joy—to desire, and waste life in a feverish quest, and never meet it more!" (732).

This is "The Minister's Black Veil" with themes of sexuality added to it. Like Hooper's parishioners, Theodore may (as his name indicates) adore God, but his faith does not extend beyond the veil. His empirical insistence on *seeing* has none of the earlier story's anxiety about sin and crime. Instead, he needs to know whether the woman under the veil is pretty or not—a consideration that outweighs her promise of "all the felicity of earth and of the future world." Still, the result is the same: all the alienation and misery that sour Hooper's life descend on Theodore as well.

"The Silvery Veil," with its eerie setting, weird characters, and cautionary plot, has all the trappings of a folk legend, and it seems the perfect story to tell in a country farmhouse among people who have come together for a common cause but who don't yet know each other very well. Like campfire stories and tales of a wayside inn, it joins separate people into an audience, entertains them, and teaches them the importance of believing in each other without insisting on hard evidence. Like all good art, it delights and instructs. And yet, that isn't exactly the final effect of Zenobia's tale. In a sort of epilogue, she explains that the no-longer-Veiled Lady attaches herself to a "knot of visionary people," and in particular to one woman among them. One day a magician presents himself to this woman and gives her a veil that will recapture the Veiled Lady: "It is a spell; it is a powerful enchantment, which I wrought for her sake, and beneath which she was once my prisoner. Throw it, at unawares, over the head of this secret foe, stamp your foot, and cry—'Arise, Magician, here is the Veiled Lady'—and immediately I will rise up through the earth, and seize her. And from that moment, you are safe!" (733). As she ends her story, in a grandly dramatic gesture, Zenobia throws a piece of gauze over Priscilla, "and, for an instant, her auditors held their breath, half expecting, I verily believe, that the Magician would start up through the floor, and carry off our poor little friend, before our eyes" (734). The effect of Zenobia's legend is to cut Priscilla off from the company in a remarkably aggressive gesture. It reinforces the mysterious hostility that drives the plot of her story, and it brings that hostility into the life at Blithedale. It also forecasts the catastrophe of the novel, in which Zenobia returns Priscilla—who is, of course, the Veiled Lady in reality—to her thralldom to Westervelt. Instead of providing social cohesion, Zenobia's legend acts like a kind of solvent, undermining the forces that have drawn the cummunards together at Blithedale.

In Stowe's works, the rituals of social cohesion are never so problematic. Chapter 30 of *The Minister's Wooing*, for example, is called, simply, "The Quilting." As part of the preparation for Mary Scudder's wedding, the women of Newport hold a quilting party. It is a scene of high energy and high spirits. Miss Prissy, a sort of tutelary spirit of New England, bustles hyperactively; Candace, the Marvyns' black servant, reveals a dream that indicates that James Marvyn has not drowned in a shipwreck, as everyone believes, but is still alive and will return in time to save Mary from marrying the minister; Madame de Frontignac, who has been a suspicious character because she is French and a woman of dubious morals, wins the approval of the other women with her needlework. After the sewing, the men join the women in a party that manifests the life of the community:

> Groups of young men and maidens chatted together, and all the gallantries of the times
> were enacted. Serious matrons commented on the cake, and told each other high and

particular secrets in the culinary art, which they drew from remote family-archives. One might have learned in the instructive assembly how best to keeps moths out of blankets,—how to make fritters of Indian corn undistinguishable from oysters,—how to bring up babies by hand,—how to mend a cracked teapot,—how to take out grease from a brocade,—how to reconcile absolute decrees with free will, how to make five yards of cloth answer the purpose of six,—and how to put down the Democratic party.[16]

For Stowe, quilting is not only an image of social life, it is also the spiritual essence of New England culture. It grows out of that native thriftiness that forbids wasting any scrap, however small, and the ceaseless, graceful industry that constitutes "faculty" in the novel.[17] It is "one of their few fine arts," and every "maiden" has her collection of scraps to sew while she talks to her "beau":

> her busy flying needle stitched together those pretty bits, which, little in themselves, were destined, by gradual unions and accretions, to bring about at last substantial beauty, warmth, and comfort,—emblems thus of that household life which is to be brought to stability and beauty by reverent economy in husbanding and tact in arranging the little useful and agreeable morsels of daily existence. (436)

So powerful an image of the "fabric" of New England life is the quilt that it softens and enlivens solitude. Mary Scudder has created a "garret-boudoir" for herself, a retreat from her mother and town life, but she has filled it with items that link her to family and history. Central among these items is a quilt, "pieced in tiny blocks, none of them bigger than a sixpence, containing, as Mrs. Katy said, pieces of the gowns of all her grandmothers, aunts, cousins, and female relatives for years back,—and mated to it was one of the blankets which had served Mrs. Scudder's uncle in the bivouac at Valley Forge" (243). The merging of female and male memory, accomplished even as the courtship is going on, make the quilt the perfect representative of marriage itself as well as of the social matrix within which marriage has its meaning.

And finally, of course, the patchwork quilt is an image of Stowe's own art. On the first page of the novel, she establishes that comparison: "When one has a story to tell, one is always puzzled which end of it to begin at. You have a whole corps of people to introduce that *you* know and your reader doesn't; and one thing so presupposes another, that, whichever way you turn your patchwork, the figure still seem ill-arranged" (1). Stowe sees her own work as the moral equivalent of a patchwork quilt, stitched together from the odds and ends of women's lives, backed with an old blanket from male history. It is a perfect description of *The Minister's Wooing* itself, as well as of *Uncle Tom's Cabin* and the rest of her fictions.

The difference between Hawthorne and Stowe is in part the difference between two contrasting temperaments and in part the difference between the American

Renaissance and the Other American Renaissance. Hawthorne's instinct—like Melville's, Thoreau's or Poe's—is always to move inward toward the psychological, the individual, the alienated. The characteristic moments of Hawthorne's fiction are moments of isolation: Dimmesdale in his closet, Hester at her needle, Clifford at his window, Coverdale in his "hermitage," Hilda in her tower. Even in those works where he is closest to the tradition of women's writing, the tales and sketches ("Little Annie's Ramble," "Sunday at Home," "Sights from a Steeple," "A Rill from the Town Pump," "The Gentle Boy") that Jane Tompkins insists were the basis of his early reputation and that formed a "perfect continuum" with the writing of Susan Warner,[18] even those works represent the solitude of a girl walking alone, a man staying home while his family goes to church, a lonely boy whose parents are outcasts.

Stowe, on the other hand, always turns outward toward the social and communal. Lonely characters are dangerous, like Simon Legree in *Uncle Tom's Cabin* or Aaron Burr in *The Minister's Wooing*. The point of many of her plots is to reconcile the alienated individual to a larger, Christian community of mutual love and support: George Harris in *Uncle Tom's Cabin*, Madame de Frontignac in *The Minister's Wooing*. For Stowe, the full meaning of human life is only revealed in community, and the novels of New England, from *The Minister's Wooing* on, not only focus on village life but are named for the communities they portray: *Pearl of Orr's Island*, *Oldtown Folks*, *Poganuc People*.

Despite these differences, however, that Hawthornean element of escape, of freedom for the imagination, never left Stowe's conception of literature. I began with a passage from the *House and Home Papers* that represented what reading Hawthorne meant to a man. I want to close with a passage from Stowe's most autobiographical novel, *Poganuc People*, about the remarkably similar use to which a girl—Dolly Cushing, Stowe's most autobiographical character—puts literature, when she discovers fiction among the dreary volumes of sermons stored in the garret of the parsonage where she lives. It suggests that the kinds of distinctions between male and female writers and readers that I have been making are artificial and that the imagination may not have gender after all:

> But oh, joy and triumph! one rainy day she found at the bottom of an old barrel a volume of the "Arabian Nights," and henceforth her fortune was made. Dolly had no idea of reading like that of our modern days—to read and to dismiss a book. No; to read was with her a passion, and a book once read was read daily; always becoming dearer and dearer, as an old friend. The "Arabian Nights" transported her to foreign lands, gave her a new life of her own; and when things went astray with her, when the boys went to play higher than she dared to climb in the barn, or started on fishing excursions, where they considered her an incumbrance, then she found a snug corner, where, curled up in a little, quiet lair, she could at once sail forth on her bit of enchanted carpet into fairy land.[19]

Notes

1. Originally collected in *House and Home Papers,* "The Lady Who Does Her Own Work" is in *Household Papers and Other Stories,* vol. 8 of *The Writings of Harriet Beecher Stowe* (1896–97; rpt. New York: AMS Press, 1967) 85–86.

2. "The Lady Who Does Her Own Work" 86.

3. Joan Hedrick, *Harriet Beecher Stowe: A Life* (New York: Oxford UP, 1994) 315. The passage in *House and Home Papers* listing "standard authors" is on p. 78.

4. Van Wyck Brooks, *The Flowering of New England* (1936; rpt. New York: Dutton, 1952) 496.

5. Brooks 432.

6. Jane Tompkins, *Sensational Designs: The Cultural Work of American Fiction, 1790–1860* (New York: Oxford UP, 1985) 147–85.

7. I adopt the term "woman's fiction" from Nina Baym's encyclopedic study, *Woman's Fiction: A Guide to Novels by and about Women in America, 1820–1870* (Ithaca: Cornell UP, 1978). Baym, interestingly, believing that Stowe "did not write any works in the genre" (15), excludes her from this study.

8. Lawrence Buell, *New England Literary Culture: From Revolution through Renaissance* (New York: Cambridge UP, 1986) 262. "Edwardsian filiation" refers to the role of Jonathan Edwards as the patriarch of the stern and inflexible Calvinism that Stowe's own father, Lyman Beecher, espoused.

9. Buell 278. A similar, though less generously phrased, view is that of David Reynolds in *Beneath the American Renaissance: The Subversive Imagination in the Age of Emerson and Melville* (Cambridge: Harvard UP, 1989) 389: "Like Hawthorne, Stowe gathered under one fictional roof both dark, iconoclastic women characters and brighter ones as well. There is a crucial difference, however, between these writers' treatment of women: because Stowe *mixes* but does not *fuse* character types, she retains a reassuringly simple division of functions absent from Hawthorne's complex texts."

10. On Hawthorne's fundamental conservatism, see, for example, Sacvan Bercovitch, "Hawthorne's A-Morality of Compromise," *Representations* 24 (Fall 1988): 1–27.

11. Hedrick 332.

12. Nathaniel Hawthorne, *Tales and Sketches* (New York: Library of America, 1982) 372.

13. J. Hillis Miller, *Hawthorne and History: Defacing It* (Cambridge: Blackwell, 1991) 51. Miller provides an extensive (though by no means complete) list of articles about "The Minister's Black Veil" in n. 9, pp. 129–30.

14. In *Stories, Sketches, and Studies,* vol. 14 of *The Writings of Harriet Beecher Stowe* (1896–97; rpt. New York: AMS Press, 1967) 205.

15. *Hawthorne: Novels* (New York: Library of America, 1983) 725.

16. *The Minister's Wooing* (1859; rpt. Hartford: Stowe-Day Foundation, 1978) 460.

17. Stowe has already defined the word: "*Faculty* is Yankee for *savoir faire,* and the opposite virtue to shiftlessness. Faculty is the greatest virtue, and shiftlessness the greatest vice, of Yankee man and woman. To her who has faculty nothing shall be impossible. She shall scrub

floors, wash, wring, bake, brew, and yet her hands shall be small and white; she shall have no perceptible income, yet always be handsomely dressed; she shall have not a servant in her house,—with a dairy to manage, hired men to feed, a boarder or two to care for, unheard-of pickling and preserving to do,—and yet you commonly see her every afternoon sitting at her shady parlor-window behind the lilacs, cool and easy, hemming muslin cap-strings, or reading the last new book" (*Minister's Wooing* 2–3).

18. See Tompkins, *Sensational Designs* 10–23.

19. *Poganuc People* (1878; rpt. Hartford: Stowe-Day Foundation, 1977) 172–73.

DISCORD IN CONCORD

Claudia Durst Johnson

In addition to works mentioned herein, the influence of
Hawthorne on Louisa May Alcott is discernible in the following
collections of her work: *Louisa May Alcott: Selected Fiction,* ed.
Daniel Shealy, Madeleine B. Stern, and Joel Myerson (Boston:
Little, Brown, 1990); *Freaks of Genius: Unknown Thrillers of
Louisa May Alcott,* ed. Daniel Shealy (Westport, Conn.:
Greenwood, 1991); and *Alternative Alcott,* ed. Elaine Showalter
(New Brunswick: Rutgers UP, 1988).

I n the tiny New England village of Concord, Massachusetts, at the height of the
American Civil War, two of the century's fiction writers, Nathaniel Hawthorne
and Louisa May Alcott, with their strong-minded artistic families, lived side-by-
side. In these few years Hawthorne's powers and reputation dwindled and Alcott's
star rose. In one of the most turbulent of political and philosophical times, the
families, deeply implicated in so many major national issues, attempted to come to
terms with their contradictory politics and clashing temperaments during personal
and national trial. Despite the unfortunate discord that surfaced between the Hawthornes and Alcotts, Louisa May Alcott would find in Hawthorne's work instructive
treatments and themes compatible with her own interests and would eventually
discover in *The Scarlet Letter* a means of coping fictionally with her often dysfunctional family.

In many ways, no two souls could be more antithetical, particularly touching the
stormy politics of race and gender, than Nathaniel Hawthorne and Louisa May
Alcott. In marked contrast to Hawthorne, Louisa Alcott was a devoted abolitionist,
a feminist, and, like her father and mother, an admirer of John Brown. Moreover,
she was in her essence the very type that Hawthorne made no secret of scorning—a
woman who wrote fiction. Yet there are vocational links between the two neighbors,
and Louisa seemed always to stand in awe and admiration of the man Hawthorne

(Gollin 188; Elbert 226–27). Moreover, her work, especially her adult fiction, continued and enlivened themes we have come to regard as part of the Hawthorne tradition—the turmoil suffered by the powerful mother and the power of and disjunction between woman's work and man's vocation which figured in the disruption of the traditional family.

Biographical Relations

The connection in life between Nathaniel Hawthorne and Louisa May Alcott, which is essentially the story of the friendship between the Hawthorne and Alcott families, is a tangled chapter of literature and politics in the history of American letters which prepares the ground for Louisa May Alcott's absorption in *The Scarlet Letter* and subsequent fictionalizing of her own disjointed family.

By reading in parallel fashion the histories available in the copious materials gathered by their biographers and the editors of their journals and letters, I hope to raise questions about the personal and political dynamics of a close and cordial relationship between neighbors and friends which came to an end abruptly just a few months before Hawthorne died, leaving for Louisa May only the poignant memory of the man she admired—always so close physically yet so distant psychologically—and the enduring influence of *The Scarlet Letter* on her work.

The two families were linked in friendship for over twenty years, embracing the two generations of Alcott and Hawthorne parents and children, beginning in the late 1830s, when Bronson and Nathaniel were introduced, until the last years of Hawthorne's life when the two families were next-door neighbors. (For information about the lives of the two families, I am heavily indebted to the biographers of Hawthorne and the Alcotts, especially Mellow, Arvin, Saxon, Stern).

The Alcotts returned to Concord in 1857 after five lean years in New Hampshire and Boston. Two years later, in 1859, Hawthorne also began plans to return to his own house in Concord, where, by this time, his closest neighbors would be the Alcotts. If we can believe Una Hawthorne's account, her father was very apprehensive about moving next-door to Bronson. In a letter to her Aunt Elizabeth, her mother's sister, Una writes, "Papa does not seem to look forward to Mr. Alcott's near neighborhood with any pleasure at all. It seems to me it would be an excellent way of getting rid of him to buy up the houses," meaning the Alcotts' property (Hawthorne, *Letters* 541). Unlike the Hawthornes, Bronson Alcott and his family were unreservedly pleased at the arrival of the new neighbors.

The high excitement in the Alcott house is attested to by Louisa in a letter to a friend in the summer of 1860:

> We are all blooming and just now full of the Hawthornes whose arrival gives us new neighbors and something to talk about besides Parker, Sumner and Sanborn. Mr. H. is

as queer as ever and we catch glimpses of a dark mysterious looking man in a big hat and red slippers darting over the hills or skimming by as if he expected the house of Alcott were about to rush out and clutch him. (L. Alcott, *Letters* 57)

The warmest connections between the families were those forged by the children. Immediately upon the arrival of the Hawthornes, the younger generation of Alcotts and Hawthornes, especially Julian, were close and constant companions, even though Louisa was twenty-eight and Julian only fourteen. In a letter to Alfred Whitman in September of 1863 Louisa still considered Julian one of her "boys" (L. Alcott, *Letters* 92). Julian describes these days in his book *Nathaniel Hawthorne and His Wife,* writing that an "unfailing spring of hospitable entertainment was always to be found at Alcotts" and that "social gayety in Concord" centered on the Alcotts (267, 322).

In December of 1862, Louisa's orders came to report to Washington to begin her duties as a nurse of Union soldiers. Sophia Hawthorne seemed to be as excited about and involved in the departure as any member of the Alcott family. Mellow writes that the news of Louisa's being called to service in Washington "created a flurry of excitement in the Alcott and Hawthorne households. Sophia had helped mark Louisa's clothing with indelible ink, in preparation for the journey" (Mellow 561). Hawthorne's son Julian saw Louisa to the train heading for Washington in December of 1862, and it was Una, Hawthorne's daughter, on whose shoulder the sick Louisa's head rested on the return trip to Concord in January of 1863. A concerned Hawthorne wrote to James Fields on 30 January that "Louisa Alcott has returned from Washington with Typhus fever which looks very threatening. I fear she will not come through it" (Hawthorne, *Letters* 533). Again, the Hawthornes, and especially Sophia, were deeply involved in the Alcotts' tribulations throughout the winter and spring of 1863. Sophia especially helped nurse Louisa and suggested that her sister May Alcott take all her meals with the Hawthornes in the darkest days of Louisa's illness.

During Louisa's recuperation, as Sophia was busy helping Abba and the Alcott daughters, Bronson was one of the few people on earth to continue to be a recipient of Hawthorne's friendship. Indeed, there appears to have been a reversal in Hawthorne's response to Bronson. The irksomeness with which he viewed Bronson in his younger days and the dread with which he may have faced moving next-door to him in 1860 seem to have been replaced by a new regard for Bronson as "the most excellent of men." Julian may have been drawing on his father's estimate of Bronson in *The Memoirs of Julian Hawthorne,* when he describes him as having "really gained in moral and intellectual stature as he advanced in age" (59).

Bronson and Nathaniel continued their rather unlikely friendship, but just months before Hawthorne died, probably sometime in the late fall of 1863 or the winter of 1862, the Hawthornes as a family broke off their friendship with their neighbors. We know from publisher William Ticknor's report that Hawthorne told

Bronson that the reason for the split was Hawthorne's and Sophia's inability to abide Bronson's wife, Abba. Yet the events surrounding the break were incontrovertibly complex, and Louisa herself may have inadvertently contributed to the break by literally "writing" her family out of their neighbors' lives. Though Louisa's own writing is part of the background of the break, it was a peculiar turn of events which had no connection at all with Hawthorne's infamous 1830 disparagement of scribbling women. There is no evidence that Hawthorne ever thought of Louisa as one of that abhorrent horde. In fact, there is no reference to suggest that he had read any of the fiction she wrote before her departure for Washington, or that he knew much about it. However, the events preceding the Hawthornes' break with the Alcotts suggests that one of Louisa's works, "Hospital Sketches" (1863), combined with the politics of the time, may have figured in the break that was blamed on Abba Alcott's difficult personality.

Differences in politics as well as differences in temperament, amplified by events following John Brown's execution, could have been expected to put a strain on the neighbors' friendship from the first. Alcott was the most fervent of the transcendentalists in speaking of Brown as a martyr while Hawthorne dismissed Brown as a criminal and scoffed at the transcendentalist characterization of Brown as a Christ-figure. In the summer of 1860, the time of Hawthorne's move to Concord, the Alcotts had held a celebrated tea for Brown's widow. Biographer James R. Mellow writes that "The politics of Concord, transcendental or otherwise, were never to Hawthorne's liking. It was, perhaps, one of the reasons he seldom ventured into Concord society after his return from Europe" (535). Even given Hawthorne's ownership of Concord property, a question arises as to why, if Hawthorne found Concord society so distasteful, he chose to settle there in his declining years and to situate himself next-door to a man whose company, not to mention politics, he had usually found irksome.

A closer examination of the chronology of the events of 1862–63 is instructive. In July of 1862 Hawthorne published an essay, "Chiefly about War Matters," based upon his firsthand observations of a battlefield, a prisoner-of-war camp, and an interview with Abraham Lincoln. The piece fell discordantly on New England ears. During the understandable patriotic fervor of wartime, Hawthorne did the unforgivable, betraying his own skepticism about the conflict, his empathy with the common soldiers of both sides, and his aversion to both John Brown and Abraham Lincoln. The lengthy correspondence about the article between Hawthorne and his publishers suggests just how removed he was from the mainstream wartime politics of his friends. The original included reference, among other things, to a Union officer who was "the stupidest looking man he ever saw" and to "the genial courtesy" of southerners contrasted to the "uncouthness of Uncle Abe's" (Hawthorne, *Letters* 462). In the Concord/Boston circles "Chiefly about War Matters" created even greater ill will because of Hawthorne's reference to Emerson's behavior after John Brown's arrest. Although Hawthorne had not returned to the United States at the time, word reached him that in a speech after Brown's execution Emerson had called him "the Saint . . . whose martyrdom, if it shall be perfected, will make the gallows as glorious as the cross" (Lusk 402). What was not expunged from the first printing of "Chiefly about War Matters" was a comment about Emerson's remark:

> I shall not pretend to be an admirer of old John Brown . . . ; nor did I expect ever to shrink so unutterably from any apothegm of a sage, whose happy lips have uttered a hundred golden sentences, as from that saying (perhaps falsely attributed to so honored a source) that the death of this blood-stained fanatic has "made the Gallows as venerable as the Cross!" ("War Matters" 327)

Hawthorne was reminded repeatedly of the cool public reception of his piece, as when, in June of 1862, he felt compelled to respond to a Mr. Woodman who objected to his treatment of Emerson.

In the summer of 1863 Hawthorne prepared for publication his last major work, and Louisa May Alcott began publishing the hospital sketches which would propel her into the literary world as a figure to be reckoned with. Both Hawthorne's and Alcott's works had political implications in a time of war. Alcott's was the well-received, politically correct piece, in marked contrast to Hawthorne's unpopular, politically inexpedient Civil War article which had appeared only eleven months earlier.

In the spring Louisa was well enough to begin work on her "Hospital Sketches," which appeared in serial form from 22 May to 26 June. She seemed to receive celebrity overnight as publishers courted her and newspapers throughout the country began reprinting the sketches. Despite the war and Louisa's still delicate health, the atmosphere in the Alcott house throughout the summer was one of jubilation. Abba and Bronson were exceptionally proud of their daughter, and tracking her success became a regular part of Bronson's journal. On 5 June he recorded that publisher Whipple was asking for the "Hospital Sketches" manuscript. On the thirteenth of that month he noted the appearance of the last of the sketches in the *Commonwealth,* all "having met with unexpected favor from various quarters." Next day he boasted about the compliment she received from Henry James Sr., and on the twenty-third he recorded the proposal from Redpath to publish the sketches as a book. On 10 July he wrote that in reviews "Hospital Sketches" is praised "highly." On 3 August he wrote that "Louisa is busy with her pen writing for the *Atlantic* and *Commonwealth.*" Later in August he appended a clipping of her poem "Thoreau's Flute." He recorded the arrival of Louisa's book and a number of favorable reviews in his journal entry of 26 August. On 4 September he indicated that James T. Fields had accepted a story of Louisa's. And on 7 September he was still proudly recording her good reviews.

To the Hawthorne house next-door, by contrast, the literary and political activity of that same summer had brought a strained and somber atmosphere. Hawthorne, still agonizing over his inability to proceed with his romances, still smarting from the hostile reception of "Chiefly about War Matters" he had received the previous year, was in the spring of 1863 preparing his memoirs of England, *Our Old Home,* for publication in book form. In July he threw this book into the turbulent political scene, as he had done his earlier piece, by determining to dedicate the book to his friend Franklin Pierce at precisely the time when the public found renewed reasons to consider Pierce a traitor to the Union cause. In May of that spring he had been undecided about how he should inscribe the volume, but by the first of July something had occurred to cause him to be very firm in his intent: "It requires some little thought and policy in order to say nothing amiss at this time; for I intend to dedicate the book to Frank Pierce, come what may" (Hawthorne, *Letters* 579). On 15 July, Fields replied, by way of a very carefully worded warning about dedicating the volume to Pierce. But Hawthorne's mind was made up, and on 18 July he replied, standing by his choice and issuing a few choice words for those who would object: "If the public of the north see fit to ostracize me for this, I can only say that I would gladly sacrifice a thousand or two of dollars rather than retain the good will of such a herd of dolts and mean-spirited scoundrels" (Hawthorne, *Letters* 587).

The subject of Franklin Pierce was a volatile topic in New England, but especially in the Hawthorne/Peabody family. Pierce had been a friend of Hawthorne's since their Bowdoin days, had offered Hawthorne assistance in his various political appointments, saving his life and family with the appointment to the Liverpool consulship. Yet Pierce had proved himself to be a copperhead and was suspected of having worked directly with the Confederacy to the detriment of the Union. The very political Peabody family's anger at Pierce's behavior was as fierce as Nathaniel Hawthorne's loyalty to him. Sophia pled repeatedly and unsuccessfully with her family to be silent on the subject of Pierce in her husband's presence. Following on the heels of his decision to dedicate his book to Pierce, on the Fourth of July Hawthorne sat on the platform while Pierce excoriated Lincoln, the Republicans, and the Union army, and at the very time when news of Gettysburg made its way through the crowd. When draft riots erupted almost immediately in New York City, resulting in the lynching of black people, many northerners blamed Pierce for helping to incite the trouble.

In political contrast to Hawthorne, who had sat on the podium with Pierce on the Fourth of July, Bronson Alcott pasted into his journal a Fourth of July speech in Boston delivered by Oliver Wendell Holmes. And Holmes's speech reads like a direct response to the arguments that Pierce reiterated in New Hampshire on the same day. Pierce excoriated Lincoln for thwarting free speech while Holmes attacked those who "damn their leaders in war time for limiting freedom of discussion." Pierce excoriated the abolitionists who had ignited the war while Holmes answered that "the combustibles were all ready on the other side of the border." Holmes's denunciation of those "whose patriotism consists in stopping an inch short of treason" seemed to be directed particularly at Pierce, in light of his reputation at the time.

The controversy tainted the Hawthornes' relations with both friends and family throughout the summer as Fields and Ellery Channing, in a move which can only be described as self-defeating, secretly urged Sophia's sister Elizabeth to convince her brother-in-law to rethink his dedication to Pierce. Hawthorne responded in a fury. To those who would call Pierce a traitor, he replied, "A traitor? Why, he is the only loyal man in the country, North or South!" (Hawthorne, *Letters* 151).

Summer for the Alcotts ended on an even more glorious note when Louisa received the bound copies of her book. Interestingly enough, while Hawthorne on principle resisted strong pressure, from friendship and wisdom, to follow political and economic expediency, Louisa viewed her Civil War piece in just the opposite way, writing in April of the same year that the *Commonwealth* thought her letters home "witty & pathetic," but, she writes, "I didn't, but I wanted money so I made three 'Hospital Sketches.' Much to my surprise they made a great hit, & people bought the papers faster than they could be supplied" (L. Alcott, *Journals* 118). The same expedient approach applies several years later, when on 1 February 1868 she writes, "Arranged 'Hospital Sketches and War Stories' for a book. By taking out all the Biblical allusions, and softening all allusions to rebs., the book may be made 'quite perfect,' I am told. Anything to suit customers" (L. Alcott, *Journals* 164). In June of 1863 she recorded in her journal that she was feeling "encouraged by the commendation bestowed upon 'Hospital Sketches' which were noticed, talked & inquired about much to my surprise and delight. Had a fine letter from Henry James, also one from Wasson & a request from Redpath to be allowed to print the Sketches in a book" (L. Alcott, *Journals* 119). In August of 1863 she was ebullient over the response to the publication: "I have the satisfaction of seeing my towns folk buying, reading, laughing and crying over it wherever I go" (L. Alcott, *Letters* 88).

Within the next few months, the Hawthornes brought their association with the Alcotts to an end. The breach must have gradually dawned on the Alcotts and puzzled them tremendously, especially in a year when the families had been so incredibly close. Finally, on a Sunday afternoon in January of 1864, Bronson called on Hawthorne to ask him what the problem was. Mellow and Saxon record Ticknor's account as reported by Annie Fields. Hawthorne had first described Bronson as "one of the most excellent of men." Ticknor went on to say that

> a few days before, Alcott had asked if there was some misunderstanding between their two families and Hawthorne had told him no, but that it "was not possible to live upon amicable terms with Mrs. Alcott." He added that in "time of illness or necessity," he was sure they would be the best of helpers to each other. "I dolled all this in velvet phrases, that it might not seem too hard for him to hear," Hawthorne said, "but he took it all like a saint." (Mellow 574)

In the report from Annie Fields's diary, quoted by Martha Saxon, Hawthorne enlarged on his comments about Abba:

"She is a person who prides herself much on her family, is busied in the desire to outshine her neighbors, is totally devoid of the power to tell the truth and occupies herself much with circulating unworthy reports; She seems to possess an oblique vision to which nothing presents itself as it is." Bronson acknowledged that this was so. "Indeed," said Hawthorne, "who should know it better?" (258)

Without doubt, Abba had driven Sophia mad for years, not just in the last months of December. She had written the following diatribe to Annie Fields two years before, on 29 May 1862:

> I was so cut to the heart by the rather ferocious and sudden announcement of Mrs. Alcott on Monday morning "That General Banks' army was entirely destroyed" and that the rebels were hurrying to Washington and that the governor had ordered off every man capable of bearing arms—and so on—that though feeling very well before hand, I became as it were a dead woman—and I have accomplished nothing this week. And that terrible news was merely all an exaggeration and I suffered for nothing. Mrs. Alcott is the most appalling sensationalist. She frightens me out of my five senses from time to time with telling me one thing and another and suggesting blood curdling possibilities. (Saxon 258)

Why, if Abba was the reason for the breach, did the Hawthornes wait for two years to cut the Alcotts? Had Louisa's summer successes heightened Abba's "pride" in her family and her "desire to outshine her neighbors"—actions of which Hawthorne complained—perhaps making too obvious her "desire to outshine her [Hawthorne] neighbors" at a time when the Concord set, in particular, was so unhappy with what he was writing? Interestingly, Julian appears to have had an opinion of Abba opposite to that expressed by the older Hawthornes. He had a high regard not only for Bronson and the girls but especially for Abba. His *Memoirs* contain these lines: "[Bronson] married a woman of beauty and charm and of great practical good sense, for whom and for his gifted and agreeable daughters I was much indebted to him" (61).

Whether Louisa ever knew the details of her father's interview with Hawthorne on that Sunday afternoon remains a mystery. She never betrayed any suspicion that her own first literary acclaim may have been politically galling to the Hawthornes, or that the Alcotts' joy that summer and fall amplified, by comparison, the Hawthorne family's agony over Pierce, over the public unhappiness with Hawthorne's own Civil War piece, and over his friends' violent disapproval of the dedication to *Our Old Home,* all of which may have just accelerated the inevitable, in light of Sophia's long-standing dislike of Abba. However, it would have been in the realm of probability, in light of the sequence of events, for Louisa to form such a supposition.

Louisa's own reaction suggests that she herself believed that Sophia and not Hawthorne was to blame for the rift. After all, Hawthorne's relationship to the

Alcotts probably never changed an iota. He had always been aloof from the first, only rarely seeing or visiting anyone in Concord, the Alcotts included.

Bronson makes no mention in his own journal of the painful talk in January about the break between the families (B. Alcott, *Journals* 362), but on 8 January he made a rare reference to Abba in his journal, which may be his private response to Hawthorne's statement that Abba was insufferable: "My wife over burthened with household chores. . . . Alas!" He followed this statement with a discussion of the cost of his way of life, which he acknowledged but did not regret. Yet Bronson's continued friendship with Hawthorne after the painful interview suggests that the breach between the families was Sophia's and not Nathaniel's doing.

At Hawthorne's death, the Alcotts, especially Louisa, were genuinely saddened and assumed some of the burden of the funeral. Louisa wrote in her journal entry for May 1864 that "We dressed the church on the 23rd for the funeral. . . . On the morning after the news came I sent in some violets from the hill where he used to walk. It pleased Mrs. H. very much and she wrote me a note" (L. Alcott, *Journals* 130). Yet Louisa and her family could plainly see that Sophia and perhaps one or more of the Hawthorne children refused to respond to any overtures to resume the friendship after Hawthorne's death. "We did all we could to heal the breach between the families," she wrote, "but they held off, so we let things rest" (L. Alcott, *Journals* 130). Yet a letter of Louisa to James T. Fields indicates that Sophia had not been remiss in expressing her gratitude, even if she continued to maintain her distance. After all the injustice that Sophia saw in Hawthorne's having been snubbed by a world which rewarded the intemperate Alcotts, it must have been particularly painful for her to see the obnoxious Abba still comforted by her husband while Sophia's own Nathaniel was gone.

The intertwined lives of the two writers and their literary families form a weave of many threads. The dynamics are composed of not only the impossible complexities and tensions of domestic life involving Sophia and Abba, the change in Hawthorne's response to Bronson in these last years, and the struggles inherent in Louisa's and Nathaniel's attempts to write fiction in America, but conflicts on matters of national import: transcendental philosophy, communitarianism, the woman question, and, notably, slavery and abolition, the Civil War, and party politics.

Literary Connections

Despite the neighbors' discordant politics and personalities, there was transcendence in Concord. It is curious to note, for example, that the friendship of the most political of the family members—Nathaniel and Bronson, standing at opposite political poles—was the most constant, remaining largely unaffected by the family feud. More important, however, was Louisa May Alcott's transcendence of the strained relations between key members of the families, as she continued to hold Hawthorne in highest regard, finding in his work subjects and a thematic stance for much of her own fiction. In 1850, Louisa, then eighteen years old, had the first documentable adult encounter with Hawthorne; she read *The Scarlet Letter* some four months after its publication, in August of 1850, writing: "Reading Mrs. Bremer and Hawthorne. The "Scarlet Letter" is my favorite. Mother likes Miss Bremer better, as more wholesome. I fancy 'lurid' things, if strong and true also" (L. Alcott, *Journals* 57). In calling Hawthorne's novel lurid, she curiously applied to it the same adjective she later used to describe her own anonymously published, sensationalistic fictions. Just a month before Hawthorne died she recorded rereading *The Scarlet Letter* (L. Alcott, *Journals* 129) and, on 28 May 1864, she wrote to Fields, "Mr. Hawthorne is gone, but [Sophia] still finds herself patiently, hopefully awaiting his return. Many of us will have the same feeling, I fancy, because he was one of those who are felt not seen, and we shall not really miss him till we turn the last leaf of his story without an end" (L. Alcott, *Letters* 106). Her journal reveals that she reread *The Scarlet Letter* on the evening of 6 March 1885 (L. Alcott, *Journals* 253). He continued to be on her mind when, in a letter to her father on 13 October 1887, she recorded her memory of Hawthorne, along with Emerson, as "a beautiful soul in prison, trying to reach his fellow beings through bars, and sad because he cannot" (L. Alcott, *Letters* 321).

Not only do Alcott's journal and letter gleanings provide every reason to believe that Hawthorne and his work had a profound impact on his neighbor, but her works themselves are evidence of his influence. Certainly she selected subjects that Hawthorne had made his own, and both wrote what she described as "lurid" fictions about the complications of love and sex (note *Behind a Mask* and other fictions for adults written under pseudonyms); both wrote about the lives of visual artists in Europe (his *The Marble Faun* can be compared with her *Diana and Persis*); both wrote fictions for young people; both wrote eyewitness accounts of the Civil War; and both wrote trenchantly of their own experiences in transcendental communities and of the transcendental school itself, which was related in the minds of both with Louisa's father Bronson Alcott (see Hawthorne's *The Blithedale Romance* and Alcott's *Transcendental Wild Oats*).

Despite Alcott's use of subjects in multiple works by Hawthorne, there seems to be little doubt that it was *The Scarlet Letter* that had the most enduring influence on her work, and that the most profound and pervasive of this novel's themes appear in two of her fictions for adults that were forged from the often painful dynamics of her own family— *Work* and *Transcendental Wild Oats*. These themes common to the works of both writers included the power of and disjunction between woman's labor and man's vocation, the turmoil suffered by the powerful mother, and the disruption in the traditional family.

A central theme in much of Alcott's fiction, and especially in the novel, *Work,* which she considered sufficiently serious and respectable to carry her true name, is the issue of work, in its narrow sense, and vocation or career, in a larger sense, a theme which is integral to Hawthorne's *The Scarlet Letter.* Reviewing the subject's importance to *The Scarlet Letter,* the reader notes that the subject of the introductory, "The Custom-House," is the narrator's conflict between his wage-earning work as a bureaucrat and his struggle as a writer attempting to recapture lost inspiration. His story is played out against that of other Custom House inhabitants who neglect their work—from the old Inspector whose fitting vocation had been that of a soldier to the lesser functionaries who spend their working hours at home in bed or snoozing in their chairs. Only when the narrator loses his work and his wages can he then resume his vocation as writer. Similarly, the theme of work pervades the story of Hester which follows. The three major characters, Hester, Dimmesdale, and Chillingworth, represent each of the vocations of which Hawthorne so often wrote: artist, minister, and scientist. Chapter headings in the novel which identify characters by their work, accentuate the theme of work: "Hester at Her Needle," "The Elf-child and the Minister," "The Leech," "The Leech and His Patient," "The Minister's Vigil," "Hester and the Physician," "The Pastor and His Parishioner," and "The Minister in a Maze." Hester's work, which includes that of seamstress and sister of mercy, both saves her and fosters her self-delusion, joins and separates her from the community.

Coincidentally, 1850 was the year when Louisa May first read *The Scarlet Letter* and when she first "went out to service" to make her living outside her family domicile, the beginning of several years of hard domestic service which formed the subject matter of her novel *Work*.

The similarities between Hawthorne's seventeenth-century seamstress and Alcott's nineteenth-century seamstress (based on her mother's experiences and hers) are remarkable. Both Hester and Christie enter the scene without supportive families, Hester's being across the ocean in England and Christie's being dead. Both women work in Boston; both are seamstresses; both are pushed to the point of suicide by their trials; both are betrayed by men; both are sisters of charity to the sick, poor, and dying; both raise their daughters without the help of husband or lover and devote themselves to troubled women in the end.

Similarly, many of Alcott's women protagonists in what she called her lurid fictions are identified by occupation, and *Work* is a narrative of the labors of its heroine, labors which include housekeeper, governess, nurse and companion, seamstress, and actress. As Hester finds some solace in her work, so does Christie.

In Hester, Hawthorne also gave Alcott the model for Christie as a strong, independent female survivor. Both heroines declare their independence, grow in endurance through their independent labors, survive work in hostile environments, and defy the expectations of the patriarchy, represented by Governor Bellingham and Reverend John Wilson in *The Scarlet Letter* and by Christie's disagreeable old uncle in *Work*.

The tragedy of *The Scarlet Letter* begins with the fractured family, proceeds without any picture in the Puritan community of the usual family of mother, father, and children, and ends with Hester taking up her mothering again, but primarily to the community of women, continuing to believe that no happiness is possible until the relationship between men and women can be altered. In similar fashion, Christie, in pursuit of her independence and freedom, begins her life of work by rejecting the idea of a marriage of convenience with a local farmer. As she proceeds, she finds relationships with men, like the wealthy Mr. Fletcher, to be untenable under the expected arrangements of the day. Only when she meets a man who is a friend first and a lover second can she consider marriage, coming closer to the ideal situation suggested by Hester, when "the whole relation between man and woman" would be established "on a surer ground of mutual happiness" (N. Hawthorne, *The Scarlet Letter* 177). Christie, in declaring her love for David, makes plain that she can be happy in marriage only if she is allowed her "independence." They join the Union effort in the Civil War together, very nearly as equals.

But the Davids and Reverend Powers of this world are rare men, and with David's demise, Christie, like Hester, must rear her daughter alone. As Hester at the end of her life "comforted and counselled" women in need, so Christie (like Alcott's own mother, Abba) devoted her life to working women like she herself had been. Hawthorne's and Alcott's descriptions of this work are similar. Hawthorne had written of Hester's last days:

> Women, more especially,—in the continually recurring trials of wounded, wasted, wronged, misplaced, or erring and sinful passion,—or with the dreary burden of a heart unyielded, because unvalued and unsought,—came to Hester's cottage demanding why they were so wretched, and what the remedy! (N. Hawthorne, *The Scarlet Letter* 177)

Note the resemblance to Alcott's description of Christie's activities:

> The workers poured out their wrongs and hardships passionately or plaintively, demanding or imploring justice, sympathy, and help; displaying the ignorance, incapacity, and prejudice, which make their need all the more pitiful, their relief all the more imperative. (L. Alcott, *Work* 425)

When Louisa and her mother first read *The Scarlet Letter* in 1850, Abba was supporting her family by working for philanthropic societies similar to the one Christie decided to devote herself to in the novel *Work*. So it was entirely fitting that Louisa dedicated *Work* to her strong, long-suffering mother:

To
MY MOTHER,
Whose Life has Been a Long Labor of Love,
This Book is Gratefully Inscribed
By
HER DAUGHTER

Ironically, then, it was Abba Alcott, the woman who so irritated the Hawthornes that they severed relations with their neighbors to avoid her, with whom Louisa saw herself sharing Hester's mantle in the Hawthornean tradition of maternal endurance, survival, moral growth, and self-sacrifice.

The writing and publication of *Work* seemed to bring Louisa May Alcott to the subject of the burden of labor and the privilege of vocation within the family as she contemplated *Transcendental Wild Oats* only a few months later. One might even suspect that the reliving of her and her mother's desperation and travail in performing menial labor for the family's survival sufficiently angered her to expose the inequities between man's vocation and woman's work and their effects on family survival.

One essential meaning of *The Scarlet Letter* would have been painfully clear to young Louisa May Alcott, even when she read the novel in 1850 as she first went out to domestic service, at a time when Bronson's entire activity was to hold conversations on transcendentalism in a room he maintained off Boston Common. That meaning was that, while the mother's work sustained the family, masculine "vocation" drained the family.

Transcendental Wild Oats (1872), her second fiction for adults based on Alcott family experiences, contains surprising echoes of Hawthorne's *The Scarlet Letter*. The themes again are the power of and disjunction between a woman's work and a man's vocation, the turmoil suffered by the powerful mother, and the disruption in the traditional family.

Transcendental Wild Oats is her fictionalized account of the family's eight-month attempt to succeed in establishing a transcendental commune in the hills of central Massachusetts. Joining them were Charles Lane, an English disciple of Bronson's, and his son William. The struggle Louisa dramatizes arises, not between the community and the outside world, but among members within the tiny group. Charles Lane, a transcendental tyrant appropriately renamed Timon Lion in the fiction, is involved in a war with Mother Hope (Abba Alcott) and, secondarily, with the children for the soul of Abel Lamb (Bronson Alcott). Lion's argument from the beginning is that Hope stands in the way of her husband's spiritual journey, yet his and Lamb's transcendental vocations are possible only because Hope takes on most of the burden of physical labor. Eventually, Lion deserts the Lambs when Abel decides, somewhat reluctantly, to remain with his wife rather than join Lion in a consociate family. Lion takes his leave, giving them a few weeks to move out, and, in dead of winter, forbids them to devalue the property by cutting wood to burn or by harvesting grain for their bread. Lamb, broken and distraught, decides to die by refusing to eat. Meanwhile Hope bestirs herself to find work for herself and rooms to rent for her family in a nearby village. Finally, Lamb emerges from his depression, decides to live, and moves away from Fruitlands with his family, led by Hope.

Behind the conflict between mother's work and father's vocation in *Transcendental Wild Oats* was Lane's and Bronson's firm conviction not to work for wages, which they considered tainted, but to wait to give themselves to their God-intended vocation. As Timon Lion answers Sister Hope, when she asks him what part of the work of the commune he proposes doing, "I shall wait till it is made clear to me" (L. Alcott, *Transcendental Wild Oats* 35). Bronson considered his vocation to be teaching and, since no teaching opportunities had arisen, he had not worked since his school in Boston had failed. Until Louisa May had been able to make a livelihood, Abba had been the parent to support the family (helped with generous gifts from Emerson and Abba's brother).

As in *The Scarlet Letter* and in *Work,* so in *Transcendental Wild Oats*—the saving qualities of physical labor are associated with woman. Mother Hope is the one who does all the work. Note her suspicion that Lion won't be lifting his finger while he pursues his vocation; the narrator's observation that only Forest Absalom helped Hope with the work:

> He it was who helped over-worked Sister Hope with her heavy washes, kneaded the endless succession of batches of bread, watched over the children, and did the many tasks left undone by the brethren, who were so busy discussing and defining great duties that they forgot to perform the small ones. (L. Alcott, *Transcendental Wild Oats* 45)

Most important, Hope is the one who, harnessing the children to clothes baskets, must harvest the grain after "some call of the Oversoul wafted all the men away" (L. Alcott, *Transcendental Wild Oats* 53). Only men like Dimmesdale, Chillingworth, Lion, and Lamb have the luxury of a "vocation"—intellectual and largely free of the physical, menial toil demanded of Hester, Christie, and Hope.

The comparison of the dynamics of *Transcendental Wild Oats* with that of *The Scarlet Letter* is startling. In both books, the dissolution of the "family" occurs simultaneously with or because of the introduction of a third man into what should ideally have been a couple, making a deadly triangle. In *The Scarlet Letter,* that triangle consists of Hester Prynne; the father of her child, Arthur Dimmesdale; and the husband she never loved and believed to be dead, Roger Chillingworth. Chillingworth it is who has a diabolical hold over Dimmesdale and says at the moment when Dimmesdale acknowledges his child and the mother of his child, "Thou hast escaped me!" In *Transcendental Wild Oats,* the trio are, similarly, Hope, Lamb who is the father of Hope's children, and Lion, the man who exercises a diabolical influence over Lamb and encourages him to shirk his rightful role as father and husband, finally trying to goad Abel into deserting them altogether.

Abel Lamb bears a remarkable resemblance to Arthur Dimmesdale. Both Dimmesdale and Abel are willing to sacrifice the good of their lovers and children to their vocations. Single-mindedly and ambitiously, Dimmesdale pursued his vocation as minister, preserving his professional reputation by denying Hester and Pearl. Abel Lamb is passionately dedicated to his "vocation" to the detriment of his family.

In refusing to work for wages, like Dimmesdale he denies his responsibility to his family and his vocations as father and husband.

Having fathered children, both men become intent on pursuits of saintliness. As Dimmesdale cultivates his saintliness, so Lamb's goal is to transcend the world. As Dimmesdale flagellates himself in the closet to purge himself of carnality, Lamb makes a religious ritual of icy cold baths. The watchword in *Transcendental Wild Oats* is transcend and "Abstain" (36). In pursuit of his own saintliness, Lamb is encouraged by Timon Lion to transcend the world and the flesh and, incidentally, his family. Though the word "abstain" is used, suggesting abstinence from sex and alcohol, the full implication is not made clear in Louisa's fictionalized account—that Charles Lane had successfully persuaded Bronson to sever his marital relations with the mother of his children and was further badgering him to dissolve the marriage/family union altogether, perhaps in preparation to join the celibate Shakers, as Lane actually did do briefly after Fruitlands folded. There seems to be no question that Bronson, so profoundly under Lane's influence, was seriously considering such a move.

The forest scene between Hester and Dimmesdale and the final sickbed scene between Hope and Abel are remarkable in their similarity of family tensions. Moreover, both are reversals of gender role expectations. In the forest scene, Arthur Dimmesdale is found to be an emotional wreck and a moral weakling. He seems to reach a nadir of despair when he pleads, "Think for me, Hester. . . . Must I sink down there, and die at once?" (N. Hawthorne, *The Scarlet Letter* 134). Hester is provoked to groan: "Wilt thou die for very weakness?" (*The Scarlet Letter* 134). So it has to be Hester, who by taking charge of the practical economic situation, gives him and herself some hope and direction, almost forcing it on him. She tells him what to think, how to justify himself, where they will go, what he can do, and how she could arrange it all: "Hester Prynne—whose vocation, as a self-enlisted Sister of Charity, had brought her acquainted with the captain and crew—could take upon herself to secure the passage of two individuals and a child" (*The Scarlet Letter* 145).

What may well have been a deathwatch near the close of *Transcendental Wild Oats* is notably similar. Abel Lamb has been destroyed by his "Brother" Lane, as the biblical Abel was killed like a sacrificial Lamb by his brother Cain. As a result, Abel lies down and turns toward the wall, "to die for very weakness," to borrow the phrase from *The Scarlet Letter*. It is not just that he is rendering up his own life, but, one must remember, in so doing he is abandoning his wife and three little girls in deepest winter in a lonely, isolated place without food or fuel. If Hope had been anything less than the extraordinary mother she was, Lamb's suicide may well have been his family's death sentence. Dimmesdale's rejection of his paternal responsibilities was scarcely greater than Lamb's. But, as in Hawthorne's forest scene in *The Scarlet Letter,* a woman—a mother—is present who can do a man's work—a woman who has grown in strength and moral stature while her mate has deteriorated. The conversation between mother and father, after Abel's decision to live, is reminiscent of the forest scene when Hester firmly and specifically answers all of Dimmesdale's frantic questions about how he can make up for what he has done, how he can continue to face Chillingworth, what he can do with his life, where they can go, and how they can get there. Like Hester, Hope has already laid plans for the family's survival. Hope speaks first:

> "Leave all to God—and me. He has done his part; now I will do mine."
>
> "But we have no money, dear."
>
> "Yes, we have. I sold all we could spare, and have enough to take us away from this snowbank."
>
> "Where can we go?"
>
> "I have engaged four rooms at our good neighbor, Lovejoy's. There we can live cheaply till spring. Then for new plans and a home of our own, please God."
>
> "But, Hope, your little store won't last long, and we have no friends."
>
> "I can sew and you can chop wood. Lovejoy offers you the same pay as he gives his other men; my old friend, Mrs. Truman, will send me all the work I want." (L. Alcott, *Transcendental Wild Oats* 61)

And so the strong and long-suffering mothers—Hester and Hope—forgive the humiliations, try to forget that paternal love has faltered, and, through work and maternal love, attempt to put their dysfunctional families together. Louisa May Alcott also transcended and tried to forget the fundamental ideological and personal friction between the Hawthorne and Alcott families and what she obviously regarded as Nathaniel's family's ill treatment of her mother, who had been so kind to Julian Hawthorne especially. She gave no hint that the family pettiness might have been caused in part by her own brilliant success at a time when Hawthorne's powers and popularity were fading.

To her, he remained the mentor, the great tragic figure, the "beautiful soul." She wrote just after his funeral that she, like Sophia, "still finds herself patiently, hopefully awaiting his return." "We shall not really miss him," she wrote, "till we turn the last leaf of his story without an end." His story continued not only in the fictions he wrote; it continued in the fictions written, as were so many of her own, in the Hawthorne tradition. Hawthorne's work likely provided Alcott a tone and a variety of themes, and *Work* and *Transcendental Wild Oats* suggest that his masterpiece, to which she turned repeatedly during her life, gave her the means for fictionally exploring the "lurid" and disruptive elements in her own difficult family.

Works Cited

Alcott, Bronson. *The Journals of Bronson Alcott*. Ed. Odell Shepard. Vol. 2. Port Washington, N.Y.: Kennikat, 1966.

——. *The Letters of A. Bronson Alcott*. Ed. Richard L. Herrnstadt. Ames: Iowa State UP, 1969.

Alcott, Louisa May. *The Journals of Louisa May Alcott.* Boston: Little, Brown, 1989.

——. *The Letters of Louisa May Alcott.* Boston: Little, Brown, 1987.

——. *Transcendental Wild Oats.* Harvard, Mass.: Harvard Common Press, 1975.

——. *Work: A Story of Experience.* New York: Arno, 1977.

Arvin, Newton. *Hawthorne.* Boston: Little, Brown, 1929.

Elbert, Sarah. *A Hunger for Home.* Philadelphia: Temple UP, 1984.

Gollin, Rita K. "Louisa May Alcott's 'Hawthorne.'" *Essex Institute Historical Collections* 118 (Jan. 1982): 42–48.

Hawthorne, Julian. *Memoirs of Julian Hawthorne.* Ed. Edith Garrigues Hawthorne. New York: Macmillan, 1983.

——. *Nathaniel Hawthorne and His Wife.* Vol. 2. Boston: Houghton Mifflin, 1884.

Hawthorne, Nathaniel. "Chiefly about War Matters." *Tales, Sketches, and Other Papers by Nathaniel Hawthorne.* Boston: Houghton Mifflin, 1850.

——. *The Letters, 1853–1856.* Vol. 17 of the *Centenary Edition of the Works of Nathaniel Hawthorne.* Columbus: Ohio State UP, 1987.

——. "The Old Manse." *Tales and Sketches.* New York: Library of America, 1982.

——. *The Scarlet Letter.* New York: Norton, 1988.

Lusk, Ralph L. *The Life of Ralph Waldo Emerson.* New York: Columbia UP, 1949.

Mellow, James R. *Nathaniel Hawthorne in His Time.* Boston: Houghton Mifflin, 1980.

Poe, Edgar Allan. "The American Scene: From Tale Writing. Nathaniel Hawthorne" (originally from *Godey's Lady's Book*). *Literary Criticism of Edgar Allen Poe.* Ed. Robert L. Hough. Lincoln: Nebraska P, 1965.

Pratt, Frederick. "Accounts of Brook Farm." *The Brook Farm Book.* Ed. Joel Myerson. New York and London: Garland, 1987.

Saxon, Martha. *A Modern Biography of Louisa May Alcott.* Boston: Houghton Mifflin, 1977.

Stern, Madeleine. *Louisa May Alcott.* Norman: U of Oklahoma P, 1985.

ELIZABETH BARSTOW STODDARD'S "IMMORTAL FEATHER"

Margaret B. Moore

Hawthornean touches in works of Elizabeth Barston Stoddard may be found in the early poem, "The House by the Sea," printed in Matlack, "Literary Career" 117; "Our Christmas Party," *Harper's Monthly Magazine* 18 (1859): 202–5; "A Partie Caree," *Harper's* 25 (1862): 466–79; and "The Prescription," *Harper's* 28 (1864): 794–800. The letters of "The Lady Correspondent" to the *Daily Alta California* of San Francisco (1854–58) portray a persona whose interest in "the woman mind" is distinctive but not unlike that of Hawthorne's.

lizabeth Drew Barstow Stoddard's first novel, *The Morgesons* (1862), almost seems to throw down the gauntlet to Nathaniel Hawthorne, an act tellingly suggesting her awareness of the Hawthorne tradition during her development as another chronicler of New England and its people. She depicts the Morgesons, a fictional family based on her own, who "had no portrait, nor curious chair, nor rusty weapon—no old Bible, nor drinking cup, nor remnant of brocade" (8). Hawthorne had used most of these items in his work, especially in *The House of the Seven Gables* (1851). That she consciously offered the list seems obvious, for she had long admired Hawthorne's work. Perhaps she was paying a kind of tribute when she and her husband, Richard Henry Stoddard, sent Hawthorne a copy of her first novel, which was in his library at the time of his death (Matlack, "Literary Career" 266). Hawthorne praised the novel in a letter to her husband as a "remarkable and powerful book" and wrote to her that the first part seemed "as genuine and lifelike as anything that pen and ink can do" (*CE* 18: 524, 531).[1] She never forgot this praise. She used it in the preface to a later edition in 1901. In describing the early poor reception of her work, she asserted in 1889: "I have one immortal feather in my cap, Nathaniel Hawthorne recognized me" (Matlack, "Literary Career" 549).

Elizabeth Drew Barstow was born in 1823 in Mattapoisett, Massachusetts, on Buzzards Bay. Her shipbuilding father, Wilson Barstow, was the younger brother of

Dr. Gideon Barstow of Salem who had married Hawthorne's first cousin, Nancy Forrester, daughter of Simon Forrester and Rachel Hathorne. Elizabeth had visited the Salem Barstows in the early 1840s and doubtless knew of the writer then but had not, so far as we know, actually met him. On 6 December 1852, she married Stoddard, a minor poet. They moved to New York City where Hawthorne helped her husband obtain a political post in the Custom House and gave him the only autobiographical sketch he ever allowed, which the poet published in 1853 (*CE* 16: 663). Stoddard became the New York "Lady Correspondent" for the San Francisco newspaper, the *Daily Alta California,* and furnished fascinating semimonthly columns from 1854 to 1858.[2] She also wrote many stories and poems for the magazines of the day and from 1862 to 1867 published three novels which received little notice, perhaps because the Civil War proved too distracting. In the last part of the century (1888–89), her novels were reissued, again with little public response.[3] An original voice, Elizabeth Stoddard nevertheless has a considerable Hawthorne connection.

Growing up in decaying seaport towns that once had intercourse with the world but had become isolated as shipping went elsewhere, Stoddard and Hawthorne had much in common, a circumstance that both enabled her to share his traditions and to expand them as they served her creative purposes. It is clear that she read Hawthorne's works. She mentioned him several times in her letters to the *Daily Alta California,* even though he was not at that time engaged in literary work. When she reviewed Henry Giles's chapter on *The Scarlet Letter* in his *Illustrations of Genius* (1854), she observed: "It is an acute analysis of the wonderful mind of Hawthorne" (5 Nov. 1854). On 8 January 1855, she praised Hawthorne as a storyteller "who stands alone here" after the "king of story tellers," Hans Christian Andersen. She wrote her lifelong friend Edmund Clarence Stedman on 21 August 1891: "three names I owe much to: Hawthorne, Lowell, Stedman" (Matlack, "Literary Career" 556).

Her readers were quick to point out that her work resembled Hawthorne's, as James H. Matlack's thorough research documents. He cites Manton Marble who in the *New York World* compared Stoddard with the Hawthorne of *The Scarlet Letter* (Matlack, "Literary Career" 224). Stedman found that Hawthorne was her predecessor in

> removing the rigid veil which hides the inner New England life—in breaking the ice which covers fervid and turbulent under-currents of soul and sense. . . . She moves in the domain of tangible facts and events, the awe and mystery of common things. She is a thoroughly original writer, the more so by this test of a locality so long the field of Hawthorne's searching regard. (Matlack, "Literary Career" 364)

Harriet Waters Preston, reviewing the reissued novels in the *Atlantic Monthly* in 1901, observed that Stoddard's art was "obviously and confessedly learned at Nathaniel Hawthorne's feet" (848). In "Hawthorne and Stoddard," Matlack traces the background of the writer, discusses her connection with Hawthorne, gives a descrip-

tion of *The Morgesons*, and suggests the reasons for Hawthorne's favorable opinion of
that book (278–302). Lawrence Buell, in "Provincial Gothic: Hawthorne, Stoddard,
and Others," compares the ways in which the two employ "gothic conventions to
anatomize the pathology of regional culture" (*New England Culture* 351). Hawthorne, he says, is "responsible for crystallizing the image of New England strangeness," while *The Morgesons* "is a more typical mid-nineteenth-century example of
the commingling of gothic devices with representational realism" (353, 354).

It should be said immediately that the two writers were unlike in many ways. New
England changed somewhat between the year of Hawthorne's birth (1804) and that
of Stoddard (1823) so that their depictions of the region were bound to differ. Their
techniques of writing were dissimilar: his polished, restrained Latinate wording
versus her often jerky, broken phrasing which seems ready to explode off the page.
Henry James thought that her books were "violently written" (Kraft 271). George H.
Boker wrote Stoddard on 21 November 1862 about *The Morgesons*:

> the book impresses me like a fragment of one of Michael Angelo's frescoes—a mass of
> powerful, struggling anatomy, which torments you while you admire, because you do
> not find anywhere, the indispensable point of repose, which the very form of Art
> demands. (Matlack, "Literary Career" 264)

The two writers also differed in their use of the past. For Hawthorne the present is
explained and surrounded by the past, whereas Stoddard makes little use of what
Hawthorne calls "the long past." This can be seen in their descriptions of a family.
When Stoddard depicts the Morgeson family, she says:

> Our family had lived in Surrey for years. Probably some Puritan of the name of
> Morgeson had moved from an earlier settlement, and, appropriating a few acres in
> what was now its center, lived long enough upon them to see his sons and daughters
> married to the sons and daughters of similar settlers. So our name was in perpetuation,
> though none of our race ever made a mark in his circle, or attained a place among the
> great ones of his day. The family recipes for curing herbs and hams, and making
> cordials, were in better preservation than the memory of their makers. . . . They had no
> knowledge of that treasure which so many of our New England families are boastful
> of—the Ancestor who came over in the Mayflower, or by himself, with a grant of land
> by Parliament. (8)

The narrator in "The Custom-House," on the other hand, tells the story of Hawthorne's family:

> It is now nearly two centuries and a quarter since the original Briton, the earliest
> emigrant of my name, made his appearance in the wild and forest-bordered settle-
> ment, which has since become a city. And here his descendants have been born and

died, and have mingled their earthly substance with the soil. . . . The figure of that first
ancestor, invested by family tradition with a dim and dusky grandeur, was present to
my boyish imagination, as far back as I can remember. It still haunts me, and induces a
sort of home-feeling with the past, which I scarcely claim in reference to the present
phase of the town. (*CE* I: 8–9)

Her tradition of the past was different from his. He saw a "dim and dusky grandeur,"
despite iniquity, whereas her version concerned "herbs and ham" and "cordials."
Richard Brodhead writes that "traditions . . . begin when the past is purged of
irrelevance" (3). And to Stoddard, recipes were, perhaps, more relevant than inexplicable grandeur.

Yet in theme the two writers were attracted by similar subjects. Of course, they
both saw "New Englandly" and coastal New Englandly at that. Each treated the sea
and the houses by them, the confining constraints for women, the remnants of
Puritanism, the mystery of the human heart, sudden death, the place of caste, the
truth in portraits, and alienation of human beings, one from another. And even
though Stoddard would probably have written about these subjects anyway, one
senses that her knowledge of Hawthorne's writings stimulated her imagination.

Having been brought up in towns on the sea, each felt a lifelong pull to the ocean
and used it in writing. Hawthorne was never happy away from the sea for long.
Richard Henry Stoddard wrote in 1853 that he and Hawthorne "fell to talking about
the sea, and the influence it had had on the childhood of both" (R. Stoddard 694–
95). Seamen abound in his stories, but Hawthorne does not venture from the shore.
The sea is there as a window on the world. In many ways, Stoddard follows Hawthorne's footsteps along the seashore, but to her the sea was an ever-present magnetic
force from which she drew strength. All three of her novels and many of her stories
are laid in coastal towns where the sea is a tangible presence.

Although the footsteps she followed as she crafted her first novel were those left
when Hawthorne wrote *The Scarlet Letter* and *The House of the Seven Gables,* Stoddard had her own story to tell, the story of Cassandra Morgeson, a young girl
growing up in Surrey, a small coastal village which is past its prime. Ships are still
built there, and sailors still sail away never to be heard from again. The port retains
to some extent a somewhat cloudy outlook on the world, but the village is inward-
looking, rigid in its ideas, intolerant of liberties. Cassandra, probably for that reason,
takes liberties and remains defiantly herself. Her father builds ships; her mother is a
product of strict Calvinistic underpinnings but whose "spiritual insight [is] confused and perplexing" (*Morgesons* 24). Her sister, Veronica, is a strange, elfish creature who reminds one of Pearl in *The Scarlet Letter* grown slightly older. Sent to
Barmouth to live with her Puritanical maternal grandfather, Cassandra experiences
her first feelings of inferiority at a school there. Despite the fact that the town's
wealthy had made their profits in slavery or piracy, or because of it, their offspring
are narrow, exclusive bigots. She next goes to Rosville to live with her cousins,

Charles and Alice Morgeson, in a town that is Unitarian and where learning actually takes place at the Academy. Cassandra is enthralled by her cousin Charles, and only his death breaks the spell. There too she meets Ben Somers of Belem (Salem), a distant cousin. He has fallen in love with Veronica and asks Cassandra to visit his home in Belem to acquaint his family with the Morgesons. At this point Cassandra enters Hawthorne's actual world where Forresters and Barstows and Dunlaps mingle. The Pickersgills are the Forresters, many of whom did have a problem with alcohol. The Somerses are the family of Dr. Gideon Barstow, who was Stoddard's uncle. The Dunlaps, recognized by Hawthorne in the book, are the family of Anstiss Dunlap who married Benjamin Barstow, another uncle of Stoddard's.[4] Cassandra encounters real hostility from Mrs. Somers but does not shrink from confrontation with her. She also meets Desmond Somers, Ben's brother, with whom she falls in love.

Back in Surrey she discovers her mother dead in her chair, a scene reminiscent of Judge Pyncheon's death in *Seven Gables*. After the traumatic death of her mother, the book rushes to climax. Mr. Morgeson marries Alice, widow of Charles; Veronica marries Ben Somers who drinks himself to death after fathering a child; and all move away save Cassandra who revels in her house by the sea. Eventually Veronica and her child and their Aunt Mercy move back. Desmond returns a reformed alcoholic, marries Cassandra, and presumably all ends well. Yet the Belem Somerses do not accept the marriage; Veronica's "eyes go no more in quest of something beyond" (*Morgesons* 252); and her child seems impassive. Cassandra herself is still trapped in provincial Surrey. In that summer home, Stoddard writes, "Before its windows rolls the blue summer sea. Its beauty wears a relentless aspect to me now; its eternal monotone expresses no pity, no compassion" (252). The reader gets no impression that in time "a new truth would be revealed"; it is more like the Pyncheon elm which whispered "unintelligible prophecies" (*CE* 1: 263, 2: 319). David Leverenz says that in *The Morgesons* Stoddard "blends passion, malice, and an eerie sense of narcissistic helplessness to portray intense women slowly stifled by small-town conventions of womanhood" (178).

There is a Hawthornesque tone or atmosphere in this book, in which the story is so much carried by dialogue that one has to leap to an understanding of characters. Yet that very fact, irritating as it is at times, makes one all the more aware of the mystery of the human heart. In each person there is more than we ever know. Stoddard also uses a light mocking manner reminiscent of Hawthorne, especially in *The Blithedale Romance*. There is, in addition, a strong resemblance in the attitude toward religion. The orthodox, tightly controlled world in which Cassandra matures is a far cry from Puritanism, but it is a descendant. These souls take religion very seriously; they have revivals; they read such orthodox papers as the *Boston Recorder*. When Cassandra finally gets to Rosville, Unitarian and broad, she feels liberated. But she goes back to Surrey and does her duty by the remnant of her family in the best female tradition. When Ben dies of alcoholism, she and Desmond cling together, and he says with heavy irony: "God is the Ruler. . . . Otherwise let this made world crush us now" (*Morgesons* 253). Fate or destiny would be closer to Desmond's God, unfeeling and unloving. Here Stoddard goes beyond Hawthorne's questioning. Although Hawthorne usually criticized the church in many of its forms or its ministers, there is, it seems to me, a somewhat muted recognition of a God who is not a God of wrath. He does, however, emphasize guilt which results from sin (in pre-Freudian days), and he seems to believe in life after death. To Stoddard, guilt comes from not being true to one's self rather than to God.[5]

Besides sharing, and going beyond, Hawthorne's theological questioning, Stoddard expanded his tradition by exploring some social issues. In *Two Men* (1865) Stoddard tells a fascinating if dark story of Jason Auster who brings to mind Hawthorne's Holgrave Maule. As a young man, Jason leaves home to "put in practice certain theories concerning the rights of men and property" (7). He takes with him two books, *Man's Social Destiny* and *Humanity in Limbo,* and, as he works as a carpenter on a new Congregational church in Crest, "a lively maritime town," he soon begins to "air theories of Socialism, Abolitionism, and Teetotalism" (9). But when Jason marries Sarah Parke of the foremost family of the town, he begins to change. His "fire was put out by the Parke sun," says Elsa, the family "help" (269). He finds he can live only by keeping silent, but as he does, he matures and finds an inner freedom. It is almost as though Stoddard were trying to imagine Holgrave after the remove to the new Pyncheon mansion. Jason learns that he has never loved his wife when he looks at her daguerreotype and sees "her cold, hard, glittering eyes" (248). Sarah, of course, is no Phoebe. Sarah too has looked at the portrait of her ancestor and has seen "that representation of sublime selfishness" (134). Like ancestor, like descendant.

Parke Auster, son of Jason and Sarah, falls in love with Charlotte Lang, a girl of mixed race, and begets a child. He plans to marry her, but she dies in childbirth. The Langs are treated sympathetically but realistically. As Matlack says: "There are no sermons on brotherhood here" ("Literary Career" 376). Phillipa Luce, a granddaughter of Squire Parke by another wife, comes to live at home and is hated by Sarah. After Sarah's death, Phillipa thinks she loves Jason but finally decides that he is "the man she had not loved, but could not endure to lose" (*Two Men* 272). The ending, in true Hawthornean tradition, is ambiguous. Phillipa and Jason do seem to marry, but the reader is aware that they probably still "looked on each other from the prison of the soul" (265).

This is a bleak story in which people live together but do not understand each other. Parke Auster sums it up when he says: "There is something appalling behind the screen of every-day life" (194). Hawthorne too has characters who do not understand each other, who feel alienated from their fellow men. Young Goodman Brown is one such; so is Hester in *The Scarlet Letter.* The difference is, I think, that Hawthorne explores the *result* of whatever is appalling or inexplicable, whereas Stoddard simply presents her characters, as though this is the way life is. Yet she wrote in the *Daily Alta California* (20 Sept. 1855): "I am disposed more to specula-tion on the interior life of man. I wish to realize the cause of things, being indifferent to their effect." In these novels, however, she is not at all indifferent to effect. Hawthorne, on the other hand, was interested in the effect of unconfessed adultery rather than its cause in *The Scarlet Letter*.

Stoddard does not react quite so much to religion in *Two Men*. Sarah Parke Auster is characterized as

> a friend to the poor and aged because it was the custom of the family. . . . [D]evoid of pious aspirations, she was a believer in the tenets of the Congregational church . . . full of the business of religion. (49)

Religion here is a habit with little passion or meaning. When the old Squire is dying, he turns to his daughter and remarks: "It all comes to this, Sarah" (24).

There is, however, a great deal said about class or caste. The mulatto family is denigrated not because it is black but because it has reached above its station. Jason soon realizes that he can never live up to the Parkes:

> From the day that Jason entered the family he suffered from an intangible something in the Squire's bearing which deprived him of his natural demeanor, and made him feel, by contrast, unfinished, awkward, incapable. (19)

Stoddard is more passionate about this than is Hawthorne, but both have shown it in their work. Hawthorne's Pyncheons are on the other side; they feel superior to other folk.

If following in someone's footsteps inevitably means being sometimes in the forerunner's shadow, Stoddard explicitly declares herself capable of making her own footprints in her last novel, *Temple House* (1867). She wrote Lilian Whiting that "there is more of my mind in it" (Matlack, "Literary Career" 544). It shows the least Hawthornean influence of the three books, although here the house itself is as important as Hawthorne's house of seven gables. "On all sides," she averred, "they were shut in from the bay, the town, and the common business of life" (*Temple House* 17). Argus Gates, a former mariner and now the possessor of Temple House, lives with his sister-in-law, Roxalana Gates, and her daughter Tempe. They live parsimoniously and simply in the house turned away from the sea in Kent, another unprosperous town. Argus and Roxalana are self-contained, each living separately. Thomas Wentworth Higginson once said of his wife's incomprehension of Emily Dickinson's family that if she had read Mrs. Stoddard's novels she would understand (Kramer 159). *Temple House* has a portrait too, that of Madame Temple, who was the last member of a "first family" who originally owned the house. A study of the portrait is like looking at Roxalana's eyes, which are cold and dense (*Temple House*

27). Argus enjoys his "strange internal liberty" and does not want to be involved with mankind, until he is forced by a shipwreck to save a sailor (31).

Near Temple House live the Brande family. Cyrus Brande possesses "a creed powerful enough to shape his actions, but not mighty enough to control a single sensation" (145). His wife is insane and finally has to be carted off to the nearest asylum. Their daughter, Virginia, is a "caged bird" who subjugates her own desires to try to help her mother and to live with her Janus-faced father, who tells her that "Mankind is a grovelling herd, beneath the pressure of a mighty hand; let no one raise his forehead above the mass, with the excuse of '*me*' written on it" (162). Virginia eventually learns that "she has a right to individual happiness" (328). This is a profoundly depressing book with something of an affinity with the subsequent poems of Edwin Arlington Robinson. Stoddard's outlook is far darker than Hawthorne's, but there are certain details in common. The novel takes place in a house in a decaying coastal town in which former Puritan convictions have turned to a code of iron duties which bring no happiness. There is no rose-gold thread in this book. There is a portrait; there is caste; there is the feeling that women have a hard life; there is the sea; and above all there is a house which traps them. But there is nothing beyond this life. The people are mysteries, but not mysteries the reader wants to probe.

Revealing less obtuseness than usual, Julian Hawthorne astutely observed that Stoddard "wrote like no other," a view that is hyperbolic but with more than a grain of truth in it. Although her style is her own, she shares with Nathaniel Hawthorne an intense feeling for the region, an attempt to make it live in words, and she uses some of the same symbols. In her first novel she is most indebted to him and grows less so. Yet she is drawn back to her roots just as irresistibly as is he. In her preface to the reprinted 1901 *The Morgesons,* she writes:

> the mystery of it is, that when I left my native village I did not dream that imagination would lead me there again, for the simple annals of our village and domestic ways did not interest me. (259)

And she ends the introduction by citing again Hawthorne's comments to her about *The Morgesons:* "Could better words be written for the send-off of these novels?" (262). She certainly felt her debt to Hawthorne, but she remained her own person. New England traditions and themes were transmitted to her but were transformed by her as she wrote her own truth.

Notes

I am indeed grateful to Professors John Idol of Clemson University and Melinda Ponder of Pine Manor College, the editors of this volume, and to Professor Eric Haralson of the State

University of New York at Stony Brook and Professor Rayburn S. Moore of the University of Georgia for perceptive readings and suggestions.

1. The *Centenary Edition of the Works of Nathaniel Hawthorne,* ed. William Charvat et al., 23 vols. (Columbus: Ohio State UP, 1962–), will be referred to as *CE* in the text with appropriate volume and page numbers.

2. It was rumored that Stoddard received $300 a year for her California letters. See Hefferman and Stecker 190.

3. More information on Stoddard not included in the "Works Cited" may be found in James H. Matlack, "The Alta California's Lady Correspondent," *New York Historical Society Quarterly* 58 (1974): 280–303; Sandra Zagarell, "Elizabeth Barstow Stoddard, 1823–1902," *Legacy* 8 (1991): 39–49; and the *DAB,* among others.

4. Richard Hall Wiswall, "Notes on the Building of Chesnut Street," *Essex Institute Historical Collections* 75 (1939): 211; *Vital Records of Salem, Massachusetts, to the End of the Year 1849,* 6 vols. (Salem: Essex Institute, 1916–18), 3: 83.

5. Hawthorne's religious views have been discussed extensively, particularly in earlier scholarship. See, for instance, Leonard J. Flick, *The Light Beyond: A Study of Hawthorne's Theology* (Westminster, Md.: Newman, 1955); Randall Stewart, *American Literature & Christian Doctrine* (Baton Rouge: Louisiana State UP, 1958); Agnes McNeill Donohue, *Hawthorne: Calvin's Ironic Stepchild* (Kent, Ohio: Kent State UP, 1985); Michael Colacurcio, *The Province of Piety* (Cambridge: Harvard UP, 1984); or Margaret B. Moore, *The Salem World of Nathaniel Hawthorne* (Columbia: U of Missouri P, 1998), especially 102–22.

Works Cited

Brodhead, Richard H. *The School of Hawthorne.* New York: Oxford UP, 1986.

Buell, Lawrence. *New England Literary Culture: From Revolution through Renaissance.* Cambridge: Cambridge UP, 1986.

Daily Alta California [San Francisco], 1854–58.

Giles, Henry. *Illustrations of Genius in Relation to Culture and Society.* Boston: Ticknor and Fields, 1854.

Hawthorne, Julian. *Nathaniel Hawthorne and His Wife: A Biography.* 2 vols. Boston: Houghton Mifflin, 1884.

——. "Novelistic Habits and 'The Morgesons.'" *Lippincott's Magazine* 44 (1889): 868–71.

Hawthorne, Nathaniel. *The Scarlet Letter,* vol. 1; *The House of the Seven Gables,* vol. 2; *The Letters, 1843–1853,* vol. 16; *The Letters, 1857–1864,* vol. 18, of the *Centenary Edition of the Works of Nathaniel Hawthorne.* Ed. William Charvat et al. Columbus: Ohio State UP, 1962–.

Hefferman, Nancy Coffey, and Ann Page Stecker. *Sisters of Fortune.* Hanover, N.H.: UP of New England, 1993.

Kraft, James. "An Unpublished Review by Henry James." *Studies in Bibliography* 20 (1967): 267–73.

Kramer, Maurice. "Alone at Home with Elizabeth Stoddard." *American Transcendental Quarterly* 47–48 (1980): 159–70.

Leverenz, David. *Manhood and the American Renaissance*. Ithaca: Cornell UP, 1989.

Matlack, James H. "Hawthorne and Elizabeth Barstow Stoddard." *New England Quarterly* 50 (1977): 278–302.

——. "The Literary Career of Elizabeth Barstow Stoddard." Diss. Yale U, 1967.

[Preston, Harriet Waters]. "Some Recent Novels." *Atlantic Monthly* 88 (1901): 848–50.

Stoddard, Elizabeth Barstow. *The Morgesons and Other Writings Published and Unpublished*. Ed. Lawrence Buell and Sandra A. Zagarell. Philadelphia: U of Pennsylvania P, 1984.

——. *Temple House*. New York: Carleton, 1867.

——. *Two Men: A Novel*. New York: Bruce and Huntington, 1865.

Stoddard, Richard Henry. "Nathaniel Hawthorne." *Harper's New Monthly Magazine* 45 (1872): 683–97.

ANNIE FIELDS'S NATHANIEL HAWTHORNE

Rita K. Gollin

A nnie Fields first met Nathaniel Hawthorne in London in June 1859, five years after marrying James T. Fields, Boston's most important publisher and Hawthorne's trusted friend. At the time of her marriage Hawthorne was the American consul in Liverpool, and he and his family had now returned from a year and a half in Italy. Almost immediately he called at the Fieldses' hotel, and Annie Fields's record of that event inaugurated a unique eyewitness record of the last five years of his life.

At twenty-five, Annie Fields was a starry-eyed worshiper of America's greatest novelist but also a sympathetic observer of her husband's old friend and privy to their business dealings. Thus, from the evidence of Hawthorne's lowered voice and the slight twitch in his face as he talked about *The Marble Faun,* she sensed his anxiety about completing the novel which her husband eagerly awaited and whose English copyright he had just arranged.[1] Hawthorne's wife and son came along on his next visit, and soon Annie's social life included both parents and all three of their children. When the Fieldses returned from the Continent the following spring and (by Hawthorne's arrangement) they all sailed back to America together, their friendship strengthened. During the next four years, until Hawthorne's death, the childless Annie served as Sophia's confidante and a fairy godmother to her children. Yet her generosity to them remained rooted in profound admiration of Hawthorne himself. Each time Anne entertained Sophia or her children in Boston or sent gifts to Concord, she could pride herself on supporting and encouraging the great writer and in the process serving her husband's publishing firm and the reading public. That pragmatic altruism continued even after Hawthorne's death, never more clearly than when Annie urged Sophia to publish Hawthorne's American journals. During his lifetime, she had concertedly recorded her firsthand and even secondhand knowledge of America's greatest novelist; and until the end of her own long life, she continued to be both a custodian of and a contributor to the reputation of Nathaniel Hawthorne.

One form of literary homage was in effect a double kind of homage: recording other celebrities' remarks about Hawthorne. The first such event occurred in Florence in the winter of 1859, where Annie enjoyed walking where Hawthorne had walked and seeing what he had seen, and where her friendship with America's greatest woman novelist began. When Harriet Beecher Stowe first visited the Fieldses' hotel, she talked "charmingly" about Hawthorne, as Annie was delighted to report. "Like old pictures, she thinks, an uncultivated taste would hardly relish him, but once understand him and you feel that the marvels of Highest Art stand before you." That common ground of admiration would expand in the spring, when Stowe arranged to cross the Atlantic on the same ship that carried the Fieldses and the Hawthornes back home. But Annie Fields's respect for Hawthorne did not keep her from recording the disparagements of another writer she revered—Ralph Waldo Emerson—even those not made in her presence. Thus an early entry in the "Journal of Important Literary Events and glimpses of interesting people" she began keeping in the summer of 1863 was her minister-friend Cyrus Bartol's report that Emerson had complained of "the distance which grew up between him and Hawthorne" and said he and Hawthorne disagreed "utterly upon politics and every theory of life." Annie was privy to one ground of disagreement: Hawthorne insisted on dedicating his "volume of English sketches" to Franklin Pierce, the man who had appointed him consul to Liverpool soon after becoming president, despite Fields's argument that dedicating *Our Old Home* to a southern sympathizer would offend abolitionists, Emerson and Stowe among them. Though Annie marveled at Hawthorne's loyalty, Stowe was indeed incensed, and Emerson "cut out the dedication" and then damned the book with faint praise: it was "pellucid but not deep."

Not until four years after Hawthorne's death did Annie discover another of Emerson's grounds for animus. In 1868 while preparing a lecture on Brook Farm, Emerson told Fields that "ever since Hawthorne's ghastly and untrue account of that community in his 'Blithedale Romance' I have desired to give what I think the true account of it." Despite her faith in Hawthorne's probity and her admiration of *The Blithedale Romance,* Annie simply recorded that statement. That James Russell Lowell shared her admiration is suggested by an exchange with Emerson a decade after Hawthorne's death, which their fellow Saturday Club member James T. Fields reported to his wife. The recent deaths of Louis Agassiz and Charles Sumner were great losses to the Saturday Club, Emerson had said, whereupon Lowell replied,

"Greater than either was that of a man I could never make you believe in as I did, Hawthorne." As Fields told his wife, Lowell's rejoinder left even Emerson silent.

Although the decorous Annie would never have ventured such a rejoinder, in the early sixties she once silently rejected a disparaging remark by one of Emerson's traditionalist friends. When Frederick Henry Hedge accused Hawthorne of being "idle," Annie felt she "could say nothing." Instead, she consoled herself by thinking about "the delicate pages woven from the fibre of his brain—for which he should be revered." Oliver Wendell Holmes also admired both the man and the writer, as evident in a bittersweet conversation that took place in her own library during the last winter of Hawthorne's life. Holmes said he would write a novel if Hawthorne were not in the field, whereupon Hawthorne ruefully replied, "I am not and I wish you would." At that point Holmes urged Hawthorne to attend meetings of the Saturday Club, and when Hawthorne protested that he could no longer drink, eat, or talk, Holmes firmly replied, "You can listen."[2] Five months later, right after Hawthorne set out from Boston for what turned out to be his final journey, Annie sadly recorded Dr. Holmes's somber professional judgment: "The shark's tooth is on him." That Hawthorne continued to remain on Holmes's mind is suggested by a few remarks he made to Annie years later. Hawthorne's "sadness" was integral with his genius, Holmes said; and "Hawthorne beginning from within was [Dickens's] contrast and counterpart." Annie herself ventured a more surprising comparison. Soon after Bret Harte came east in 1871, Annie concluded that his "pleasant acceding to both sides in politics, and other traits of like nature, gives him affinity with Hawthorne." Better still, the western humorist turned out to be "a true appreciator of Hawthorne" and particularly of his humor: simply thinking about Hawthorne's "sly" notebook description of Margaret Fuller's obstreperous cow made him erupt in "merriment."

In her own role as "a true appreciator of Hawthorne," Annie recorded and even pursued biographical lore about him. Thus she set down what the two daughters of Hawthorne's old friend Frederick Howes told her when she visited their Beverly Farms estate in the summer of 1866. For example, when Hawthorne was "blamed most unjustly as they knew well because of his introduction to the Scarlet Letter about Salem," their family were "almost the only friends Hawthorne had in Salem," and their house was "one of the few he was willing to visit." They also reminisced about their aunt Susan Burley, a benefactor of the Hawthornes about whom Annie had "often heard Mrs Hawthorne speak in terms of friendly admiration." As for the old man Hawthorne "showed up" in "The Custom-House," he "was a dishonest fellow who had defrauded the government but as the matter was hushed up few knew how much in the right Hawthorne was"; and Mr. Upham, "no exalted character either, . . . was shown in his true colors" as Judge Pyncheon in *The House of the Seven Gables*. On one of her visits to the Howes sisters, Annie met Mrs. Nathaniel Silsbee, whose husband was mayor of Salem during Hawthorne's term in the Custom House, and who made the curious remark that Hawthorne "was born in Salem, but we never knew anything about him." According to Miss Howes, however, Mr.

Silsbee had probably been "one of his persecutors." But what struck Annie most during her visits to Beverly Farms was one of the sisters' observations: "Hawthorne wore the air of a banished lord!" In her journal she recorded that remark and her own reaction: "Nothing ever described him better." Her husband would later appropriate the remark for his essay on Hawthorne.

Hawthorne died in May 1864, while staying in the Pemigewasset House in Plymouth, New Hampshire. When the Fieldses passed through Plymouth a year later, the thought of "Hawthorne's dying eyes looking out on the hills of Plymouth" intensified Annie's appreciation of their beauty. Then, on the third anniversary of his death, in the very inn where he had died, she heard the "keeper of the house" recall that he had assisted Hawthorne to his bed that night. Most of what he then said the Fieldses already knew: Hawthorne had died in an "easy posture," his death discovered only when his friend Pierce "placed his hand upon him lovingly in one of the wakeful pauses of the night and found that he was cold." But the innkeeper's concluding remark was a poignant supplement: "The distress of Mr Pierce was indescribable. . . . He hardly ever saw a man suffer more."

Annie's own memories of Hawthorne often surfaced when she was vexed by Sophia Hawthorne's demands on her friendship and on James T. Fields's checkbook. Thus, when Sophia demanded increased royalty payments, Annie lamented that Hawthorne's family had become "virtually beggars" though he himself had left his affairs in remarkably good shape. Implicitly reprimanding Sophia, she recalled that Hawthorne had been "so just and careful himself, never spending a cent he could not afford." A brief visit to Hawthorne's sister Elizabeth in July 1866 provoked a more thoughtful comment. Elizabeth's "rusting powers" made Annie conclude that "utter solitude" lames a woman's powers more than a man's, after which she firmly declared that "solitude fed [Hawthorne's] genius, solitude and the pressure of necessity." Next, she recalled "his reply to me when I offered to brush his coat one morning 'no no I never brush my coat, it wears it out!' "

Because her sympathy for the man intertwined with her reverence for the writer, in the very process of reading Hawthorne's American journals Annie Fields became his ideal reader. He seemed "always to be teaching himself to observe and record with accuracy," Annie marveled, resolving to emulate him in her own journals. "What a picture of character laid bare such a book is!" she once exclaimed. "Such impatience under the discipline of days! He lacked the Jove-compelling power to drive his genius, so he was driven thereby." And as testimony to the power of Hawthorne's "great truthfulness," she said that "the man himself rises up as I read." Even more dramatic is her response to his Italian journals three years later. Again she felt the man rise up, and his words made her relive her own Italian experiences. But she now credited Hawthorne with expanding her mind and sympathies. "Nothing has ever made me comprehend more vividly the fullness of the world and the weight of the most trivial observation upon the mind of man than Hawthorne's religiously kept journal," she said, then poignantly mused, "I do not wonder that he was tired of pen and ink when those latter days came."

When she read *Septimius Felton* soon after, she first agreed with Browning and other critics who considered it "one of his greatest productions" and then ventured a shrewd judgment of her own: through his "vast weird analysis" of the restless seeker who tries to transcend the limits of mortality and ends up perhaps eternally alone, Hawthorne presented his "own character and motives under a slight viel [*sic*] of fiction." Next, she confidently expanded on one of her own previous insights into Hawthorne's working methods: "the patience and microscopic power with which Hawthorne wrote his journals was a kind of perpetual preparation for his books." Then, with an even firmer voice of authority, she declared, "Never a day elapsed that he did not work in this fashion." Perhaps one reason for such confidence was that she had not only been making her own meticulous journal entries but putting them to further use—for her recently published poetic idyll about the Shakers entitled "The Children of Lebanon" as well as for the obituary of Dickens and the memoir of Hawthorne signed by her husband alone.

Annie Fields's contributions to her husband's essay on Hawthorne merit separate attention. Soon after reporting in her journal in November 1870 that her husband was about to retire and would "occupy himself with literature," she was "Consulting this diary for notes about Hawthorne yesterday which I found very scanty." Almost certainly her husband requested that consultation. In his essay on Hawthorne, he drew from Annie's journal and also her letters from Sophia, presenting her observations as his and simply saying Sophia's letters had been addressed to "us." Fields's essay on Hawthorne—later republished in his best-respected book, *Yesterdays with Authors*—skillfully incorporates excerpts from Annie's journal. He used Annie's own descriptions of Hawthorne as a houseguest who always stayed in the third-floor room overlooking the water where he had "unmolested habitation" and the freedom to read in their library. He took out of context the bittersweet story Hawthorne told of the friend who kept such close watch over him after publisher William Ticknor's death that he forgot to pack his slippers, presenting it as an example of Hawthorne's amusing anecdotes. Annie once advised Hawthorne what to write in an admirer's album during a breakfast party she gave in London in May 1860; her husband placed that incident at an English friend's evening party and cast himself as the adviser. And he repeated as his own Annie's accounts of their jaunting car expedition with the Hawthornes in Ireland a day after sailing from Liverpool, as well as Annie's accounts of Hawthorne's last visits to them—including his account of attending Mrs. Pierce's funeral in December 1863 and his happy reminiscences about his adolescent years in Raymond, Maine.

Hawthorne had already inspired Annie herself to write a poem—a solemn blank-verse elegy entitled "The Traveller," inscribed "In memory of, and in love of, Nathaniel Hawthorne."

He rose upon an early dawn of May
And looked upon the stream and meadow flowers
Then on the face of his beloved, and went;

And passing gazed upon the Wayside haunt,
The homely budding gardens by the road
And harvest promise.—Still he said, I go!

Once more he mingled in the midday crowd
And smiled a gentle smile, a sweet farewell,
Then moved towards the hills and lay him down.

Lying he looked beyond the pathless heights,
Beyond the wooded steep and clouded peaks,
And looking, questioned, then he loved and slept.

And while he slept his spirit walked abroad,
And wandered past the mountain, past the cloud
Nor came again to rouse the form—at peace.

Though like some bird we strive to follow him,
Fruitless we beat at the horizon's verge
And fruitless seek the fathomless blue beyond.

We work and wait and water with salt tears,—
Learning to live that living we may sleep
And sleeping cross the mountains to God's rest.[3]

It is easy to fault the poem's epithets as conventional and even cliché—"pathless heights," "wooded steep," "clouded peaks." Yet Annie managed to incorporate the bounded yet boundless quality of the New Hampshire landscape, and her analogue of a bird beating "at the horizon's verge" is particularly fresh. Further, the poem movingly expresses her feelings of loss and yearning, which was perhaps her main purpose in writing it. It exists only in manuscript, and there is no way of knowing if she showed it to anyone or if she hoped to publish it.

Even before Hawthorne's death, Annie shared her appreciation of Hawthorne with other women. Often it was a form of nurturance, as in the case of her sister Lissie, who was living at Charles Street in the winter of 1866 and trying to support herself as a portrait painter. At one point she sat down with Lissie and "studied up the Dolliver Romance for a picture," hoping that "perhaps she will paint Pansie." And on another occasion when she read "Rappaccini's Daughter" to Lissie, she might well have hoped her sister would paint Beatrice.

Her admiration for Hawthorne also figured in her correspondence with the *Atlantic*'s women contributors. Rebecca Harding Davis's fascination with Hawthorne began during her childhood, she told him after the success of her *Atlantic* story "Life in the Iron-Mills"—he had made her see "mystery and charm" in the commonplace though she did not then know his name. During a ten-day visit with the Fieldses, she would later rhapsodically recall, she met Sophia Hawthorne and such luminaries as Lowell and Holmes along with many women contributors to the *Atlantic,* among them Celia Thaxter, Elizabeth Peabody, and Louisa May Alcott. Her next two days were spent in Concord with the Hawthornes, where her greatest pleasure came from her conversations with Hawthorne himself. Understandably, she treasured his farewell: "I am sorry you are going away. It seems as if we had known you always." Her reverence for Hawthorne was now another bond with Annie Fields, and a topic for discussion in their letters.[4] It is hardly surprising that Annie never repeated to her Sophia Hawthorne's remark that both she and her husband disliked the flabby style and narrative "squalor" of "the gifted Rebecca." When Hawthorne died, Rebecca mournfully declared that his death was "a people's loss." In that same spirit, Annie sent Rebecca a tender account of his "going to rest" in Sleepy Hollow Cemetery, which then prompted Rebecca to recall the time he had sat in that cemetery with her, "his hands clasped about his knees & the quaint smile with which he said 'Yes it *is* pleasant.'" For both women, the irony of his next remark surely took on new meaning: "The most beautiful pleasure grounds you will find in New England are our grave-yards. *We* only begin to enjoy ourselves when we're dead.'"[5]

Though Hawthorne did not play as large a role in Annie's friendship with Harriet Prescott (later Spofford), the Newburyport woman whose lively stories dazzled early readers of the *Atlantic,* they shared their enthusiasm for Hawthorne's work, and in 1863 Annie was delighted to hear from Hawthorne himself that he "had some conversation with her and liked her." In 1871 when the Spoffords stayed at Charles Street, Annie put them in what she called "Hawthorne's room." Harriet claimed the next day that "his restless ghost kept sleep away."

But the woman who most fully shared Annie's reverence for Hawthorne was Laura Johnson, the Staten Island woman who became her most intimate confidante in the sixties. Whenever Hawthorne came to Charles Street, Annie told Laura what he said and did, often allowing herself more freedom than in her journal. An example is her account of Hawthorne's return from Philadelphia after Ticknor's death. Because he looked unwell and retired early, the Fieldses began breakfast without him the next day.

> Presently he came gently in with the same pale solemn look and when we said, did you sleep well, has all been well with you since we parted, he answered "Yes! all is well with me except life!" He soon recurred to his late experience. "I hate all undertakers" he said, "there are some callings which no man ought to follow."

"These are things I never can repeat to anybody," Annie said, meaning anybody else. As she assured Laura, "I believe you will understand them, will take them as we should take every thing from such a man, sacredly, to be held with judgment and reverence." Next came a remarkable tribute:

> We regard Hawthorne as the greatest genius our country has produced and if he had never written a word, to watch a spirit more sensitive to every influence than a ripe wheatfield to passing breezes . . . is of greater value . . . than can be expressed.

Then, as if talking aloud, she compared him to the poet she most revered: "The solemnity of Hawthorne is something I have never met with except in Tennyson indeed they are more alike than either of them know." When she later gave Laura a report of Hawthorne's funeral, she included her own thoughts and emotions as she sat in the Old Manse afterward and watched the Musketaquid "gleaming down among the apple blossoms from his study window." In reply, Laura shared Annie's mourning and reaffirmed her reverence for Hawthorne's genius but added a discordant note: her neighbor Mrs. Shaw "did not like or think well of him on acct of his engagement to Miss E. P. his sister in law. We will talk about this when we meet."[6] Clearly, anything about Hawthorne was worth talking about, though usually Annie called the turns. Thus, after reading "Septimius, the story of a deathless man," Annie told Laura it was "autobiographic" and urged her to read it.

Annie's role as custodian of Hawthorne's reputation took several new turns after she was widowed in 1881 and became a biographer of writers who had been her friends. Thus when her friend Moncure Conway was preparing to write his *Life of Nathaniel Hawthorne* in 1889, he asked Annie if she had any advice for him, or perhaps some reminiscence. And the year before, Thomas Wentworth Higginson had asked more specific questions while preparing his own biography of Hawthorne.

> Your good husband . . . told me that Hawthorne wrote some of the early Peter Parley books, & I have several times mentioned this as a fact, but am now asked to substantiate it. There is much internal evidence in their style; but can you help me to any external evidence? I don't think Goodrich mentions it in his Recollection; nor does Julian H. in his Biography. Also, do you know where "The Hollow of the Three Hills" first appeared?

Higginson's inquiry prompted Sarah Orne Jewett's essay on Hawthorne's style, and possibly also the comments on Hawthorne in Annie's unpublished survey of American literature.[7] In 1899 she published a short biography of Hawthorne. That same year, when Houghton Mifflin was preparing to issue a new edition of Hawthorne's work, Horace Scudder asked her to help out with the Miscellany text. Specifically, he said the passages Fields had asked Hawthorne to eliminate from "Chiefly about War

Matters" because "injudicious in 1862 would be harmless and quite interesting in 1900," and if she had the manuscript "if you wd allow the dropped passages to be restored"—a somewhat curious request, since they had been restored in subsequent publications of "Chiefly about War Matters." Then in 1908 Barrett Wendell wrote to ask her if Hawthorne could possibly have written a story about old-time Boston that he had recently read, and she replied that it was possible but "Miss Jewett and I feel the only way to tell is through style." As that reply attests, she and her beloved companion Sarah Orne Jewett often discussed Hawthorne's work, and one of Jewett's unpublished manuscripts suggests they did so with some passion.[8]

Annie Fields's brief biography of Hawthorne clearly and sympathetically chronicles the life of the Great Romancer, testifying to his probity and truthfulness, his generosity and wit, ranging from such personal matters as his solitary habits and his reliance on Sophia to such professional matters as his infinitely careful journal records, incorporating details she alone knew together with quotations from his letters and passages from her predecessors Henry James and George Lathrop, and concertedly setting a few records straight.[9] In her account of his childhood, she drew from her own journal his recollection that in Maine he had lived "like a bird of the air, so perfect was the freedom I enjoyed." Defending him as she had felt unable to do when Hedge charged him with idleness three decades before, she insisted that "He could not be called idle" even though he made that accusation against himself. But some of her praise of Hawthorne was doubly honed, as when she chided Sophia and defended her husband by saying "No temptation ever lured him into buying, or letting any member of his family buy, anything which he could not pay for at once," adding that Hawthorne never fancied "his books should bring more than the market for them warranted, and never mortgaged his brains in advance."

Further, she insisted that her husband had earned Hawthorne's trust. His publishers "were generous to him, though their wishes far outran anything they could do for him," she declared. Not only did they constantly reprint his books, but (as Hawthorne had said) Fields smote the rock of public sympathy on his behalf, and no author had a publisher he valued as much. As for two occasions when Hawthorne took issue with her husband, Annie predictably sided with her husband. He had been right to persuade Hawthorne to eliminate unflattering descriptions of Lincoln from his "Chiefly about War Matters," descriptions she still considered "petty" even though her husband had published them in *Yesterdays with Authors*. And in assessing Hawthorne's dedication of *Our Old Home* to Pierce, she said he "didn't know himself at that time" since he loved Pierce but "also loved his other friends and his country."

Shrewdly aware that Hawthorne habitually looked "at every side of a question," she traced the pathetic deterioration of his health to his agitation about the Civil War. Describing his appearance at that time, she said he remained handsome but had become a "large, slow-moving, iron-gray man, with marvellous dreamful eyes"—eyes which were "soft and kind, but in-seeing." As Annie then mused, she never "had the impression of being looked at by Hawthorne," yet always had "a very keen sense of . . . being understood by him." Even more precisely injecting herself into the end of her account, she said that when he "came to our house in Boston" in March 1864 "[w]e were much shocked by the change in his appearance." And after reporting on his death two months later, she said whenever she stood in the room where he died, "as I have frequently done since he passed out silently into the skies, it is easy to imagine the scene on that spring morning."[10]

Annie Fields may well have offered her final pronouncements on Hawthorne in an undated and unpublished nineteen-page manuscript on American literature. By celebrating the great writers of New England including Lowell, Longfellow, and Holmes but concentrating on Hawthorne and Emerson, she was perhaps deliberately addressing Emerson's statement that he and Hawthorne were completely at odds.[11] In some respects she agreed:

> The habits of Hawthorne, as is now well known, were in entire contrast to those of Emerson. They long inhabited the same town yet they rarely met. His method of writing too was quite unlike, for whereas Emerson would bring home his poems from the field or wood and also doubtless many a noble sentence of prose, he found in his study a method of his own for putting his prose together and giving it such continuity as he could.

Then, focusing on the novelist's working habits, she said:

> Hawthorne made a footpath by frequent walking to & fro on the crest of a small hill behind the "Wayside" where he lived in Concord. There and in other walks and other places he wove the texture of his great romances so firmly together in his mind that when he came to write them down they sped on in one continuous flow scarcely needing a correction. Sometimes he would write the word he did not intend and blur it out speedily with his finger writing over it before the ink was dry; but once thought out in his great walks at Redcar in England at the Villa Montauto in Florence or at home on the little hill, there it lay clear in his mind and ready for the page. . . . [I]n the pages of the "House of the Seven Gables" which is preserved entire, this method can easily be seen.

In praising Hawthorne's financial probity, Annie also praised the way her husband maximized the writer's income and implicitly criticized Sophia both for poor management and for criticizing Fields:

> Hawthorne was a poor man as the world counts riches[.] He had no resources beyond his pen and his books never had very large sales, but his *publisher* made the most of them and Hawthorne himself was a man of few wants. Sometimes he may have felt the need of money for his family but they also, the children being young, and Mrs

Hawthorne being a woman of small expenditure, were content with little. Hawthorne's probity in money matters and his real generosity were the traits of one of Nature's noblemen. He could never be induced to buy a thing which he could not pay for neither did he ever wear an air of poverty but bore himself with the dignity of one who had what he needed and otherwise spent no time in considering the question. I can believe that petty economies were seldom if ever a subject of discourse between husband and wife and whatever anxieties he suffered were borne in silence. Occasionally if it were proposed to buy something which he considered unnecessary he would say so and that was the end of it—

Next, she acknowledged the writer's profound psychic privacy:

Hawthorne's inner life was largely his own: neither wife nor child nor friend shared freely in his experiences. His wife knew him more nearly than any other but although he rested on her and loved to hear her talk sometimes his whole heart seems to have unveiled to no living soul.

Then, returning to her project of comparing Hawthorne and Emerson, Annie Fields celebrated their similarities:

In spite of the contrasted natures of the men I have spoken of, their ideals and general habits of life were not superficially very unlike. They loved simplicity of manner, dress and behavior and instilled these ideas into the minds of their children. They felt strong kinship with Wordsworth. His "plain living and high thinking" might have been said by one of themselves. Their highest pleasure was in their work and beyond that in the society of the men and women of their time. They were not generally frequenters of theatre nor seekers after entertainment. . . . Such is it to have had a habit of work, and love to others, and high aspirations, for one's country and oneself. In this spirit they lived and died leaving a legacy to their country which leavens it and lifts it up even when the mechinations [*sic*] of politicians take arms against its welfare.

In conclusion, she offered a paean of praise for "these teachers of America":

It is humanity and not a nation to which they address themselves. It is the human soul, the soul of their brother, they are calling, urging him to embrace the opportunities of life under the fresh conditions America has offered and to cherish these opportunities for the uplifting of the spirit into a larger and more indestructible happiness.

All in all, Annie Fields stretches our understanding of how Hawthorne was judged by his famous and not-so-famous contemporaries, including Annie herself. Conscientiously, she was witness, recorder, publicist, and custodian of Nathaniel Hawthorne's reputation, and she also participated in its creation.

Notes

1. The sixty-one volumes of Annie Fields's diaries in the Fields Papers at the Massachusetts Historical Society begin with the travel diaries she kept in England and on the Continent.

2. Mark DeWolfe Howe did not include the exchange with Holmes in his *Memories of a Hostess: A Chronicle of Eminent Friendships Drawn Chiefly from the Diaries of Mrs. James T. Fields* (Boston: Atlantic Monthly Press, 1922) but did include Longfellow's comment to Fields about receiving a sad note from Hawthorne and wishing to "have a littler dinner for him, . . . of two sad authors and two jolly publishers."

3. The poem is dated Plymouth, New Hampshire, 19 May 1864; it is written in ink in a notebook containing manuscript poems dated between 1864 and 1873 at the Huntington Library. The notebook containing poems written between 1857 and 1864 includes a poem of five six-line stanzas entitled "Loss and Gain," Gain—5 6-li stanzas—dated Campton, 16 June 1864, "After Hawthorne's death," Annie noted. Trying to with "unforgotten pain," the speaker says, "We count our loss and still the river flows / And still we drink the fragrance of the rose," then receives spiritual consolation from "the light of Love whose gleam is permanent."

4. In *Bits of Gossip* (Boston: Houghton Mifflin, 1904) 30–64, Davis recalled that as a child she had once spent a whole day in a tree devouring an unsigned collection of "moral tales," unaware of the author's name until she encountered a volume of *Twice-told Tales* in 1862. Responding to her letter saying so, Hawthorne said he would try to see her when he traveled to Washington, though battles in the area prevented it. Their only meeting was in Concord, where while conversing with Alcott and Emerson she especially relished seeing "Hawthorne's sagacious eyes watch us, full of mockery."

5. Rebecca Harding Davis to Annie Fields (AF), 27 June [1864], U of Virginia Library.

6. AF to Laura Johnson, [April 1864] and 24 May 1864, Huntington Library; and Laura Johnson to AF, 17 July 1864, New York Public Library. Sarah Sturgis Shaw presumably heard of the "engagement" from her friend Elizabeth Peabody, who misinterpreted Hawthorne's interest in her during his secret courtship of Elizabeth's sister Sophia.

7. Moncure Conway to AF, 14 December 1889, T. W. Higginson to AF, 24 June 1888, and Horace Scudder to AF, 21 August 1900, Huntington Library; and AF to Barrett Wendell, 24 July 1900, Houghton Library, Harvard. Jewett's brief and unpublished manuscript comparing Hawthorne's style to Scott's is at the Houghton Library; Annie Fields's survey at the Huntington Library is discussed below.

8. Jewett's page-long manuscript now at the Houghton Library rhetorically invites some venturesome "critic in these days of statue building to Hawthorne" to assess his debt to Scott without fearing charges of envy or iconoclasm.

9. Annie Fields's volume in the Beacon biographies of Eminent Americans edited by her good friend M. A. DeWolfe Howe—*Nathaniel Hawthorne* (Boston: Small and Maynard, 1899)—runs to only 132 duodecimo pages. Although DeWolfe had asked Annie to write a preface, she told him she thought that was unnecessary, then dispatched a postcard saying, "My taste revolts at the idea of such a preface! I think the little book ought to be taken as it is

or left alone." The next day she told him that she had accepted Small and Maynard's terms because he asked her to, though Houghton Mifflin paid 15 percent and that would be her price in the future. AF to Howe, 29 and 30 Aug. 1899, Houghton Library.

10. In *Yesterdays with Authors* (Boston: Osgood, 1872) 124, the "I" in that statement is James T. Fields.

11. Annie Fields's manuscript titled "American Literary Life" is a relatively recent addition to the Fields Addenda at the Huntington Library.

MARY RUSSELL MITFORD

John L. Idol Jr.

From the tireless pen of Mary Russell Mitford (1787–1855) came plays, poems, essays, sketches of English village life, introductions to compilations of many types of literature, letters, and recollections. Starting with a distaste for writings of American authors, she came in time to be an ardent champion of American letters. In her estimate, no American author stood higher than Nathaniel Hawthorne. To the utmost of her ability, she worked eagerly and well to see that English readers came to know and admire Hawthorne.

From her discovery of *The Scarlet Letter* in 1851 until her death in 1855, she read Hawthorne's work and declared that America had at last produced a great, if sometimes flawed, author. Whenever she could, she boosted his fiction, lending copies of Hawthorne works to friends and reviewers, mentioning his name and the titles of his books in her letters, and endorsing him enthusiastically when she published her memoirs, *Recollections of a Literary Life; or, Books, Places, and People* (1852).

She evidently missed seeing the pirated edition of *Twice-told Tales* (1849), "The Celestial Railroad" (pirated in 1844), and *Mosses from an Old Manse,* first printed in England in 1846. Her introduction to Hawthorne came early in 1851 when James T. Fields sent her a copy of *The Scarlet Letter* along with works by John Greenleaf Whittier and Oliver Wendell Holmes. Her first remark was brief; she described the novel as "a wild romantic tale of the elder days of Boston" (*Letters of Boner* 199). Two weeks or so after this first notice (11 Feb. 1851), she spent more time with the romance and now lamented the fact that it was not available in England. (A pirated edition did appear two and a half months later.) She told Charles Boner that the novel was "very striking and poetical" (*Boner* 206). She was already looking forward to the publication of his next work, which, as she had heard in a letter from Mrs. Jared Sparks, could be counted on as finer than anything that had seen print (*Letters* 2: 38). That work, of course, was *The House of the Seven Gables,* a copy of which James Fields sent her. By July, she was ready to agree that it surpassed the earlier romance in some ways: "The legendary part dim, shadowy, and impressive, and the living characters exquisitely true, vivid, and healthful. The heroine, Phoebe, is almost a Shakespearian creation, as fresh and charming as the Rigolette of Eugene Sue" (*Boner* 189–90). On the same day (20 July 1851) that she expressed this estimate to Boner, she was writing much the same to Fields, turning to him for additional information about Hawthorne, inquiring about his age and profession. So impressed was she by Hawthorne's romances that she told Fields she was already sure Hawthorne was "one of the glories of your most glorious part of great America" (qtd. in Fields 289). Some months later when Fields visited her home, he answered her queries about Hawthorne. Meanwhile he passed along her praise of Hawthorne in her letter to him. Graciously, Hawthorne returned the compliment, writing (18 Aug. 1851) that he was "glad . . . the Seven Gables have pleased Miss Mitford, whose sketches [*Our Village*], long ago as I read them, are as sweet in my memory as the scent of new hay" (*CE* 16: 475).[1] Mitford, at this time, was busy preparing her *Recollections* for the press. Taking time out to read the newly published two-volume edition of *Twice-told Tales* which Fields had shipped her, she confided to Boner that she found the work "inferior" to Hawthorne's novels (*Boner* 215). When Fields finally arrived at her home (mid-October), he came bearing not only news of Hawthorne but a copy of the just issued *Wonder Book for Girls and Boys.* Mitford rushed to spread word of Hawthorne the man to her circle of friends, writing to W. C. Bennett (17 Oct. 1851) that Fields had reported: "[Hawthorne] blushes like a girl when praised—is still young—and a magnificent specimen of manhood almost a giant (I thought he was tall and large)—Mr. Fields says he would cut out into four of Dr. Holmes who is a compact little man. Hawthorne is upon the model of Webster. . . . [Hawthorne] thinks himself the most overrated man in all America" (Egerton ms. 3774, British Library).

Besides these extravagant "facts" about Hawthorne's physique, Fields, continuing in his expansive mood, told her a great deal more about his rescued author, including the story of his own role in publishing *The Scarlet Letter.* Mitford seized upon his account and hastened to share it, telling a number of correspondents how Fields had found Hawthorne in "extreme penury" in Salem, how Fields upon hearing of Hawthorne's poverty had gone to him and declared his confidence in Hawthorne's power, promising to print 2,500 copies of any work that Hawthorne would give him and allowing a 25 percent royalty. He capped his tale by revealing that Hawthorne had reluctantly put a part of *The Scarlet Letter* into his hands and by confiding that he had instantly recognized its greatness, assuring Hawthorne of success if only he would complete the work (*Boner* 217).

She immediately took up the book Fields had brought with him, *The Wonder Book* and found its charm irresistible. She told Francis Bennoch, who was to become Hawthorne's closest English friend, "I always love children's books, but this is fit for any age. I am not sure (with the exception of George Sand) that Hawthorne is not the best living writer of prose fiction" (*Letters* 2: 229). She began to think of ways to promote Hawthorne's work, telling Fields early in 1852 that she had had "the honor of poking [Hawthorne] into the den of the Times, the only civilized place in England where they were barbarous enough not to be acquainted with 'The Scarlet Letter.' I wonder what they will think of it. It will make them stare" (qtd. in Fields 295).

Opinions that Mitford had been forming and expressing privately she now was ready to declare publicly, for after much work, her *Recollections* was published. Here she could place Hawthorne's fiction among the work of other American novelists. Fine as were Cooper's novels, especially *The Pioneers,* William Ware's *Zenobia,* Robert Montgomery Bird's *Nick of the Woods,* and as brilliant as were the stories of Washington Irving, no one, she proclaimed, excelled Hawthorne, the "new star . . . lately sprung into light in the Western horizon . . . [who] will hardly fail to be a bright illumination over both Europe and America" (517). Mitford then undertook blending a critical estimate of *The Scarlet Letter* and *The House of the Seven Gables* with a synopsis of each before extracting more than ten pages of Hawthorne's prose as a sample of his achievement. In her commentary, she expressed a special liking for Hepzibah, confessing that, once in an effort to support herself in the midst of financial straits, she had thought of setting up as a shopkeeper herself. "Ah, I have a strong fellow-feeling for that poor Hepzibah—a decayed gentlewoman, elderly, ugly, awkward, near-sighted, cross!" (520). Preferring the realistic to the legendary, Mitford extracted from the portions of the novel dealing with Hepzibah and Phoebe. Herself adept in using realistic detail, Mitford likened Hawthorne's use of realism to Balzac's and to Dutch painting. It was this same love of realism that led Mitford to downgrade *The Blithedale Romance* when she compared it to *The House of the Seven Gables.* Like Herman Melville, Mitford hungered for larger servings of roast beef (realism) than Hawthorne set before her. In this call for more realistic treatment of his narrative line and characters, Mitford anticipated the response Hawthorne had when *Transformation* (*The Marble Faun*) appeared to English readers far too vague and allegorical.

While Mitford was doing her utmost to champion the work of this newly discovered star, Hawthorne settled down to a job he had never done before, writing a letter of introduction to an English author, in this instance a letter to Mitford to present Grace Greenwood (Sara Jane Clarke). As he accepted the request, he said, "I suppose it would be more than a courtesy to write, as she has made such kind mention of me in her book [*Recollections*]; and I shall be glad to requite her kindness so abundantly as by introducing Grace Greenwood" (*CE* 16: 533). Before Greenwood left for her fifteen-month sojourn in England and her visit to Mitford's home, Hawthorne completed his letter of introduction and asked Greenwood to "tell the good old lady everything that you think will please her, about my gratitude and appreciation of her good opinion—and it will every word be true" (16: 535). Besides her introductory note from Hawthorne, Greenwood probably arrived with a copy of Hawthorne's newest work to present to Mitford, *The Blithedale Romance.* Mitford speedily thanked Fields for sending it, frankly adding what she found wrong. "It seems to me too long, too slow, and the personages . . . ill chosen." Zenobia she disliked because she linked her to Margaret Fuller or some other unsexed female. Hollingsworth reminded her of a disgusting English preacher of loathsome memory, and Westervelt and Priscilla were "almost equally disagreeable." She complained again of Hawthorne's "want of reality," convinced that the lack of realism in his early tales delayed his climb to fame. She was also sure that his practice of allegory, his projection of thought through some "ideal medium," would prevent the extension of his fame "if he do not resolutely throw himself into the truth." The fine parts of the book, she insisted, were the realistic: the search for Zenobia's body, the "burst of passion in Eliot's pulpit," and "likeable" and "honest" Silas Foster, "who alone gives one the notion of a man of flesh and blood." She added that she found the plot well constructed. Flawed as this new romance was, she nonetheless was pleased to recommend it to friends, saying, "with all its faults [the book] is one that nobody but Hawthorne could have written" (qtd. in Fields 304–5; L'Estrange 383). Writing to Hawthorne to thank him for autographing the copy sent to her by Fields, Mitford told him that his writing reminded her of Balzac's, "not by imitation, but by resemblance." She praised "the passion of the concluding scenes, the subtle analysis of jealousy, and the exquisite finish of style." Her reservations were not so strong that she backed away from her practice of boosting Hawthorne, for she sent her autographed copy to Willmott of the *Times,* where, she told Fields, it had gotten a "highly eulogistic critique" (qtd. in Fields 313).

More exciting than her effort to see that *The Blithedale Romance* received good press in England was the news in the fall of 1852 that Fields expected to come to England the following spring and would bring Hawthorne with him. Infirm as she was at the time, Mitford hoped to rally before they arrived so that she could be up "to show Mr. Hawthorne all the holes and corners of my own self" (qtd. in Fields 309). While waiting for them to come, she continued championing Hawthorne's work in letters to her friends. She boasted, for example, of having had "the pleasure of sending [Hawthorne] word a month ago [Dec. 1852] about the Russian translation of *The House of the Seven Gables.*" She also explained to Fields that an appointment to a public office by Franklin Pierce would be good for Hawthorne's art. "It will be an excellent thing for his future books,—the fault of all his writings, in spite of their great beauty, being a want of reality, of the actual, healthy, every-day life which is a necessary element in literature. All the great poets have it,—Homer,

Shakespeare, Scott" (qtd. in Fields 320). Here was her diplomatically indirect way of getting word to Hawthorne that he could widen his audience and strengthen his chance for lasting fame if he would overcome his self-admitted tendency to rely too heavily on allegory.

As the time for Hawthorne's arrival in England (23 July 1853) drew near, Mitford could scarcely contain her excitement. But time and again she would be disappointed, first by the fact that William Ticknor, not Fields, would be accompanying Hawthorne, and then by Hawthorne's inability to leave behind his consular duties in Liverpool. Finally, every obstacle overcome, the visit was set for 6 August. She hastened to tell such friends as Charles Kingsley to be there when Bennoch, Ticknor, and Hawthorne arrived, but once again Hawthorne had to postpone the visit. Her letter to Hugh Pearson on 8 August reveals the depth of her disappointment: "Ah! dearest friend, how we wished for you! Hawthorne did not come." She then told Pearson why, adding that Hawthorne would leave Liverpool for London at the end of the month. "*Then* he will certainly come here, and you *must* meet him" (*Letters* 2: 207). But there was never to be a visit by Hawthorne, though Ticknor did call, finding "little of [her] available except the head and heart." Yet, she still looked forward to better health and another opportunity to meet Hawthorne, "whom I can never think of except as a friend" (Ticknor to Hawthorne, 2 Oct. 1853, New York Public Library).

A recently arrived book, *Tanglewood Tales,* sent by Fields, had renewed her longing to meet Hawthorne. Difficult as writing was now for her, she rushed to tell Hawthorne how much she admired his further recasting of classical fables. "In addition to that wash of prose poetry which is so peculiarly your own, and which reproduces in so exquisite a manner the early history of your country—you have contrived to blend your own fancy with some of those lovely classical fables. . . . How many thousands will think of you as the name of some glorious old legend comes to them! It is a fine thing to make a holiday book of that to which to school boys has too often been a dry lexicon" (qtd. in J. Hawthorne 2: 35). The close of 1853 did not mark an end to the hope that Hawthorne could meet his staunch English admirer, a fact borne out by his note to her on 16 January 1854: "The Steamer (just arrived from Boston) has brought the enclosed letter from Fields. . . . I am glad it gives me an opportunity to say what a pleasure it is to me to be in the same country with you. When Mr. Fields comes over again (which he tells me will be in May) I cherish the hope of seeing you in company with him; but even if that should not happen, I shall still feel like a neighbor—the sense of inaccessibleness being removed" (*CE* 17: 165). By May, Mitford's health had declined so much that she felt she could see only her dearest friends. She wrote Fields that she still wanted him to visit, "but any stranger—even Mr. Hawthorne—is quite out of the question" (qtd. in Fields 344).

Her death later in 1855 prompted her countrymen to think of raising funds for a monument, and Hawthorne found himself an auditor to part of the discussion behind that drive when he accompanied Bennoch to government offices in Downing Street, where Bennoch and Mitford's longtime friend William Harness talked about the monument. Their conversation revealed that the British public seemed cool to erecting a monument. Hawthorne was "surprised to hear allusions indicating that Miss Mitford was not the inevitably amiable person that her writings would suggest: but the whole drift of what they said tended, nevertheless, towards the idea that she was an excellent and generous person, loved most by those who knew her best" (*English Notebooks* 323–24).

Hawthorne indeed had ample reason to settle on the word "generous," for Mitford had spared no effort to encourage her circle of literary friends and the reading public at large to enjoy Hawthorne's work. Although she lagged behind her countryman Henry Fothergill Chorley in discovering Hawthorne and recommending him to others, her endorsement of him counted heavily. Much better known both in England and the United States than Chorley, Mitford reached a larger readership. Here was a busy, well-respected woman, one whom Hawthorne in a moment of pique might have called a scribbler, who helped establish him as one of the leading writers of prose fiction. And for that generosity he was grateful. Had he been privy to all her strictures, to her concern that his "want of reality" limited his appeal to many readers, Hawthorne could have nodded his agreement. After all, for all his success as a symbolist and practitioner of the romance, he relished the beef and ale served up by writers like Anthony Trollope. To her credit, Mitford was able to take Hawthorne pretty much as she found him, praising what she liked and hoping that he would learn to correct what she saw as his faults.

Note

1. Quotations from Nathaniel Hawthorne's letters are from the *Centenary Edition of the Works of Nathaniel Hawthorne*, ed. William Charvat et al. (Columbus: Ohio State UP, 1962–), hereafter cited as *CE* with volume and page numbers.

Works Cited

Fields, James T. *Yesterdays with Authors*. Boston: Osgood, 1872.

Hawthorne, Julian. *Nathaniel Hawthorne and His Wife*. Boston: Osgood, 1885.

Hawthorne, Nathaniel. *The English Notebooks*. Ed. Randall Stewart. New York: Modern Language Association, 1941.

——. *The Letters, 1843–1853* and *The Letters, 1853–1856*. Ed. Thomas Woodson. Vols. 16 and 17 of the *Centenary Edition of the Works of Nathaniel Hawthorne*. Columbus: Ohio State UP, 1985, 1987.

L'Estrange, A. G. *The Friendships of Mary Russell Mitford*. New York: Harper, 1882.

Mitford, Mary Russell. *The Letters of Mary Russell Mitford*. 2nd ser. Ed. Henry F. Chorley. 2 vols. London: Bentley and Son, 1872.

——. *Memoirs and Letters of Charles Boner with Letters of Mary Russell Mitford to Him during Ten Years.* Ed. R. M. Kettle. London: Bentley, 1870.

——. *Recollections of a Literary Life; or, Books, Places, and People.* New York: Harper, 1852.

——. Unpublished Letters. Egerton ms. 3774. British Museum Library.

Ticknor, William. Letter to Hawthorne, 2 Oct. 1853. New York Public Library.

VIRGIN SAINT, MOTHER SAINT

Patricia Marks

In addition to *Middlemarch,* many of George Eliot's works show
Hawthornean influence. Traces of Hawthorne's *Scarlet Letter* may
be seen in almost all of her novels, and other examples abound:
The Blithedale Romance may be found in *The Mill on the Floss;*
The Marble Faun in *Romola;* and *The House of the Seven Gables* in
Felix Holt. Students and scholars of both writers will find that
Hawthorne's influence is pervasive in obvious and in subtle ways.

Thanks be to the Saviour, and the Blessed Virgin and the saints, and this good father, there
is no more trouble for poor Teresa!

The Marble Faun

By the time George Eliot published *Middlemarch* in 1871, seven years after
Nathaniel Hawthorne had died, she herself had read most of his major works.
It is not just *Romola* that is reminiscent of Hawthorne's last completed novel, as is
often suggested; rather, *Middlemarch,* with Dorothea as mother saint, rewrites the
hagiographic imagery associated with Hilda. The differences between the two figures reside very much in their authors' temperament and education, yet the son of
Puritans and the translator of *Leben Jesu* agree on one point: the normative conception of sainthood is inadequate. It follows the rule of the heart, not of the church or
of the world, and the path that rule dictates is various. For Hawthorne, inhabitant of
that space where the real and the imaginary intersect, sainthood leaps over theological differences to possess the Godhead in its own way, preserving both mystery and
internal sanctity. For Eliot, influenced by Comtean positivism, sainthood is activity,
a movement from willing the good to bringing it about in human terms. Dorothea
thus seems the fulfillment of Hilda, a corrective for a saint too virginal, too self-
contained, too unwilling to embrace the world.

In no sense did Eliot announce such an intention; rather, Hawthorne's influence seems to have been more subtle. Her letters suggest that she read the earlier novels of her "grand favourite,"[1] and also that she read *The Blithedale Romance*[2] by 11 September 1852, reread *The Scarlet Letter* in March 1857, and tried to find a copy of *The Marble Faun* in May 1860. Critics generally agree that *Romola* was influenced by *The Marble Faun,*[3] and some have suggested that both the theme of the legacy of evil and the characters in *Middlemarch* are allied with similar aspects in *The House of the Seven Gables* and *The Scarlet Letter* (Stokes 198–207). Yet *Middlemarch* bears the marks of a considered revision of Hawthorne's heroine Hilda as well as a rewriting of his romance aesthetic.

Hawthorne's well-known definition appears in the Preface to *The House of the Seven Gables,* where he juxtaposes "Romance" to "Novel." The former, he says, calls for "latitude" and enrichment of the "atmospherical medium," not "minute fidelity"; connects a "by-gone time" with the "present" instead of focusing on "the realities of the moment"; and, rather than being "impale[d] . . . with its moral, as with an iron rod," possesses "[a] high truth, indeed, fairly, finely, and skilfully wrought out, brightening at every step, and crowning the final development of a work of fiction" (2–3). The one law of the romance writer is not "to swerve aside from the truth of the human heart"; the one latitude is to choose the way truth is presented. Eliot, who insists that "Art must be either real and concrete, or ideal and eclectic" (*Letters* 2: 362), might agree with the law of "psychological realism" (Stokes 107) but would add to it a further element. The artist, she says in *Adam Bede,* must "give a faithful account of men and things as they have mirrored themselves in my mind . . . without trying to make things seem better than they were; dreading nothing, indeed, but falsity" (221–22, ch. 17). Adhering to the "truth of the human heart" and avoiding "falsity" are related;[4] but Eliot's aesthetic is repositioned as a moral stance, that if art does not picture the "ugly, stupid, inconsistent people" who are given as companions to "tolerate, pity and love, . . . we may happen to leave them quite out of our religion and philosophy and frame lofty theories which only fit a world of extremes" (222–24, ch. 17).

In Hilda, Hawthorne presents the kind of "angel . . . a face paled by the celestial light" or "Madonna, turning her mild face upward and opening her arms to welcome the divine glory" that Eliot rejects in her artistic manifesto in *Adam Bede* in favor of "the old women scraping carrots with their work-worn hands" (224, ch. 17). Yet Eliot, like Hawthorne, uses the iconography and nomenclature of sainthood as a marking and isolating device for Dorothea, and both authors define sainthood through the responses of the other characters. The two would agree that a pattern of behavior motivated by internal ethical standards is the key, but beyond that, on how these standards are derived and put into practice, they would differ.

For Hilda and Dorothea, clothing is associated with a moral stance. Hilda chooses white as a statement about purity, both literally when she feeds her doves (*Marble Faun* 52, ch. 6) and figuratively when she refuses to console Miriam, after the model has been murdered: "I am a poor, lonely girl, whom God has set here in an evil world, and given her only a white robe, and bid her wear it back to him, as white as when she put it on" (208, ch. 23). The "white-souled" Hilda, as Miriam calls her, engenders a "pure, white atmosphere" as a barrier; her goal is preserving her self, rather than helping others. In contrast, Dorothea's clothing is tinted, or tainted with a hint of "worldly" color: she wears pale colors, like the Quaker gray that attracts the attention of the painter Naumann or the pale blue pelisse that blends with the faded upholstery in her boudoir. Her movement toward selflessness is mirrored in the neutrality of her dress; during her married life, her most characteristic outfit is the "plain dress of some thin woolen-white material . . . as if she were under a vow to be different from all other women" (*Middlemarch* 354, ch. 37). She conveys a personal style, her dress notable for its plainness, her shapeliness such that "she could wear sleeves not less bare of style than those in which the blessed Virgin appeared to Italian painters" (7, ch. 1). Her dress seems to belie her passionate response to her mother's jewels, those "fragments of heaven" (13, ch. 1), yet Dorothea herself becomes like a jewel, associated with light, her religious belief centered on "desiring what is perfectly good" and so "widening the skirts of light and making the struggle with darkness narrower" (382, ch. 39). Hilda's statement is static: she seeks to preserve her goodness. Dorothea's is dynamic: the operative words—"desiring," "widening," "making"—forecast openness and action.

The visual iconography of dress is expressed verbally in the nomenclature and epithets of divinity, and again the focus in Eliot is on inclusiveness. Kenyon, who worships Hilda's "remote and shy divinity" (*Marble Faun* 122, ch. 13), sees her as a figure of "peaceful beatitude," as "Saint Hilda" (363–64, ch. 40). In her tower where she tends the Virgin Mary's lamp, she is figured as "far above" and "unattainable," a "spirit, . . . with the evening glory around her head" (372, ch. 40). Her aloofness is a matter of space and spirit: the disconsolate Miriam sees Hilda's moral repugnance as appropriate for an angel but judges that her womanhood is hardened by her sinlessness (209, ch. 23). Like Hilda, Dorothea is divinized by those around her. In a generalized sense, Will, like Kenyon, sees her as divine: she is an "angel beguiled" (*Middlemarch* 204, ch. 21); he appreciates the "divineness," not the artistry, of her pose as Santa Clara (212, ch. 22); and in her he sees "heaven" (621, ch. 62). These and other commonplace observations speak of Will's attraction; yet Lydgate, whose definition of perfect womanhood lies in a narrower vein, validates the nomenclature, going even further by identifying Dorothea with the Virgin Mary.

The Marian associations by which both Dorothea[5] and Hilda are identified express their differing attitudes toward community and service. Hawthorne's heroine persistently rejects the terminology, while Eliot's seems largely unconscious of it. Although she devotedly tends the flame at the Virgin's shrine in her tower, thereby earning the veneration of the common folk, Hilda insists that she is only giving due honor to "divine Womanhood." For Hilda the concept remains an abstraction, however. Distraught over witnessing the murder, she searches the altarpieces in

Rome for a "virgin mother" but is unable to find the mixture of earthliness and heavenliness, understanding and forgiveness, that she needs:

> a face of celestial beauty, but human as well as heavenly, and with the shadow of past grief upon it; bright with immortal youth, yet matronly and motherly; and endowed with a queenly dignity, but infinitely tender as the highest and deepest attribute of her divinity. (*Marble Faun* 348, ch. 38)

What she looks for seems figured in Dorothea, who, for Lydgate and others, "has a heart large enough for the Virgin Mary" (*Middlemarch* 758, ch. 76). Both Hilda and Dorothea are motherless; the one searches for comfort, and the other comforts.

In her desire for the "perfectly good," Dorothea seeks to participate in human affairs, not to isolate herself. She is, moreover, associated with multiple hagiographical figures whose martyrdom suggests personal pain and self-abnegation as well as connection to a larger historical/theological process. Before her marriage, she is said to have the quietude and "air of repose . . . of Santa Barbara, looking out from her tower" (*Middlemarch* 86, ch. 10); Barbara, who converted to Christianity when her father imprisoned her in a tower, presents a figure of virginal faith, much as Dorothea does. During her honeymoon, however, Dorothea poses as Santa Clara for Naumann's painting, a pose both ironic and appropriate, for like the Poor Clares, who were devoted to a life of austerity, she wishes to dispose of the wealth she has gained by her marriage. Finally, after Casaubon's death, when she longs for action, she rejects the prospect of sitting "like a model for Saint Catherine looking rapturously at Celia's baby" (523, ch. 54). These specific references are commentaries not just on her immediate actions but also on her development: she moves to reject a position of submissive idealism.

That decision is also exemplified spatially. While Hilda and Dorothea view the world from above, from tower and boudoir, Hilda's promise to deliver Miriam's packet plunges her only momentarily into the liveliness of the streets. Hilda is imprisoned and sequestered by the Roman Catholic establishment, and, set free again, she puts herself in Kenyon's care. She is involved only tangentially and unwittingly in the political undercurrents of the novel, for it is said that if her lamp goes out, as it does when she is kept sequestered in the convent after delivering the packet, then the property reverts to the church (*Marble Faun* 52, ch. 6). Dorothea, on the other hand, involves herself deliberately with people she knows, the vista from her boudoir changing with her growth in moral understanding. At first the focus is on the lime tree avenue with all of the figures frozen into blue-green tapestry art (*Middlemarch* 73, ch. 9); then, when the Casaubons return from their honeymoon, the decor appears ghostly, heightening the tension between the outdoors and the indoors, between static purity and active moral life. The "white earth" and "white branches" and "uniform whiteness" that make up the "crystalline purity of the outdoor snow" are reminiscent of the merciless "pure, white atmosphere" in which Hilda seeks to discern the truth; and both kinds of atmospheres contrast with the "sentient commingled innocence" of Dorothea's own "breathing whiteness" and clinging "white fur" (267, ch. 28). Dorothea's vista changes to encompass human beings; after her night of despair over the apparent love affair between Rosamond and Will, she looks beyond the gates into the road and the fields and sees the living, working humans of whom the blue-green tapestry men and women are a pale reflection (777, ch. 80). Like Hilda, Dorothea leaves her tower, but rather than taking refuge in a conventional prison, a return to virginal innocence, she goes to Rosamond to offer sympathy and forgiveness.

The iconography of the hand bears out these differing ideas of service. Kenyon has sculpted Hilda's hand in marble: it is dainty and beautiful; Miriam recognizes its "maiden palm" and "delicate fingertips" (*Marble Faun* 120, ch. 13). Its very delicacy implies fragility, a separation from the active workaday world. In contrast, Dorothea's "were not thin hands; or small hands, but powerful, feminine, maternal hands" (*Middlemarch* 38, ch. 4); her "beautiful," "wonderful" hand is partly what appeals to the artist Naumann (184, ch. 19). This contrast is indicative of the way in which Eliot both redefines "feminine" and re-creates Hilda as a figure with greater moral breadth.

Hilda's hand is used to create art at one remove, not to depict the old women or the "heavy clowns taking holiday in a dingy pot-house" of Eliot's favorite Dutch paintings, but rather to copy what other artists have produced. In terms of Hawthorne's aesthetic, Hilda has called upon "the warmth and richness of a woman's sympathy; not by any intellectual effort, but by this strength of heart, and this guiding light of sympathy, she went straight to the central point" (*Marble Faun* 56–57, ch. 6). She venerates the old masters religiously as Dorothea venerates Casaubon as an "affable archangel" (*Middlemarch* 277, ch. 29), and the old masters return her regard by "guiding her delicate white hand" (*Marble Faun* 58, ch. 6). Indeed,

> assisted by the delicate skill and accuracy of her slender hand . . . the girl was but a finer instrument, a more exquisitely effective piece of mechanism, by the help of which the spirit of some great departed Painter now first achieved his ideal, centuries after his own earthly hand, that other tool, had turned to dust. (59, ch. 6)

While Hilda sacrifices herself to art, she does not respond to human need in the same way. Dorothea, who feels ignorant and stupid in front of the old masters, figures as a corrective: her inexperience and warm sensibilities combine so that she feels the "weight of unintelligible Rome" as a "vast wreck of ambitious ideals, sensual and spiritual, mixed confusedly with the signs of breathing forgetfulness and degradation" (*Middlemarch* 188, ch. 20). Her sympathies are at once more theoretical and more human than Hilda's. The old masters she venerates are philosophical; "learned men kept the only oil," and knowledge is the lamp she seeks (85, ch. 10). Hilda, who wants to remain innocent, dislikes explaining away mystery and wonder (*Marble*

Faun 104, ch. 12), and her sympathies are poured into art. While Hawthorne condones her choice of the higher and nobler road on which her own desires are sublimated to those of the "great departed ones" (51, ch. 6), Eliot shows how such veneration is a dead end, unable to satisfy Dorothea's yearning for well-defined duties (44, ch. 5), for "action both rational and ardent" (85, ch. 10).

Unlike Hilda, Dorothea discovers that the "dead hand" of the past is both stifling and restrictive. She yearns to turn toward others: her theory about goodness—that desiring the good is a way of combatting evil—is applied in a communal, rather than an isolationist way. The record of whom Dorothea helps—Casaubon, Will, Lydgate, Rosamond, Farebrother—is long and blends the moral with the material. From the first she has wanted to help others by providing new cottages, clothing, and a village school but is frustrated in her efforts; she is disturbed that she should "have so much more than [her] share without doing anything for others" (*Middlemarch* 382, ch. 39). This sense of serving others is strong; she wishes to divide her income with Will, feeling that he has been unfairly deprived; and she espouses a universalist Christian teaching, one that "brings in the most people as sharers in it" (486, ch. 50). Her income is burdensome to her because "it is so difficult to make shares at all even" (757, ch. 76).

Hawthorne's passing reference to Teresa, adopted by Eliot as a kind of coda for her novel, figures as a touchstone for the differing perspectives of the two characters. The Teresa whom Hilda meets as she searches fruitlessly for a virgin mother in St. Peter's is a simple Italian woman rejoicing over newfound spiritual happiness; confession has relieved her of "trouble," as it will relieve Hilda (*Marble Faun* 356, ch. 39). Both are freed of their burdens, and being thus freed, Hilda walks into imprisonment by delivering Miriam's packet, effectively disappearing from the surface action of the novel. Dorothea, on the other hand, receives no external comfort and, indeed, finds her best refuge in trouble itself—taking action, making a difference in someone's life. Just as Hilda was unable to identify a mother Madonna, the father figure Dorothea sought for in Casaubon is unavailable. Her confessions are made by herself to herself in her boudoir. The first ends with the realization that "the energy that would animate a crime is not more than is wanted to inspire a resolved submission when the noble habit of the soul reasserts itself" (*Middlemarch* 418, ch. 42); that is, she understands that the same energy expended in rebuffing Casaubon might also be directed toward compassion and self-discipline. Her second confession ends with the similar but more pointed realization that her actions affect not just her life but others' lives—Rosamond's, Will's, Lydgate's. In both instances, then, she refocuses from self to others and finds relief in moral action.

Perhaps the same tendency is obvious in the Preface and Prelude, with Hawthorne writing about himself and Eliot about Saint Theresa[6] and the readerly "we." Hawthorne writes about writing, maintaining that he has always performed for the "gentle reader," without ever having met that audience face to face; Eliot plunges into a story about Saint Theresa, the context for Dorothea, thereby immediately beginning the *action* of writing. Again, Hawthorne protests that the text is "merely a fanciful story, evolving a thoughtful moral," rather than a picture of "Italian manners and character"; Italy is "a sort of poetic or fairy precinct, where actualities would not be so terribly insisted upon" (*Marble Faun* 3). Eliot insists upon the serious actualities, the "meanness of opportunity," at the beginning (*Middlemarch* 3). In *Middlemarch* "fairy" Italy is where Dorothea discovers the inadequacies of romance, not its satisfactions; the very texture of the novel is the England of railroads and politics and journalism and pawnbrokers. Hawthorne seeks to transform these actualities into romance to showcase the triumph of a character who begins from a high moral stance, while Eliot shows the way in which Dorothea learns to transform her "actualities" into a field of moral action. The very development of the two characters, Dorothea a psychologically realistic rewriting of Hilda, mirrors the aesthetic and critical postures of the authors.

Notes

1. Edward Stokes comments that Hawthorne was Eliot's "grand favourite" because "both believed in the moral . . . function of fiction; they were both intensely interested in the inner life; they both recognized the subjective nature of the novel or romance" (113).

2. The problem of whether Eliot commented formally on *Blithedale Romance* remains unsolved, with the evidential weight against her authorship of the October 1852 *Blithedale* commentary in *Westminster Review.* Edward Stokes surveys the entire controversy (90–92). James D. Rust's argument that the review is stylistically reminiscent of Eliot is discussed by Gordon Haight in his edition of the *Letters* and elsewhere and contested by Thomas Pinney and Richard Stang on the basis of critical disparity (Eliot, a realist, would be unlikely to call for reality as a mere backdrop to the ideal).

3. Stokes conveniently groups the arguments, making useful references to discussions by Ellin Jane Ringler, Mario Praz, and Curtis Dahl (173–89). He refers as well to his own contention that both Hilda and Romola undergo a "transformation . . . from Virgin to Madonna" (179).

4. Eliot's interest in real figures rather than idealized ones is related to her delight in the truthfulness of Dutch paintings. Not adverse to paintings of angels or of Madonnas, Eliot nonetheless finds greatest beauty in "the secret of deep human sympathy" (*Adam Bede* 224, ch. 17). Hawthorne also uses the analogy but, with reference to *The House of the Seven Gables,* is concerned with the finish, rather than the subject matter: on 3 Nov. 1850, he writes to J. T. Fields, "Many passages . . . ought to be finished with the minuteness of a Dutch picture, in order to give them their proper effect. . . . [T]he fact is, in writing a romance, a man is always—or always ought to be—careering on the utmost verge of a precipitous absurdity, and the skill lies in coming as close as possible, without actually tumbling over" (*Letters* 371).

5. Jill Matus, who gives a gendered reading of the connection between Madonna iconography and art, argues that the Madonna imagery reinterprets and validates social expectations of actual maternity (286). More than that: the sequence of "motherhood, sexuality, and

saintliness" is fulfilled when Dorothea becomes a metaphorical mother in her anguish over Will's supposed betrayal (293, 295). Matus also brings together other, scattered Marian references related to manuscript deletions (290), Naumann's artistic comments (291), and the Renaissance use of hands (295).

6. In contrast to Gordon Haight, who sees the Theresan imagery as a signpost to reform, Franklin E. Court suggests that the Prelude is an ironic commentary on the dangers of mystical egoism (23) and that eventually Dorothea becomes a "Positivist Madonna," one of the women who, through "ethical superiority . . . have the capacity to consecrate their rational and imaginative faculties to the service of feeling rather than blessedness" (25).

Works Cited

Attwater, Donald. *A Dictionary of Saints*. New York: Penguin, 1981.

Court, Franklin. "The Image of St. Theresa in *Middlemarch* and Positive Ethics." *Victorian Newsletter* 63 (1983): 21–25.

Eliot, George. *Adam Bede*. Vol. 1 of the *Complete Works of George Eliot*. 12 vols. New York: Sproul, 1899.

——. *The George Eliot Letters*. Ed. Gordon S. Haight. 9 vols. New Haven: Yale UP, 1954–78.

——. *Middlemarch*. Ed. David Carroll. Clarendon Edition. Gen. ed. Gordon S. Haight. Oxford: Clarendon, 1986.

Hawthorne, Nathaniel. *The House of the Seven Gables*. Vol. 2 of the *Centenary Edition of the Works of Nathaniel Hawthorne*. Ed. William Charvat et al. Columbus: Ohio State UP, 1965.

——. *The Letters, 1843–1865*. Vol. 16 of the *Centenary Edition*. Ed. William Charvat et al. Columbus: Ohio State UP, 1985.

——. *The Marble Faun; or, The Romance of Monte Beni*. Vol. 4 of the *Centenary Edition*. Ed. William Charvat et al. Columbus: Ohio State UP, 1968.

Matus, Jill. "The Iconography of Motherhood: Word and Image in *Middlemarch*." *English Studies in Canada* 3 (1991): 283–300.

Pinney, Thomas. *Essays*. New York: Columbia UP, 1963.

Rust, James D. "George Eliot on *The Blithedale Romance*." *Boston Public Library Quarterly* 7 (1955): 207–15.

Stang, Richard. *The Theory of the Novel in England, 1850–1870*. New York: Columbia UP, 1959.

Stokes, Edward. *Hawthorne's Influence on Dickens and George Eliot*. St. Lucia and New York: U of Queensland P, 1985.

"PARTLY SYMPATHY
AND PARTLY REBELLION"

Carol M. Bensick

Fruitful studies in Ward's fiction will result from a comparative/
contrastive look at how she and Hawthorne treat social issues and
explore the claims of the heart and head.

My subject is a four-page letter written by the then famous English novelist Mary Augusta Arnold (who published as "Mrs. Humphry") Ward (1851–1920) to U.S. Ambassador Joseph Choate for publication in a volume of the *Essex Institute Historical Collections* commemorating the hundredth anniversary of the birth of Nathaniel Hawthorne.[1] I apologize in advance for a certain amount of confessionalizing at the start. If an excuse is required, let it be the example of Hawthorne's own practice.

As the flexible title of our collection shows, each of us faced a choice of emphasis. In my case, I could write an essay *on Hawthorne* (through Mrs. Humphry Ward); or I could write an essay *on Mrs. Humphry Ward* (through Hawthorne). In both the precomposition moments I invoked when I began, I wanted to write on the most substantial topic I could. In my first moment I assumed this was the former. In my second this assumption had vanished. For others, the choice might still be automatic, or axiomatic, but for me, when and where (like Georgiana Aylmer) I found myself, it was at least temporarily unavailable. I had no confidence, because no experience, in the latter choice. But I also saw no option. And unlike the entrapments I was accustomed to live with on a daily basis, this was an entrapment that was strangely exhilarating.

Now, quickly. To have wound up seeming to draft Mrs. Humphry Ward into service as some sort of feminist heroine is admittedly strange. Here was a woman who married at twenty-one, immersed herself in the career of a son, spurned conventional women's topics in fiction, and publicly campaigned against women's suffrage. To suggest that such a woman lacked—in an age which, like our own, made the possession of such a thing an explicit possibility—"a feminist consciousness" would be a poor joke.

I would conceal nothing. According to the impersonal report of mid-twentieth-century literary history speaking in the voice of Edward Wagenknecht, while women writers like Olive Schreiner, Kate Chopin, Charlotte Perkins Gilman, and more obliquely, Edith Wharton were pioneering a distinctively feminist Anglophone fiction, Mrs. Ward wrote about "politics," "religion," "history," and "war." At a time when men and women alike were debating woman's nature and women's rights, the particular public controversy that Mrs. Ward chose to enter was over religion and science.[2] And when all else has been said, there is always that matter of her name. How can a woman who calls herself "Mrs. Humphry Ward" be—if not a feminist—at least of service to feminism? *Can* a woman who calls herself "Mrs. Humphry Ward" be of service to feminism?

Obviously I think she can. Not only on the weak account (malgré lui) but on the strong one. Reconstructing Mrs. Ward as a feminist is worthwhile above all for what it implies. To tease or torture feminist implications out of the text of (say) Olive Schreiner would be of scant force. Everyone *knows* Schreiner is a rebel against contemporary social constructions of gender, and only people already sympathetic to feminism are likely to read either her or her critics. But Mrs. Ward is someone whom traditional men and women, then and later, embraced. Indeed, she was a woman a man could point to in triumph as proof that feminism was at best unnecessary to female happiness or achievement. As long as certain women persist in denying reality to feminist accounts of women's experience and legitimacy to women's complaints, so long will feminism doubt its own founding insights. "I *thought* women were being oppressed but geez, if *she* so confidently *denies* it, maybe I was wrong . . . (again) . . ."

If even a woman who repressed even her own name can be reconstructed for feminism, I am supposing, maybe Christina Sommers, Phyllis Shlafly, Marabel Morgan, Sally Jessy Raphael, and whoever each reader will, need not be causes of despair. As for Hawthorne: he can take it.

To conclude this long preamble, then, the claims I initially entertained turned on treating Mrs. Ward either as a Hawthorne critic or as a kindred novelist. It is in frank hopes of making a statement, not only of unaccustomed timeliness, but of greater real substance than I judge any of those initial claims had potential to found that I have challenged my timidity to set them aside. Instead of a(nother) literary-historical reading of a literary-historical reading, then, what I have attempted to do is to explore Mrs. Ward's letter for traces of her personal response to Hawthorne as a reader. These traces in turn I have, as a matter of frank premeditation, attempted to interpret in terms of gender. That this is my first such attempt will undoubtedly be clear; such an effect, however, in the words of Margaret Fuller anticipating derision in response to a foible, "can't be helped."

With a brief contextualization of Mrs. Ward and her letter and a final, reiterated admission that to do this to Mrs. Ward is to read her, very much, "against the grain" (and, also, perhaps to put some strain on the project of this collection), we begin.

In 1904, a mixed group of distinguished individuals—American and foreign writers, and American diplomats and statesmen—contributed letters to a special issue of the *Historical Collections* of the Salem, Massachusetts, Essex Institute, an issue devoted to the commemoration of exercises it held in honor of the centenary of Nathaniel Hawthorne's birth. One of these individuals was the English novelist Mary A. Ward, who published as Mrs. Humphry Ward.

The invitations came about in this manner. The president of the Essex Institute, Robert Rantoul, had initially invited Joseph Choate, then U.S. ambassador to Great Britain, to join the mayor of Salem, the pastor of the First Church in Cambridge, one of the overseers of Bowdoin College, and the son of Ralph Waldo Emerson (to name only the individuals who actually spoke) in delivering an address at the Salem ceremony. Choate, as he wrote to Rantoul, found himself prevented by "public duties" from attending the ceremony. In intended compensation, Choate solicited letters from "celebrated writers and critics" in England. These "eminent writers and persons" were Henry James, Andrew Lang, M.P. James Bryce (evidently the "person" of Choate's peculiar phrase), and Mrs. Ward.[3]

In asking Mrs. Humphry Ward to write a letter on the subject of the Hawthorne centenary, Joseph Choate was asking a literary eminence. In point of output, when her works were collected in 1909 they would run to sixteen volumes, and she still had eleven more years of productivity ahead. In point of esteem, according to Edward Wagenknecht, "for many years Mrs. Ward was regarded as George Eliot's successor." (One must admit that this estimate would not have impressed Hawthorne.) But in her lifetime Mrs. Ward achieved an even greater coup: she won, from no less a figure than Tolstoy, the name of "the greatest living English novelist." When we recall that her contemporaries included such individuals as Hardy and Conrad, not to mention Henry James, one hardly knows by which phenomenon (besides Tolstoy's unsexist cosmopolitanism) to be more greatly awed: Mrs. Ward's contemporary renown, or her near invisibility in standard twentieth-century literary history.

We can now turn to explore our specific concern of how gender inflects Mrs. Ward's letter. Stated preferences for texts, for scenes within texts, and explicit terms of approbation can provide an initial basis for interrogation.

The entire list of works Mrs. Ward mentions or invokes (in order) in her letter includes *The Scarlet Letter, The Marble Faun, The House of the Seven Gables* (twice), "Malvin's Burial" (*sic*), "The Ambitious Guest," "Rappaccini's Daughter," "The Notebooks" (*sic;* twice), "The Seven Vagabonds," and "The Custom-House." (As a matter of comparison, Henry James in his letter to the institute mentions only the four novels.) Not forgetting that Mrs. Ward herself does not make her own list from our point of view, our question is, Can deliberately considering this list as one made by a woman yield any interesting results?

(With its central female parts) the absence from her list of *The Blithedale Romance* is perhaps most striking. Similarly so, for the same reason, when we turn to the stories is the omission of "The Birth-mark" and "The Artist of the Beautiful." The appearance, instead, of *The House of the Seven Gables* with its choice of the apparently ultraconventional Phoebe and comical Hepzibah, of *The Marble Faun* with its prim Hilda and shamed Miriam, of "Malvin" with its domestic Dorcas, of "Guest" with its stereotypical family, of the male-only "Custom-House," and of "Rappaccini" with its martyred Beatrice suggests an indifference if not hostility to untraditional women. Which way we think "The Seven Vagabonds" cuts will depend on whether we see its gypsy as a realistic historical portrait of a liberated woman or the projection of a prurient (white) male fantasy.

Ward's reading of *The Scarlet Letter,* however, is different. It is the one text she stresses the most. There is nothing, we may think, particularly *gendered* about that. Given that most people would make the same choice, is there anything distinctive about Mrs. Ward's? Assuming there is, can it be interestingly related (in spite of her own opaqueness on the category) to gender?

Attending to the particular *scenes* from the novel which Ward cites bears out these possibilities. As we proceed we must recognize that even as we are analyzing Mrs. Ward she is simultaneously analyzing us. We learn about our selves as she tells us about hers.

The scenes Ward likes in *The Scarlet Letter*—or rather does not like but was (as a child) moved by to "a sort of aching and painful joy"—are two. One is the scene when Pearl compels Hester to resume the "scarlet letter." The second is the death of Dimmesdale.

What is there to say about an account which, mentioning only two scenes from the novel, mentions just those? To give this question point, we need merely ask what other scenes from the book a reader might recall. What about, for instance, "The Minister's Vigil"? Or the opening scene on the scaffold? Not Ward's choice of scenes only but her choice of characters as well might come to seem strikingly limited. Had Hester (and Dimmesdale) sinned alone? We might not expect to hear about Mistress Hibbins or the Reverend John Wilson, but where is Roger Chillingworth? (It is true Mrs. Ward will mention him later. The reference, however, is noticeably vague ["the grim vengeance of"] and, uniquely among her examples as a group, lacks reference to any "scene.") It seems Ward (as little Mary Arnold) related to *The Scarlet Letter* exclusively "as a Love Story."[4]

Relating to it so, what was her response? In her own contemporary analysis, it was "partly sympathy and partly rebellion."

The account that follows her reading begins to fill in the content of this hybrid feeling. It is perhaps the most naive moment of a letter which quickly becomes quite public and professional. Ward tells Choate that she read the scene "Again and again," "insisting with myself that it must end" with the characters' escape, "and hardly able—though always conscious of its shadowy approach—to bear the moment" when Pearl returns the letter.

Ward's implicit interpretation of Dimmesdale's death scene adds further specification to her childish reaction. Speaking now as adult (and critic) she can evaluate the scene ("one of the most poignantly beautiful in literature," "one of the greatest things of imagination") and analyze it ("deriving its power from that stern spiritual energy which is its ultimate source"). But far more interestingly, what it left her with as a juvenile reader was an "awe and shudder." What could have produced this result?

Presumably Ward's reaction was due to the meaning she gave the scene. To her, Dimmesdale's dying evidenced one concrete thing. Precisely, his death represented his refusal to answer Hester's plea for an assurance that they two would meet in heaven. Nothing here about sin or guilt or salvation or redemption. And what this refusal meant to Ward was "a last denial of hope."

Twice, then, Ward's letter speaks of hope. But hope for what? Putting the two scenes together, the answer to that question seems to be a man's and woman's happy romantic union. The fascination of *The Scarlet Letter* for Ward seems to be that it raises the plausible specter of this hope—indeed, creates it—and then—twice—crushes it. The novel, so her account suggests, teaches readers to believe that a woman could find fulfillment in romantic-sexual-domestic relations with a man, and then it refuses to pay up. "And"—we are tempted to say, regarding Hawthorne—Mrs. Ward "was enough of a woman scarcely to forgive him."

Ward proceeds to theorize that the thing which leads Hawthorne to deny Hester and his women readers is his trait of "austerity."[5] Though she refers this immediately to a somewhat stereotyped explanation of "his deep-rooted Puritanism" (an explanation which she does not even bother to pretend is original by elaborating it with an admitted but not referenced quotation as "what has been [,]" ho-hum, "often pointed to as 'the sense of sin' in him"), the unusual word reverberates as a genuine contribution to the problem. Would a male critic respond to Hawthorne as "austere"?

It may be doubted. A male reader has for his (hetero)erotic delectation bevies of lavishly described opulent females. Where the male reader has these "dark ladies" (as well as attractive female extras, including, for example, Dimmesdale's parishioners with their "white bosoms"), the female reader, seeking a (hetero)erotic object, gets the reiterated choice between two types I have theorized privately as the Jock and the Nerd: on the one side, rude and hairy present and former blacksmiths (Hollingsworth, Robert Danforth, Aminadab, Robert), on the other pale, sick, skinny (omitting Owen Warland's "fat" phase) artist-intellectuals (Dimmesdale, Fanshawe, Aylmer). Those few males who are explicitly represented as normatively good-looking have other drawbacks: Donatello is underwitted (and violent); Coverdale and Giovanni Guasconti are suspicious and critical.[6] The Hawthorne male whose good looks are most insisted on, Westervelt, is offered as a pimp and associated with the devil. Worst of all, whereas the Hawthorne male has the additional life choice, portrayed as quite desirable, of bachelorhood, the Hawthorne female can only be happy with a man.

For a man who desires to do so, to read Hawthorne for his sexual plot "as a man" is to enjoy a fantasy scenario in which a succession of gorgeous women throw themselves at him and in which, what is much more, he has the satisfaction of ultimately *rejecting* them. This leaves the woman reading Hawthorne as a woman to experience over and over again unrequited love: to be vicariously insulted, ignored, suspected, accused, rejected, poisoned, hushed, insulted. Apart, admittedly, from *Fanshawe,* the only heterosexually successful marriages (in a universe where marriage is the only hope of happiness a woman has) Hawthorne women make are (in "The Artist of the Beautiful" and *Septimius Felton*) with redneck blacksmiths. Males of education and refinement flee or refuse women. In contemporary legal terms, the woman in Hawthorne's universe is condemned to sexual discrimination, sexual harassment, and sexual abuse.[7]

If anything like this is anything like true, for an actual woman to write a "tribute" to Hawthorne will require stupendous repression. Happily, according to the distinctive character that literary history has given her, this Mrs. Humphry Ward *was.* In the words of the ever-serviceable Wagenknecht, Mrs. Ward stars in a chapter of *Cavalcade of the English Novel* called "Victorian Sunset" as "naturally the first" of "the conservatives" who make up the "current" against which the "counter-currents" of "Progressives" flowed during "the latter end of Victoria's reign." For Wagenknecht, Mrs. Ward is "the perfect symbol of everything that was stuffy in Victorianism." Similarly, for Samuel Chew of BaughBrookChewMaloneandSherburn, Ward forms the mainstream, establishment, status-quo background against which Olive Schreiner can appear as a specimen of "the 'new' feminism which was to gain ground during the last years of the century." If we admit these things are true, but deny that Ward was repressed, we must hold that she lacked anything that needed repression. In view of our account of her letter on Hawthorne (which Wagenknecht and Chew have, understandably, not read), we may doubt this.

Is a reaction of (part) "rebellion" merely, to use a self-description from elsewhere in her letter, "irrational"? Is there any other way for us, if not for her, to see this demand for a happy ending other than as an embarrassing instance of some rather conventional wishful thinking?

To dignify a feeling like the one Ward admits having had of indignation or betrayal toward Hawthorne for Dimmesdale and Hester's failure to end up together it must be possible to think that the novel could have allowed the couple to do so. Only if the couple's failure to end up together is a result, not of historical and psychological probability and necessity, but of authorial fiat is rebellion appropriate. If Ward does (or did) think that Hawthorne kept his lovers apart arbitrarily—an act of aggression against the (women?) readers he had previously seduced into hoping for a happy outcome—does she have grounds?

If Mary Arnold reacted to the *Scarlet Letter,* to any degree that we have imagined, as a defraudment of the trusting reader—a very seduction and betrayal mirroring Dimmesdale's of Hester (to what salvation for the author is the already enjoyed reader being sacrificed?)—even Ward's situation as the writer of this letter is suddenly awkward. How shall she convey such a reaction to Joseph Choate without coming across inappropriately as a girl—as a very girl of girls?

A hypothesis that Ward did feel some inchoate uneasiness in view of her audience seems necessary to explain an element in the sentence at hand which otherwise would seem redundant. For if not to placate Choate, why preface the predicate, the business end of the sentence, the one concerning *The Scarlet Letter* and the other texts that she recalls from childhood, with a phrase like "long before I truly understood" them? I do not mean to imply that Ward does not believe her own words when she wrote them. On the contrary, I feel sure she thinks that there has been a growth, amounting to a qualitative or at least categorial improvement in her response to these texts. I notice merely that this phrase has the effect of turning the reaction she will go on to divulge, of mixed sympathy and rebellion, as the result of less than true understanding into false understanding. In short, it characterizes the reaction to *The Scarlet Letter* in terms of half rebellion as false. It falsifies to repudiate it.

Is such a conclusion on Ward's part inevitable? I am not sure. The effect of reading her account of that conflicted childhood reaction—which in fact is not unequivocally limited to childhood, as the phrase "I have read" could theoretically refer to that same morning—is just to experience such a reaction at least momentarily oneself. Or to feel momentarily that if such a reaction is not true to the novel the novel had been better if it were.

When Ward gets so far as to say of Dimmesdale's death scene that "the awe and shudder of such a last denial of hope has always remained with me as," I imagine that the noun we expect will follow is something like "an outrage." I imagine we expect her to charge Hawthorne with a three-way betrayal, embracing the characters, the readers, and his own self. When instead of anything like this I read the phrase "one of the greatest things of imagination" I fancy *we* feel betrayed by *her.* In midsentence, she has shifted from reader-response to classification and evaluation. To invoke the terms of classic Hawthorne criticism, from addressing my "heart" Ward suddenly switches her appeal to my "head."

And yet how can she do otherwise? She is writing a prescribed "tribute" to Hawthorne. How can she come out in her first paragraph attacking him? If we consider the matter from this point of view, we may well want to exchange our disappointment for gratitude. If she never mounts an attack on Hawthorne for his treatment of women readers through his treatment of his woman character, she succeeds remarkably in provoking us to do so.

Ward's claim to "rebellion" may come, it is true, *sous* the quadruple *rasure* of "long before I truly understood," "hardly rational," "partly," and ascription to childhood. Still it does come. And a reader (as one may suppose) can pick and choose, within the letter, which elements she may.

Notes

1. *Essex Institute Historical Collections* 41.1 (Jan. 1906): 49–54.

2. Edward Wagenknecht, *Cavalcade of the English Novel*, rev. ed. (New York: Holt, 1954) 386–90, 606–7. Needless to say, Ward's sense of these things would differ from contemporary ones. We would need to prefix the qualifier "male" in order to be sure to designate the same object of reference. If indeed Ward chose to write on the same subjects that male novelists did, this fact should make it all the easier to use a juxtaposition of her works with theirs to investigate the possibility of differences other than subject matter between male and female novelists.

According to Samuel Chew, Ward "took part" in a "lively discussion" between Thomas Henry Huxley and the Reverend Henry Wace, principal of King's College, London, on agnosticism, with special reference to Darwin. See Samuel C. Chew, "The Theory of Evolution and Its Repercussions," *Literary History of England*, ed. Albert C. Baugh et al. (New York: Appleton-Century-Crofts, 1948) 1307.

3. Of seven other letters or tributes rounding out the issue, two appear to have been solicited directly by Rantoul (from J. M. Barrie and Harriet Prescott Spofford); one (from D. G. Mitchell) seems to have been solicited by the secretary of the Essex Institute; four (from E. C. Stedman, W. R. Thayer, Mrs. E. S. P. Ward, and the author of an "account" of a 1904 Hawthorne family reunion) are identified by a footnote as being "selected" from "many letters received in connection with the Centennial"; from its placement after the "Appreciation of Hawthorne" by Lang, one " 'Estimate of Hawthorne' by Doctor Anton E. Schonbach of the University of Gratz" seems as if it might have been one of those solicited by Choate.

4. Ernest Sandeen, "*The Scarlet Letter* as a Love Story," *PMLA* 77 (1962): 425–35.

5. Curiously, the word "austerity" is a word that Edward Wagenknecht applies to Mrs. Ward herself.

6. The types of the Hawthorne (Heterosexual) Male in his relations with women would make an astonishing study. Bad manners (the Jock) and poor looks (the Nerd) are the least of the problem he poses for the Hawthorne Female, and therefore the female Hawthorne reader. For Robert S. Levine, Coverdale is "at times loathesome": "Fiction and Reform I," *Columbia History of the American Novel*, ed. Emory Elliot (New York, 1991) 135.

7. I find some of these concerns sharply articulated in an early article by Nina Baym. Baym, however, keeps up a critically correct distinction between Hawthorne and his bad male characters that I wish experimentally to waive. I applaud her pithy statement that "the recurrent image of a woman dead at a man's feet and through his efforts cannot be ignored" and would use it to authorize a more engaged analysis than she chose to pursue. Baym crucially and convincingly flags what she calls "the minor sexual sadism of 'Endicott and the

Red Cross,' 'The Snow Image,' and 'The Hollow of the Three Hills,'" and "the prurient relation between narrator and female auditor in 'Alice Doane's Appeal'" but concludes her essay, which is conducted in an even, almost urbane tone, by making these things matters of "art." I cannot imagine noticing such things and not undertaking a reinterpretation of Hawthorne from the point of view of gender from the ground up. Can any sadism be minor? "Thwarted Nature: Hawthorne as Feminist" is a crucial and was a pathbreaking essay, however, and I want to spread its fame. See Fritz Fleischmann, ed., *American Novelists Revisited: Essays in Feminist Criticism* (Boston: Hall, 1982).

HAWTHORNE'S LEGACY TO REBECCA HARDING DAVIS

Janice Milner Lasseter

In addition to the works treated herein, Hawthornean influence can be traced in the following pieces: "Anne," "The Wife's Story," "A Pearl of Great Price," "Marcia," "Earthen Pitchers," "A Wayside Episode," "An Ignoble Martyr," "Gray Cabins," "Tirar y Soult," "A Grumble," "Women in Literature," *Dallas Galbraith, A Law unto Herself, Frances Waldeaux,* and *Kitty's Choice; or, Berrytown.*

Rebecca Harding Davis, who was born 24 June 1831 and spent her first five years in Huntsville, Alabama, lived until her marriage in Wheeling, Virginia (later West Virginia). She was schooled informally by her mother and various tutors until at age twenty-four she entered Washington Female Seminary where she graduated with honors in 1848. Little is known about the period of her life between 1848 and the 1861 publication of *Life in the Iron-Mills,* her first and most significant work. This startling story about the laboring class began her work as a pioneer of American realism. In addition to fiction, Davis wrote extensively on women's issues and other social issues in newspapers and periodicals. Toward the end of her life, her fame was eclipsed by that of her son Richard Harding Davis, a glamorous celebrity and writer (Langford x). It is quite ironic that her *New York Times* obituary characterizes her as the mother of Richard Harding Davis, an irony repeated more recently in James Mellow's biography of Hawthorne. The book notes that Julian Hawthorne, on a trip as a journalist to Cuba to cover the Spanish-American War, was accompanied by Richard Harding Davis, but makes no mention of the visit of his now more famous mother's visit to the Hawthornes' home at the Wayside in 1862 (587). A prolific fiction writer, essayist, reviewer, and journalist who was well known during her publishing life, Davis virtually disappeared for almost eighty years until Tillie Olsen discovered Davis's first book serialized in musty, coverless copies of the *Atlantic Monthly* in an Omaha junkshop. In her unprecedented depiction of the grim lives of the working class, Davis inaugurates literary realism twenty years before those usually credited for its advent. This novella launched a fifty-year career which yielded a corpus of 500 published works including short stories, novellas, novels, sketches, and social commentary. Late in her life, Davis recalled the young Rebecca's avid reading of books by Bunyan, Maria Edgeworth, and Sir Walter Scott, but to Nathaniel Hawthorne she attributed the commonplace subject matter in her writing, although the Hawthorne effect surfaces variously in her work.

Davis considered herself the literary progeny of Nathaniel Hawthorne. Describing Hawthorne as "the greatest of living romancers," Davis reveals that Hawthorne's classic status was firmly in place as early as the 1860s. In naming him her literary forebear, she linked herself not to his artistic vision of romance but to "the commonplace folk and things which [she] saw every day" when, as a young girl, she read three of his unsigned early sketches.[1] The primary legacy Hawthorne bequeathed to Davis was subject matter. The characters who inhabit realist fiction were the common folk who became the center of her literary theory, a program she announces in her second work of fiction: "I want you to dig into this *commonplace,* this vulgar American life, and see what is in it. Sometimes I think it has a new and awful significance that we do not see." Expounding on this realist aim midway through the book, the author interjects:

> I live in the *commonplace.* Once or twice I have rashly tried my hand at dark conspiracies, and women rare and radiant in Italian bowers; but I have a friend who is sure to say, "Try and tell us about the butcher next door, my dear," . . . I must show men and women as they are in that especial State of the Union where I live. (*Margret Howth* 6, 102, 105)

Writing about the here and now, Davis participated in the creation of a national literature. In the "Boston in the Sixties" chapter of her memoir *Bits of Gossip,* she descried the prevailing philosophical discussions in pejorative terms amid an account of an evening spent at the Wayside, the Hawthornes' home in Concord. Arguing that the transcendentalist pawing over and dissecting the eternal verities lack "some back-bone of fact," she associates herself with Hawthorne's skepticism: "Whether Alcott, Emerson, and their disciples discussed pears or the War, their views gave you the same sense of unreality, of having been taken, as Hawthorne said, at too long a range" (36). From her perspective, Hawthorne "was an alien among these men, not of their kind," because they were out of touch with the "real world" and "never would see it as it is" (*Bits of Gossip* [hereafter *BOG*] 32–33). Those whose visions she found more authentic, more real, were credited with the flowering of American literature: "We were in the flush of our triumph in the beginnings of a national literature. We talked much of it. Irving, Prescott, and Longfellow had been English, we said, but these new men—Holmes, Lowell, and Hawthorne—were our own, the indigenous growth of the soil" (*BOG* 47). Her ambition to join this literary pantheon, the influence her early reading of Hawthorne's sketches exerted over her, and their similar attitudes toward the Civil War deepened her awe of Hawthorne.

Respect for other writers was characteristic of Davis, but not reverence. In her memoir, awe characterizes her analysis of Hawthorne. He replied to her youthful letter, "saying that he was then at Washington, and was coming . . . to see coming to see . . . me. *Me.* Well, I suppose Esther felt a little in that way when the king's sceptre touched her" (*BOG* 31). That scepter imbued her, she believed, with a magic touch which issued her into "his enchanted country" (*BOG* 31, 64). Its magical properties did not grant her a place alongside him in the literary canon emerging in the 1860s, but Hawthorne's "touch" did steep her in a literary practice that has earned her, finally, a place in the canon as a pioneer of American realism.

Davis's debut into American letters with *Life in the Iron-Mills* in the *Atlantic Monthly* (1861) almost coincided with her reading of Hawthorne's *Twice-told Tales.* In this his first collection, she learned the name of the author whose literary art had enchanted her as a child. Her memoir recalls her climbing into a tree-house erected in a cherry tree back of her Wheeling (not yet West) Virginia, home with a two-volume set titled *Moral Tales.*

> It was in two volumes; the cover was of yellow paper and the name was "Moral Tales." . . . The publisher of "Moral Tales," whoever he was, had probably stolen these anonymous papers from the annuals in which they appeared. Nobody called him to account. Their author was then, as he tells us somewhere, the "obscurest man of letters in America." (*BOG* 30–31)

Among the tales were "two or three unsigned stories" she recalled with precision:

> One was a story told by a town-pump, and another the account of the rambles of a little girl like myself, and still another a description of a Sunday morning in a quiet town like our sleepy village . . . in these papers the *commonplace* folk and things which I saw every day took on a sudden mystery and charm. (*BOG* 30)

The stories mentioned—"Little Annie's Ramble," "A Rill from the Town Pump," and "Sunday at Home"—do not appear in *Moral Tales,* but the specificity in her naming and description of the book leaves no doubt that she did indeed read such a book and recognized some of Hawthorne's work there.

Moral Tales is "a collection of anonymous pieces, probably pirated from annual gift books," as Jane Atteridge Rose plausibly explains (4). Published in 1840 by Littlefield Press under the name of Samuel Griswold Goodrich, *Moral Tales* contains six works by Hawthorne: "The Wedding Knell" and "David Swan" appear in volume 1; "Night Sketches, beneath an Umbrella," "The Canterbury Pilgrims," "The Haunted Mind," and "Sights from a Steeple" in volume 2. But the stories Davis recalled were published elsewhere. Of Hawthorne's stories that did appear in *Moral*

Tales, only two seem akin to the three she recalls as having influenced her. "Sights from a Steeple" shares with "Little Annie's Ramble" a narrator surveying town life. But storms, boiling seas, and darkness infuse "Sights from a Steeple" with Gothic undertones. "Night Sketches, beneath an Umbrella" has a lonely narrator noting the people he meets on a stormy night's walk. The spectral quality of "The Wedding Knell," the oneiric ambience in "David Swan" and "The Haunted Mind," and the parabolic elements of "The Canterbury Pilgrims" would have interested Davis. Similar qualities in Edgeworth, Bunyan, and Scott had engaged her interest (*BOG* 31). Not these Gothic qualities alone but also the authors' knights, pilgrims, and fiends shared the "magic world" of the commonplace folks in the three sketches she recalls as having influenced her (*BOG* 30).

The gloomy tone of Hawthorne's work in *Moral Tales* may account for the specificity of her recall of the book itself. That eerie quality emanating from human doubt and moral gloom as glosses on the commonplace coexists, even complements, her sense of herself as one who tends to see both sides of any issue, a trait she believed she shared with Hawthorne, as we will see later (*BOG* 109). Davis employs Hawthorne's use of the common folk and common places for her stories about people and places not traditionally thought proper subjects for artistic expression in the early 1860s. She wants to convey the underside of conventional precepts and social mores, to lead her readers into "the fog and . . . foul effluvia" as a means of correcting demeaning and destructive social practices. As Howells would say in 1881, realists want "to know and to tell the truth," and the truth of the commonplace in American culture for Davis was all too often fiercely realistic.

The correspondences between those three sketches in which she discovered the magic of the commonplace may be detected in *Life in the Iron-Mills, Margret Howth: A Story of To-Day, Waiting for the Verdict,* and some of her short fiction. *Life in the Iron-Mills'* treatment of the commonplace resonates with the somber mood of her invitation into a new kind of fiction:

> I want you to hide your disgust, take no heed to your clean clothes, and come right down with me,—here, into the thickest of the fog and mud and foul effluvia. I want you to hear this story. This is a secret down here, in this nightmare fog, that has lain dumb for centuries: I want to make it a real thing to you. (13–14)

The moral gloom resident in much of Hawthorne's work is usually associated with sin, guilt, and doubt, not specifically social reform. Still as Richard Brodhead posits, despite his attempt to detach himself from the social dramas of his time, Hawthorne wound up exploding them into narratives "afflicted with intense unreality" (147–48). The gloom in Davis's work also associates guilt with social issues, but her social dramas are treated with intense reality. What Davis valued in Hawthorne's sketches appears unabashedly in her best-known and first-published story, *Life in the Iron-Mills.* Hawthornesque doubt coexists with grim reality in the pall industrialism casts on Davis's artistic vision. It surfaces in her soliciting her readers' empathy for the lives of factory workers who eke out a meager existence in the dank, dark underside of their lives and in the questions art asks of God. The commonplace lives Davis depicts in *Margret Howth* differ in depth and kind from the more lighthearted characters of the commonplace in "Little Annie," "Sunday," and "Rill." Annie's ramble occurs in the sunshine, her good life assured by a loving father who escorts her. The sequestered narrator of "Sunday at Home" peeps through his window at the parade of commonplace folk entering church—children, elderly women and men, pretty girls, the clergyman, and long lines of others. It too is a primarily lighthearted sketch, a candidate for the kind of writing that may have gotten Hawthorne the reputation as the "man who means no meanings," an interpretation Melville overturned in "Hawthorne and His Mosses." The sketch that has more in common with Davis's commonplace characters is "A Rill from the Town Pump." In it, the pump as narrator is a character who surveys all the town's citizens, both the young and the old, the pauper, the drunkard, Indians, governors, and even the animals, but keeps them all at a distance, never permitting the dust, "the turbulence and manifold disquietudes of the world" to sully what may be called its "soul" (*CE* 9: 147–48). The everyday lives of everyday people in the three sketches were endowed with meaning and mystery for young Rebecca. For her the commonplace folk are usually working-class people, slaves or former slaves, women, and the middle class, the people among whom she lived. Industrialism's dire consequences for the working class and American culture in general, the class warfare pivotal to the slavery issue, the competing claims of domesticity for women which shape much of the social impetus of her work coincide with its realist qualities.

To limn the human condition of lives she could only imagine, she employed a Hawthornesque narrative strategy. As in "Sunday at Home" and "Sights from a Steeple," the narrator of *Life in the Iron-Mills* stands above the folk about whom she writes; the narrator inhabits the third story of the house in which the puddlers occupied the cellar. Looking out the street window at the "slow stream of human life" plodding to the great mills, the narrator pleads for a new subject matter for fiction—"I am going to be honest. This is what I want you to do"—and implores readers to risk identifying with "massed, vile, slimy lives" (13–14). She aims to expose the misconception that the higher, nobler traits do not exist in the common folks. *Life in the Iron-Mills* illustrates the utter waste of human potential when economic plight blights the spirit. The story imagines such waste in artistic terms. The artist's predicament that appears both in *The Marble Faun* and in "The Artist of the Beautiful" lies at the heart of Hugh Wolfe's sculpture of the Korl Woman, the image that grips the men inspecting the mill with unflinching force. Social reform is demanded implicitly by Hugh's interpreting the sculpture's meaning as "She be hungry" and by the question the sculpture asks, "What shall I do to be saved?" One of the onlookers realizes that "money" would provide not only the requisite spiritual freedom but the economic redemption as well. When people of means exonerate themselves of the guilt they bear for the desperate straits of workers imprisoned by oppressive class structures, as do overseer Clarke, Kirby, the Doctor, and even Mitchell, the whole culture is impoverished and endangered. The Dantean fires form part of the mythic dimensions Judith Fetterley notices in *Life in the Iron-Mills,* the white-hot fire reminiscent of the same in "Ethan Brand." The infernal fires of the mills suggest not only the hell of the puddlers' existence but also the callous hearts of the mill owner, overseers, and their companions; the fiery lime kiln calcifies the heart of one who had hovered, as have the puddlers and their superiors, over a white-hot, richly symbolic fire of mythic magnitude (Fetterley 310). The civil and moral lapse, the inefficacy of the church, and the malaise of the mill workers, which forecast Hugh's death, bespeak hellish proportions.

Hawthorne's sense of history, his historical settings and subjects appear to have inspired another realistic impetus in Davis's work. Sharon Harris links Davis's literary theory of the commonplace to her abiding interest in national and local politics. Davis sought to understand current politics by examining the history that gave it rise. Harris attributes to Hawthorne (and Sedgwick) Davis's "acute interest in historical locales and in how the ideologies of the past informed the present." Furthermore, Harris concludes, Hawthorne influenced "Davis' own belief that to study American history and . . . to expose the mythos of the past were requisite preliminary stages if one was concerned with artistically recording the 'accurate history' of the present" (7). The "unhindered progress" intrinsic to expansion was invested with a grim underside because expansion and economic success relied on slavery. For Davis, this dilemma in American culture arose from "corrupted history" (27). Comparisons may be drawn between Hawthorne and Davis's affinity for writing fictional accounts of historical events with Davis's "A Faded Leaf of History" and a number of Hawthorne's stories—the Salem witchcraft trials ("Young Goodman Brown"), pre-revolutionary overthrows of monarchical intervention ("My Kinsman, Major Molineux"), and trials that dramatize the consequences for humanity caught in the interstice of theocratic Puritan rule and individual autonomy ("The May-Pole of Merry Mount" and *The Scarlet Letter*).

Although the history-making Civil War was a rich imaginative historical source, Hawthorne's writings about it were nonfiction prose, such as "Chiefly about War Matters," "Northern Volunteers," and *A Biography of Franklin Pierce*. In Davis's work, repeated explorations of the bitter internecine struggle become recurrent. During her 1862 visit to Concord, she was shocked at the prevailing optimism in the "Areopagites'" philosophizing about everything from the eternal verities to pears to the war. Nothing she heard among most of the inhabitants of the "modern Athens" gripped her more than their wrongheaded analyses of the Civil War.[2] In the parlor at the Wayside, Bronson Alcott described the war as "an armed angel . . . wakening the nation to a lofty life unknown before" with Emerson's "profound submissive attention," while Hawthorne's "laughing, sagacious eyes" watched "full of mockery" (*BOG* 34). Both Davis and Hawthorne had actually seen the war. Hawthorne had recently visited several battle sites and had just composed "Chiefly about War Matters" for the *Atlantic*. Davis, whose home state (Virginia) was about to split over the war issue and whose first five years had been lived in the slave-holding state Alabama, had herself witnessed the war's brutality. Hawthorne responded to Alcott, the man he described as "the Sage of Concord": "We cannot see that thing at so long a range. Let us go to dinner" (*BOG* 35). Davis's reply to Alcott appeared much later, in her memoir: "War may be an armed angel with a mission, but she has the personal habits of the slums" (*BOG* 34). Hawthorne's restrained chiding of his cohort confirmed Davis's private remonstrance. She interpreted Hawthorne's perceptions to be intellectually and politically kin to her own, a melding, a collapsing of identities comparable to that frequently detected in Melville's relationship with Hawthorne. In casting Hawthorne as the "unfortunate man who saw both sides" of the issue, Davis repeats a characterization of herself as one who always "had a perverse inclination to see the other side of the question" ("Men's Rights" 212). Not only did Hawthorne and Davis have a penchant for taking the opposing side, or seeing two sides of all questions, they also were the only persons in the Wayside parlor who had seen the War itself. Both were in touch with the gloomier aspects of the war and of life. As was true of the later realists, the war decidedly affected her intent to write about the gloomy, the vulgar in American life. The entire conversation in the Wayside parlor effected in Rebecca the recognition that Hawthorne was here—as he was in Boston—"an alien among these men, not of their kind" (*BOG* 55). The clash of transcendental optimism with Hawthorne's cautious objectivity and Rebecca's pessimism about the waste and destruction of the war is drawn in sharp relief in Rebecca's memoirs. She recalls Bronson Alcott standing before the fireplace in "the little parlor of the Wayside, . . . his long gray hair streaming over his collar, his pale eyes turning quickly from one listener to another to hold them quiet, his hands waving to keep time with the orotund sentences" (34). All the while "Mr. Emerson stood listening, his head sunk on his breast, with profound submissive attention, but Hawthorne sat astride of a chair, his arms folded on the back, his chain dropped on them, and his laughing, sagacious eyes watching us, full of mockery" (34). Appalled by Alcott's rhapsodizing, Rebecca inwardly fumed: "I had just come up from the border where I had seen the actual war, the filthy spewing of it; the political jobbery in Union and Confederate camps, the malignant personal hatreds wearing patriotic masks, and glutted by burning homes and outraged women. . . . This would-be seer who was talking of [the war], and the real seer who listened, knew no more of war as it was, than I had done in my cherry-tree when I dreamed of bannered legions of crusaders debouching in the misty fields" (34).

For Davis, witnessing partitioning of her own state and dealing all too closely with the war's realities made the Civil War a ripe subject for imaginative examination. The galvanizing effects of her sensing in Hawthorne a kinship with her perception of the war were evident in the subjects of her fiction after her visit to Concord. Among her many writings about the war, *Waiting for the Verdict, David Gaunt,*

"John Lamar," "The Yares of Black Mountain," and "Blind Tom" rank among the best. After *Life in the Iron-Mills,* most critics rate *Waiting for the Verdict* second among her writings. The novel's title conveys the dilemma the nation faced after the war. The issue is raised by slave mother Anny: "de black man . . . is waitin' for de whites to say which dey shall be—men or beasts. Waitin' for the verdict" (354). This book exposes the illusory hope at war's end that the nation might fully heal and thus be able to achieve its early ideals. On the subject of the national rupture we call the Civil War, Davis creates a history chronicling the catastrophic consequences to the lives of all Americans in all classes.

Davis's admiration for Hawthorne never waned. His scepter never lost its enchantment for her. It is less certain, though, that Hawthorne would have appreciated her claiming him her literary ancestor. If Sophia Hawthorne's assessment of Davis is, as she claims, Hawthorne's as well, he was unimpressed, especially with *Margret Howth.* Sophia wrote a note to Miss Harding, as she preferred to call Rebecca, shortly after Harding's departure from Concord. A few months later, in November of 1862, Sophia wrote Annie Fields: "Mr. Hawthorne and Julian think [Gail Hamilton] . . . the only good lady-author in America" (Stewart 303). Then in a May 1863 letter to Annie, Sophia castigates "Miss Harding":

> Tell Heart's Ease that he must objurgate Miss Harding (I like to call her so) for her use of that bominable unenglish, affected word "pulsing" and "Pulses" (as a verb) and "pulsates" in her papers. It is unpardonable, Mr. Hawthorne cannot read her productions now, they are so distasteful to him from her bad style and slimy gloom—alas! that I should say so. I always read what she writes, because of the ability she shows but I also tire of the mouldiness, east wind and grime which she will mix in with her pictures of life. (Stewart 304)

Sophia's credibility is undermined by the pettiness implied in the "I like to call her so" remark. Whether or not Hawthorne did refuse to read Davis's work, it is clear that the distinctions drawn here do distinguish romance from realism in almost definitive terms. This issue needs further examination in Davis's work, for she felt that her freedom to express her own vision was hampered by her publishers. Jean Fagan Yellin's cogent essay on the detrimental effect of Fields's insisting on a sunnier ending to *Margret Howth* leaves no doubt that in her attempt to satisfy her publisher Davis dramatically diminished the artistic achievement of her second novel. Another example of the conflict she experienced in this regard is noted in Harris's discussion of Davis's story "John Lamar." When "Fields accepted the story without admonishing its dark vision," Davis remarked that she needn't have written it "with one hand tied behind my back . . . after all" (qtd. in Harris 73). She fought this battle most of her publishing life, especially until the 1870s when she moved into journalism as a commentator on pressing current social issues.

An especially important parallel to Hawthorne is the nineteenth-century concern with domesticity. A muzzled critique of the relations between man and woman so integral to Hawthorne's novels permeates much of Davis's short fiction, such as "Marcia," the powerful "In the Market," "Doctor Sarah," "The Wife's Story," and several other of Davis's stories and essays. Hester of "The Wife's Story" decidedly resembles the Hester of *The Scarlet Letter* in her struggle with a self-definition at odds with that her culture expects. The protagonist of most of these stories would have to commit intellectual suicide much as Zenobia committed literal suicide in *The Blithedale Romance* to experience autonomy and definition in a world where female independence wars against domesticity. The young woman writer in "Marcia" faced the same fate Hawthorne had implied should happen to "ink-stained Amazons" in his essay "Mrs. Hutchinson." As did Hawthorne, Davis grappled with the inward complexities of women's lives. Her women usually opt for marital happiness, aiming simultaneously to find meaningful work outside that role. It is interesting that Davis's memoirs include her assessment of the Hawthornes' marriage as admirable, and of Sophia as the perfect wife to Hawthorne.

When Davis attributed to Hawthorne her commonplace subject, she is most in line with genre theorists who tend to believe that American realists get from their romanticist ancestors subject matter that the realists then treat more objectively. Although Davis believed that she and Hawthorne were more objective in their view (both were certainly nay-sayers to transcendentalism), still she knew the difference. She knew she was writing an innovatively objective fiction that borders on naturalism at times, but she knew she was no writer of romance. Of him, she concluded in her memoir, "America may have great poets and novelists, but she never will have more than one necromancer" (*BOG* 59). The nightmarish quality of the inner life of most of Hawthorne's characters is translated in Davis's fiction to the nightmarish quality of a culture tottering on the brink of disaster as industrialism and war wreaked havoc on the lives of the common folk.

It was not the influence of Hawthorne's best fiction that Davis acknowledged as influencing her but the common folk in those three little sketches written about people she believed she might have known, someone potentially like herself. Not only did his writing for children get replicated in her own long career, but primarily the sketches about Annie, the town pump, and the invisible narrator watching the townspeople go to church sparked her youthful and mature imagination immeasurably and interminably. When she left Concord, she reports, Hawthorne "hesitated shyly," held out his hand, and said: "I am sorry you are going away. It seems as if we had known you always." Her final analysis leaves no doubt about the enormous awe she always had for him: "because of the child in the cherry tree, and the touch which the magician laid upon her [his farewell words] seemed to take me, too, for one moment into his enchanted country" (*BOG* 64). Little wonder then that one of her last publications followed Hawthorne's earliest model—a collection of short tales about indigenous American soil entitled *The Silhouettes of American Life*. These tales, which lack the naturalistic cast of Davis's early realism, depict the lives of colonists, slaves, and women of all ages. They delicately nuance the dilemmas of persons seeking autonomy in a subtly menacing social context.

Having abandoned the stark realism which won her acclaim in her own time and canonical stature now in ours, the aging Davis focused on creating a distinctly American literature, writing what she believed was indigenous fiction—far from the interior fiction James perfected. Melville's dictum that Hawthorne "says NO, in thunder" might be said as well of Davis, and not just because she, like Hawthorne, rejected transcendentalism. Her resistance to James's high-culture realism is one reason her work did not fit within the ensuing course of American realism. Despite quibbles among some of Davis's contemporaries and high modernist objections of many twentieth-century readers, a growing number of current scholars find the bulk of her work compelling, as evidenced by *American Literary Scholarship: An Annual 1996:* "Rebecca Harding Davis's literary stock is rising" (Oliver 257). Her elevated stature may be explained by the success with which Davis fulfilled her own goal of leaving behind a story that would "make history live and breathe" (*BOG* i). From Hawthorne as well as from her own insights into the human condition, Rebecca Harding Davis learned to invest the commonplace with an imagination that captured the history, the national character, and the social issues of her own time.

Notes

1. She was in good company in this regard, for Longfellow, who was Hawthorne's Bowdoin classmate and a well-known poet, also noted how his friend invested the "commonplace" with poetry and romance (Hawthorne, *Centenary Edition* 9: 508; hereafter cited as *CE*).

2. Rebecca Harding's visit to the Hawthornes in Concord took place during her visit to her new friends James T. and Annie Fields. Fields, editor of the *Atlantic* and friend, publisher, promoter of Hawthorne, had been responsible for publishing *Life in the Iron-Mills.* At 138 Charles Street, as she did for so many literary figures, Annie Fields introduced Rebecca to prominent people, such as Oliver Wendell Holmes and Louisa May Alcott. At the Wayside on Wednesday, 18 June, Rebecca, as guest of the Hawthornes, because of the discussion with Emerson and Alcott about the war, was disappointed in the "Atlantic coterie" from a realist's perspective: "while they thought they were guiding the real world, they stood quite outside of it, and never would see it as it was" (*BOG* 32–33).

Works Cited

Brodhead, Richard H. *The School of Hawthorne.* New York: Oxford UP, 1986.

Davis, Rebecca Harding. *Bits of Gossip.* New York: Houghton Mifflin, 1904.

——. *Life in the Iron-Mills and Other Stories.* Ed. Tillie Olsen. New York: Feminist, 1972.

——. *Margret Howth: A Story of To-Day.* Ed. Jean Fagan Yellin. New York: Feminist, 1990.

——. "Men's Rights." *Putnam's Magazine* ns 3 (1869): 212–24.

——. *Waiting for the Verdict.* Upper Saddle River, N.J.: Gregg, 1968.

———. "The Wife's Story." *Life in the Iron-Mills and Other Stories.* 177–222.

Fetterley, Judith, ed. *Provisions: A Reader from 19th-Century American Women.* Bloomington: Indiana UP, 1985.

Grayburn, William F. "The Major Fiction of Rebecca Harding Davis." Diss. Pennsylvania State U, 1965.

Harris, Sharon M. *Rebecca Harding Davis and American Realism.* Philadelphia: U of Pennsylvania P, 1991.

Hawthorne, Nathaniel. *The Centenary Edition of the Works of Nathaniel Hawthorne.* Ed. William Charvat et al. Columbus: Ohio State UP, 1984.

Hawthorne, Sophia Peabody. "Sophia Hawthorne's Diary for June 1861." Ed. Thomas Woodson. *Nathaniel Hawthorne Review* 15 (1989): 1–5.

Herbert, Walter T. *Dearest Beloved: The Hawthornes and the Making of the Middle-Class Family.* Berkeley: U of California P, 1993.

Hesford, Walter. "Literary Contexts of *Life in the Iron-Mills.*" *American Literature* 49 (1977–78): 70–85.

Jones, Wayne Allen. "The Hawthorne-Goodrich Relationship." *Nathaniel Hawthorne Journal* 1975: 91–140.

Langford, Gerald. *The Richard Harding Davis Years: A Biography of a Mother and Son.* New York: Holt, 1961.

Mellow, James. *Nathaniel Hawthorne in His Times.* Boston: Houghton Mifflin, 1980.

Oliver, Lawrence J. "Late-19th-Century Literature." *American Literary Scholarship: An Annual 1996.* Ed. David J. Nordloh. Durham: Duke UP, 1998. 215–42.

Pfaelzer, Jean. Introduction. "Marcia." By Rebecca Harding Davis. *Legacy* 4 (1987): 3–10.

Quinn, Arthur Hobson. *American Fiction: An Historical and Critical Survey.* New York: Appleton, 1936.

Rose, Jane Atteridge. *Rebecca Harding Davis.* New York: Twayne, 1993.

Schaeffer, Helen Woodward. "Rebecca Harding Davis, Pioneer Realist." Diss. U of Pennsylvania, 1947.

Smith, Henry Nash. *Popular Culture and Industrialism, 1865–1890.* New York: Doubleday, 1967.

Stewart, Randall. "Hawthorne's Last Illness and Death." *More Books* 19 (1944): 303–13.

Yellin, Jean Fagan. Afterword. *Margret Howth: A Story of To-Day.* By Rebecca Harding Davis. New York: Feminist, 1990.

HAWTHORNE, JEWETT,
AND THE MEDITATIVE SUBLIME

Gayle L. Smith

In addition to the works examined here, *Deephaven* (1877) and *Country By-Ways* (1881) would offer interesting landscape descriptions to be read alongside Hawthorne's.

I n *The School of Hawthorne,* Richard Brodhead argues that for the generation of American writers of prose fiction that followed him Hawthorne was virtually "synonymous with literature itself," and to write was "inevitably to enter into an intercourse with him" (51).

While a number of contemporaneous reviews of Sarah Orne Jewett's works do invoke Hawthorne's example, the limited published comments we have indicate that Jewett had, at best, mixed feelings about Hawthorne as a literary model. In 1903 Julia R. Tutweiler defends Jewett's digressive style by citing Hawthorne, along with Irving, Thackeray, Charlotte Brontë, "and a score of other illustrious artists" (rpt. 28). In his 1904 essay, Charles Miner Thompson wonders whether "this accusation . . . of undergoing the influence of Hawthorne [which] is made against almost every New England writer of gloomy stories" is justified. At the same time, however, he feels "some confidence that this writer of exquisite English had a share in showing Miss Jewett how to write" and even suggests likely "traces of his influence" in specific stories and characters (rpt. 40). In a 1915 article devoted to Mr. and Mrs. James T. Fields, Henry James identifies Jewett as "mistress of an art of fiction all her own, even though of a minor compass, and surpassed only by Hawthorne as producer of the most finished and penetrating of the numerous 'short stories' that have the domestic life of New England for their general and their doubtless somewhat lean subject."[1] Brodhead too comments on shared subject matter, observing that Hawthorne served, or was pressed into serving, as a "prototype" for regionalist writers (66). Thus he refers to Jewett's *The Country of the Pointed Firs* as her "beautiful fusion of Hawthorne's fictions of New England as backwater and his fables of monomania" (50). He points out that Jewett, as a member of the literary society that revolved around the powerful publisher and patron James T. Fields (Hawthorne's publisher as of 1850) and "the most literary of the regionalists," would have felt Hawthorne's influence especially keenly (64).

In two letters Jewett denies Hawthorne's influences. Writing in 1890 to Mrs. Fields, by then her longtime companion, she says, "I . . . have read part of Hawthorne's American Journal volume but didn't care for it as much as I used to" (Fields 72). "This was a volume of Hawthorne's younger journals," she continues, perhaps by way of explanation for its deficiencies, "a conscious effort after material and some lovely enough notes of his walks and suggestions for sketches; but these last lack any reality or imagination, rootless little things that could never open seed in their turn, or make much of any soil they were put into, so 'delicate' in their fancy as to be far-fetched and oddly feeble and sophomorish" (72–73). Acknowledging that her opinion seems like "high literary treason," she rejects Hawthorne's deliberate search for material and finds Charles W. Brewster's *Rambles about Portsmouth* more rewarding for its "mere hints of description" (72). She says nothing here, however, about Hawthorne's finished works. She responds to Charles Miner Thompson's essay, mentioned above, in which he concluded that Hawthorne had considerable influence on her content and style, and freely discusses her fondness for Turgenev but declares, "I never was a Hawthorne lover in early life!" (Fields 196). Perhaps Turgenev, Flaubert, and Tolstoy seemed to invite less simplistic and reductive comparisons.

Brodhead points out that all manner of writers, internationalists and local colorists, radicals and conservatives, romantics and realists, found ways to claim authority for their approaches through various aspects of Hawthorne's work.[2] The last pair of "opposites," romantics and realists, represents the most profound connection between Hawthorne and Jewett. Hawthorne specifically addressed this issue, articulating the concept of the "neutral territory" in "The Custom-House" and discussing the domain of the romance versus that of the novel in the Preface to *The House of the Seven Gables*. As a closer look at these works reveals, Hawthorne's conception of writing in visual, painterly terms allows him to describe a sensibility that is both realistic and romantic. Jewett habitually refers to her own writings as though they were sketches or paintings, and so have many critics. Like Hawthorne, Jewett achieves this subtle, shifting perspective by using a wide range of visual elements in her writing. Settings, landscapes, and houses take on aesthetic, even symbolic value without losing their literal, earthy presence, and artist characters invite direct examination of romantic and realist theories. Most specifically, both writers share a great deal with the aesthetics of the American landscape painters we have come to know as the luminists, especially Fitz Hugh Lane, Martin Johnson Heade, John Frederick Kensett, Sanford Gifford, and somewhat arguably, Frederic Church.[3]

Hawthorne's entire "neutral territory" scene, so theoretical and far-reaching in its aesthetic implications, is thoroughly visual and luminist. From the "protoluminist" Washington Allston to the classic luminists to Church, all experimented repeatedly with the effects of different kinds of light. Art historian John Wilmerding traces a movement from preference for bright, noontime light to occluded, filtered, hazier light, twilight, and evening light in the course of the luminist movement itself.[4] Heade painted multiple versions of various marsh scenes at different times of day, sunrise, sunset, twilight, emphasizing the subtle, shifting effects of time, light, and atmosphere on subject and observer. Hawthorne reveals a parallel sensitivity to the importance of light when he describes himself in his parlor late at night, trying to "*picture forth* imaginary scenes, which, the next day, might flow out on the *brightening* page in *many-hued* description" (*CE* I: 35; emphases mine).[5] Moonlight renders landscape, sailboats, and figures mysterious, even slightly otherworldly, in Washington Allston's 1819 *Moonlit Landscape*.[6] It is the moonlight streaming into Hawthorne's familiar parlor that brings out the new, strange, and wonderful:

> There is the little domestic scenery of the well-known apartment; the chairs, with each its separate individuality; the centre-table, sustaining a work-basket, a volume or two, and an extinguished lamp; the sofa; the book-case; the picture on the wall;—all these details so completely seen, are so spiritualized by the unusual light, that they seem to lose their actual substance, and become things of intellect. Nothing is too small or too trifling to undergo this change, and acquire dignity thereby. A child's shoe; the doll, seated in her little wicker carriage; the hobby-horse;—whatever, in a word, has been used or played with, during the day, is now invested with a quality of strangeness and remoteness, though still almost as vividly present as by daylight. Thus, therefore, the floor of our familiar room has become a neutral territory, somewhere between the real world and fairy-land, where the Actual and the Imaginary may meet, and each imbue itself with the nature of the other. (*CE* I: 35–36)

Although at first the everyday objects seem to lose their substantial reality, finally both states coexist and even intermingle; the imaginary does not dislodge the ordinary but seems to have been liberated, become more palpable and usable to the writer as the spiritual depths of the ordinary are retrieved in this light. The mirror on the wall goes one step further, organizing and framing the images scattered around the room, presenting everything "one remove farther from the actual, and nearer to the imaginative" (*CE* I: 36). No longer is it a dichotomy, real versus imaginary; it is a vast and shifting continuum.

Rebecca Harding Davis seems to have responded to this sensibility as she read some of Hawthorne's sketches, works more valued by late-nineteenth-century readers. "In these papers," she writes, "the commonplace folk and things which I saw every day took on a sudden mystery and charm, and, for the first time, I found that they, too, belonged to the magic world of knights and pilgrims and fiends" (Brodhead 219n24).[7] Similarly, in an 1893 letter to Annie Fields, Jewett discusses the importance of the everyday in art, prompted by her rereading of Flaubert, saying, "People talk about dwelling upon trivialities and commonplaces in life, but a master writer gives everything weight, and makes you feel the distinction and importance of it, and count it upon the right or the wrong side of a life's account" (Fields 82). Arguing more explicitly for a neutral or commingled realistic/romantic vision, she confronts her differences with her editor, William Dean Howells, who rejected her story "A White Heron." She writes, "Mr. Howells thinks that this age frowns upon the romantic, that it is no use to write romance anymore; but dear me, how much of it there is left in the every-day life after all" (Fields 59). It is the artist's job to bring out the meaning, to show how the real and ideal coexist, whether in the parlor in the moonlight or in the marsh at sunrise.

Hawthorne's long-standing admiration for the Dutch realist painters reveals his commitment to the same point of view. At the huge Manchester Exhibition in 1857, Hawthorne comes back to this preference, marveling at the Dutch painters' ability to depict reality more accurately than the photographer. Whereas he finds many works of the Pre-Raphaelites too mechanical, too labored in their transcription of details that reveal nothing beyond themselves, in the Dutch works he finds suggestions of a deeper reality. He describes a dented metal vase in a painting by Gerard Dou as "absolutely more real than reality" (*English Notebooks* 556). He sums up his response saying, "And it is strange how spiritual, and suggestive the commonest household article—an earthen pitcher, for example—becomes when represented with entire accuracy. These Dutchmen get at the soul of common things, and so make them types and interpreters of the spiritual world" (556).[8] As he completes *The House of the Seven Gables,* he writes to Fields, "Many passages of this book ought to be finished with the minuteness of a Dutch picture, in order to give them their proper effect" (*CE* 16: 371). Like so many reviewers, Th. Bentzon (pen name, Marie Therese Blanc) discussed Jewett's work in painterly terms; she even likens her character portraits to those done by the Dutch realists (Bentzon, rpt. 4).

The popularity of Hawthorne's literary sketches doubtless made it possible for Jewett and many others to adopt and refine this genre, expanding on its twin characteristics, an emphasis on detailed description rather than action or narrative and an air of experimentation and incompletion.[9] Just as Hawthorne describes his theory of the neutral territory in pictorial terms in "The Custom-House," in the Preface to *The House of the Seven Gables,* he speaks of the romance in general and his work in particular as visual compositions. Creating a romance, he says, the writer "may so manage his atmospherical medium as to bring out or mellow the lights and deepen and enrich the shadows of the picture" (*CE* 2: 1). Furthermore, he suggests that the reader may want to allow the "legendary mist" of the story "to float almost imperceptibly about the characters and events, for the sake of a picturesque effect" (2: 2). In fact, he admits that the narrative may be so thin as to require this dimension. In sketches such as "Footprints on the Seashore," "The Old Manse,"

"The Toll-Gatherer's Day," and even "My Visit to Niagara," there is just enough action to create an occasion for the narrator's meditations on his surroundings. Jewett and her critics regularly refer to her as a "painter" or sketch artist, sometimes, like Tutweiler, praising her "byways of reflection and meditation," other times, with Paul Elmer More, citing her creation of scenes "petrified into motionlessness" and her inability to depict action or passion, a quality More attributed to "Brahmin writers of New England fiction" in general, presumably including Hawthorne (Tutweiler, rpt. 28; More, rpt. 50, 49).

If Hawthorne frequently relied on carefully crafted tableaux and occasionally longed to write a big, realistic novel, or at least to wrest a story from the business of the Custom House, Jewett too struggled with the demands of lengthier fiction. Her 1873 letter to editor Horace Scudder, who had already accepted two of her early stories, reveals that even at this point she is aware of two deep-seated and interconnected aspects of her prose. First, she already understands her own writing process in painterly terms. Her earlier stories, she says, were written very quickly and the more recent ones Scudder criticized were written and revised more carefully, perhaps too carefully, though she still calls them "experiments." She compares her stories to her own paintings: "the more I worked over pictures the stiffer and more hopeless they grew," she observes (Cary, *Letters* 29). The stories she wrote more impulsively she finds to have the most reality and individuality. Secondly, she responds to Scudder and Howells, both of whom suggested she make her stories longer. However, she knew her strengths and her weaknesses: "In the first place, I have no dramatic talent. The story would have no plot. I should have to fill it out with descriptions of character and meditations" (29). More than twenty years later she advises Rose Lamb on her writing, stressing the experimental and visual elements: "If something comes into a writer's or a painter's mind the only thing is to *try it,* to see what one can do with it, and give it a chance to show if it has real value. Story-writing is always experimental, just as a water-color sketch is" (Fields 118; emphasis Jewett's). A few years later in one of a series of letters critiquing the work of the aspiring writer John Thaxter, she compliments his landscape and description but finds the sketch as a whole confusing, "as if one saw a beautiful, quiet piece of landscape painting with its figures hastily done, and crowded and even puzzling to the eye" (Cary, *Letters* 119). Obviously, she could see the danger in a work separating into two unrelated parts, descriptive and narrative, and the surest way for her to conceive of it was by seeing it.

Hawthorne's and Jewett's descriptive, visual styles allowed them to create rich, detailed, but deliberately imprecise settings for their fiction. Hawthorne's exploration of his conflicted, complex relationship with Salem as his home in "The Custom-House" opens up a theme Jewett returns to in many stories. Most poignantly perhaps, she confirms her own idea of the impact of landscape on personality when she visits the "dreadfully sad old village" near the home of the Brontës: "Nothing you ever read about them can make you know them until you go there. . . . Never mind people who tell you there is nothing to see in the place where people lived who interest you. You always find something of what made them the souls they were, and at any rate you see their sky and their earth" (Fields 158). In his Preface to *The House of the Seven Gables,* Hawthorne insists that while the reader may "choose to assign an actual locality" he would prefer to have the book read as a romance, with characters, and presumably settings, admitted to be of his "own making, or, at all events, of his own mixing" (*CE* 2: 3). Hawthorne's comments may have been necessitated by his earlier criticism of Salem, but Jewett was more consistently evasive about the existence of any real-life counterparts to her village settings. As much as Deephaven resembled York, at one point she maintains that she created her setting before so much as staying overnight in York (Cary, Introduction to *Deephaven* 12). In 1888 she tells a correspondent that *A Marsh Island* is set somewhere in Essex (called "Sussex" in the novel); she claims never to have found the exact place herself but allows that a mere glimpse of an island farm from the railroad may have given her the idea for the setting (Cary, *Letters* 56). Likewise, she is willing to locate the setting for *The Country of the Pointed Firs* somewhere between Tenants Harbor and Boothbay but denies that any actual landing or harbor served as model for Dunnet Landing (Cary, *Letters* 116). Rather like Hawthorne, by mentioning an area by name, Jewett claims a measure of verisimilitude and the credibility that goes with it; at the same time she claims a more general province and relevance for her sketches. An anonymous reviewer of *The Country of the Pointed Firs* agreed, saying Jewett has "made a seacoast of her own, a mirage lifted just above the horizon of actual land, and peopled it with figures that are images of reality, also."[10] In his 1877 review of *Deephaven,* Howells surmises that "some particular sea-port sat for Deephaven" but maintains that Deephaven actually represents an entire "class of old shore towns" (rpt. 25). Moreover, he almost paraphrases Hawthorne's description of the "neutral territory," declaring *Deephaven* "imbued with a true feeling for the ideal within the real" (26).

If Hawthorne and Jewett shared a preference for literary forms that were simultaneously realistic and romantic and if they understood their own creative efforts in visual, even painterly terms, we might expect these propensities to culminate in a similar pictorial quality to the descriptive elements in their prose. Hawthorne, Jewett, and their contemporaries could and did discuss their works in relation to the Dutch realists, Claude Lorrain, and the cult of the picturesque, but they could not discuss the luminist aesthetic as such because it would not be identified as a distinct entity until 1954.[11] I have described elsewhere how, particularly in his notebook entries and sketches, Hawthorne moves away from the Claudean-inspired picturesque landscape style of Hudson River school painters like Thomas Cole, Asher Durand, and Thomas Doughty and toward a more open, stilled, light-filled landscape, effectively anticipating the style and vision we now call "luminist."[12] Lane, Heade, Kensett, and Gifford, central to the luminist group, generally paid more attention to actual locations, to light, and to atmospheric effects than their predecessors did. Frederic Church, whose stunning experiments with landscape, color, and light connect him with these painters, tended to a more dramatic, conventionally sublime total effect.

Basic to the luminist vision is a meditative, reflective quality, a deeper interest in the individual's subjective experience of nature than in sheer physical phenomena. In his essay "Luminism and the American Sublime," Earl A. Powell observes, "The placid, quiescent canvases of the luminists, austerely composed and tightly painted, were American equivalents of Kantian and neo-Kantian visualizations of the sublime" (72). In "My Visit to Niagara," published in 1835, Hawthorne's focus is not so much the great natural attraction of the falls but the narrator's very gradually evolving, personal experience of Niagara. And his most satisfying views little resemble the traditional sublime versions of its awesome power; instead, they anticipate several paintings John Kensett would do in 1851, focusing on calmer stretches of the river above and below the falls themselves. Repose, silence, stillness, a sense of arrested motion and infinite space characterize many luminist landscapes. Discussing Lane's 1852 *Entrance to Somes Sound from Southwest Harbor,* for example, Franklin Kelly refers to the combination of reasonably accurate topography and depiction of everyday reality with an arresting feeling of absolute order and tranquillity as "a compelling synthesis of reality and imagination," terms again suggestive of Hawthorne's stated and Jewett's implied aesthetic (144). Hawthorne's meditations on the Concord River finally celebrate (quietly) its calm, literally and metaphorically reflective qualities, and the narrator of "The Toll-Gatherer's Day" is most enchanted when a schooner becomes stuck under the open bridge and all commerce ceases for several hours.

Barbara Novak is discussing the silence and repose of luminist paintings when she says that in their space "everything happens while nothing does," but she could almost be describing a sketch by Hawthorne or Jewett as well (28). As Richard Cary says in his Introduction to *Deephaven,* "Not much ever happens in Miss Jewett's best stories"; instead, they are suffused with "a calm sense of eternality" (20–21). Jewett's characters often adopt the pose of the meditative observers in luminist paintings, inviting us to contemplate the landscape with them. In *The Country of the Pointed Firs,* natives as well as the vacationing narrator deliberately seek out commanding views of sea and shore. When the narrator and Mrs. Todd, with whom she is spending the summer, visit Mrs. Todd's mother and brother William out on Green Island, William takes her up along the great rock ledge to the highest point on the island. "It gave a sudden sense of space," she says, "for nothing stopped the eye or hedged one in,—that sense of liberty in space and time which great prospects always give" (63). When she thinks they are too far inland to gain a view of shore, they climb a hill and discover "a wonderful great view" of the upper bay (123). Beyond the bay are "distant shores like another country in the midday haze which half hid the hills beyond, and the far away pale blue mountains on the northern horizon" (123–24). Again, though the vantage point is more elevated than that of the typical luminist landscape, we have the sense of space and an interest in light and atmosphere, suggestive of Sanford Gifford's many depictions of haze and mist. This "noble landscape" also includes "a schooner with all sails set coming down the bay from a white village that was sprinkled on the shore," a sight that both puts man's efforts into perspective and celebrates the commercial sailing past of the region (124). Significantly, at the end of her stay, she climbs a hill to take one last look at the view and also to watch for her steamer, successor to the romantic schooner. Later as she watches from her steamer, more than the summer seems to be coming to an end:

> The little town, with the tall masts of its disabled schooners in the inner bay, stood high above the flat sea for a few minutes, then it sank back into the uniformity of the coast, and became indistinguishable from the other towns that looked as if they were crumbled on the furzy-green stoniness of the shore. (235)

There are more disabled schooners, relics of an earlier time, than there are sailing ones, and in many ways Dunnet Landing is indistinguishable from the other shore towns "crumbled" here and there along the harsh coast. As Josephine Donovan observes, Jewett's vision was often "elegiac," mourning the passing of an entire way of life in her region (11). Even as a young girl, she had seen the results of the long decline of commerce, ship building, and even agriculture in her area of Maine.

While Hawthorne's landscape descriptions often anticipate the luminists' experiments with light, color, atmosphere, and tone, Jewett seems to look back to the subjects and mood of Lane and Heade in particular. Lane's New England harbor scenes of the 1840s and early 1850s are full of everyday images of fishing, shipping, and lumbering, images that were becoming all too scarce by the time Jewett was imaginatively reconstructing them in her sketches and fiction, often through the reminiscences of long-retired sailors or their widows. Realism and romanticism coalesce in many of these paintings; in the busy foreground of *Gloucester Harbor,* 1847, men split and saw wood and coat a small boat with pitch, and in *Gloucester Harbor,* 1848, fishermen are cleaning their catch. These very unromantic activities go on, however, against exquisitely calm, balanced backgrounds of shore, islands, water, and sky. In each, the sky occupies more than half of the canvas. Earl A. Powell discusses two Boston Harbor paintings from 1854 and 1856 in which steamships occupy prominent positions in the midst of sailing vessels; the sailboats are still, waiting for the tide perhaps, while the steamers move by their own power toward the viewer. Powell reminds us that, like the railroad, the steamship was the "new symbol of the industrial revolution" ("Boston Harbor Picture" 56). Even earlier, in 1849, the year in which Jewett was born and just after his first trip to Maine, Lane depicted a steamer in *Twilight on the Kennebec,* an even more suggestive painting. The steamship, though small and somewhat undefined against the background on account of the half light, moving upriver toward Augusta, contrasts powerfully with the stilled sailboats and the lumber schooner lying aground, awaiting repairs or perhaps abandoned. The twilight setting also suggests that he was consciously depicting the end of an era. Franklin Kelly concludes that this painting is about more than Lane's personal experience with Maine's wilderness, that "it is also about his awareness of the inevitable conflict between civilization and the wilderness" (134). This painting, with the story it suggests, and a pair of later paintings, *Lumber Schooners at Evening on Penobscot Bay*, 1860, and *Owl's Head, Penobscot Bay, Maine*, 1862 (fig. 1), with their sense of time suspended and action subdued, share an elegiac, almost reverential mood similar to Jewett's at the end of *The Country of the Pointed Firs*. Like Lane, whose latest paintings include the fewest people and manmade details, Jewett seems to seek a stay against the turmoil of change.

Her earlier novel *A Marsh Island* deals with several of the same themes and throughout evokes a luminist sense of landscape, space, and time. As the story opens, the young painter Dick Dale is at work at his easel. Most of those who pass by on the road find the landscape he is painting "in no way remarkable" and would have directed the painter to a better site. More specifically, "They saw a familiar row of willows and a foreground of pasture, broken here and there by gray rocks, while beyond a tide river the marshes seemed to stretch away to the end of the world" (3). Dale's landscape is unframed, vast, and common, as many luminists' landscapes were. The work on the easel could be one of Martin Johnson Heade's many studies of the marshlands of Essex County, the area in which Jewett's novel is set. *Marshfield Meadows*, 1878 (fig. 2), for example, depicts an unspectacular set of landscape features that, through repetition, composition, and lighting, suggest that the marshes extend into infinity. In a discussion of Heade's tireless experimentation with different views of the marshes at different times of day, Lisa Fellows Andrus connects his paintings with the larger issues of the real and the ideal: "The marsh scenes are a compendium of the luminist purpose: the portrayal of the particular facts of a specific place arranged to reveal universal truths through a measured and balanced composition and tonal modulations of light" (46).

Dale's aesthetic, like Hawthorne's and Jewett's, embraces the familiar, especially when it is enriched by various lights. The fact that Dale is a painter affords Jewett ample opportunities to describe the landscape from different perspectives and, like Heade, in changing lights. Dale turns around and suddenly notices the hills behind him, growing purple in the late afternoon light; the light disappears in a haze for a time and returns, "transfiguring" the trees and willows with its golden light (*Marsh Island* 12). Early in the morning, she tells us, "The marshes looked as if the land had been raveled out into the sea, for the tide creeks and inlets were brimful of water, and some gulls were flashing their wings in the sunlight, as if they were rejoiced at the sight of the sinking and conquered shore" (66–67). During haying, we see the whole farm from the marsh, and the hills take on different colors in the morning haze. When hay making is concluded, we are treated to another Heade-like description: "The marshes were dotted as far as eye could see by the round haystacks with their deftly pointed tops. These gave a great brilliance of color to the landscape, being unfaded yet by the rain and snow that would dull their yellow tints later in the year"

Fig. 1. Fitz Hugh Lane, *Owl's Head, Penobscot Bay, Maine*, 1862. Oil on canvas, 15¾ x 26⅛″. Bequest of Martha C. Karolik for the M. and M. Karolik Collection of American Paintings, 1815–1865. Courtesy, Museum of Fine Arts, Boston.

Fig. 2. Martin Johnson Heade, *Marshfield Meadows,* 1878. Oil on canvas, 17¾ x 44″. Courtesy, The Currier Gallery of Art, Manchester, N.H. Currier Funds, 1962.13. Photo, Frank Kelly.

(106–7). The sense of a quiet, eternal order that emerges from a Heade scene applies here too as Jewett reaffirms the meaning and beauty of the farmers' simple but rich lives.

Jewett need not have been especially concerned about being regarded as a slavish follower of Hawthorne. With Irving and others, Hawthorne helped establish a literary climate that at least tolerated the prose sketch, a shifting blend of narrative and personal essay, although that climate was changing quickly for Jewett. More profoundly, Jewett, like Hawthorne, also sought to create a literature that was both realistic and romantic because that was how she perceived everyday life. Hawthorne and Jewett both approached the writer's task with visual analogues in mind. More than any other single aspect of their works, their still, meditative, luminist landscapes confirm their successful blending of the real and the ideal.

Notes

1. The James article, "Mr. and Mrs. James T. Fields," originally appeared in the *Atlantic Monthly* 116 (July 1915): 21–31. Richard Cary uses the passage my quotation comes from as headnote to his *Appreciation of Sarah Orne Jewett*.

2. See Brodhead, esp. 15–16 and 64; the entire book makes this point by way of examples.

3. For an excellent survey of American luminism, see John Wilmerding et al., *American Light: The Luminist Movement, 1850–1875* (Washington, D.C.: National Gallery of Art, 1980), the catalogue to the exhibit. Wilmerding's Introduction, 11–20, and Barbara Novak's "On Defining Luminism," 23–29, are particularly useful starting points.

4. See Wilmerding's "The Luminist Movement: Some Reflections," *American Light* 97–152, esp. 108.

5. References to Hawthorne's writings are to the *Centenary Edition,* unless otherwise noted, and are cited in the text as *CE* with volume and page number.

6. For detailed discussions of Allston's protoluminist works, see Barbara Novak's *American Painting of the Nineteenth Century* (New York: Praeger, 1969), esp. 54–55, and Bryan Jay Wolf's *Romantic Re-Vision: Culture and Consciousness in Nineteenth-Century American Painting and Literature* (Chicago: U of Chicago P, 1982), esp. 60–62.

7. Brodhead specifies the sketches Davis refers to as "Little Annie's Ramble," "A Rill from the Town Pump," and "Sunday at Home." He cites Davis's *Bits of Gossip* (London: Archibald, Constable, 1904) 30.

8. For a thorough examination of Hawthorne's relations to the visual arts, see Rita K. Gollin and John L. Idol Jr., *Prophetic Pictures: Nathaniel Hawthorne's Knowledge and Uses of the Visual Arts* (New York: Greenwood, 1991).

9. For a discussion of the literary sketch, especially with respect to Irving, Hawthorne, and James, see Thomas H. Pauly, "The Literary Sketch in Nineteenth-Century America," *Texas Studies in Literature and Language* 17 (1975): 489–503.

10. This review originally appeared in the *Atlantic Monthly* 79 (Feb. 1897): 272–73. It is reprinted in Nagel 37.

11. See John Baur's "American Luminism: A Neglected Aspect of the Realist Movement in Nineteenth-Century American Painting," *Perspectives USA* 9 (Autumn 1954): 90–98.

12. See Gayle L. Smith, "The Light of Reflection: Hawthorne and the Luminist Sublime," *Prospects: An Annual of American Cultural Studies* 16 (1991): 171–204.

Works Cited

Andrus, Lisa Fellows. "Design and Measurement in Luminist Art." Wilmerding et al., *American Light* 31–56.

Bentzon, Th. "Le Roman de la Femme-Médecin." *Revue des Deux Mondes* 67 (1 Feb. 1885): 598–632. Rpt. in Cary, *Appreciation of Sarah Orne Jewett* 3–15.

Brodhead, Richard H. *The School of Hawthorne.* New York: Oxford UP, 1986.

Cary, Richard, ed. *Appreciation of Sarah Orne Jewett.* Waterville, Me.: Colby College P, 1973.

——. Introduction. *Deephaven and Other Stories.* New Haven: College and University P (1966): 7–23.

——, ed. *Sarah Orne Jewett Letters.* Waterville, Me.: Colby College P, 1967.

Donovan, Josephine. *Sarah Orne Jewett.* New York: Ungar, 1980.

Fields, Annie, ed. *Letters of Sarah Orne Jewett.* Boston: Houghton Mifflin, 1911.

Hawthorne, Nathaniel. *The Centenary Edition of the Works of Nathaniel Hawthorne.* Ed. William Charvat et al. Columbus: Ohio State UP, 1962–.

——. *The English Notebooks.* Ed. Randall Stewart. New York: Russell and Russell, 1962.

Howells, William Dean. Rev. of *Deephaven. Atlantic Monthly* 39 (June 1877): 759. Rpt. in Nagel, *Critical Essays on Sarah Orne Jewett* 25–26.

Jewett, Sarah Orne. *The Country of the Pointed Firs.* New York: Avon, 1977.

——. *A Marsh Island.* Boston: Houghton Mifflin, 1885.

Kelly, Franklin. "Lane and Church in Maine." Wilmerding et al., *Paintings by Fitz Hugh Lane* 129–56.

Nagel, Gwen L., ed. *Critical Essays on Sarah Orne Jewett.* Boston: Hall, 1984.

Novak, Barbara. "On Defining Luminism." Wilmerding et al., *American Light* 23–29.

More, Paul Elmer. "A Writer of New England." *Nation* 91 (27 Oct. 1910): 386–87. Rpt. in Cary, *Appreciation of Sarah Orne Jewett* 49–51.

Powell, Earl A. "The Boston Harbor Pictures." Wilmerding et al., *Paintings by Fitz Hugh Lane* 47–59.

——. "Luminism and the American Sublime." Wilmerding et al., *American Light* 69–94.

Thompson, Charles Miner. "The Art of Miss Jewett." *Atlantic Monthly* 94 (Oct. 1904): 485–97. Rpt. in Cary, *Appreciation of Sarah Orne Jewett* 32–48.

Tutweiler, Julia R. "Two New England Writers—in Relation to Their Art and to Each Other." *Gunton's Magazine* 25 (Nov. 1903): 419–25. Rpt. in Cary, *Appreciation of Sarah Orne Jewett* 26–31.

Westbrook, Perry D. *Acres of Flint: Sarah Orne Jewett and Her Contemporaries.* Rev. ed. Metuchen, N.J.: Scarecrow, 1981.

Wilmerding, John, et al., eds. *American Light: The Luminist Movement, 1850–1875.* Washington, D.C.: National Gallery of Art, 1980.

——, eds. *Paintings by Fitz Hugh Lane.* Washington, D.C.: National Gallery of Art, 1988.

Women and Genteel Poverty
in the Fiction of Hawthorne and Freeman

THE UNFORTUNATE FALL

Melissa McFarland Pennell

In addition to the works treated herein, Hawthornean influences
can be traced in numerous short stories from the collections *A
Humble Romance* and *A New England Nun,* as well as in novels
such as *Jane Field* and *The Shoulders of Atlas.*

In 1891, Mary E. Wilkins Freeman published her best-known collection, *A New
England Nun and Other Stories.* That year the first review to link her work and
Nathaniel Hawthorne's also appeared. Since then, similarities between the work of
Hawthorne and Freeman have been highlighted in critical responses to her work,
many focusing on the New England sensibility reflected by both authors.[1] For
instance, an early review of *Pembroke* indicates that both Hawthorne and Freeman
provide "the same wonderful pictures of New England life—pictures that are at once
a revelation of the depth and steadfastness of human nature and the capacity for
dogged, passionless suffering born and bred in the Puritan temperament" (Marchalonis 34). While Hawthorne and Freeman share an awareness of the power of
residual Calvinism in shaping New England experience, they also share a personal
understanding of the role class status and expectations played in the process of self-
definition. Each experienced the vulnerability of the individual in the rise and fall of
family fortunes, a vulnerability that also shapes the lives of some of their characters.[2]
Both authors confront in their fiction what Hawthorne identifies in *The House of the
Seven Gables* as the "inherent instability of human affairs" (366, ch. 1). *Seven Gables,*
Hawthorne's most extended treatment of the decline of family and fortune, articulates a set of values and expectations that governed the world into which Mary
Wilkins Freeman was born and in which her characters struggle to maintain a sense
of self-worth and independence. In his treatment of Hepzibah Pyncheon, Haw-

thorne creates a prototype for some of the women who later appear in Freeman's work. Aspects of Hepzibah's character important to Freeman's genteel women include: her intense valuing of the familial past, especially in light of the reduced circumstances of the present; her use of form and decorum to create emotional distance and self-protective barriers; and, most significantly, her acceptance of economic poverty to preserve a sense of integrity and independence.

Although Hawthorne claimed that *The House of the Seven Gables* was a "healthier product of [his] mind [than *The Scarlet Letter*]" (*Letters* 421), in it too he probes the darker sides of human experience, especially those influenced by social expectations. Keenly aware, in light of his own experiences, of the ways financial poverty and familial decline can contribute to emotional poverty and isolation, Hawthorne sympathetically portrays the struggles of Hepzibah Pyncheon, whose fantasies of miraculous rescue through the arrival of a mysterious fortune sustain her. Hepzibah's New England heritage, which Hawthorne sketches in this fiction, allows him to consider her character within the context of both a personal and historical past, to invest her with a sense of place and purpose. In *Seven Gables,* Hawthorne focuses upon the familial past of the Pyncheons, a history intertwined with that of his fictional town modeled on Salem. That this familial past also reverberates in the present is no surprise, for the narrative states that "a weighty lesson [comes] from the little regarded truth, that the act of a passing generation is the germ which may and must produce good or evil fruit in a distant time" (356, ch. 1). Hawthorne continues to develop this theme as his narrative recounts the self-serving acts of Pyncheons that have elevated some in terms of wealth but isolated others at the margins of society. The Pyncheons' illusive claim to lands in Maine have "resulted in . . . an absurd delusion of family importance" (367), while the family itself has dwindled in size and some, like Hepzibah and Clifford, have been denied full engagement with life. Despite this mixed history, Hepzibah is proud of her lineage, evident in her "reverence for the pictured visage" in the ancestral portrait that hangs in the house (380, ch. 2).

For Hepzibah, the importance of this history and of the house as its tangible symbol cannot be overstated. As Steven Mintz explains, "during the Victorian era, the family represented the most important symbol of stability and continuity, the only embodiment of a tangible past in a period of rampant change and self-seeking individualism" (13). However, the immediate Pyncheon family tree, in contrast to the "Pyncheon elm" which, though great in years, "was still in its strong and broad maturity" (374, ch. 1), now stands reduced to Jaffrey, his son, Hepzibah, Clifford, and cousin Phoebe. Hawthorne links this reduction to the actions and choices of various family members, introducing the notion of individual responsibility for the larger family fortunes. In nineteenth-century New England, where family name and history strongly influence one's place in the social fabric and one's sense of self, this responsibility is great indeed. When they result in decline, actions and choices are also interpreted through the New England Calvinist legacy that accepted, in practice if not in doctrine, the belief that poverty or financial failing was punishment for sin, a public sign of God's displeasure with an individual or family. Thus the depiction of a family's decline, either in numbers or in wealth, suggests the potential loss of place, social and psychological, for individuals confronting changes in the modern world. Hepzibah herself gives voice to the inner turmoil this creates for her when she tells Holgrave, "I wish I were dead, and in the old family tomb, with all my fore-fathers! . . . This world is too chill and hard" (389, ch. 3).

In addition to the burden of responsibility for preserving the family history, Hepzibah also bears the burden of maintaining some sign of the family's status. This is difficult, however, given her situation: she is "wretchedly poor" and though she has "fed herself from childhood with the shadowy food of aristocratic reminis-cences . . . [she] must [now] earn her own food, or starve!" (383, ch. 2). To explore Hepzibah's plight, Hawthorne examines her concepts of gentility, for she has been socialized to believe that "a lady's hand soils itself irremediably by doing aught for its bread" (383). Many nineteenth-century American genteel practices reflected aspira-tions toward a life of leisure as enjoyed by the English aristocracy and gentry, and women especially were charged with the responsibility of enacting them, especially as women's roles evolved within the "cult of domesticity." To fulfill her role within the genteel world and within the cult of domesticity, a woman began early in life to cultivate the talents and virtues that make this lifestyle possible, including the ability to interpret the symbolic significance of each gesture, article of clothing, and mate-rial good. According to the code of gentility, a set of values that exerted influence in Freeman's day as well, a woman's sense of self and her concepts of success (and failure) were shaped in accordance with her ability to conform to these expectations. Though Hepzibah readily admits that her values were shaped in another time and that she will never understand "new notions" (391, ch. 3), she too remains conscious of underlying meanings and how her own actions will be interpreted.

The values that have shaped her life allow Hepzibah to see herself as guardian of the house and repository of Pyncheon family lore and tradition, but such a role is unimportant to a world preoccupied with technological progress and change. Hepzibah exists at the margins of Salem's social world, her life circumscribed by a code of gentility and decorum, even though her house stands not far from the center of town. While the Pyncheon ancestors are described as men of temper and ire as well as fortune, Hepzibah, the first living Pyncheon to appear, is "the old maid" alone in the house. Hawthorne's repeated use of this pejorative is important, for it conveys the presumed stasis of Hepzibah's life and indicates how the community defines a woman of Hepzibah's age, marital status, and prospects. Even though Hepzibah has tried to remain invisible, accepting her marginality as part of her self-sacrifice, the community still exercises influence over her identity. The first scene in which she appears is filled with references to "restraint" and to an avoidance of "indecorum," indications that Hepzibah is governed by the expectations she inter-nalized years earlier. That she has "dwelt in strict seclusion; taking no part in the business of life, and just as little in its intercourse and pleasures" (377, ch. 2) reveals that Hepzibah (or any woman alone) has no role according to the conventions of her day. She cannot be part of that masculine world of competition and production nor can she fulfill the expectations of the cult of domesticity, for she has no family present and no social life.[3] Hawthorne further provides evidence of the community's standards of judgment through the gossip of the two laboring men and a few women of the neighborhood whose bits of dialogue offer the public assessment of Hepzibah Pyncheon.[4]

Hepzibah's distance from the world and her lack of interaction have created a false impression of her. Her black silk gown of outdated line and "the strange horror of a turban on her head" (386, ch. 2) are almost comical, while "her scowl had done Miss Hepzibah a very ill-office, in establishing her character as an ill-tempered old maid" (380). The narrative reveals, however, that "her heart never frowned. It was naturally tender, sensitive, and full of little tremors and palpitations" (380). Such tenderness of heart engenders vulnerability, and Hepzibah's strict adherence to the rules of decorum, that she was "born a lady, and [has] always lived one—no matter in what narrowness of means" (390, ch. 3), has served as a form of self-protection.[5] When Hepzibah speaks with Holgrave, who tells her that her attitudes suggest "not privilege, but restriction" (390), Hepzibah cannot relinquish the values that have defined her, as she replies "with a manner of antique stateliness, to which a melancholy smile lent a kind of grace" (391). This self-defensive use of decorum remains evident during the early stages of Phoebe's visit as well. Hepzibah's initial responses to Phoebe are governed by the standards according to which Hepzibah lives, establishing a formal distance between them. However, after a period of growing acquaintance, Hepzibah "kissed Phoebe, and pressed her to her heart" (435, ch. 6), finding new warmth in Phoebe's presence. This change in relationship occurs for Hepzibah in part because Phoebe accepts her as she is.[6] While Phoebe may be an example of the "new Plebianism" (421, ch. 5) that will supplant Hepzibah as shopkeeper and housekeeper, she also provides Hepzibah an important outlet for her affections.

One event that will allow Hepzibah to reclaim a portion of her role as a dutiful daughter of the Pyncheons is the return of her brother Clifford, released from years of wrongful imprisonment. Hepzibah has maintained a "continual devotedness" (378, ch. 2) toward her brother, and when he once again resides with her, she feels a "sorrowful affection" for him (443, ch 7). Hepzibah "had asked nothing of Providence, but the opportunity of devoting herself to this brother whom she had so loved" (466, ch. 9), yet his return brings her another failure. She cannot please her petulant brother, for "she was a grief to Clifford, and she knew it" (468). Though she feels a "strange mingling of the mother and sister" toward him (480, ch. 10), her acts of self-sacrifice cannot erase the impact of the outer world on Clifford, nor can she physically embody the signs of beauty that he craves. Not until Clifford has spent himself at the end of the "Flight of Two Owls" when "he forthwith began to sink" does he turn to Hepzibah, stating " 'You must take the lead now' " (581, ch. 17). But at the lonely station where they have landed, Hepzibah is separated from everything that has defined her life and her role. Fearing that her own reserves of love and affection will once again prove ineffective, Hepzibah cries out, " 'Oh, God—our Father—are we not thy children? Have mercy on us!' " (581), hoping for a safe return to their familiar, if limited, world.

Were this the extent of Hepzibah's character, she would fade into the background and take her place on the shelf as society expects. However, Hawthorne reveals another side to Hepzibah's character that anticipates the inner strength of the women in Freeman's fiction. Hepzibah has subsisted for a period of time, relying in part on a meager garden and the few eggs her chickens provide, but she has barely sustained herself and needs income to support herself and her brother. Even in this situation, she is bound by the expectations that have directed her life. Since she is not suited to sewing or teaching, "this business of setting up a petty shop is almost the only resource of women, in circumstances at all similar to those of our unfortunate recluse" (384, ch. 2). In spite of the desperate situation in which she finds herself, Hepzibah does not wish to be a charity case, even within her family. As the narrative explains, Hepzibah occupied, in "an extremely retired manner, the House of the Seven Gables, in which she had a life-estate. . . . [S]he was understood to be wretchedly poor, and seemed to make it her choice to remain so" (372, ch. 1). The crucial phrase here is "to make it her choice to remain so," for Hepzibah, like many of Freeman's later protagonists, has accepted her poverty and marginal existence as a means of maintaining her independence. Her rejections of Jaffrey's offers of income or shelter on his country estate symbolize her refusal to submit to Jaffrey's power or to accept his version of family history and destiny. When Jaffrey intrudes, hoping to coerce Clifford and Hepzibah into moving to his estate, Hepzibah stands up to him, seeing through his "loathsome pretense of affection," and "for once, Hepzibah's wrath had given her courage" (548, ch. 15). She ultimately accedes to Jaffrey's wishes that she call Clifford, but Hepzibah's moment of resistance and the willful anger that supports it signify the act of resistance her entire life has been.

As the romance draws to a close, Hawthorne sets in motion a process of restoration for Hepzibah. Upon Jaffrey's death and that of his son, the remaining Pyncheons inherit the family fortunes and estate. As they prepare to adjourn to their new country seat, Hepzibah clearly prefers the role of "Lady Bountiful" that her new wealth allows her to enjoy, as her gesture to Ned Higgins suggests. But Hawthorne's interest has been in the struggle Hepzibah endures to maintain her dignity and sense of self-worth. In telling her story, Hawthorne has invested her with a nobility that relies not on financial wealth but on the richness of character that lies beneath the surface of her too easily overlooked life.

This same underlying strength of character shapes many of the women in Freeman's fiction who must deal with the impact of financial and familial decline. Like Hawthorne, Mary Wilkins Freeman was born into a middle-class New England family that had strong ties to the region's history dating to the colonial period. She spent her childhood and young adulthood in two communities that had rigid social and religious codes that shaped an individual's view of self and the world. According to Edward Foster, it was in this sphere that Mary Wilkins learned what might be termed her own "five points" of New England life: "Work, Thrift, Family, Gentility," and Religion (14). Because of her personal experiences with social and financial decline, Freeman was able to create convincing portraits of the genteel poor, too "aristocratic" to "go into trade" and too proud to accept acts of charity. Like Hepzibah Pyncheon, these genteel poor became invisible as they retreated from village life, hidden behind the facades of houses that reflect the now lost prominence (and wealth) of their families. Throughout her life Freeman sought stable households that offered her the security that had been lost in her own family's decline, yet in some of her best works of fiction she depicts women who choose to stand on their own, who accept their marginal lives and meager finances as a means of preserving an uncompromised self. As Michele Clark notes, "having lost their status, their prosperity, and often their men [these women have] nothing to rely on but their pride, their capacity for a frugal independence, and their sense of self-esteem" (167).

The importance of gentility and the material wealth that helps to convey it appear in numerous stories and novels by Freeman. Often not the dominant issue of a story, the preservation of gentility proves an important undercurrent in the lives and expectations of characters. Emphasis on suitable attire, proper decor, and even the quality of food one consumes shapes the world in which many of Freeman's female characters live.[7] These women struggle to conform to the expectations of their world, conscious of both family tradition and the social parameters that limit the choices they can make. Aware of the middle-class pressure for upward mobility, especially through marriage, they also suffer the fear of falling, economically and socially. Many await the long-anticipated return of a loved one, usually in Freeman's stories a suitor, for whom they have maintained a steadfast devotion. Women who, like Hepzibah, have remained single, frequently consider sewing or teaching as a means of meeting their financial need, believing that such choices preserve their genteel status by avoiding the appearance of open competition for resources. Yet even in dire circumstances such women avoid accepting charity, seeing it, as does Hepzibah, as a loss of independence and a surrender of self to the control or influence of another. In every exchange, some level of parity must be preserved in order to maintain personal dignity. In works such as "Old Lady Pingree," "A Gala Dress," and *Pembroke,* Freeman creates "old maids" who resemble Hepzibah Pyncheon and share her values and struggles. But they are never simply copies; rather, Freeman treats each woman as an individual whose story deserves telling.

Nancy Pingree, the central character of "Old Lady Pingree," most closely resembles Hepzibah, even in her style of dress. Nancy "was lame in one hip; but for all that, there was a certain poor majesty in her carriage. Her rusty black dress hung in straight long folds, and trailed a little. She held her head erect, and wore an odd, black lace turban" (148). She too lives in an old family mansion, alone but for her two boarders. Nancy has already experienced a more severe dispossession than Hepzibah, for the "immense old mansion, which had been the outcome of the ancient prosperity of the Pingrees, was [now] owned entirely by [Deacon Holmes] through foreclosed mortgages" (153). Though by the Deacon's goodwill she has a "life-estate" there, "down in the depths of her proud old heart rankled the knowledge that an outsider owned the home of her fathers" (153). As for Hepzibah, family history and tradition are everything to Nancy, and being the "last of the hull family" she sees a need to uphold a certain standard, even though she claims " 'I ain't nothin' " (152). Having reached the age of eighty, Nancy focuses on the end of her life, and her way of upholding standards is "to be buried independent, like the rest of [her] folks" (152). She views the family burial plot as her final home: like the mansion "its singularity had been in subtle accordance with the Pingree character, and she was a Pingree" (159). She has been saving "a few cents at a time," though "all Nancy had to live on was the rent of [the] rooms, besides the small proceeds from her three hens and her knitting, and neighborly donations. Some days she had not much for sustenance except her pride" (154). But Nancy's pride and independence will be put to the test.

Raised in the genteel tradition, Nancy maintains a formality in her encounters with others and uses her sense of decorum as a means of self-protection. In her conversations with Mrs. Holmes, who serves as an intermediary between Nancy and the Deacon, Nancy speaks with an "air of resolution" and "a solemn tremor in her voice" (151). Mrs. Holmes is fully aware of Nancy's financial situation, and Nancy assumes that Mrs. Holmes will carry out the last offices at Nancy's death, yet this does not create a comfortable intimacy between them. Nancy requires that a certain distance be maintained in order to preserve her sense of social, if no longer economic, equality. When Mrs. Holmes concludes a visit, she leaves payment for Nancy's knitting in a basket in the vestibule. Nancy

> carried it into the sitting room, and opened it; it was packed with eatables. Done up in a little parcel at the bottom was the pay for the three pairs of stockings.
>
> This was the code of etiquette, which had to be strictly adhered to, in the matter of Nancy's receiving presents or remuneration. Gifts or presents openly proffered her were scornfully rejected, and ignominiously carried back by the donor. Nancy Pingree was a proud old woman. (153)

Refusing to perceive herself as a charity case, Nancy performs these small rituals as her own acts of resistance.

In her relationship with Jenny Stevens, one of her boarders, Nancy also relies on a level of formality. Like Hepzibah's early encounters with Phoebe, Nancy's early exchanges with Jenny reflect both her pride and a reluctance to become emotionally vulnerable by becoming too attached. When speaking with Jenny she exhibited a "stately manner of extending her arm" and "held her wide mouth stiff" (150). She resents that Jenny "seems to have the idea that [she's] so awful poor" (150), especially since Jenny and her mother have also fallen on hard times. When they disagree about Jenny's attempt to pay the rent, though her mother is desperately ill, "the two poor, proud souls stood confronting each other" (155), indicating that they have more in common than they admit. Upon her mother's death, Jenny reveals that she must ask the town to provide burial because Jenny lacks sufficient funds. Allowing her sympathy for Jenny to dictate her actions, Nancy parts with the money she has saved for her own funeral, finding that "this harsh charity . . . was almost like giving a piece of her own heart" (157). At first, she "felt for herself the respect which she would have felt for an Old Pingree in his palmiest days," but soon "she simply felt intense humiliation at having to confess her loss of independence" (157). Nancy, however, has gained by her sacrifice, for "she never regretted what she had done. She grew very fond of Jenny" (157) and Jenny returns her affection.

As does Hawthorne at the end of *Seven Gables,* Freeman supplies a means of financial restoration for Nancy, though less grand. In one of her conversations with Mrs. Holmes, Nancy admits that she has sacrificed her small hoard for Jenny, but she refuses Mrs. Holmes's offer to replace it. The railroad, which had provided Hepzibah with one of her encounters with the modern world, indirectly provides a means of rescue for Nancy. Mrs. Holmes, knowing that Nancy will not accept charity, tells her that the new rail line will be laid through the Pingree land and the depot built there as well. She goes on to explain that the Deacon wishes to compensate Nancy: "It isn't a present. It's no more than your just due. I don't think the Deacon would ever feel just right in his conscience if he didn't pay you a little something. You know the property wasn't considered worth so much when he foreclosed" (161). The $200 of this settlement gives back to Nancy the security she thought she had lost. As the narrative explains, "All her heart was full of a sweet, almost rapturous peace. She had had a bare, hard life; and now the one earthly ambition, pitiful and melancholy as it seemed, which had kept its living fire was gratified" (162).

As her writing progresses, Freeman creates figures who seem less closely modeled on Hepzibah but who still reflect aspects of her character. In *A New England Nun and Other Stories,* Freeman again includes a story of women coping with genteel poverty, though in this tale she uses humor to lighten the mood. The Babcock sisters of "A Gala Dress" are as proud a pair of New England spinsters as can be, who refuse "to be beholden to other folks" (38) even though they subsist on bread and butter and weak tea served in "china cups" with "thin silver teaspoons" (41). For Elizabeth and Emily Babcock, "there had been in their lives the faint savor of gentility and aristocracy" (43). They too live in the old family home that represents their heritage and their independence; "they might have had more if they would have sold or mortgaged their house, but they would have died first" (43–44). Their pride and desire to uphold standards extend to their public appearance, and for years they have faced a dilemma: they have been reduced to one acceptable black silk dress between them. The situation is dire indeed, for "to their notions of etiquette, black silk was as sacred a necessity as feathers at the English court" (44). To conceal the truth from the village, they take turns attending public functions, each time retrimming the dress to disguise its sameness. The two sisters, victims of "excessive shyness and secrecy" (40), are also "very fond of society, and their reserve did not interfere with their pleasure in the simple village outings" (44), but they most fear public exposure of their poverty.

To create dramatic tension in the story, Freeman introduces an adversary in the person of Matilda Jennings, a woman whose brash intrusiveness is not unlike that of Jaffrey Pyncheon, whom she even resembles.[8] She barges into the private world of the Babcock sisters' home obviously intending to snoop. Though she attempts "innocent insinuation [it] did not sit well upon Matilda . . . and the pretence was quite evident" (42). Hoping to find evidence that will corroborate her suspicion as to the true state of affairs within the Babcock home, Matilda spies the black silk dress awaiting its transformation. In her efforts to elicit the truth about the dress, "Matilda Jennings, in her chocolate calico, stood as relentlessly as any executioner before the Babcock sisters" (43). Her opportunity to force the issue comes the next day at the July Fourth picnic, when she allows Emily to walk into a cluster of exploding firecrackers. The dress is irreparably scorched, and Emily believes her and her sister's fate is sealed.

But here too Freeman introduces a reprieve that comes to the sisters out of the past. News of their Aunt Elizabeth's death allows Elizabeth to trim the black silk with mourning crepe, hiding the burn marks from prying eyes. A short time later, a trunk arrives containing many of Aunt Elizabeth's clothes, including two black silk dresses. The sisters appear together in public, and "the wonder and curiosity were certainly not confined to Matilda Jennings [since] the eccentricity which the Babcock sisters displayed in not going into society together had long been a favorite topic in the town" (49–50). Matilda, eager to gain insight, insinuates that townsfolk claim the sisters have finally resolved a feud. Stung by this comment, Elizabeth reveals the truth. But the reaction from Matilda is unexpected, for instead of gloating, she admits "I s'pose I begretched you that black silk. . . . I never had a black silk myself, nor any of my folks that I ever heard of" (52). In a moment of generosity that transcends their usual reserve, the Babcock sisters offer Matilda the old black silk, since they had "mended it nice" (52). Matilda, "with a fine light struggling out of her coarse old face," confesses her responsibility for the damage, achieving an honesty and intimacy rare among these village folk.

In her best-known novel, *Pembroke,* Freeman considers the threatened fall from genteel security in a subplot. Sylvia Crane is one of the younger of Freeman's "old maids," a spinster whose eighteen-year courtship with Richard Alger has been her long period of hopeful anticipation. Like Hepzibah, Sylvia lives in the family home, proud that it is "the oldest house in the village" (50) in which her traditions and memories are rooted.[9] While preserving the family home, Sylvia has made changes according to fashion, conscious of the demands of gentility and of the way she is perceived in the community. She exhibits a "perfect decorum and long-fostered maiden reserve" (53) that keeps her at the margins of familial and community activity and often appears "in the background" (45), as self-effacing as Hepzibah, observing the interactions of others. Though her family believes she has sufficient means to endure, Sylvia's pride keeps her from revealing the truth of her poverty. She has assumed that marriage to Richard, a man of some means, will alleviate this concern, but when this falls through, she must confront her plight.

Knowing that the few eggs from her hens and the "meagre moneys on her little lands" that the town selectmen have advanced her will no longer sustain her, Sylvia resigns herself to surrender. Her sister Hannah Berry acknowledges that "there wa'n't any chance for a woman like [Sylvia] to earn [her] livin' in Pembroke" (224). Sylvia has "conducted herself as if [her dealings with the town] were a guilty intrigue . . . to keep her poverty hid as long as may be" (207), but ultimately admits that the poorhouse is her only choice. To perpetuate her concealment a bit longer, Sylvia invites her family to tea, even though it will drain her financial resources and "reduce terribly her little period of respite and independence" (210).[10] Trapped by the demands of custom, Sylvia rages, but appears "like a wilful child who hurts itself because of its rage and impotent helplessness to hurt aught else" (211), as she recognizes her lack of power, social and economic. After holding the tea, the last office of her genteel life, Sylvia parts with possessions that have signified this life for her, the sofa and the "old thin silver spoons of the Crane family" (216), offering them as wedding gifts for her niece. As she readies the house for her departure, Sylvia feels "beyond any frenzy of sorrow or tears," working "hard all night" to create "neat order" in the hopes of preserving the last vestiges of her reputation (217).

Though her family's social and economic standing was never as high as that of the Pyncheons or of some Freeman's genteel women, Sylvia's fall entails what they all dread: public exposure.[11] Her ride to the poorhouse is marked by the struggle between her pride and her sense of defeat, for "she sat up straight in the chair[,] . . . [wearing] her best bonnet and shawl," but "she looked at everything . . . with a pang of parting forever" (218). On her way to the poorhouse, Sylvia must pass Richard's home; shocked by what he sees, Richard takes Sylvia back to the old Crane house. There he overcomes his pride and reticence, confessing his love for her. Through Richard Alger's actions, Freeman provides Sylvia a means of restoration. As Deborah Lambert notes, "penniless and half-starved, Sylvia is humiliated and powerless beyond all normal circumstances" and "Richard's response to Sylvia's plight demonstrates his economic power" (Lambert 204), but this power allows Sylvia to return to security after her trial. Like Nancy Pingree and the Babcock sisters (as well as Hepzibah Pyncheon), Sylvia ultimately has her wish fulfilled, though it comes through the more conventional agency of marriage.

The above stories are all written during the early years of Freeman's career, but the plight of women trapped within the strictures of genteel poverty continued to interest her.[12] Even in her last collection, *Edgewater People,* Freeman returned to this problem in "Value Received" when the Matthews sisters who are "stranded in a backwater of the intensely genteel and decorous past" teach a lesson about the "undersmart of charity." Late in her own life, Mary Wilkins Freeman denied being directly influenced by the work of any other writer, specifically distancing herself from Nathaniel Hawthorne (Kendrick 385). However, if one traces the echoes of Hawthorne's treatment of Hepzibah Pyncheon through Freeman's stories, a degree of influence seems undeniable. Both authors, writing from personal experience and observation, attempt to assert the dignity and meaning of their characters' lives in spite of their reduced circumstances. Both create endings that offer characters respite from the trials endured, suggesting their shared need to offer hope for recovery from "unfortunate falls." In his fiction, Hawthorne conveys the integrity and resiliency of a New England woman who endures a period of decline while struggling to preserve a sense of self. Freeman, writing decades later, sees New England women facing the same challenges and limits that Hawthorne perceived. Her ability to draw upon the model Hawthorne has created, while interweaving her own variations, makes each of her characters individual and unique. Her portrayals of genteel poverty reflect both a line of continuity between her work and Hawthorne's and the artistry that makes Mary Wilkins Freeman's fiction her own.

Notes

1. The first review to link their work appeared in *Bookman* [London] 1 (Dec. 1891): 102–3; rpt. in Marchalonis, *Critical Essays on Mary Wilkins Freeman* 22–25. Recently critics have identified certain Freeman stories as revisions of specific Hawthorne tales: see Susan Allen Toth in *Critical Essays* on "Wakefield" and "A Slip of the Leash"; John Getz in *Critical Essays* for an analysis of "The Birth-mark" and "Eglantina"; and Mary R. Reichardt's *A Web of Relationship* for discussion of "The Wedding Knell" and "Three Old Sisters and an Old Beau" as well as "Wakefield" and "A Slip of the Leash."

2. In his *Nathaniel Hawthorne in His Times,* James R. Mellow provides extensive discussion of the financial difficulties that beset Hawthorne from the time of his father's death through his own adulthood. Edwin Miller also considers Hawthorne's anxieties about the poorhouse in *Salem Is My Dwelling Place.* Freeman's experiences with the economic and social upheavals of the post–Civil War period are discussed in Edward Foster's *Mary E. Wilkins Freeman* and Mary Reichardt's *Web of Relationship.*

3. For a discussion of the conflicts between the "old gentility" and the "cult of the true woman," see Gillian Brown's "Women's Work and Bodies in *The House of the Seven Gables*" in her *Domestic Individualism* 63–95, and Joel Pfister's *Production of Personal Life.*

4. Both Foster and Reichardt offer comments on Freeman's use of gossip as a valuable narrative technique; see especially Reichardt 118–23.

5. Hawthorne's metaphor for Hepzibah's experiences, that "every added day of seclusion had rolled another stone against the cavern-door of her hermitage" (*Seven Gables* 385; ch. 2),

also foreshadows the literal practice of Sylvia Crane in Freeman's *Pembroke,* who rolls a stone before her door whenever she leaves.

6. This relationship between Hepzibah and Phoebe reappears with modifications in Freeman's *Shoulders of Atlas* (1908) in the relationship between Sylvia and Rose. Sylvia initially keeps Rose at a distance, fearing her judgment and rejection, but the barrier of decorum falls as she too finds an outlet for her affection.

7. The importance of gentility and decorum appears in numerous Freeman stories. In some, like "Robins and Hammers" from *A Humble Romance* and "The Givers" from *The Givers,* Freeman focuses on the material goods that are the tangible evidence of one's station. In "The Willow-Ware" from *The Fair Lavinia and Others,* Freeman offers insights into how a young woman is socialized under the rigors of genteel behavior.

8. In *Seven Gables,* Jaffrey is described as "portly," "with a dark square countenance," "[an] almost shaggy depth of eyebrows, and the massive accumulation of animal substance about the lower region of his face, a kind of fleshy effulgence" (452). Matilda of "A Gala Dress" is "short and stout, with a hard, sallow, rotundity of cheek, her small black eyes were bright pointed under fleshy brows" (42).

9. In front of the old Crane homestead stands "a great elm tree" (*Pembroke* 60), reminiscent of the Pyncheon elm in its grandeur.

10. Freeman also creates a link between Sylvia's need to conceal her poverty and her need to conceal her emotions, including her embarrassment over mistakenly revealing her feelings to Barney Thayer. In one scene Sylvia dons a Hawthornesque black veil to prevent her family from discerning her discomfort.

11. Freeman sets "Sister Liddy" from *A New England Nun and Other Stories* in a poorhouse. The recitation of loss by the various inhabitants gives a disturbing picture of the pain Sylvia anticipates on her journey.

12. See also "Bouncing Bet" in *Understudies* (1903).

Works Cited

Brown, Gillian. *Domestic Individualism.* Berkeley: U of California P, 1990.

Clark, Michele, ed. *The Revolt of Mother and Other Stories by Mary E. Wilkins Freeman.* Old Westbury, N.Y.: Feminist, 1974.

Foster, Edward. *Mary E. Wilkins Freeman.* New York: Hendricks House, 1956.

Freeman, Mary E. Wilkins. *Edgewater People.* New York: Harper, 1918.

——. *The Fair Lavinia and Others.* New York: Harper, 1907.

——. "A Gala Dress." *A New England Nun and Other Stories.* New York: Harper, 1891.

——. *The Givers.* New York: Harper, 1904.

——. "Old Lady Pingree." *A Humble Romance and Other Stories.* New York: Harper, 1887.

——. *Pembroke.* Ed. Perry Westbrook. New Haven: College and University P, 1971.

Getz, John. " 'Eglantina': Freeman's Revision of Hawthorne's 'The Birthmark.' " Marchalonis 177–84.

Hawthorne, Nathaniel. *The House of the Seven Gables. Novels.* New York: Library of America, 1983.

———. *The Letters, 1842–1853.* Vol. 16 of the *Centenary Edition of the Works of Nathaniel Hawthorne.* Ed. Thomas Woodson et al. Columbus: Ohio State UP, 1985.

Kendrick, Brent L., ed. *The Infant Sphinx: Collected Letters of Mary E. Wilkins Freeman.* Metuchen, N.J.: Scarecrow, 1985.

Lambert, Deborah G. "Rereading Mary Wilkins Freeman: Autonomy and Sexuality in *Pembroke.*" Marchalonis 197–206.

Marchalonis, Shirley, ed. *Critical Essays on Mary Wilkins Freeman.* Boston: Hall, 1991.

Mellow, James R. *Nathaniel Hawthorne in His Times.* Boston: Houghton Mifflin, 1980.

Miller, Edwin Haviland. *Salem Is My Dwelling Place.* Iowa City: U of Iowa P, 1991.

Mintz, Steven. *A Prison of Expectations: The Family in Victorian Culture.* New York: New York UP, 1983.

Pfister, Joel. *The Production of Personal Life: Class, Gender, and the Psychological in Hawthorne's Fiction.* Stanford: Stanford UP, 1991.

Reichardt, Mary R. *A Web of Relationship: Women in the Short Stories of Mary Wilkins Freeman.* Jackson: U of Mississippi P, 1992.

Toth, Susan Allen. "Defiant Light: A Positive View of Mary Wilkins Freeman." Marchalonis 123–31.

Hawthorne Student, Teacher, Critic,
and Respondent

KATHARINE LEE BATES

Melinda M. Ponder

Readers interested in other travel writing by Hawthorne will
want to read various sketches of American sites as well as *Our
Old Home* (1863), the *English Notebooks* (1870), and the *French
and Italian Notebooks* (1871). Bates's other travel writing is on
Spain: *Spanish Highways and Byways* (1900).

Katharine Lee Bates (1859–1929), best known today as the author of "America
the Beautiful," was a popular New England writer of fiction, poetry, and
literary criticism who admired, promoted, learned from, and responded to Hawthorne's writing. A student of his poetic and realistic artistry, she widened his
readership by her praise of him in her 1898 widely read textbook on American
literature, and in 1902 she further popularized him by writing the introductory
material for a complete edition of his fiction, the only such woman critic to do so. As
a teacher, critic, and writer, her interest in Hawthorne was important to her own
career, and her published work on him is significant today for its contribution to
Hawthorne studies. In the context of this book she can be seen as a transition figure
who reviewed, taught, discussed, introduced, and helped keep Hawthorne before
the reading public, especially in academe, while she herself was developing as an
educator, critic, and writer who used Hawthorne's subject matter and approaches
in her fiction and travel writing, eventually responding to his negative ideas of "literary women."

Bates was also a spokeswoman and advocate for women's education, having
graduated in 1880 from Wellesley College and joined its English Department in
1885, where she served as its chairman from 1891 to 1925. She eventually published
thirty-two volumes of creative or scholarly works in addition to hundreds of shorter
pieces in such periodicals as the *Atlantic Monthly* and the *New York Times,* many

focused on the lives and work of both fictional and historical women. As she became increasingly successful as a "scribbling" woman herself and a professional scholar and educator dedicated to training a new generation of female academics, Bates moved from focusing as a critic on the women in Hawthorne's life and writing to totally revising his images of women in *Our Old Home* (1863). Her own armchair travel book on England, *From Gretna Green to Land's End* (1907), is of special interest as it brings together two concerns of her professional life—women and Hawthorne—and provides a place where she can offer her own version of a "literary woman" (*CE* 5: 105).[1]

Bates had entered the Hawthorne "school" as a twenty-one-year-old graduate of the fledgling Wellesley College with her article in the *Boston Transcript* defending Hawthorne from Henry James's criticism of *The Marble Faun*. She had already been recognized as an important young writer with Longfellow's praise of her poem published by William Dean Howells in the *Atlantic Monthly*. Unlike the first generation of Hawthorne's women reviewers and promoters, Bates saw Hawthorne as a writer to emulate and study as much for the sake of her own career as for his. As Richard Brodhead notes, to post–Civil War authors Hawthorne was the founder of a tradition who "established the work they [sought] to continue" (51). And Bates saw herself entering into this literary and critical tradition open to women and men alike. As a professional writer, especially as a poet, Bates felt she could teach her readers about Hawthorne's artistry:

> Hawthorne's strange and shadowy tales linger among the mysteries of man's moral nature, which he reveals half mockingly, half mournfully, and withal lovingly, like the circling wind that rustles, with sobbing and dreary laughter, the colored leaves of autumn, in whose decay and corruption it finds a fascinating beauty. ("James")

She defends the "purely imaginative" element in Hawthorne, so much more interesting to her than James's realism: "Hawthorne . . . understood how to count the paving stones while he pointed to a star." She confidently disagrees with James, anticipating what she herself would attempt in her own poetry in the next four decades:

> Mr. James says rightly that Donatello is of a different substance from his companions, but reading further, we are tempted to mend the simile. It is as if a painter should give magic to his canvas by a strain of music, in obedience to whose cadences the figures of the picture should move and dance and live, and *wonderland* be opened to the gazer for an hour. ("James"; my emphasis)

As a hopeful writer herself, Bates may have been interested in Hawthorne initially because she shared his New England roots. Born of Yankee clergy and educators, Bates's paternal grandfather had been president of Middlebury College and her mother an early graduate of the Female Seminary, later Mount Holyoke College (Burgess 10). Like Hawthorne, she had grown up in a household impoverished by her father's early death where her youthful literary ambitions had been encouraged by the intellectual stimulation and verbal talent of the female members of the family.

As Bates began to write fiction, poetry, and children's literature, she found in Hawthorne a useful model of a professional writer. Like him, Bates was not able to live on the earnings from her writings and was forced to take jobs which supported her and several family members so that she could write. Hawthorne had worked at Brook Farm, the Custom Houses of Boston and Salem, and finally the Liverpool consulship; Bates worked as a professor of English at Wellesley College and earned a significant income from her commercial publications.

Bates advanced Hawthorne's reputation for several generations of student readers by her treatment of him in her 1898 *American Literature* published by the Macmillan Company and designed for use by secondary schools.[2] Setting literary history in the context of American cultural and political history, she discussed individual writers as distinct creators of American literature. Like Brander Matthews (10–14), Bates saw American literature as "a branch" of English literature and "the individual expression of an independent nation" (v), a literature with which its citizens ought to be familiar.[3]

Bates's enthusiasm for Hawthorne's writing, including his notebooks, is apparent throughout her *American Literature*.[4] Drawing on material from George Lathrop's *Study of Hawthorne,* Henry James's *Hawthorne,* and primarily from Hawthorne's own prefaces, notebooks, and material in the family memoirs of Julian Hawthorne and Rose Hawthorne Lathrop, Bates discusses Hawthorne's literary development, analyzing the strengths of each work and its place in his aesthetic development. She has a writer's interest in his methods, observing that his notebooks "testify to that self-imposed discipline of strict observation and accurate expression, which constituted his technical training for the art of literature" (305).[5] Like James, she explains Hawthorne's use of Puritan history in terms of its artistic potential: its "picturesqueness . . . attracted him" while the contrasts between "the divineness of the venture and the prosaic fashion in which it was pursued, between the burning soul of faith and its matter-of-fact, dismal body of Puritanism, rejoiced him with a pure artistic joy" (306). She depicts him "enveloping" and "draping" "rich, soft, dreamy shadow . . . a dusty ermine of romance" around "that iron age" (306). However, unlike James, she sees Hawthorne's "heredity and environment," "that crushing sense of human responsibility, of conscience, sin, and doom, those tremendous Puritan convictions sealed by blood and tears," not as restricting his talents but as provoking in him "aesthetic appreciation" (307). Of all the makers of "American literature," Hawthorne is Bates's choice as the writer on whom teachers should focus supplemental study throughout the year for his range of subject matter and the "charm" of his writing (328).

Bates's success with *American Literature* was important to her both professionally and financially. In the year of its publication, she recorded earning a sum nearly equal to that of her teaching salary of $1,700.[6] In the following year, 1899, her introduction to the T. Y. Crowell edition of *The House of the Seven Gables* appeared and was followed in 1900 by her introduction to Crowell's edition of *Twice-told Tales*. She was then chosen to write all the introductory material for Crowell's 1902 edition of Hawthorne's works.[7] Again, this represented a substantial professional honor as well as a financial achievement, as she once more earned a sum from Crowell nearly that of her teaching salary at Wellesley (Diary, 1905–26; Salary Receipt Register, 1899–1902). Because such an extensive edition was not again published until Ohio State University's *Centenary Edition,* Bates's presentation of Hawthorne remained the most current in his collected works for sixty years.

This introductory material in the 1902 Crowell edition, read as a whole, narrates the story of Hawthorne's literary career, expanding Bates's earlier discussions of him. In each volume, she discusses the historical, literary, and personal contexts of the work, its publication history, its reception history in both America and England, and the importance of the particular volume in his development as a writer. Writing with a keen interest in the women in Hawthorne's life and career, Bates adds to Hawthorne biography by including the voices and ideas of his mother, sisters, sister-in-law, and wife—material missing from earlier work by George Parsons Lathrop, Henry James, and George Woodberry[8]—and calls attention to other women such as Margaret Fuller, Hannah More, Elizabeth Barrett Browning, Harriet Beecher Stowe, and the Cary sisters, whose careers touched Hawthorne's.

Bates assessed Hawthorne from her own professional experience as a writer, as she had begun to do in her analysis of him in her *American Literature.* She was interested in his working habits, his material, his craft, and his genius, and she drew on her own experience to dramatize the small details of a writer's professional life. Writing from the perspective of her own knowledge of the difficulties of publication, of the layouts and readership of periodicals, of the critical importance of the reviewers' opinions, and of the arduous work of transforming ideas and notes into polished work, Bates pictures Hawthorne's slow climb to popularity as a drama best told by another writer, evoking the appearance and material context of Hawthorne's first pieces, describing both the quality of the publication and the placement of his work on the page. Analyzing Hawthorne's growth as a writer no doubt gave Bates insight into her own accumulating oeuvre and helped prepare her to respond to Hawthorne's presentation of England in *Our Old Home,* a subject on which she was also beginning to be an authority.

In 1906 Bates wrote an introduction to Crowell's edition of Hawthorne's *Our Old Home,* published as a small red volume, perfect for carrying in one's pocket on sightseeing excursions, and then left on her own trip to England, with a contract from *The Chautauquan,* the popular home-study movement's publication, for a series of articles describing her literary journey through England. Whereas Hawthorne had revised his *Atlantic Monthly* articles into *Our Old Home,* Bates parlayed her articles into *From Gretna Green to Land's End.* In this 1907 book, Bates's gender interests led her to remodel Hawthorne's "old home" and his view of intellectual women.

In *Our Old Home,* Hawthorne had written little that was positive about the few women he includes, instead focusing on their appearance or eccentricities. He spends several pages complaining of "the awful ponderosity of frame," the "elephantine" advance, and the "enormous bulk" of English matrons (*CE* 5: 48, 49). Then, centering his chapter on Shakespeare country around his role in Delia Bacon's attempt to prove that Shakespeare's plays were authored by a conclave of Elizabethan philosophers, he makes the phrase "Gifted Woman" of his chapter title almost an oxymoron with his story of Bacon's misdirected obsession.[9] Commenting at length on her appearance as well as on her ideas, he describes his stereotype of an intellectual woman without bothering to apologize for it:

> I had expected (the more shame for me, having no other ground of such expectation than that she was a literary woman) to see a very homely, uncouth, elderly personage. (*CE* 5: 105)

While Bates could explain Hawthorne's insulting comments about the girth of British matrons as part of his "imperfect and unfriendly conception of the English character" (Intro. to *Our Old Home* [*OOH*] xi), and call his generosity to Bacon worthy of any "knight" or "saint" (xvii), her whole book *From Gretna Green to Land's End* responds to his notions of gifted women with an alternative portrait of what a "literary woman" was like. Bates countered his persona of a male writer and American consul recording his experiences in England with her own persona of a female writer and scholar whose adventures and specialized knowledge of England's literary history expands her reader's cultural legacy to include intelligent and significant women, both the women Bates writes of and herself as narrator.

Bates had first traveled to England in 1890–91 for a sabbatical year at Oxford and had seen England through Hawthorne's eyes, carrying *Our Old Home* with her, perhaps as she describes in her introduction to it, "a dumpy volume in yellow paper covers" which could be picked up for a shilling as a guidebook "on the humblest bookstalls of Warwick, Lichfield, and Old Boston" (*OOH* xii). In her letters home, she referred her family to it, advising them to consult their own copies of Hawthorne to imagine her travels.

Familiar with both Hawthorne's essays on England and their source in his *English Notebooks,* Bates had analyzed their strengths and weaknesses in her introduction to Crowell's edition of *Our Old Home.* About to write about her own travel articles, Bates saw Hawthorne's work not as a collection of Addisonian sketches whose details illustrate Hawthorne's philosophical, cultural, and personal questions but as a book for armchair travelers. She saw his poor choice of material as regrettable since his notebooks abound with memorable and vivid sketches, particularly of the beautiful

Lake Country which Hawthorne, with his "full sympathy with the poetic associations" and "delight in noble scenery," could have made pleasant reading, "brightened," as it was in the notebooks, "by some of his most characteristic human touches" (*OOH* xiii). Hawthorne's charm in the notebooks from "the freshness of the impressions," and "the frank informality of the tone" unfortunately, Bates wrote, was absent from the essays. However, she did find some of Hawthorne's revised descriptions striking—his appreciation of England's " 'veiled sky, and green lustre of the lawn and fields' " (xvi), of its Gothic cathedrals, Tower of London, Warwick Castle, and Leicester's Hospital. Above all, for Bates, it was Hawthorne's persona as "an active man of affairs, sustaining his due part in social intercourse and supremely delighting in London,—a man generous to human need and tender of human infirmity" (xvii), so moved by the children in the slums, which made his book noteworthy. Bates therefore chose to write about material omitted by him, particularly the Lake Country and Oxford, and create her unusual persona of a woman scholar successfully traveling through the home of her literary ancestors.

Hawthorne had given his readers valuable advice on the secret of good travel writing, gleaned, perhaps partly, during his own extensive reading of travel literature borrowed from the Salem Athenaeum. While writing in the chapter "Up the Thames" about the "air-castle" of the Crystal Palace "glimmering afar in the afternoon sunshine like an imaginary structure" (*CE* 5: 258), he describes the travel writer's difficulties:

> While writing these reminiscences, I am continually impressed with the futility of the effort to give any creative truth to my sketch, so that it might produce such pictures in the reader's mind as would cause the original scenes to appear familiar, when afterwards beheld. (5: 258)

Then, revealing the secrets of his own craft, he advises the travel writer instead to "Give the emotions that cluster about [the scene], and, without being able to analyze the spell by which it is summoned up, you get something like a simulacrum of the object in the midst of them" (5: 259). Bates had already heeded this advice in her first popular travel book, *Spanish Highways and Byways,* published in 1900 at the close of the Spanish-American War. Now, in writing about England, she structured her book around the distinctive impressions and "cluster of emotions" which she felt as a woman traveler, teacher, and writer.

Bates makes her persona of a female traveler in quest of intellectual adventure clear from the start of her journey. The covers of her book, especially the first deep-red edition, suggest a quest, with heraldic designs in gold leaf, and there is an enclosed map for her readers to follow on their pilgrimage. As a female critic of English poetry (she had published *The Ballad Book* in 1893 and then textbook editions of Shakespeare, Coleridge, Keats, and Tennyson), Bates authoritatively enters England's literary past. Her tone is exuberant and welcoming to her readers, now her students, as she shows the English landscape to be alive with the voices of its poets, dramatists, and novelists.

Where Hawthorne had ushered his readers into his "dusky and stifled" consul office in Liverpool (*CE* 5: 9), Bates welcomes her readers to join her on the train. Knowing that many of her readers could afford to travel only vicariously with her, Bates asks them imaginatively to join "us," Bates and her traveling companion, Katharine Coman, a social economist and feminist whose beautiful photographs illustrate Bates's prose guide. Even those who can afford only her book can share her all-female compartment, a private space large enough for their enthusiasm:

> well worth the honest price of first-class tickets, for as the rain sped on from the Ribble into the Eden Valley, with the blue heights of the Pennine range and the long reaches of the Yorkshire moors on our right, and on our left the cloud-caressed summits of Lakeland, we needed all the space there was for our exultant *ohs* and *ahs,* not to mention our continual rushing from window to window for the swiftly vanishing views of grey castle and ruined abbey, peel tower and stone sheep-fold, grange and hamlet, and the pearly, ever-changing panorama of the mist. (*Gretna Green* 1–2)

Following Hawthorne's advice about conveying her own impressions and associations, Bates sees the area around Carlisle from her perspective as a female scholar in the periods of its Roman occupation, settlement by the Britons, and its border warfare "as Scotch balladry well remembers" (14), using the voices of past singers to vividly dramatize the history whose ruins she visits. From the beginning of her book, Bates reminds her readers of the role played by women in English history and literature, of the women of Carlisle who held off the Scots with boiling water, of Mary Queen of Scots, of Queen Eleanor, and of Lady Carlisle, "a vigourous worker in the causes of Temperance and Woman Suffrage" (24). Her first chapter, like Hawthorne's "Consular Experiences," situates the reader in his or her new country and in the professional life and mind of its interesting narrator. Not only is she a female scholar, she is at heart an imaginative writer who concludes her first chapter by making her persona clear:

> It was already evening, but such was the witchery of the scene, still with something eerie and lawless about it despite an occasional farmhouse with stuffed barns and plump ricks and meadows of unmolested kine, that we would gladly, like the old Borderers whose armorial bearings so frequently included stars and crescents, have spent the night in that Debatable Land, with the moon for our accomplice in moss-trooping. (29)

Clearly, Bates was an improvement over Hawthorne's Delia Bacon. Well-trained in careful research techniques, intelligent, and resourceful, Bates was a woman critic healthily invigorated by her scholarly pursuits.

Where Hawthorne had frequently wrestled with the problem of seeing the reality of a place which his imagination had constructed from his reading and then finding that the reality never measured up to the imagined landscape (one thinks of him looking in vain for the exact spot of Dr. Johnson's penance or Warwick Castle, which could only be a dream if seen from the safe distance of the bridge [*CE* 5: 66–67]), Bates presents herself as relishing her adventures in the landscapes most associated with writers she loves. Proceeding to the Lake Country from the Border, she becomes a guide with whom the reader can identify, as she recounts the difficulties of finding lodgings, of being "banged and clanged along a few miles of fairly level road" in a "motor-bus, of all atrocities" (*Gretna Green* 31), and of enjoying Ambleside and Grasmere without compulsively consulting Wordsworth's "Excursion" for apt lines. Although her Lake District, with its Wordsworthian "opalescent hills and silver meres" (50), was full of rain, her scholarly work on early English drama enabled her to see a significance in ceremonies which might have been overlooked by those, like Hawthorne, without her training. She links the pagan rites in honor of nature gods with the Christian rituals, describing the rush-bearing processions as survivals of the medieval miracle plays, all presided over by Wordsworth's beloved circle of mountains (59). In such a chapter, Bates energetically brings her extensive scholarly expertise to a landscape already rich with literary associations and thus creates a Lake Country uniquely her own.

In her long central section on Shakespeare's country, Bates inevitably must confront Hawthorne's material, especially the specter of Delia Bacon and women scholars whose intellects have been developed by "overmastering ideas" and "deep political philosophy" which then unbalance their sanity. Instead, Bates shows herself to be a sound scholar of both Shakespeare and English drama who, having spent several of her sabbatical years in Oxford, can show her readers the Shakespeare whom Hawthorne had missed. Where Hawthorne had been unable to feel much emotion while in Shakespeare's birthplace, Bates effectively connects her reader to him by describing the Shakespeare landscapes of meaning to her—"the noble symmetries of St. Michael's, its companion spires of Holy Trinity and Grey Friars, the narrow streets and over-jutting housetops, the timber-framed buildings, the frescoed walls and carven window-heads, all that we see to-day of the medieval fashion he must have seen in fresher beauty, and far more" (147). Moving from nearby Coventry where Shakespeare could have watched the " 'rude mechanicals' " playing the Nativity (153), through Warwick and Kenilworth to "Leycester's Hospital, so inimitably described by Hawthorne" (to which Bates adds her own lovely description), into Stratford and the traditional Shakespeare sites, Bates, always interested in the women connected with male writers, adds a trip to Wilmcote, the birthplace of Shakespeare's mother.

Beyond the Cotswolds where Shakespeare traditions cling "like a silver mist," Bates describes Oxford as he would have approached it, through Woodstock, noting his status as an outsider, one she had experienced herself as a woman scholar in the university town:

I would give half my library to know with what feelings Shakespeare used to behold its sublime group of spires and towers against the sunset sky. This "upstart crow," often made to wince under the scorn of those who, like Robert Greene,—the red-headed reprobate!—could write themselves "Master of Arts of both Universities," what manner of look did he turn upon the august town

> "gorgeous with high-built colleges,
> And scholars seemly in their grave attire,
> Learned in searching principles of art?"

(Gretna Green 202)

Bates drew for her description of Oxford on her own familiarity with such places as the grounds of Magdalen College, "where deer browse peacefully beneath the shade of giant elms and where Addison's beloved Water Walks beside the Cherwell are golden with the primroses and daffodils of March and blue with the violets and periwinkles of later spring, [which] are even more tempting to the book-fagged wanderer than Christ Church Meadow and 'Mesopotamia'" (207–8). She includes the May Day rite at dawn (which she enjoyed at 5:00 a.m.), when "the ending of the rite is made known to the multitude by the flinging over of the caps,—black mortar-boards that sail like a flock of pensive rooks—then away it streams over Magdalen Bridge toward Iffley" (208), and wonders what "the thronging student life of Oxford [could] have meant to the author of 'Hamlet.'" Where his teachers and rivals were at home beside the rivers of Oxford and Cambridge, "did those fluttering gowns, those gaudy-hoody processions, stir in him more than a stranger's curiosity?" And, critical of the brotherhood of scholars closed to women as well as to those who disagreed with the strong philological orientation of contemporary Oxford criticism, she writes: "Even now, when his name is blazoned on rows upon rows of volumes in window after window of Broad Street, I doubt if the Oxford dons would deem Shakespeare capable of editing his own works" (228).

In addition to presenting her own views of places described by Hawthorne, Bates extends her journey to additional places—especially those of women who were significant in England's history and literature. She writes of her pilgrimage to Swarthmoor for the sake of Quaker leader Margaret Askew Fell, the descendant of Anne Askew, " a beautiful woman of twenty-four, thoughtful and truthful, [who] had been burned as a heretic" (94) and was tried with her four daughters for refusing to take the oath of supremacy in 1663. Bates describes the women martyred as witches who were burned in Lancashire, "poor old crones, doubled up and corded thumb to toe . . . [and] flung into the Calder to see whether they would sink or swim" (103). Bates warms the brass tablet in Cheshire's Church of St. Michael by recounting a woman's story, a ballad of a "Spanish Lady's Love for Sir Uryan, an offish personage," whose "blunt English manners" she puts to shame (114). Cheshire, for Bates, is also the home of Mrs. Gaskell, with Knutsford her Cranford, whose Mary Barton gave such a sympathetic presentation of the Lancashire mill hands and who "served the poor of Manchester not with the pen alone" (119) but, during the cotton famine brought on by our Civil War, organized sewing rooms and other means of employment for women.

Paralleling Hawthorne's similar centrally placed excursion into Robert Burns country with her own central section on a woman writer's home, Bates describes "The Heart of England" as the place that shaped George Eliot's development. Up to this point, Bates's female gender has seemingly caused her no problems as a scholar-traveler making her way through England. However, as if to underscore the difficulties faced by a woman such as George Eliot whose career is apparently invisible even in the town of her birth, Bates describes the lack of control and mobility she faced as a tourist. Taking trains where possible, Bates and Coman decided to "post" through the country, having tried "an automobile scamper" across Staffordshire where the driver had not listened to their directions or requests. As Bates notes, even with a cart, the women wanted to drive themselves (both literally and metaphorically), "but the English hostlers, shaking their stolid heads, preferred that we should be driven" (138). In the Lake Country, they had been lucky to find a "broad-minded butcher" who would trust them on short expeditions with a pony and cart, but they were not so fortunate near George Eliot's Nuneaton, still off the tourist path today, and so engaged a "victoria" pulled by a single horse for a shilling a mile, controlled, of course, by the reins of the male driver. The driver, representative of a far larger male population, had never heard of "George Eliot" and thus could not understand their quest, both physical and spiritual.

Eliot's town also seemed oblivious of her renown: "Nuneaton was as placidly engaged in making hats and ribbons as if the foot of genius had never hallowed its soil, and went its ways regardless while we peered out at inns and residences mirrored in George Eliot's writings"—while Bates perseveres to find her school and the rectory where she had been a child in Chilvers Coton which, "like Nuneaton, [had] no memories of its famous woman of letters" (141). Indeed, the only time the women see her name is on a poster advertising "George Eliot Sauce" (141). Even in the local church, her brother, Isaac Evans, had dedicated his window in memory of his wife, not his sister, and the sexton can only tell Bates "in rambling, gossipy fashion, what a respectable man Mr. Isaac Evans was, and that he never would have anything to do with 'his sister for years'" until she married Mr. Cross (143). It is only when Bates visits the "quiet brown house set among laden apple-trees . . . with a bright, old-fashioned garden of dahlias, sweet peas, and hollyhocks" where George Eliot was born (144) that she feels the congruence between her sense of the writer and her place, the kind of association suggested by Hawthorne.

In her final chapter, Bates continues her identification with all adventurers, female and male, ending her journey in Devon and Cornwall, appropriately at the seacoast long the launching place of such explorers as Sir Francis Drake and Sir Walter Raleigh. Having grown up on coastal Cape Cod, Bates is at home in a landscape "freshly discovered by each new lover of the moorland and the sea, of soft air and the play of shadows, of folklore and tradition, of the memory of heroes" (335). At Biddeford, Kingsley's "hero-town," she honors those who fought against the Spanish fleet and then visits King Arthur's landmarks, bravely casting a stone, for lack of an Excalibur, into the bottomless tarn of legend through that "wet, white air" (360). Making their final pilgrimage to Tintagel, Bates and Coman climb the slippery paths to the site of Arthur's castle with its dramatic views of the "Holy Headland," and Bates rides on to Land's End, a female quester looking toward her American home in "the land of hope and promise" (378). Like Hawthorne, who leaves his readers watching him attempt to "save both countries, or perish in the attempt," Bates looks homeward as she ends her book. Because she has made England unforgettable with her adventures in it, *Our Old Home* seems far more interesting with her female and scholarly perspective expanding its dimensions. Not surprisingly, Bates's work was more popular than Hawthorne's, going through at least five editions.

As a writer, Hawthorne had taught Bates about style and the ideal world existing beyond the commonplace. She wrote, "For an author, style must be the body of personality," and she loved "the inevitable grace" of Hawthorne's speech, "words that fall like the music of a voice" (*OOH* xviii). His voice and life were also rich models for her, giving her a sense of how a writer could shape both the readers and the culture of America by opening "wonderland" for their gaze. However, as she came into her own as a writer, with her appealing creative mind, verbal power, and twentieth-century sexual politics, Bates made "our" England the home of both her male and female readers and complicated Hawthorne's definition of gifted and literary women.[10]

Notes

I gratefully acknowledge the help of Wilma R. Slaight, archivist at Wellesley College, for her suggestions and assistance with my research.

1. References to Hawthorne's *Our Old Home* are to the *Centenary Edition,* hereafter cited as *CE* with volume and page number. Bates's editions of Hawthorne's works are cited by title and page number.

2. Her textbook joined others by Brander Matthews, Fred Pattee, and Moses Coit Tyler (Vanderbilt 132).

3. Spencer discusses the "correlation of American literature with the American character" (292–96).

4. See, for instance, her use of Hawthorne's description of Thoreau (221).

5. Likewise Leslie Stephen, one of the sources recommended by Bates, praises Hawthorne's "fineness of observation" (298).

KATHARINE LEE BATES

6. Bates listed the earnings from her publications in her Diary, 1905–26. I am indebted to Wellesley College for its release of information to me in the Salary Receipt Register, 1896–99.

7. Known as the Lenox Edition, the set was entitled *Hawthorne's Romances* and included the following: *Twice-told Tales* (vols. 1 and 2); *Mosses from an Old Manse* (vols. 3 and 4); *The Scarlet Letter* (vol. 5); *House of the Seven Gables* (vol. 6); *A Wonder Book for Girls and Boys* (vol. 7); *Tanglewood Tales* (vol. 8); *The Blithedale Romance* (vol. 9); *The Marble Faun* (vols. 10 and 11); *The Snow Image* (vol. 12); *Fanshawe* (vol. 13); *The Whole History of Grandfather's Chair* (vol. 14). *Our Old Home* was published separately by T. Y. Crowell in 1906 with Bates's introduction. Crowell also published a more compact set of seven volumes, known as the Popular Edition, in 1902 in which he used the same introductions by Katharine Lee Bates. My references are to the Lenox Edition. Rose Hawthorne Lathrop wrote a general introduction for the 1900 Autograph Edition. Limited to 500 copies, each work had introductory notes by H. E. Scudder.

8. See my article in the *Nathaniel Hawthorne Review* for an extended discussion of this topic.

9. See Nina Baym's article for an interesting discussion of Hawthorne's promotion of Delia Bacon.

10. See the Introduction to this volume for a detailed discussion of Hawthorne's exploration of gender issues.

Works Cited

"Annual Reports of the President and Treasurer of Wellesley College." 1894, 1895, 1896, 1897, 1898, 1900, 1903. Wellesley College Archives. Boston: Frank Wood.

Bates, Katharine Lee. *American Literature.* New York: Macmillan, 1898.

——. Diary, 1893–97; 1905–26. Katharine Lee Bates Papers. Wellesley College Archives.

——. *From Gretna Green to Land's End.* New York: Crowell, 1907.

——. Introductory notes to *Hawthorne's Romances.* Vols. 1–14. New York: Crowell, 1902.

——. Introductory notes to *Our Old Home.* New York: Crowell, 1906.

——. "James on 'The Marble Faun.'" *Boston Evening Transcript* 24 Sept. 1880.

Baym, Nina. "Delia Bacon: Hawthorne's Last Heroine." *Nathaniel Hawthorne Review* 20.2 (Fall 1994): 1–10.

Brodhead, Richard H. *The School of Hawthorne.* New York: Oxford UP, 1986.

Burgess, Dorothy. *Dream and Deed.* Norman: U of Oklahoma P, 1952.

Cady, Edwin H. "The Wizard Hand: Hawthorne, 1864–1900." *Hawthorne Centenary Essays.* Ed. Roy Harvey Pearce. Columbus: Ohio State UP, 1964. 317–66.

Hawthorne, Nathaniel. *Our Old Home.* Vol. 5 of the *Centenary Edition of the Works of Nathaniel Hawthorne.* Ed. William Charvat et al. Columbus: Ohio State UP, 1970.

Hutton, Richard H. *Essays in Literary Criticism.* Philadelphia: Coates, 1876.

James, Henry. *Hawthorne.* 1879. Ithaca, N.Y.: Cornell UP, 1956.

Matthews, Brander. *An Introduction to the Study of American Literature.* New York: American Book, 1896.

"Nathaniel Hawthorne." Department of English Literature, Course Catalogues (1895–1900). Courses of Instruction, outlines, syllabi, reading lists, exams. Wellesley College Archives.

Ponder, Melinda M. "Katharine Lee Bates: Hawthorne Critic and Scholar." *Nathaniel Hawthorne Review* 16.1 (Spring 1990): 6–11.

Rathbun, John W., and Harry H. Clark. *American Literary Criticism, 1860–1905.* Boston: Twayne (Hall), 1979.

"Review of *American Literature.*" No source or date. Reviews of Miss Bates's Publications. Katharine Lee Bates Papers. Wellesley College Archives.

Salary Receipt Registers, 1896–99; 1899–1902. Wellesley College Archives.

Smith, Alexander. *Dreamthorpe.* Boston: Tilton, 1864.

Spencer, Benjamin T. *The Quest for Nationality.* Syracuse: Syracuse UP, 1957.

Stephen, Leslie. *Hours in a Library.* London: Smith, Elder, 1874.

Vanderbilt, Kermit. *American Literature and the Academy.* Philadelphia: U of Pennsylvania P, 1986.

CATHER AND HAWTHORNE

John J. Murphy

In her essay on Sarah Orne Jewett, Willa Cather selected *The Scarlet Letter* as one of the "three American books which have the possibility of a long, long life" and "confront time and change so serenely" ("Best Stories" 58). She also praised Hawthorne's masterpiece in her seminal statement "The Novel Démeublé" as an example of artistic selection: "The material investiture of the story is presented as if unconsciously; by the reserved, fastidious hand of the artist, not by the gaudy fingers of a showman or the mechanical industry of a department-store window dresser" (41). She might have had "The Birth-mark" in mind when she wrote "The Profile," an early story of a woman with a facial disfigurement (Woodress 125). Certainly she read Hawthorne extensively; a complete edition of his works was in her childhood home in Red Cloud, Nebraska (Woodress 40). In her early piece on Poe in the *Lincoln Courier*, she lists Hawthorne, Poe, and James as our only masters of pure prose (*Kingdom of Art* 382). There is little doubt she admired Hawthorne greatly, and she shared with him a sense of locale, a sense of the past, superior descriptive powers, and an interest in rendering landscape.

There are thematic similarities as well; for both writers, the conflict between good and evil was an inherent aspect of settling the wilderness. Roy R. Male's summary of this combination in Hawthorne and of the search it generated might well be applied to Cather:

The wilderness offered freedom from time's ravages, a dream of renascent youth, but it was also the realm of the devil. Since in its untrammeled spaciousness no guiding path from past experience could be discerned, what appeared to be freedom was likely to prove delusory wandering and waste. . . . In [Hawthorne's] own life, he restlessly sought a home that would combine the rich density of accumulated time with freedom and novelty of open space. (40–45)

Cather's prairie novels (*O Pioneers!* [1913], *My Ántonia* [1918], *One of Ours* [1922], and *A Lost Lady* [1923]) chronicle the failure of pioneers to accomplish much beyond repeating the evils of older societies but without their redeeming cultural achievements. As a result, for her protagonists, westward movement reverses to eastward movement and an escape into art and history. This direction, of course, reflects Hawthorne's capping his completed novels with *The Marble Faun,* which can be seen as instigating a tradition that Cather, through James and Wharton, embraced as her own. At her death in 1947 she left unfinished her first novel to be set entirely in Europe (papal Avignon); however, prior to that she discovered a fruitful combination of accumulated time and space in the American Southwest which she utilized in *The Song of the Lark* (1915), *The Professor's House* (1925), and most successfully in her masterpiece *Death Comes for the Archbishop* (1927). She had found a substitute for Europe in the pueblo cultures of the mesa country and was among the first to explore it in fiction.

Both thematic similarities, the failed gambol in space and the discovery of a culture of accumulated time, should be considered in placing Cather in the Hawthorne tradition. The following comparison of *The Blithedale Romance* and *My Ántonia* (their authors' only novel-length experiments in first-person narrative) should illustrate the initial theme, and the consideration subsequent to that of *Death Comes for the Archbishop* with reference to *The Marble Faun* should illustrate the second.

At the beginning of *The Blithedale Romance,* Miles Coverdale, having "faith and force enough to form generous hopes of the world's destiny," travels "far beyond the strike of city clocks, through a drifting snowstorm" (9–11). The air beyond the limits of Boston "had not been breathed once and again," and "wave-like drifts" have buried the stone fences. There are few human traces: the dwellings are scattered, the villas deserted "with no footprints in their avenues" (10–12). Hawthorne takes his narrator to the fringes of settlement, to a miniature frontier where a somewhat misguided agricultural effort at reforming the world will be observed.

Although Coverdale initially admits some "generous hopes" regarding the world's destiny, his experiences at Blithedale soon motivate him toward a literary interest in it. Refusing to pursue the attraction he feels for Zenobia and the love he finally admits for Priscilla because there is nothing he so much fears as proving himself a fool or an ass, he remains aloof, prying into the affairs of others, impatiently wishing for a conclusion: "I began to long for a catastrophe. . . . I would look on, as it seemed my part to do, understandingly, if my intellect could fathom the meaning and the moral" (157). Coverdale returns to Blithedale at the end "with a yearning interest to learn the upshot of all my story" (205). Before Zenobia's body is taken from the dark river, he has a dream, "all the circumstances of which . . . converge to some tragical catastrophe" (228). His stance toward life is objectified in his hermitage, "A hollow chamber of rare seclusion" formed by the decay of some branches in a pine tree. From here he can spy on others as material for his study and protect himself from involvement: "This hermitage was my one exclusive possession while I counted myself a brother of the socialists. It symbolized my individuality and aided me in keeping it inviolate" (99).

While the experiences Jim Burden narrates in *My Ántonia* lack the mystery of Coverdale's, his stance is surprisingly similar. There is a curious passage beyond the middle of Cather's novel where Burden admits his reluctance to leave the green enclosure behind an overhanging elm, "where the sunlight flickered so bright through the grapevines" (179), to join the hired girls for their picnic. Burden has other retreats—the bedroom where he confines himself after his struggle with Wick Cutter, the study in Lincoln where he conceives his Black-Hawk friends as literary figures. (While reading Virgil he hears the hired girls' laughter, and the image of "Lena coming across the harvest-field in her short skirt" floats like a picture above the line "*Optima dies . . . prima fugit*" [204].) His withdrawal began before he left Black-Hawk ("I sat at home with the old people in the evenings now, reading Latin that was not in our High-School course" [174]), and by the Lincoln section Burden's mind and responses are dominated by music, poetry, and theater. Thrilled by fictional people and situations rather than real life, he responds to Lena's renunciation with less feeling than when watching Marguerite renounce Armand in *Camille*. Indeed, his whole narration, from the snake episode with its St.-George-and-the-dragon motif to the final stylized idealization of Ántonia, is dominated by a literary vision.

The need in both novels for a world of one's own making accompanies a feeling of loss in dealing with reality, frustration that life is not turning out the way one would like it. Burden entered a place much less touched by humanity than Coverdale had, "not a country at all, but the material out of which countries are made." He had "the feeling that the world was left behind, that we had got over the edge of it, and were outside man's jurisdiction. . . . Between that earth and that sky I felt erased, blotted out" (12–13). "Everywhere, as far as the eye could reach, there was nothing but rough, shaggy, red grass. . . . [T]he grass was the country, as the water is the sea. . . . I felt motion in the landscape; in the fresh, easy-blowing morning wind, and in the earth itself" (18). Surely not many descriptions are as inspired about new beginnings.

But their promise is short-lived. The corpse of Mr. Shimerda, which will not fit in a standard coffin and is rejected by the Catholics because of their creed and the Norwegians because of their clannishness, announces that this unmade country will be molded according to old patterns unrelieved by the cultural life Burden will discover at university. The pettiness he contemplates as he paces the streets at night indicates how inadequately people realize the potential of new beginnings and how quickly the cultural deprived among them (read American-born in Cather) succumb to materialism. The life that went on in the flimsy frame houses "was made up of evasions and negations; shifts to save cooking, to save washing and cleaning; devices to propitiate the tongue of gossip. The guarded mode of existence was like living under a tyranny" (168). Burden's disappointment with the outcome of the place makes him want to flee: "I wanted to get away as soon as possible" (174). How similar this is to Coverdale's confession: "Blithedale was no longer what it had been. Everything was suddenly faded. . . . I felt an inexpressible longing for at least a temporary novelty" (138–40). Coverdale returns to Boston. Unfulfilled desire, selfishness, and hypocrisy, suggested here in the stiffened, distorted corpse of Zenobia, are the upshot of this attempt at new beginnings, and Coverdale admits "an intolerable discontent and irksomeness" (138). The discontent is partially with himself, as is Jim Burden's. Like Coverdale, Burden refused or was not able to establish satisfactory relationships with women. Perhaps they required too much, for Ántonia became involved with the snakelike Wick Cutter just as Zenobia and Priscilla were bound to the evil Westervelt. In Cather's novel social class plays an important role in this regard. Marriage to Ántonia or Lena seems beneath Burden, would frustrate his going the privileged route to Harvard and law school. He also shares with Coverdale a quality ironic in one so condemning of society, a fear of the opinions of others: "Disapprobation hurt me, I found—even that of people whom I did not admire" (174).

In each novel the final regret of the narrator is obvious, regret that he had not gone a different route. Coverdale admits, "Life . . . has come to rather an idle pass with me" (247), while Burden's desire to be numbered among Ántonia's children is defeatist, considering his own unsuccessful, childless marriage, and the final estimate of his relationship with Ántonia betrays emptiness: "Whatever we had missed, we possessed together the precious, the incommunicable past" (273). The failure of each becomes poignant when juxtaposed with a response to the earth that betrays desire for involvements missed in human relationships. In Cather's novel this is revealed early, when the boy Jim sits in the hollow of his grandmother's garden: "The earth was warm under me, and warm as I crumbled it through my fingers. . . . I was something that lay under the sun and felt it, like the pumpkins, and I did not want to be anything more. . . . that is happiness; to be dissolved into something complete and great" (20). Coverdale betrays similar feelings when he returns to Blithedale: "I could have knelt down, and have laid my breast against that soil. The red clay of which my frame was moulded seemed nearer akin to those crumbling furrows than to any other portion of the world's dust. There was my home, and there might be my grave" (206). The soil of Blithedale becomes the grave of Zenobia and the prairies at the crossroads the grave of Mr. Shimerda, both victims of new beginnings in a more dramatic but no less definite way than either narrator.

In *The Marble Faun* Hawthorne's subject is accumulated history and its confrontation, negative in its potential to annihilate and positive in growth opportunities. Both Miriam and Donatello mature through struggle with the sinful element embodied in the model, while Hilda and Kenyon, their American counterparts, compromise such opportunities through withdrawal, hesitancy, and return to a less encumbered America. As if to link the world of Hawthorne's final novel to her own, Cather set the prologue of *Death Comes for the Archbishop* in Rome of 1848, ten years before the Hawthornes arrived there from Liverpool. Richard Brodhead marvels at the silence in *The Marble Faun* regarding the explosive contemporary events of Italian nationalism, yet he recognizes that Hawthorne's interest was in "another Italy quite differently conceived . . . , not social but aesthetic, the sum of the art works and art history assembled there" (xi–xii). Cather's novel places Italian politics up front, although in a somewhat backhanded way; her Italian, French, and Spanish cardinals (she is as culturally inclusive as possible—the Spanish cardinal has an English mother), while discussing evangelization of New Mexico territory newly acquired by the United States, "avoided politics as men are apt to do in dangerous times. Not a word was spoken of the Lombard war, in which the Pope's position was so anomalous" (13). This reference hints that the aesthetically conceived history to be confronted will not be European but the accumulation of "thirty Indian nations, . . . each with its own customs and languages" and set in a "world . . . cracked open into countless canons and arroyos . . . sometimes ten feet deep, sometimes a thousand" (7–8). Also reversed in Cather is the role of literary heritage; usually the source of Old World legends for Americans (Hawthorne's inherited Rome, for example, is the product of other writers), literature here defines America for Europeans. The Spanish cardinal defends his ignorance of the pueblo culture of New Mexico by blaming his novel reading: "My knowledge of your country," he tells the American missionary, "is chiefly drawn from the romances of Fenimore Cooper, which I read in English with great pleasure" (10). In Cather, a French priest will experience in America cultural and self-confrontation remarkably similar, as I shall indicate, to that of Hawthorne's principals in Europe.

The first episode that comes to mind in *Death Comes for the Archbishop* relative to *The Marble Faun* is "The Legend of Fray Baltazar," arguably the dramatic center of the first six books, that part of the novel in which Bishop Jean Marie Latour attempts to unravel the "unimaginable mystery" (81) of his vast diocese and prepares to turn inward and recognize the self-serving nature of his plans to build a cathedral and keep his vicar, Father Vaillant, with him. In Baltazar's story the embodiment of evil is thrown to death from a cliff in a scene reminiscent of "On the Edge of a Precipice" (*Marble Faun*, ch. 18), complicating Cather's light and dark, good and evil dynamic by making evil Franciscan (Hawthorne does the same in making evil Capuchin). The labyrinth of evil suggested by the legend invites the reader to make an unlikely comparison between Cather's idealized bishop and Baltazar, thus adumbrating Latour's self-questioning in books 7 and 8.

Preparation for these introspective complications as well as the friar's demise begins in "The Lonely Road to Mora" as icy, "lead-coloured drops" explode against Latour's nose and cheeks (*Death Comes* 64). The diabolical dimension of the struggle is suggested in frequent references to amphibian and reptilian life: the raindrops are the shape of tadpoles, and the "horny backbones" of the mountains beetle above the missionaries. When villainous, infant-killing Buck Scales emerges from his adobe on the edge of a steep ravine, anticipating the setting of Baltazar's loggia, he possesses a "snake-like neck, terminating in a small, bony head," and, like Miriam's model, seems "not more than half human" (66–67). He has in his clutches an inarticulate Mexican woman named Magdalena, who, detecting the bishop's silver cross, warns the missionaries away by drawing the edge of her palm across her throat. She turns up at Mora battered enough to satisfy Miriam's prescription for a convincing Michael, her clothing cut to rags, her legs, face, and hair plastered with mud. After Scales's execution, she is employed by the nuns and transfigured into a handsome, Hilda-like keeper of doves that flash and dissolve in light "as salt . . . in water" before settling on her person and eating from her lips: "she put a crust of bread between her lips, two doves hung in the air before her face, stirring their wings and pecking at the morsel" (209).

This rescue by the church and resulting dove scene can mislead the reader into a facile view of the novel's conflict until Cather casts priests as degenerates and varies her chiaroscuro of Euro- and Native American cultural strains when the bishop travels toward Acoma in exploring his diocese. Kit Carson's revelation in the Magdalena episode that he "was brought up [in Missouri] to think all priests were rascals" (76) prepares us and Latour for Gallegos, the fandangoing gambler padre of Albuquerque; sexually notorious Padre Martinez of Taos; Arroyo Hondo's miser padre, Lucero; and for the legend of Baltazar. However, Padre Jesus de Baca, a man of "golden goodness" (85) in the dazzlingly white Isleta pueblo, qualifies our view, even though he is "very superstitious," a parrot worshiper who reveres an ancient wooden pattern of these birds much as the Acomas revere their miraculous, rain-making portrait of St. Joseph.

The chiaroscuro pattern progresses on the journey from Isleta to Acoma when Latour and his Indian guide Jacinto battle "curling," sun-obscuring sand while surrounded by clusters of wild pumpkin resembling "great colon[ies] of grey-green lizards . . . arrested by fear" (88) which repeat the mood of the encounter with Scales. In the clarity of the following dawn at Laguna, however, harmony is evident in a tapestry of "gods of wind and rain and thunder, sun and moon" decorating the altar of the mission church there (89). But this fails to alleviate the lapse from Indian culture Latour suffers in his conversation with Jacinto about stars and later at Acoma when he doubts the impact of Calvary on the turtlelike population (100). The bishop takes recourse in responding to the mesa country through his own cultural orientation; he views mesas as cathedrals "Gothic in outline" so scattered as to suggest the Creator had "left everything on the point of being brought together" (94–95). Hawthorne's use of clouds in "On the Battlements" (*Marble Faun,* ch. 29) to indicate psychological or spiritual reality may well have inspired Cather's rendering, through Latour, of mesa country sky: "every mesa was duplicated by a cloud mesa, like a reflection. . . . The great tables of granite . . . were inconceivable without their attendant clouds . . . as the smoke is part of the censer, or the foam of the wave" (95). The meanings of Acoma are anticipated in these clouds, and the "international myth" is reversed in Cather's having an expatriated European enumerate comfortable Old World meanings of rock (the Jewish idea of God, the Christian one of church) before fathoming the "strange" and "shocking and disconcerting" literalness of Indian life: "The Acomas . . . had their idea in substance" (98).

The ambivalence of Acoma to Latour is embodied in the poisonous, artificial looking nightshades that blossom like Easter lilies at the base of the rock and in the ambitious mission church itself, built on a scale to suggest to him exploitation by missionaries (an unexpected response considering Latour's own plans for a Romanesque cathedral in Santa Fe). More blatantly exploitive are the cloister and loggia adjacent to the church, doubtlessly built to transport the missionaries in spirit to "some cloister hung on a spur of the Pyrenees" (102). Latour spends the night in the loggia "homesick for his own kind," for European progress in contrast to these Acoma "rock-turtles on their rock" and their "reptilian" kind of life "that had endured by immobility" (103). This New World life now seems an older and unintelligibly darker mystery than Hawthorne's Rome. At this juncture Cather inserts "The Legend of Fray Baltazar," about the priest who ruled Acomas early in the eighteenth century, to dramatize the confrontation between two worlds.

Baltazar suffers at the hands of the Acomas a fate startlingly similar to Miriam's model at the hands of Donatello. The padre typifies at least four of the great sins (pride, covetousness, gluttony, and anger)—the other three (envy, lust, and sloth) are represented in other cities. Placed immediately after Latour's contemplation of the positive achievements of Europeans, the story assumes an irony possibly unintended by Cather. That "glorious history of desire and dreams" is played out here by a Spanish friar who "bore hard on the natives," took the best of their produce, and "exacted a heavy tribute in labour" (104). The Acomas served as pack animals to carry soil from the plain below for the cloister garden; women were taxed water to keep it green, and servant boys ran errands to distant places for household goods and delicacies for the padre's table. Baltazar kept his vow of chastity ("his sensuality went no further than his garden and table") because breaking it would compromise his power (106). The natives murmured but feared the padre's magic, especially his control over the portrait they believed brought them rain.

Once this background is sketched, the action moves swiftly and effectively, much like that in "On the Edge of a Precipice." Baltazar prepares a magnificent dinner for neighboring priests in order to show off "his fine garden, his ingenious kitchen, his airy loggia" (107), an event echoing the clerical dinner set "in the gardens of a villa in the Sabine hills, overlooking Rome" (3) in the novel's prologue. When a serving boy accidentally spills gravy over the head of one of the guests, Baltazar, who "had been drinking freely of . . . fiery grape brandy" (110), flings his heavy mug at the boy's head and kills him instantly. The guests flee, but Baltazar hesitates to leave behind his good life. From the loggia he detects the black hair of a guard at the exit of the mesa and can only await the outcome. At moonrise, the Acomas invade the loggia, silently bind him (to his credit Baltazar too remains silent and refuses to struggle), and "after a few feints" drop him from the highest cliff of the mesa, where the "women flung broken pots and such refuse as the turkeys would not eat" (113). A single detail incapsulates the diabolical pride of the man: "No sound but hissing breath came through his teeth."

Subsequently, when Latour and his guide get caught in a blizzard on their way to Father Vaillant, who lies dying of black measles in a mountain village, and take shelter in a cave, the novel's cultural conflict turns inward and develops psychological dimension. Latour has heard stories attributing snake and fire worship to the Pecos tribe, of which Jacinto is a member; there is even a legend about babies being sacrificed to an enormous serpent kept in the mountains. It is hardly surprising that when Jacinto grudgingly takes him into a sacred space of his people, the priest is reluctant, feels distaste for the place, detects a fetid odor there, and is dizzied by the hum of a river flowing far below. In order to enter, he must climb between two liplike formations in a rock wall; hence, entering the cave has oral connotations emphatically sexual, one feels, when once inside the space (which Latour construes as Gothic in shape, like a chapel) the focus becomes a hole "about as large as a very big watermelon, of an irregular oval shape" (128). When this is painstakingly closed up with rocks and mud by Jacinto without explanation, its genital implications combine with Indian mysteries deep within the earth to challenge the rationally orchestrated mystery of Latour's mission and celibacy, and the priest has Jacinto repeat a Paternoster with him as protection, one feels, before they retire. However, in the middle of the night Latour discovers his guide pressed against the oval listening for something. At dawn they emerge into "a gleaming white world" (132); yet the dark experience remains to haunt, and the serpent legends are confirmed by a Yankee trader raised in these mountains. Thus Cather returns us to the beginning of this journeying part of her novel, to the phallic neck and head of Buck Scales in "The Lonely Road to Mora."

Willa Cather's debt to Hawthorne is not a matter of borrowing but one of tradition. Because she read his fiction during her formative years and that of other writers (particularly Henry James) influenced by him, his work impacted hers in multiple ways. I am convinced that without Hawthorne's Hester, Alexandra Bergson in *O Pioneers!* would be less stalwart, and without Hawthorne's forest the marsh woods in

A Lost Lady less evocative. The stance of narrator Jim Burden toward his text in *My Ántonia* would be less complex without Hawthorne's experiment with point of view in *Blithedale.* The "international myth" Cather inherited through James emphasized morals over manners because of Hawthorne, and without that emphasis *Death Comes for the Archbishop* would lack its otherworldliness, its chiaroscuro of good and evil, its landscape of mystery.

Works Cited

Brodhead, Richard H. "Introduction." *The Marble Faun; or, The Romance of Monte Beni.* By Nathaniel Hawthorne. New York: Viking Penguin, 1990. ix–xxix.

Cather, Willa. "The Best Stories of Sarah Orne Jewett." *Willa Cather on Writing.* New York: Knopf, 1962. 47–59.

——. *Death Comes for the Archbishop.* New York: Vintage, 1990.

——. "Edgar Allan Poe." *Lincoln Courier.* 12 Oct. 1895. Rpt. in *The Kingdom of Art: Willa Cather's First Principles and Critical Statements, 1893–1896.* Ed. Bernice Slote. Lincoln: U of Nebraska P, 1966. 380–87.

——. *My Ántonia.* New York: Viking-Penguin, 1994.

——. "The Novel Démeublé." *Willa Cather on Writing.* New York: Knopf, 1962. 35–43.

Hawthorne, Nathaniel. *The Blithedale Romance.* Boston: Houghton Mifflin, 1900.

——. *The Marble Faun: or, The Romance of Monte Beni.* New York: Viking-Penguin, 1990.

Male, Roy R. *Hawthorne's Tragic Vision.* New York: Norton, 1964.

Woodress, James. *Willa Cather, Her Life and Art.* New York: Pegasus, 1970.

"DEMONS OF WICKEDNESS, ANGELS OF DELIGHT"

Elizabeth N. Goodenough

In addition to works cited herein, the culture of Victorian childhood and influences on Virginia Stephen may be traced in *Stories for Children, Essays for Adults: The Unpublished Writings of Julia Stephen,* ed. Diane Gillespie and Elizabeth Steele; "Lewis Carroll" in *The Moment and Other Essays;* "Mr. Hudson's Childhood" and "A Russian Schoolboy" in *The Essays of Virginia Woolf,* vol. 1, ed. Andrew McNeillie; and "A Sketch of the Past" in *Moments of Being: Unpublished Autobiographical Writings,* ed. Jeanne Schulkind.

There is something that almost frightens me about the child—I know not whether elfish or angelic, but, at all events, supernatural.

Hawthorne, *American Notebooks*

To be a child is to be very literal: to find everything so strange that nothing is surprising; to be heartless, to be ruthless, yet to be so passionate that a snub or a shadow drapes the world in gloom.

Woolf, *Collected Essays*

Interactions between children and adults, children's books and books for adults, and reading as a child and writing as an adult are issues central to contemporary critical theory and cultural studies.[1] Among the many nineteenth- and twentieth-century authors who have written for children and for adults—from William Makepeace Thackeray, Frances Hodgson Burnett, and Oscar Wilde to Sylvia Plath, Isaac Bashevis Singer, and Ken Kesey—Nathaniel Hawthorne (1804–64) and Virginia Woolf (1882–1941) stand out because of the unusual ways they represent what Hawthorne termed the "unestimated sensibility" of the child (*CE* 7: 4).[2] Rarely conforming to the sentimental pieties of his day, children appear in unprecedented number in Hawthorne's domestic essays and tales, juvenile literature, and late romances. Among the first to speak in American literature, Hawthorne's children are also strikingly voluble in lifelike talk, inscrutable outbursts, and precocious questions. All of Woolf's major works sketch some aspect of infancy, childhood, or adolescence to show how the formative life of an individual gives rise to the multiple identities of the adult. Not only is consciousness in her art determined by the impressionability of early life, but the central drama of her fiction is the relation which a character forms with the past. Idealizing the separate integrity of the child, the narratives of Hawthorne and Woolf eschew "the adult obsession with facts" (Dusinberre 1991) for the nonconformist vision of those who find with Woolf "the only exciting life is the imaginary one" (*Writer's Diary* 126). Finally, the revolution in juvenile literature, which Hawthorne hoped to instigate with Henry Wadsworth Longfellow in the 1830s and which later influenced Victorian childhoods like Virginia Stephen's, also advanced both writers' redefinitions of the novel—as romance or elegy, play-poem or novel-essay. Thus, despite differences in gender, class, education, and nationality, the temperamental affinity of these memory-ridden artists centers on the child. Their use of this protean figure throughout their pioneering careers is complex, related to their concern with origins and the past, their early emotional deprivations, self-doubts as authors, and their protracted sense of being literary outsiders. The isolation and receptivity of the young symbolize their highest ideal: the creative power and freedom of the unfettered imagination to live in a world of its own making.

Had Hawthorne lived into his eighties, the young Virginia Stephen might have encountered this "classic" American author as Victorian sage or hoary storyteller like the one he created in *Grandfather's Chair* (1841), a generation older than her father and other "great men" like Henry James (1843–1916) who were his friends (*Moments of Being* 136). Yet it is striking that although Leslie Stephen (1832–1904) read Hawthorne aloud to his children, along with Shakespeare and Austen (*Essays* 1: 128), Woolf does not discuss his works in her essays, letters, or memoirs. Three years before her death, however, when she attempted to sum up the year 1938 in her diary, she cut to the quick, questioning her concern with writing:

> On the whole the art becomes absorbing—more? No, I think it's been absorbing ever since I was a little creature, scribbling a story in the manner of Hawthorne on the green plush sofa in the drawing room at St. Ives while the grown ups dined. (*Writer's Diary* 298)

Looking back at fifty-six, Woolf seems less pessimistic about aging than Wordsworth in the Intimations Ode or than Mrs. Ramsay, who asks why her children must grow up and "lose it all" (*Lighthouse* 91). But the manner in which the writer situates her nascent self in the "border territory" of romantic tradition (Swingle 271) is striking: a child in a house by the sea, rapt in invention, pens a tale in a green world of her own. Like the strange effect of mingled fire and moonlight on his deserted study in "The Custom-House," where Hawthorne dramatizes the conditions congenial to the creation of romance, this scene of writing pointedly contrasts the solitary child (a little "scribbling woman") and the conventionality of adult life. Like Hawthorne, intimately cited here as precursor, Woolf saw her work as a fusion of opposites—of inner and outer realities, vision and fact, dream and reality—which, like the attempt to represent the interior life of a child, requires an artistic sleight of hand, the capacity to write out of both sides of the mind at once.

Coming late in life, as her revelation of sexual abuse as a child did, this diary entry is provocative in suggesting how formative experiences may escape registration. It reminds us that what is unspoken in Woolf functions like Hawthorne's stylistic reticence: from her early desire to write "a novel about Silence" or "the things people don't say" (*Voyage Out* 216) to the wordlessness of her fictional children, ellipsis or absence may magnify significance. Like her kinship with Walter Pater, the reclusive misogynist and university patriarch whose suppressed influence is documented in Perry Meisel's *The Absent Father,* Woolf's feminist revision of her first literary model must be inferred. For example, during her fifteenth summer, when she was still reading Hawthorne "after her light was supposed to have been put out" (Bell 57), she began imitating the Elizabethans. "Entranced" by the "large yellow page" and "obscure adventures" of Hakluyt's *Voyages,* "lugged home" by her father from the London library, Virginia Stephen wrote essays entitled *Religio Laici,* a history of women and a history of her own family "all very longwinded and Elizabethan in style" (*Writer's Diary* 147). This adolescent passion for the sixteenth century, like Hawthorne's obsession with the Puritans and his effort to relate his own family heritage (especially the infamous Judge Hathorne of the Salem witch trials) to the New England past, did not flag with maturity. It flowered in middle age with the "child's play" (*Diary* 3: 264) of *Orlando* (1928) where her "Proustian fascination" with old families and great homes (Brewster 121) surveys cultural transformations from the English Renaissance to the present. As in Hawthorne's juvenile work, *Grandfather's Chair,* where children, conceived from Calvinist and Wordsworthian points of view, reflect on anecdotes symbolic of colonial history, the sex-changing and cross-period-dressing Orlando challenges the gender stereotypes of her 300-year prime of life. Like the romantic poets, who permeate her work but whom Woolf never discusses, Hawthorne's romances are an unwritten premise of her art. The elusive child—in the paradoxical ways they present this prismatic figure—embodies their common preoccupation with the transfiguring imagination and the fluctuating, spectral self.

The way in which adults conceived of childhood altered radically during the first half of the nineteenth century. Romantic ideas about the child's divine innocence permeated transcendentalist thought, educational reforms, the Sunday School movement, the growth of pediatrics, and the spawning of a new secular literature for and about children. The Calvinist notion of infant damnation was finally discarded, and gentler discipline was advocated in the child-rearing manuals, now addressed to mothers, which proliferated after 1830. The egalitarian American marriage and child-centered family impressed Alexis de Tocqueville on his visit in 1831. Reflecting on this shift in sentiment occurring during his own generation, Ralph Waldo Emerson quoted a friend, a "witty physician," who lamented that "it was a misfortune to have been born when children were nothing and to live until men were nothing" (qtd. in Cable 101).

The energetic career of Hawthorne's sister-in-law, Elizabeth Palmer Peabody, who was converted by William Ellery Channing's reading of Wordsworth's Intimations Ode, conveys the scale of expectation associated with children and their education during this period. With her older sister Mary, who married Horace Mann in 1843, she opened schools, wrote texts for the nursery, guides for teachers, and pioneered the kindergarten movement in this country. Not surprisingly, one of Elizabeth's first pupils, her youngest sister Sophia, anticipated motherhood and domestic education as ideal extensions of her former vocation as an artist. The adults surrounding Hawthorne's early life could have had little such confidence in the purity of childhood or maternal power. The author's early orphanhood—his father's death at sea when the boy was four, the loss of a parental home, subsequent adoption by uncles, and lengthy separations from his mother—suggests the deprivations which inspired sentimental and serious writers throughout the nineteenth century. After Captain Hawthorne died in Surinam, his widow returned to her family home on Herbert Street in Salem and depended on her Manning brothers to become surrogate fathers for the three children. Pragmatic Uncle Robert Manning, who supervised Nathaniel's schooling in Salem, may also have imparted to his nephew the suspicion that the artistic side of his nature was morally weak or effeminate. Early letters from Salem indicate that as an adolescent the boy felt chastised by his aunts and that he deeply missed his mother, who had moved to the family home in Raymond, Maine. After visits there, he always looked back on this northern frontier as paradise, penning at sixteen an elegiac poem, "Days of My Youth." Hawthorne's parental loss and early sense of displacement may explain his nostalgia, as well as his need to remain at home, in his "natal spot" of Salem, with his mother and two sisters for "twelve dark years" after graduating from Bowdoin College.

The author's uncertainty about his origins is reflected in his literary focus on childhood and detailed observations he made of his own children. Remembered as a doting parent, he recorded vicissitudes of the nursery in *The American Notebooks*. His empiricism was tempered, however, by his scrutiny of two-year-old Julian for "recollections of a pre-existence" (*CE* 8: 400) and his belief that "it is with children as Mr. Emerson . . . says it is with nature . . . the best manifestations of them must take you at unawares" (8: 409). That he did not always maintain his wife's rhapsodic faith in the perfection of their offspring is evidenced by the ironic humor of "Twenty Days with Julian & Little Bunny," a diary kept while playing nurse to Julian in Sophia's absence and the problematic, even frightening experience of watching first-born Una: "I now and then catch an aspect of her, in which I cannot believe her to be my own human child, but a spirit strangely mingled with good and evil" (8: 430–

31). His haunted regard of this "elfish or angelic" daughter conjures up his insubstantiality and self-doubt, recalling Emerson again: "Nature is a mere mirror, and shows to each man only his own quality."

In Hawthorne's case, shifting representations of the child mirror multiple qualities of the author: his artistic calling, bizarre feeling of unreality, and obsession with "the foul cavern of the heart" his fiction explores. On the one hand, Hawthorne personally identified with the special, unspoiled perception of the child in Rousseau, Blake, Coleridge, and Wordsworth. A lifelong pattern of defining or renewing himself artistically through young females culminated in his marriage to the delicate and unworldly Sophia Peabody, who "looked upon herself as a little girl" (Pearson 267). It is also reflected in the innocent wonder of such characters as the "sinless" child in "Little Annie's Ramble" (1835); Alice, "a flower bud fresh from paradise," in *Grandfather's Chair* (*CE* 6: 51); and Pansie Dolliver in Hawthorne's last unfinished romance, all of whom dispel the gloom of their aged male companions. In "The Gentle Boy" (1832), however, the brokenhearted Quaker child who is abandoned and then martyred functions as a tragic projection of the artistic sensibility. Despite Hawthorne's resistance to transcendentalism, the contemporary setting of "The Snow Image" (1851), where realistic infantile speech constitutes almost the entire dialogue (Hurst 10), shows the vulnerability of "a childish miracle": adults inevitably lose belief and casually disregard children's godlike way of seeing. On the other hand, the "brood of baby-fiends" (*CE* 9: 92) who stone Ilbrahim and the savage children who taunt Pearl in *The Scarlet Letter* dramatize a darker, more Augustinian view of the young. Whether absorbed from his upbringing or reading of Puritan sermons, essays, and memoirs, inherent perversity as well as spiritual precocity distinguish Hawthorne's metamorphic representation of the child.

The wild and prescient behavior of Pearl, partially modeled on Una's, illustrates how unresolved tensions in Hawthorne's imagination created "the most enigmatic child in literature." As Barbara Garlitz has argued, Pearl "can become all things to all men," having been variously interpreted by critics as childlike and unchildlike, as prelapsarian innocent and "darksome fairy," as disordered nature and "symbolized conscience," as a manifestation of the id and of our hopeful future, as an example of moral indifference and Rousseauian natural goodness, as an unnatural recluse from society and a redemptive agent (689). In fact the kaleidoscope of responses to Pearl surveyed constitutes a history of juvenile vice ranging from Puritan superstition about demon offspring to the physico-theological laws of bad heredity of Hawthorne's day to the natural lawlessness or animality ascribed to childish aggression in the last third of the nineteenth century (695). A microcosm of Hester's moral chaos, Pearl is filled with hate and bitterness even as she manifests an uncanny instinct for truth. As Melville, who recognized the subjectivism of his own reading, said of Hawthorne, Pearl is "immeasurably deeper than the plummet of the mere critic" (16). Unsettling the Puritan community's (and the critic's) attempt to name, or fix the identity of, this problematic outcast, Hawthorne's Pearl, like his other unfathomable types, prefigures the use of indeterminacy by modernist writers like Woolf.

Such contradictory views of childhood make the juvenile works Hawthorne published between 1835 and 1853 strikingly uneven. The myths, or purely imaginative works, he was proudest of now seem an odd cul-de-sac in the history of American juvenile fiction. The frame stories, however, he constructed for all six collections— *The Whole History of Grandfather's Chair* (originally published in three volumes: *Grandfather's Chair, Liberty Tree,* and *Famous Old People*), *Biographical Stories for Children* (1842), and the two *Wonder Books* (1851, 1853)—rely on native, contemporary settings which forecast the local and realistic trends of subsequent children's books like *The Widow and the Parrot* (1982), Woolf's tongue-in-cheek tale of the English village, Rodmell. Especially striking is the fireside setting of *Grandfather's Chair,* a "neutral territory" or flickering mental space between child and storyteller, which emerged a decade later in the preface to *The Scarlet Letter:* "somewhere between the real world and fairyland, where the Actual and the Imaginary may meet, and each imbue itself with the nature of the other" (*CE* 1: 36). Whether hearing Una play outside his study inspired him, as Julian claimed, or this middle ground from his first children's book empowered him, the dreamy and democratized perspectives which inaugurated the great age of English children's books are foreshadowed in Hawthorne and developed in modernism. Just as Woolf remarked about Carroll's two Alice books they are not "books for children; they are the only books in which we become children" (*The Moment and Other Essays* 70–71), Hawthorne and Woolf display a childlike consciousness—cocooned, specular, weightless—even when they are not writing about children (Coveney 314).

Indeed, children, the only artists (these writers might think) who draw with complete authority, inspired their masterpieces: *The Scarlet Letter* (1850) and *To the Lighthouse* (1927). Written in response to the death of the mother, both works allowed the authors to exorcise the past. Although Hawthorne married the angel in the house, and Woolf was her daughter, both writers expressed their antipatriarchal rage in the idealization of a childlike inwardness and creative potential (Herbert 258). Organized in response to the unanswered question of a persistent child, these family romances are less plots than tableaux juxtaposed, static scenes frozen in Time. Pearl's insistent "Whose child am I?" and James's urgent query as to when he will go to the lighthouse instigate quests for autonomy which move from enchanted dependence on a beautiful maternal heroine to a humanized, more "objective" awareness of resolution and independence. Caught between regal, sadly reflective, enigmatic mothers and self-centered, dependent, puritanical fathers, both Pearl and James perversely mirror and displace what their parents' withhold—Hester who can't explain "A," Mr. Ramsay stuck at "R." They fixate instead on their own symbol making, Pearl's seaweed letter critiquing Hester's scarlet one and James's boar's skull signifying the stark knowledge of his father. Nailed to the bedroom wall, this totem of danger and death cannot be touched by Mrs. Ramsay, and although its shadows keep his sister awake, James will not sleep without it.

Dimmesdale and Mr. Ramsay, unable to speak to children "as children," are unnerved by their passion—Pearl's tantrum in the forest and James's ruthless will. Coldly frustrating desire, each father creates a hostile, "mother's child" until a gesture of paternal acknowledgment breaks the spell. Pearl leaves her mother and New England, marries and bears children in Europe, while James at sixteen, steering the boat with grim determination, exchanges the fantasy of killing his father for the less heroic achievement of earning his praise. Like the delayed "recognition" scene acted out by the strange complicity of Dimmesdale and Chillingworth (Ragussis 67), James's identification with Mr. Ramsay's power to dominate others finally enables him to let go of the torment of the past, when his mother left him for his father, "impotent, ridiculous, sitting on the floor grasping a pair of scissors" (*Lighthouse* 278).

In his autobiography, Frederick Buechner describes childhood as "a waiting for you do not know just what and living, as you live in dreams, with little or no sense of sequence or consequence or measurable time" (39). The expedition to the lighthouse which James has dreamed of making "for years and years it seemed" is a symbol of frustration precisely because he is a child and any postponement is thus not simply a matter of time—another day or week—but intensifies that exquisite impatience which is childhood itself. Like the artist, the lover, and the "true romantic," Woolf's children do not homogenize or generalize experience. That James—lacking detachment or a sense of proportion—is embedded in his perceptions lends his awareness special vividness and truth. Sitting with his army and navy cut-outs, James sees one detail or absolute quality at a time, cutting out each picture in its fresh singularity. Woolf praised Aksadoff for revealing this curious aspect of the child's mind, how it is "taken up with what we call childish things together with premonitions of another kind of life, and with moments of extreme insight into its surroundings" (*Books and Portraits* 102).

That children's language goes largely unrecorded in Woolf does not indicate that she thought them voiceless creatures, seen but not heard by their elders. Unlike Hawthorne, however, she gives their silence a vital narrative and thematic role, seeing early epiphanies as the elusive core of life and entrapment in adult roles as tantamount to the dulling of perception. Mary Jane Hurst has shown that in *The Scarlet Letter* heuristic, regulatory, and informational-interpretative speech categories account for only two thirds of Pearl's discourse while "the remainder of her speech falls into expressive, imaginative, and poetic categories, elements almost entirely absent from the reported direct discourse of the adults to her" (73). But the question of James, who at six has no doubt asked his mother about the expedition more than once, is pointedly deleted from the beginning of *To the Lighthouse:* at the critical juncture where text begins, only the mother's response is recorded. Likewise the speechless vulnerability of George Oliver in *Between the Acts* (1941) is paradoxically related to his primitive, invincible power: seeing a flower whole, the bound-

aries of the toddler's being dissolve in a mystical revelation of perception and sensation. The elder Mr. Oliver, like the callous grownups in "The Snow Image," terrifies
his grandson out of this private theater of rapture by putting on a snout of newspaper, coming at him like a "peaked, eyeless monster," and then calling George "a
crybaby—a crybaby" (13).

The "blackness" Melville saw in Hawthorne no doubt seemed to Woolf a vestige
of "the old-fashioned Calvinism, with all its horrors," she found in Oliver Wendell Holmes's upbringing. In a rare allusion to Hawthorne (in the same essay on
Holmes) she ascribes to both Americans a "pathetic effort to mix the elements of his
childhood with melancholy and beauty" (*Essays* 1: 294). With Mrs. Ramsay's death
in *To The Lighthouse* she moved beyond the Victorian pessimism and sentimentality
about childhood which characterized her mother's generation. But the more complex of Hawthorne's dramatizations of sin prefigure Woolf's demonizing psychology
and her converse celebration of the child's anonymity and possibility. Both writers
depict evil as overweening selfhood, an egocentrism which violates the boundaries
and perspectives of another person. Dr. Bradshaw, like Dimmesdale's leech, Roger
Chillingworth, forces the soul of Septimus Smith, causing the acutely sensitive,
unfused man to destroy himself. Miss Kilman, a name worthy of Hawthorne, feeds
on Elizabeth Dalloway with a greedy need which startles the girl at tea. Situating the
Dalloway daughter in a jealous triangle, which pits her undetermined being between two grownups whose vicarious needs she is oblivious of, Woolf reveals the
ugly struggle for power endemic to selfhood. That this disturbing reality grasps at
the roots of even the detached, richly appreciative Mrs. Dalloway indicates Woolf's
profound distrust of the adult ego. Thinking of Miss Kilman, Mrs. Dalloway reflects
as her party begins that what one needs in middle age is hate, not love, to galvanize
the self (*Mrs. Dalloway* 265–66), a sentiment reminiscent of Roger Chillingworth's
demise. Torn from his object of revenge, the unhappy doctor, "like an uprooted
weed that lies wilting in the sun," leads the narrator to ponder "whether hatred and
love be not the same thing at bottom" (*CE* 1: 260).

In *Jacob's Room* (1922) the suspense generated by incipience is like a Hawthorne
mystery: the growing Jacob Flanders, who rarely speaks, is brooded over, scrutinized,
and commented upon by the hovering narrator and other outsiders. Investing
maturation itself with the sphinxlike qualities of Dimmesdale's dying or Wakefield's
self-making venture (Weinstein 25), Woolf finally seals the secrets of Jacob's twenty-
six years by premature death. Yet this culminating event, craftily withholding what
youth's reckless imagination and perfect self-absorption might become, is conceived
ironically—not as tragic waste but as escape from the closure and corruption of
adulthood. That "the world of the adult made it hard to be an artist" is, as William
Empson has said, a theme running throughout romantic and Victorian literature
(260). Woolf's rendering of this idea, especially in the early *Voyage Out* (1915)
and *Jacob's Room*, reflects the temperamental links between her pessimism and the
nostalgic and escapist attitude of the 1890s epitomized by *Peter Pan; or, The Boy Who*

Would Not Grow Up (1905).[3] When Virginia was ten, Sylvia Lewellyn Davies, the original Mrs. Darling, had spent part of her honeymoon in the Stephen home at St. Ives (*Passionate Apprentice* 46n). Barrie's charismatic, protective mother in the lamp-lit nursery foreshadows Mrs. Ramsay's perfect attunement to her children's moods at bedtime, the poignant moment before the dark hiatus of "Time Passes" steals all childhoods away.

Although Woolf, not Hawthorne, suffered from madness and committed suicide, the earlier writer seems less able to survive the loss of faith in perceptual innocence. If writing and marriage to Sophia were how Hawthorne opened an "intercourse with the world," Una's near fatal Roman illness closed the door on a broken man (Herbert 267). The childless Woolf, on the other hand, once she distanced herself from the protective illusions of Mrs. Ramsay, combined the survival of the virginal spinster artist, Lily Briscoe, with the adult perspectives fortifying James through Mr. Ramsay. Although as a feminist she knew Leslie Stephen's life precluded hers as a writer, she also believed that as professionals they were "in league together." While the late works— *The Waves* (1931), *The Years* (1933), and *Between the Acts*—place the child in contexts calculated to show the fragility of the artistic potential, Woolf offers escape from selfhood in the passive recapitulation of undifferentiated moments of being. In the approach of death Woolf glimpses the dissolution of identity which congeals over a lifetime—a destination, or liberation, akin to her affirmations of divine childhood, those mystical, fluid moments when nature is first anonymously apprehended.

Notes

Portions of this essay were originally published in *"The Magnetized Observer": Hawthorne's Romantic Vision,* an exhibition catalogue (Salem, Mass.: Essex Institute; Cambridge, Mass.: Houghton Library, 1988).

1. See, for example, U. C. Knoepflmacher, "The Balancing of Child and Adult: An Approach to Victorian Fantasies for Children," *Nineteenth Century Fiction* 37 (1983): 497–530; Richard N. Coe, *When the Grass Was Taller: Autobiography and Childhood Experience* (New Haven: Yale UP, 1984); Juliet Dusinberre, *Alice to the Lighthouse: Children's Books and Radical Experiments in Art* (New York: St. Martin's, 1987); *Romanticism and Children's Literature in Nineteenth-Century England,* ed. James H. MacGavran (Athens: U of Georgia P, 1991); James R. Kincaid, *Child-Loving: The Erotic Child and Victorian Culture* (New York: Routledge, 1992); Karen Lesnik-Oberstein, *Children's Literature: Criticism and the Fictional Child* (Oxford: Oxford UP, 1994); *Infant Tongues: The Voice of the Child in Literature,* ed. Elizabeth Goodenough, Mark Heberle, and Naomi Sokoloff (Detroit: Wayne State UP, 1994); 1993 MLA Session and volume on "Cross-Writing," *Children's Literature* 25, ed. U. C. Knoepflmacher and Mitzi Myers (New Haven: Yale UP, forthcoming).

2. Quotations from Hawthorne's works are from the *Centenary Edition,* hereafter cited as *CE* with volume and page numbers.

3. Barrie's play, a treat on her twenty-third birthday, Virginia Stephen found "imaginative & witty . . . but just too sentimental" (*Passionate Apprentice* 228). Likewise, she worried that reviewers would deem *To the Lighthouse* "sentimental" and "Victorian" (*Diary* 3: 107).

Works Cited

Bell, Quentin. *Virginia Woolf: A Biography.* Vol. 1. New York: Harcourt, 1972.

Brewster, Dorothy. *Virginia Woolf.* New York: New York UP, 1962.

Buechner, Frederick. *The Sacred Journey.* San Francisco: Harper, 1982.

Cable, Mary. *The Little Darlings: A History of Child-Rearing in America.* New York: Scribner, 1972.

Coveney, Peter. *The Image of Childhood: The Individual and Society: A Study of the Theme in English Literature.* Baltimore: Penguin, 1957.

Dusinberre, Juliet. *Alice to the Lighthouse: Children's Books and Radical Experiments in Art.* New York: St. Martin's, 1987.

Empson, William. *Some Versions of Pastoral.* London: Chatto and Windus, 1935.

Garlitz, Barbara. "Pearl: 1850–1955." *PMLA* 72 (1957): 689–99.

Hawthorne, Nathaniel. *The Centenary Edition of the Works of Nathaniel Hawthorne.* Ed. William Charvat et al. Columbus: Ohio State UP, 1962–.

Herbert, T. Walter. *Dearest Beloved: The Hawthornes and the Making of the Middle-Class Family.* Berkeley: U of California P, 1993.

Hurst, Mary Jane. *The Voice of the Child in American Literature.* Lexington: UP of Kentucky, 1990.

Meisel, Perry. *The Absent Father: Virginia Woolf and Walter Pater.* New Haven: Yale UP, 1980.

Melville, Herman. "Mosses from an Old Manse." *Critics on Hawthorne.* Ed. Thomas J. Rountree. Coral Gables: U of Miami P, 1972.

Pearson, Norman Holmes. "Elizabeth Peabody on Hawthorne." *Essex Institute Historical Collections* 94 (1958): 256–76.

Ragussis, Michael. *Acts of Naming: The Family Plot in Fiction.* New York: Oxford UP, 1986.

Swingle, L. J. "The Romantic Emergence: Multiplication of Alternatives and the Problem of Systematic Entrapment." *Modern Language Quarterly* 39 (1978): 264–83.

Weinstein, Arnold. *Nobody's Home: Speech, Self, and Place in American Fiction from Hawthorne to DeLillo.* New York: Oxford UP, 1993.

Woolf, Virginia. *Between the Acts.* New York: Harcourt, 1941.

——. *Books and Portraits: Some Further Selections from the Literary and Biographical Writings of Virginia Woolf.* Ed. Mary Lyon. London: Hogarth, 1977.

——. *Collected Essays.* Ed. Leonard Woolf. Vol. 1. London: Hogarth, 1966.

——. *The Diary of Virginia Woolf.* Ed. Anne Olivier Bell, assisted by Andrew McNeillie. Vol. 3, *1925–1930.* New York: Harcourt, 1980.

——. *The Essays of Virginia Woolf.* Ed. Andrew McNeillie. Vol. 1, *1904–1912.* New York: Harcourt, 1986.

——. *Jacob's Room & The Waves.* New York: Harcourt, 1959.

——. *The Moment and Other Essays.* London: Hogarth, 1947.

——. *Moments of Being: Unpublished Autobiographical Writings.* Ed. Jeanne Schulkind. New York: Harcourt, 1976.

——. *Mrs. Dalloway.* New York: Harcourt, 1953.

——. *Orlando: A Biography.* New York: Harcourt, 1956.

——. *A Passionate Apprentice: The Early Journals, 1897–1909.* Ed. Mitchel A. Leaska. New York: Harcourt, 1990.

——. *To the Lighthouse.* New York: Harcourt, 1955.

——. *The Voyage Out.* New York: Harcourt, 1948.

——. *The Widow and the Parrot.* New York: Harcourt, 1982.

——. *A Writer's Diary.* New York: Harcourt, 1953.

EMILY DICKINSON'S PEARLS

Karen Kilcup

I n a striking 1852 letter to his friend and editor James T. Fields, Nathaniel Hawthorne wrote, "*All* women, as authors, are feeble and tiresome. I wish they were
forbidden to write, on pain of having their faces deeply scarified with an oyster-
shell" (*CE* 16: 624).[1] The violence inherent in this remark is the more noteworthy
given its symbolic expression of the oyster shell, since it was only two years earlier
that Hawthorne had published a book in which the female image of Pearl figured
centrally. Emily Dickinson, obviously, could not have known of this letter to Fields,
and when she herself wrote to Thomas Wentworth Higginson that "Hawthorne
appalls, entices" she may or may not have been alluding to *The Scarlet Letter*. At first
glance Dickinson's relationship to Hawthorne as literary precursor is only slight; for
example, we know of only a handful of direct references to his work in her letters
(Johnson, *Letters* 2: L622).[2] Jack Capps observes that Dickinson's reading was eclectic; "she was seeking ideas with poetic potential"; "she was shopping in the literary
market place" (Capps 24, 25).[3] Given the poet's characteristic independence, it is
more appropriate to speak of Hawthorne as a resource, a "mine," rather than an
influence; nevertheless, Dickinson shares with Hawthorne a number of attitudes
and images that render her familiarity with his work both likely and significant. The
tension between revelation/publication and concealment is perhaps the most obvious connection. For Hawthorne's "inmost Me behind its veil," we have Dickinson's "supposed person"; for his "Coverdale," we have her "I'm Nobody!"; for his

"Veiled Lady," we have her "still—Volcano—Life" (*CE* 1: 4; Johnson 2: L268; *CE* 3: 5; Johnson 1: P288; *CE* 3: 108–16; Johnson 2: P601).[4] Beyond this connection, there are many others (Railton 190–92; Lease 101, 110–28; Lowe 45–46), but what I will focus on here is "Pearl" in Hawthorne's and Dickinson's work as both image and perspective, and I will concentrate on its specifically sexual resonances.

As someone acutely interested and well educated in science, Dickinson would likely have known how pearls were formed: when external grit or sand makes its way into an oyster, the mollusk exudes a substance that forms a hard, smooth coating to protect itself. The result borders on poetry: a luminous, beautiful, precious stone that is wholly concealed until the oyster is captured and opened. This gem enters Dickinson's poems time and time again, and many that employ the image are among her most well known: "'Arcturus' is his other name," "I taste a liquor never brewed," "Your riches taught me poverty," "We play at paste," "The Malay took the Pearl," "I started early, took my dog," "She rose to his requirement, dropt." A disproportionate number of these references occur in the early part of Dickinson's career; if we are to accept Johnson's speculative dates, poem 998, which was written about 1865, was the last. In nineteenth-century symbology, pearls were associated not only with the biblical "pearl of great price," or immortal soul, but also with women's purity (and therefore sexuality) (see *CE* 1: 89). In *The Scarlet Letter* Pearl encodes the outsider, mystery, wildness or nature, the child, Hester's "publication," and Hester's sexuality, while Dickinson's Pearls suggest, variously, creativity, life, mystery, power, value, truth, virtue. Beyond these associations, it is noteworthy that oysters and other mollusks creating pearls suggest a striking analogy with female genitalia. In this connection, Paula Bennett observes that "the existence of a pattern of imagery involving small, round objects in Dickinson's writing cannot be disputed." She goes on to assert, "Dickinson was replacing the hierarchies of male-dominated heterosexual discourse—hierarchies that disempowered her as woman and poet—with a (paradoxical) clitorocentrism of her own, affirming her specifically female power" (Bennett, "Pea" 113, 114).[5]

I wish to expand on Bennett's insights on adult female sexuality here in relation to Hawthorne as well as Dickinson by discussing the sexuality of the female child. That is, I will suggest that Pearl represents not only an image but a perspective: in both Hawthorne and Dickinson (though with differential inflections), she is the female child who claims her own discrete identity, voice, and most significantly, in direct opposition to the culture that has engendered her, her sexual power. In mid-nineteenth-century America, as middle-class culture separated officially into more public and more private spheres, children gained both ideological status and increased opportunities for adult attention. Barbara Finkelstein observes that between 1835 and 1870 it was assumed that "very young children required guidance, not repression, activity rather than confinement, sensitive tutoring from a totally available, benevolent mentor" (124). This nurturing involved "the social isolation of mother and child and an intensification in their relationships" (125). Though it is born from necessity, Hester and Pearl's relationship epitomizes this ideal. Such relationships were considered more "natural" because of the common belief, explored by both Hawthorne and Dickinson, that like women, children "experienced the world through their feeling (their 'hearts'), unlike [men] who operated through reason" (Boylan 154, 157). Hence, if an important emphasis was against "premature mental exertion," another was that "mothers ought to drench their children in sensuous experience, surrounding them in a world of natural and attractive objects" (Finkelstein 125, 126). Lydia Maria Child urges in the *Mother's Book:* "First stimulate bodily senses, by presenting attractive objects to the child . . . things of bright and beautiful colors . . . and sounds pleasant and soft to the ear" (cited in Finkelstein 126). This sensual experience was encouraged in spite of reformers' fears of "sexual and social precocity" (125); oddly, these reformers seem not to have made the connection between sensuality and sexuality. Hester's desire to clothe Pearl in the most ornate and sensual garb suggests her (and Hawthorne's) at least subconscious acknowledgment of this connection.

Both Hawthorne and Dickinson were surrounded by a white middle-class culture that promoted these ideologies; both had important relationships with children; both, if we acknowledge the poet's letters to her nephews and nieces, wrote for children (Phillips 159–67). In addition, both express fascination for children's capacity for "feeling" and celebrate, if they question, children's capacity for an appreciation of the sensuous world. Although writers have for many years remarked on Dickinson's use of the child's perspective, often holding that the child voice freed her to write (Gilbert and Gubar 591), from another vantage Barbara Clarke Mossberg argues that the culturally enforced image of the child proved frustrating and limiting for Dickinson (10–13). Joanne Dobson investigates how the poet conveys her ambivalence about the little girl persona while she observes that this persona "screened out the mature woman with her disconcerting potential sexuality and guaranteed the woman writer a comfortable, and thus approving, audience" (62).[6] These perspectives seem to assume the child perspective is not sexual, yet both Hawthorne's and Dickinson's "Pearls" intimate that sexuality and childhood are not only *not* mutually exclusive but are sometimes troublingly continuous. Whether consciously or not in the case of each writer, literally or figuratively, the voice of "Pearl" speaks (of) sensuousness and desire.

Bennett's observations about "small, round objects" resonate in *The Scarlet Letter*'s acknowledgment of the affiliation between desire and Pearl herself. When Hester ponders her daughter's wild, ruleless nature, she echoes mid-nineteenth-century beliefs when she recalls "what she herself had been, during that momentous period while Pearl was imbibing her soul from the spiritual world, and her bodily frame of its material of earth. The mother's impassioned state had been the medium through which were transmitted to the unborn infant the rays of its moral life" (*CE* 1: 91). Similarly, Hawthorne underscores that "there was a trait of passion, a certain depth of hue, which [Pearl] never lost"; the author goes on to suggest a comparison between passionate Pearl and an intensely sexual adult woman, Shakespeare's Cleopatra. Echoing Enobarbus's speech about Cleopatra, "Age cannot wither her, nor custom stale / Her infinite variety," Hawthorne observes, "Pearl's aspect was imbued with a spell of infinite variety" (Bevington 2.2.245–46; *CE* 1: 90; Farr 170–76; Byers 35–38).[7] Just as Cleopatra casts her spell over Antony, Hester *and* Pearl throw theirs over the hapless lover Dimmesdale (*CE* 1: 214), although he is explicitly fearful of Pearl's (and by extension Hester's) passionate nature: he tells the latter, "I know nothing that I would not sooner encounter than this passion in a child" (210).

Left to her own desires, Pearl claims her identity, and her relationship with her mother, only apart from a masculine sexual economy; she does so when the pair are wandering outdoors on a summer day and Hester is questioning the fiendishness of her daughter (and hence the nature of her own sexuality):

> "Child, what art thou?" cried the mother.
> "O, I am your little Pearl!" answered the child. (*CE* 1: 97)

In a psychoanalytic reading of this relationship, Lois Cuddy notes that "Pearl is never seen without Hester in this novel because it is not her function to stand alone. . . . Pearl is everything that Hester would deny about herself" (102). Furthermore, Cuddy indicates that Pearl *speaks for* Hester: she is "free to express the emotions for both her mother and herself" (110); "Pearl can sense her mother's turmoil and becomes her mother's voice" (104).[8] If we use Bennett's terms, however, the conversation just cited could be a dialogue between Hester and herself; that is, Pearl enacts the freedom of Hester's "clitorocentric" self. Later, in the forest, Pearl refuses to acknowledge her mother without the scarlet letter, in part because of the latter's renewed role as Dimmesdale's partner. Pearl reclaims her only after Hester has replaced the letter on her breast, saying "Now thou art my mother indeed! And I am thy little Pearl!" (*CE* 1: 211). The scarlet letter emblematizes Hester's self-defined and independent sexual identity; without it, not only does Pearl lose her own presence in the world, but so does her mother.

Significantly, given Bennett's discussion of how flowers were universal nineteenth-century figures for female sexuality, Pearl affirms this presence by repeatedly adorning herself with flowers: "Pearl gathered the violets, and anemones, and columbines, and some twigs of the freshest green. . . . With these she decorated her hair, and her young waist" (*CE* 1: 205). This scene recalls the advice to middle-class mothers that they "ought to drench their children in sensuous experience" (Finkelstein 126). Hester's comment to Dimmesdale about this self-adornment is telling: "Dost thou not think her beautiful? And see with what natural skill she has made those simple flowers adorn her! Had she *gathered pearls,* and diamonds, and rubies, in the wood, they could not have become her better" (*CE* 1: 206; emphasis added).[9] Here we see a convergence of the language of flowers and gems; as Bennett notes, "according to

Robert Scholes, 'jewel' or 'gem' is the clitoris's only secondary meaning in classical Greek" (Bennett, "Critical Clitoridectomy" 237). Hawthorne's Pearl represents female sexuality incarnate, desire made flesh. What is perhaps even more significant, however, is his representation of her, even more than her mother, as self-contained, independent; this independence signifies a freedom that is the source of her mystery, her power, and of her ability to inspire fear in conventional male sexuality represented by Dimmesdale, the father. Pearl's independence must—and will—ultimately be repressed.

This passage in *The Scarlet Letter* anticipates Dickinson's famous "man of noon" letter to her friend and future sister-in-law Susan Gilbert: "How dull our lives must seem to the bride, and the plighted maiden, whose days are fed with gold, and who *gathers pearls* [emphasis added] every evening; but to the *wife*, Susie, sometimes the *wife forgotten,* our lives perhaps seem dearer than all others in the world" (L93). As I have observed elsewhere, not only does the content of this letter gesture toward sexual passion, but so does its increasingly breathless and climactic structure (Oakes 193–94). Both Hawthorne and Dickinson associate Pearls with sensuous, preheterosexual experience. In the "man of noon" letter, significantly, it is the "plighted maiden" who "gathers pearls." More explicitly, in a poem that invokes the child's perspective and voice, Dickinson's Pearl enacts the voice of an intimate with nature, a voice that elaborates the elemental and independent source of female desire, pleasure, and power:

> I taste a liquor never brewed—
> From Tankards scooped in Pearl—
> Not all the Frankfort Berries
> Yield such an Alcohol!
>
> Inebriate of Air—am I—
> And Debauchee of Dew—
> Reeling—thro endless summer days—
> From inns of Molten Blue— (P214)

This poem has been catalogued as one of Dickinson's poems about art, but we should remark how nature figures here (Farr 31–32; Bennett, *Dickinson* 108–10; Wolff 187, 361; Keller 155). The speaker performs Lydia Maria Child's advice cited earlier: "First stimulate bodily senses, by presenting attractive objects to the child . . . things of bright and beautiful colors . . . and sounds pleasant and soft to the ear." Dickinson's vision underscores the freedom, the limitlessness ("endless summer days"), and the excess of the natural world, including but not limited to the sexual excess figured in the comic "Debauchee of Dew." By encoding desire initially in the image of "Dew," Dickinson suggests the speaker's childlike affinity with a bee or a butterfly, miniaturizing and familiarizing desire to make it acceptable, while at the same time encoding a clitorocentric image. Like Hester's Pearl, this speaker is situated firmly in the natural world, and also in the language of flowers and gems.

As the poem concludes, however, the speaker exceeds this affinity, as she renders her experience of/in nature orgasmic:

> When "Landlords" turn the drunken Bee
> Out of the Foxglove's door—
> When Butterflies—renounce their "drams"—
> I shall but drink the more!
>
> Till Seraphs swing their snowy Hats—
> And Saints—to windows run—
> To see the little Tippler
> From Manzanilla come!

The sexuality that the poem represents is autoerotic, for the speaker is both its agent and its object; furthermore, the taxonomy of the pearl genders this sexuality female. As a declaration of independence from rules, from convention, the poem's world expands beyond the human and extends into the divine, calling on "Seraphs" and "Saints" to bear it witness. In contrast to Dobson's affirmation that Dickinson's child voice "screened out the mature woman with her disconcerting potential sexuality," the poet here—and repeatedly—celebrates the freedom of a child's sexuality. This freedom is perhaps possible because of adult blindness to its possibility.

On the other hand, perhaps this blindness is semiconscious; because in both Hawthorne and Dickinson, the Pearl voice becomes the focus of repression, although with different sources in each case. If Pearl is Hester's "publication," one whose bodily person she embroiders with all her art, nevertheless, she will not permit her daughter an identity via a voice. In fact, her constant purpose is to prevent Pearl from acquiring an independent voice; during the procession preceding the Election Sermon, Pearl asks her mother about Dimmesdale's identity: " 'Mother,' said she, 'was that the same minister that kissed me by the brook?' " Hester's reply is emblematic of her attitude: " 'Hold thy peace, dear little Pearl! . . . We must not always talk in the market-place of what happens to us in the forest' " (*CE* 1: 240). The message here, that sexuality must not be voiced, at least in the public realm, occurs on an earlier occasion that again points us back to Dickinson. Returning home from their walk on the seashore, Pearl insistently asks her mother why Dimmesdale keeps "his hand over his heart." Hester's reply is telling: " 'Hold thy tongue, naughty child!' answered her mother, with an asperity that she had never permitted to herself before. 'Do not tease me; else I shall shut thee into *the dark closet!*' " (181; emphasis added). Once again, Hester enforces silence about female sexuality; this silence is both self-imposed (she refuses to reveal the name of her own sexual partner to the authorities) and culturally imposed (the Puritan women gossip about the shame of Hester's "self-publication," her pregnancy). Paradoxically, the community desires, in voyeuristic fashion, to know more about her sexual misconduct and seeks to publicize it (in the form of the scarlet letter) at the same time that it seeks to suppress it. Most important for our purposes here, however, is the regime of silence that Hester attempts to impose on Pearl.

In Dickinson's terms, Pearl is a "poem" whom the community—and Hester as its representative—would have be "prose":

> They shut me up in Prose—
> As when a little Girl
> They put me in the Closet—
> Because they liked me "still"— (P613)

To be "prose" is to be a good "little Girl"; Dickinson affirms the advice that "very young children required guidance, not repression, activity rather than confinement," described by Finkelstein (124). In particular, here and in poems like "I taste a liquor never brewed" and "Wild nights—wild nights," she critiques cultural norms and refuses this repressive silencing, of both the body and the voice, affirming the value of her "small" size:

> It was given to me by the Gods—
> When I was a little Girl—
> They give us Presents most—you know—
> When we are new—and small. (P454)

She imagines herself as "Rich" because of this power from "the Gods" that she is able to keep in her "Hand," but the wealth is in part self-defined: "*To take* the name of Gold— / And Gold to own—in solid Bars— / The Difference—made me bold—" (emphasis added). The speaker's affirmation is *not only* of the "small" sexual power located in the clitoris and its metaphorical images *but also* of the "small" sexual power of the female child.

In this context, it is worth recalling that while from one perspective Hawthorne's Pearl represents wildness, freedom, she also performs the voice of culture, repression: it is she who paradoxically insists that Hester reassume the badge of the scarlet letter when Hester has cast it off, as well as she who renders that symbol literally meaningful to the Puritans. Even more importantly, Pearl is finally reintegrated into the community as an adult woman who conforms to social norms. When Dimmesdale claims her as his daughter, "Pearl kissed his lips. A spell was broken." At this point, Pearl enacts the role of the sentimental heroine: "her tears" on "her father's cheek" were "the pledge that she would grow up amid human joy and sorrow, nor for ever do battle with the world, but be a woman in it" (*CE* 1: 256). Hawthorne echoes cultural terms in which a woman is a child until she is paired with a man; for being a woman in the world of *The Scarlet Letter* means becoming a wealthy heiress who is normalized and synthesized into the heterosexual community via marriage. Not only does Pearl catapult past puberty, she also disappears—from New England and from the text, her story having been completed by that marriage. Her voice is never heard again, as she is finally, effectively silenced, no longer Hester's Pearl, or Hester's clitoral pleasure, but a man's.

In poem 732 Dickinson explores the meanings of marriage and of cultural silencing in terms similar to Hawthorne's but from a very different perspective:

> She rose to His Requirement—dropt—
> The Playthings of Her Life—
> To take the honorable Work
> Of Woman, and of Wife—
>
> If ought She missed in Her new Day,
> Of Amplitude, or Awe—
> Or first Prospective—Or the Gold
> In using, wear away,
>
> It lay unmentioned—as the Sea
> Develope Pearl, and Weed,
> But only to Himself—be known
> The Fathoms they abide—[10]

In "normal" terms, a woman can have the "Playthings" of the child *or* the "Work" of the mature woman, low ("dropt") or high ("rose") status. The second stanza quickly undermines these norms and hierarchies, however, claiming "Amplitude," "Awe," and "first Prospective" for the *child,* not the woman. The final stanza works to clear a space of subversive sexual freedom for the married woman, the self-defined (if selectively silent) sexual being in possession of control of her own "Pearl" and "Weed." Dickinson signals this transposition of power and independence by making the "Sea"—the source of "Pearl" and "Weed"—masculine. Nevertheless, silence, whether chosen or imposed, remains silence. While Hawthorne is satisfied that Pearl is finally "still," Dickinson's adult voice explores the difficulties and pain of speaking, especially by the sexual self (P505, P601, P754, P1247, P1261). In a poem like "I'm ceded, I've stopped being theirs" (P508), she appears to be giving up childhood entirely, as she relinquishes her "Dolls" and her "childhood," when she was "Crowned—Crowing—on [her] Father's breast." What she relinquishes, however, is not childhood but an other-defined childhood "shut . . . up in Prose," seeking instead to "Look down upon Captivity / And laugh" (P613) and to revel in the sensuous experience expressed in "I taste a liquor never brewed."[11]

Similarly, Hawthorne's Pearl displays an intriguing (to Hawthorne) independence, refusing to obey her mother at the most critical times, often when sexuality is at issue. Children are and always have been sexual, but it is even more important to observe that for both Dickinson and Hawthorne the child's desire exceeds the adult's ability to control it. Pearl is the embodiment of Hester's "child-self," her "immature" inability to relinquish control over her own pleasure and rage. This connection emerges in a passage whose images anticipate those of "She rose to His Requirement—" as they echo once again the ostensible encouragement in sensual experience afforded mid-nineteenth-century middle-class children. Walking on the beach with her mother, Pearl underscores her position in her mother's life:

> Her final employment was to gather sea-weed, of various kinds, and make herself a scarf, or mantle, and a head-dress. . . . As the last touch to her mermaid's garb, Pearl took some eel-grass, and imitated, as best she could, on her own bosom, the decoration with which she was so familiar on her mother's. A letter,—the letter A,—but freshly green, instead of scarlet! The child bent her chin upon her breast, and contemplated this device with strange interest; even as if the one only thing for which she had been sent into the world was to make out its hidden import. (*CE* 1: 178)

Decorating herself with the emblem that defines her mother, Pearl translates it into another language altogether. More publicly than the woman in Dickinson's poem, she subverts intended symbolic meanings into uncanny and "hidden import," in so doing clearing a space for the wild freedom of independent and "childish" female sexuality, whose meaning is pleasure figured in Dickinson's "Amplitude," "Awe," and "first Prospective." In "She rose to His Requirement," Dickinson echoes, whether deliberately or not, Pearl's role as "author" in her own right, apart from her mother, who ultimately serves as the guardian of cultural norms, even as she, like Dickinson's "Wife," may silently and privately refute them.

Finally, Pearl's self-containment and self-sufficiency, like Hester's, seem both alluring and problematic to Hawthorne. As the "publication" of Hester's transgression (to rephrase Dickinson, "the Auction / Of the Mind of Woman" [P709]), Pearl has through most of the book only a mother as "author," recalling Anne Bradstreet's claims to literary maternity in "The Author to Her Book." In Dickinson, such sexual self-publication also remains problematic:

> Best Things dwell out of Sight
> The Pearl—the Just—Our Thought.
> Most shun the Public Air
> Legitimate, and Rare— (P998)

Dickinson kept herself and her pearl poems out of the sight of all but her intimates. Nevertheless, the poet's kaleidoscopic child perspective resonates with the power and pleasure of that vision. Time after time we see her assuming the knowing child's superiority to the adult woman. In a letter to her young friend Eugenia Hall, Dickinson wrote:

> Dear "Genie."
>
> The lovely flower you sent me, is like a little Vase of Spice and fills the Hall with Cinnamon—
>
> You must have skillful Hands—to make such sweet Carnations. Perhaps your Doll taught you.
>
> I know that Dolls are sometimes wise. Robins are my Dolls.
>
> I am glad you love the Blossoms so well.
>
> I hope you love Birds too.
>
> It is economical. It saves going to Heaven
>
> Lovingly,
> Coz. Emily. (L455)

In both letters and poems, Dickinson intimates the child's connection with nature, sensuality, and creativity.[12] I'll conclude with a Dickinson poem in the child voice that intimates its power and worries about its potential loss:

> I held a Jewel in my fingers—
> And went to sleep—
> The day was warm, and winds were prosy—
> I said " 'Twill keep"—
>
> I woke—and child my honest fingers,
> The Gem was gone—
> And now, an Amethyst remembrance
> Is all I own— (P245)[13]

Intensely sexual, the poem enacts a consummation and the loss of a "Jewel" that is, finally, not a loss, as it is translated climactically into "an Amethyst remembrance" that suffuses all of Dickinson's work.

Notes

1. Quotations from Hawthorne's works, letters, and notebooks are from the *Centenary Edition of the Works of Nathaniel Hawthorne,* ed. William Charvat et al. (Columbus: Ohio State UP, 1962–), hereafter cited as *CE* with volume and page numbers. Hawthorne's desire to disfigure women is all the more menacing because the disfigurement of a woman's face carries such a strong cultural and psychological penalty. It is possible that Hawthorne could

have been referring to fiction writers more than poets, who might threaten his career's success less directly. For a persuasive account of the complexities of Hawthorne's relationships with women writers, see Wallace.

Since this essay was accepted for publication, additional work has appeared that deals with the erotic and Dickinson or the erotic in nineteenth-century American women's poetry more generally. Although these essays are of adjacent interest, none of them deals with the concerns that I focus on here. See, for example, Runzo, Sullivan ("Running the 'Double Risk'" and "Suing Sue"), Pagnattaro, Henneberg, Koski, Smith, Hagenbüchle, and Bennett ("'Pomegranate-Flowers'").

2. References to Emily Dickinson's letters and poems use Johnson's numbering and are hereafter cited as L (*Letters*) and P (*Poems*). See also L62, L290, L292, L542 (not an accurate reference to Hawthorne), and L93.

3. As Capps points out, "since her opinions, except those pertaining to the Bible and Shakespeare, are not reliably reflected either in her direct statements or in the frequency of her reference to the author, perhaps her true evaluation lies not in what she says about an author's work but rather in what she does with it" (24).

4. There has been increasing agreement that Johnson's printed versions of Dickinson's poems represent an edition, and that such a form cannot indicate the diversity of her manuscript forms or, accurately, her intentions. Among the most persuasive arguments for reading Dickinson's holograph versions are Martha Nell Smith in *Rowing in Eden: Rereading Emily Dickinson* and Susan Howe's *The Birth-mark: Unsettling the Wilderness in American Literary History*.

5. As Bennett states, many of the images to which she refers are "neutral," having "no sexual significance" (Pea 113). I am grateful to Paula Bennett for discussing my ideas in personal conversations, June 1994, 21 Aug. 1994.

6. In spite of Dobson's assertions that "the percentage of little girl poems in [Dickinson's] work is comparatively small" and that "there exist only about a dozen poems with a distinctly little-girl persona," she acknowledges that "in many more the voice has a childlike quality" (62–63). When we look at the letters as well as the poems, this voice expands its scope significantly. Dobson does the crucial work of locating the poet's child voice in its contemporary literary context, although she focuses more on fiction than poetry, as does David S. Reynolds. Reynolds comments on Dickinson's facility for "impersonation," which we might note here is a skill much perfected by children (424; see Walker, passim).

7. In spite of the apparent difference between kinds of passion, we might observe that, as Antony and Cleopatra themselves demonstrate, the distance between anger and desire is very short.

8. Cuddy's Freudian/Eriksonian perspective is one that Bennett would see as masculinist and that she puts aside in the development of her clitorocentric theory of female pleasure. Nevertheless, these insights of Cuddy's are not incompatible with Bennett's. I am grateful to Lee Person for reading an earlier draft of this essay and for pointing me to Cuddy.

9. See also Dickinson's P137, P168.

10. P493, "The world stands solemner to me," represents an ambiguous telling of the

marital drama performed by Hawthorne's Pearl and enacted in P732; Dickinson reflects: "A doubt—if it be fair—indeed— / To wear that perfect—pearl— / The Man—upon the Woman—binds— / To clasp her soul—for all—"

11. Farr identifies a group of poems as the "Sue cycle," a subset of which are some of the lyrics with the pearl as a central image (100–177). Among these are P732, which she suggests was written of Sue (193). Farr identifies the Pearl in these poems with Sue, which is provocative but possibly too limiting, as my discussion suggests.

12. Not only does the poet write in a child voice to children, of course; she also does so to her adult friends. See L397 to Susan, for example, written when the poet was in her early forties.

13. See Dickinson's P136 for a similar perspective, in which the brook figures female sexuality; compare this poem to Dickinson's "man of noon" letter (L93).

Works Cited

Bennett, Paula. "Critical Clitoridectomy: Female Sexual Imagery and Feminist Psychoanalytic Theory." *Signs* 18.2 (1993): 235–59.

——. *Emily Dickinson, Woman Poet.* Iowa City: U of Iowa P, 1990.

——. "The Pea that Duty Locks: Lesbian and Feminist-Heterosexual Readings of Emily Dickinson's Poetry." *Lesbian Texts and Contexts.* New York: New York UP, 1990, 104–25.

——. "'Pomegranate-Flowers': The Phantasmic Production of Late-Nineteenth-Century Anglo-American Women Poets." *Solitary Pleasures: The Historical, Literary, and Artistic Discourses of Autoeroticism.* Ed. Paula Bennett and Vernon A. Rosario II. New York: Routledge, 1995. 189–213.

Bevington, David, ed. *Antony and Cleopatra.* Cambridge: Cambridge UP, 1990.

Boylan, Anne M. "Growing Up Female in Young America, 1800–1860." *American Childhood: A Research Guide and Historical Handbook.* Ed. Joseph M. Hawes and N. Ray Hiner. Westport, Conn.: Greenwood, 1985. 153–84.

Byers, John R., Jr. "The Possible Background of 3 Dickinson Poems." *Dickinson Studies* 57 (1986): 35–38.

Capps, Jack. *Emily Dickinson's Reading, 1836–1886.* Cambridge: Harvard UP, 1966.

Cuddy, Lois A. "Mother-Daughter Identification in *The Scarlet Letter.*" *Mosaic* 19.2 (1986): 101–15.

Dobson, Joanne. *Dickinson and the Strategies of Reticence.* Bloomington: Indiana UP, 1989.

Farr, Judith. *The Passion of Emily Dickinson.* Cambridge: Harvard UP, 1992.

Finkelstein, Barbara. "Casting Networks of Good Influence: The Reconstruction of Childhood in the United States, 1790–1870." *American Childhood: A Research Guide and Historical Handbook.* Ed. Joseph M. Hawes and N. Ray Hiner. Westport, Conn.: Greenwood, 1985. 111–52.

Gilbert, Sandra M., and Susan Gubar. *The Madwoman in the Attic: The Woman Writer and the Nineteenth-Century Literary Imagination.* New Haven: Yale UP, 1984. 580–650.

Hagenbüchle, Roland. "'Sumptuous—Despair': The Function of Desire in Emily Dickinson's Poetry. *Amerikastudien/American Studies* 41.4 (1996): 603–21.

Hawthorne, Nathaniel. *The Blithedale Romance.* Vol. 3 of the *Centenary Edition of the Works of Nathaniel Hawthorne.* Ed. William Charvat et al. Columbus: Ohio State UP, 1962–.

——. *The Letters, 1843–1853*. Vol. 16 of the *Centenary Edition of the Works of Nathaniel Hawthorne*. Ed. William Charvat et al. Columbus: Ohio State UP, 1962–.

——. *The Scarlet Letter*. Vol. 1 of the *Centenary Edition of the Works of Nathaniel Hawthorne*. Ed. William Charvat et al. Columbus: Ohio State UP, 1962–.

Henneberg, Sylvia. "Neither Lesbian nor Straight: Multiple Eroticisms in Emily Dickinson's Love Poetry." *Emily Dickinson Journal* 5.2 (1996): 1–19.

Howe, Susan. *The Birth-mark: Unsettling the Wilderness in American Literary History*. Hanover, N.H.: UP of New England, 1993.

Johnson, Thomas H., ed. *The Letters of Emily Dickinson*. 3 vols. Cambridge: Belknap-Harvard UP, 1958.

Johnson, Thomas H., ed. *The Poems of Emily Dickinson*. 3 vols. Cambridge: Belknap-Harvard UP, 1963.

Keller, Karl. *The Only Kangaroo among the Beauty: Emily Dickinson and America*. Baltimore: Johns Hopkins UP, 1979.

Koski, Lena. "Sexual Metaphors in Emily Dickinson's Letters and Poems to Susan Gilbert." *Emily Dickinson Journal* 5.2 (1996): 26–31.

Lease, Benjamin. *Emily Dickinson's Readings of Men and Books: Sacred Soundings*. London: Macmillan, 1990.

Lowe, James. "The Poetry of Emily Dickinson: A Landscape of Hierophancy." *Dickinson Studies* 70 (1989): 36–47.

Mossberg, Barbara Antonina Clarke. *Emily Dickinson: When a Writer Is a Daughter*. Bloomington: Indiana UP, 1982.

Oakes, Karen. "Welcome and Beware: The Reader and Emily Dickinson's Figurative Language." *ESQ: A Journal of the American Renaissance* 34 (1988): 181–206.

Pagnattaro, Marisa Anne. "Emily Dickinson's Erotic Personae: Unfettered by Convention." *Emily Dickinson Journal* 5.2 (1996): 32–38.

Phillips, Elizabeth. *Emily Dickinson: Personae and Performance*. University Park: Pennsylvania State UP, 1988.

Railton, Stephen. *Authorship and Audience: Literary Performance in the American Renaissance*. Princeton: Princeton UP, 1991.

Reynolds, David S. *Beneath the American Renaissance: The Subversive Imagination in the Age of Emerson and Melville*. Cambridge: Harvard UP, 1989.

Runzo, Sandra. "Dickinson, Performance, and the Homoerotic Lyric." *American Literature* 68.2 (1996): 347–63.

Smith, Martha Nell. *Rowing in Eden: Rereading Emily Dickinson*. Austin: U of Texas P, 1992.

Smith, R. McClure. " 'He Asked If I Was His': The Seduction of Emily Dickinson." *ESQ: A Journal of the American Renaissance* 40.1 (1994): 27–65.

Sullivan, David. "Running the 'Double Risk': Emily Dickinson Fleeing the Worm's Secretions." *Emily Dickinson Journal* 5.2 (1996): 190–96.

——. "Suing Sue: Emily Dickinson Addressing Susan Gilbert." *Emily Dickinson Journal* 5.2 (1996): 45–70.

Wallace, James D. "Hawthorne and the Scribbling Women Reconsidered." *American Literature* 62.2 (1990): 201–22.

Wolff, Cynthia Griffin. *Emily Dickinson*. New York: Knopf, 1986.

Some Observations on the
Fiction of Hawthorne and Gilman

"SUCH A HOPELESS
TASK BEFORE HER"

Denise D. Knight

In addition to the works treated herein, the Hawthornean themes
of obsession, sin, and morality can be seen in the following
Gilman pieces: "Her Beauty," *Forerunner* 4 (Feb. 1913): 29–33;
"His Mother," *Forerunner* 5 (July 1914): 169–73, rpt. in Denise D.
Knight, ed., *The Yellow Wall-Paper and Selected Stories of
Charlotte Perkins Gilman* (Newark: U of Delaware P, 1994) 73–
80; and "The Vintage," *Forerunner* 7 (Oct. 1916): 253–57, rpt. in
Knight 104–11.

While she was vacationing on Martha's Vineyard in the summer of 1882,
Charlotte Perkins (Gilman)[1] settled herself one morning in a shady orchard
where, according to her diary, she spent the day reading, among other things, "a
book on beauty," and "some *Mosses from an Old Manse.*"[2] While Gilman's diary
entry for that August day doesn't record her opinion of Hawthorne's fiction, she later
hailed him as a "great and deep" writer whose work was "honored as one of the
distinctive glories of American literature."[3]

That Charlotte Perkins Gilman admired Hawthorne's writing is not surprising:
he was the country's preeminent literary figure in the second half of the nineteenth
century and enjoyed extraordinary popularity. Gilman, in fact, became familiar with
his work at an early age. When she was just sixteen, she was present for the opening
night performance of the stage version of *The Scarlet Letter,* produced at the Boston
Theatre, which was also attended that evening by William Dean Howells, James
Russell Lowell, and Henry Wadsworth Longfellow.[4] Gilman's exposure to Hawthorne's work continued over the years; in addition to reading *Mosses from an Old
Manse,* she counted among her Christmas presents in 1883 a new "silk umbrella & a
book of Hawthorne."[5]

Although Gilman praised Hawthorne's writing, few of the pieces in her extensive
body of fiction, with one notable exception, would suggest that she was strongly

influenced by his work. While one review of her classic short story, "The Yellow Wallpaper," proclaimed it "worthy of a place beside some of the weird masterpieces of Hawthorne and Poe"[6]—a comparison dismissed by writer Amy Wellington as "only a lazy classification for a story which stands alone in American fiction"[7]—the heavily steeped didacticism that characterizes the majority of Gilman's fictional works, comprising nearly 200 short stories and eight novels, betrays the rather singular vision of her agenda for social reform. As one of the intellectual leaders of the late-nineteenth-century women's movement, Gilman advocated such advancements for women as economic independence, socialized motherhood, and the kitchenless home.[8] The purpose of nearly all of her writing, she insisted, was to show readers how a reformed society might operate to the benefit of all of its inhabitants; her goal in writing fiction was not to produce works that could be lauded for their artistic merit but rather to "alter the ideas, feelings and habits" of her readers.[9] "I have never made any pretense of being literary," she confessed in her autobiography (*Living* 284). Indeed, when William Dean Howells requested permission in 1920 to include "The Yellow Wallpaper" in his anthology, *Great Modern American Stories,* Gilman "assured him that was no more 'literature' than any of my other stuff, being definitely 'written with a purpose' " (*Living* 121).

In his eloquent study tracing the impact of Hawthorne's writing on a host of American authors, Richard H. Brodhead acknowledges that, despite his reputation as a literary giant, Hawthorne's influence was felt to a much lesser extent in the late nineteenth century "on writers who take a stand against the newly institutionalized literary domain."[10] Gilman was among those who opposed traditionally masculine literature. She vociferously condemned not only the existing fiction but also the magazines in which much of it appeared. She also rejected the depiction of women characters as too narrow: "Fiction, under our androcentric culture, has not given any true picture of woman's life, very little of human life, and a disproportioned section of man's life," she complained in *The Man-Made World.*[11] Moreover, Gilman argued that too many women characters had been viewed from the male perspective and defined not by their individualism but by their relationship to a male character: as his wife, his lover, his sister, his daughter.[12]

Gilman's answer to these deficiencies was to produce fiction that would not only break from the masculine tradition but also reduce the marginalization of women in literature. At the same time, her purpose in writing was always, emphatically, to educate society.

"If I can learn to write good stories," Gilman wrote in the early 1890s, "it will be a powerful addition to my armory."[13] For Gilman, however, learning to write good stories did not mean honing her literary skills but producing works that would demonstrate viable alternatives to long-ingrained and oppressive habits that were inherent in a patriarchal society. "Literary virtuosity" and financial success were never her aim (*Living* 308). Furthermore, while Gilman's allusion to her "armory" might sound a bit militant, she was acutely aware of the power of the printed word to arouse the complacent, to persuade the undecided, to effect political and social change.

This is not to say, however, that Gilman, like so many other writers, did not appropriate some of Hawthorne's most prominent themes. Indeed, the Hawthornesque themes of sin, morality, guilt, redemption, and obsession figure prominently in Gilman's fiction; however, she reshaped the conflicts, the characters, and particularly the resolutions in the majority of her stories to argue more explicitly her central thesis: that a reformed society—one that promotes the peaceful, progressive, ethical, and democratic improvement of the human race—is not only desirable but also within reach. Whereas Hawthorne's Hester Prynne could only look forward, vaguely, to "some brighter period, when . . . a new truth would be revealed, in order to establish the whole relation between man and woman on a surer ground of mutual happiness,"[14] Gilman's characters are able to effect a "new truth" and to enact a positive change. Again and again, Gilman's fiction offers solutions to seemingly untenable social and domestic problems.

Only a single selection from Gilman's extensive oeuvre can be properly attributed to the "School of Hawthorne," to borrow Brodhead's phrase. That one story, "Clifford's Tower,"[15] was part of a "Studies in Style" that Gilman inaugurated early in her career, when she became editor of the *Impress,* a literary weekly published in California in 1893–94. The Studies in Style series was designed to provide readers with "a wider knowledge and more delicate appreciation of distinctive literary methods"[16] and featured imitations of writings by such prominent authors as James, Twain, Alcott, Poe, Garland, Freeman, and Hawthorne. But here again, Gilman's literary representations served a practical rather than an artistic purpose. Struggling to balance the demands of writing articles, verses, editorials, and reviews, as well as keeping the paper afloat, Gilman found that she didn't have sufficient time to also "write a good story every week" (*Living* 173), nor could she afford to buy one. Thus her Studies in Style was born—stories produced in "avowed imitation of a well-known author" (173). The first reader to guess correctly whose work Gilman was imitating would receive a copy of one of that author's books.

Of the seventeen sketches that she produced, Gilman found the writing of "Clifford's Tower," in imitation of Hawthorne, to be among the most difficult. "Not the greatest and deepest characteristics of so great and deep a writer [as Hawthorne] could be rendered in this brief story," she lamented.[17] "Indeed its brevity was one of the essential difficulties in this case, the style of Hawthorne being comparitively [*sic*] diffuse," she continued. While Gilman was satisfied with her rendering of Hawthorne's "elegant diction" and "the old New England background," she was less pleased with the story's "most Hawthornesque features . . . the tone of sadness and hint of supernaturalism, the family strain of pride and unforgiven injury long past, and the sudden dark catastrophe which brings it to an end." Space constraints had left these elements inadequately developed, she conceded in the 3 November 1894 *Impress* (4).

Indeed, the plot of "Clifford's Tower" is predictable, the characters underdeveloped, and the dialogue weak. Set in the charming and colorful New England countryside, "Clifford's Tower" recounts the story of Herndon Clifford, one of the country's original settlers, who sets out to build a castle "which should rival in this new world the ancestral glory of his family in the old." Clifford's intention is to build the castle as a tribute to his bride-to-be, Mabel Hurd. When Mabel undergoes a change of heart and returns to her first love, Clifford abruptly halts construction of the castle and spends the remainder of his life in exile. Generations later, one of Clifford's descendants, the "fair pale Agnes whose short life was passed in the very shadow of the [castle] tower," falls in love with Robert Hurd, grandson of the woman who had left Clifford to return to her first love. Agnes's mother, Catharine Clifford, a chronically ill but exceedingly strong-willed woman, forbids the union between the two young lovers. "While I live, and while this tower shall stand, you shall not marry this man!" she commands Agnes. An obedient daughter, Agnes reaffirms her duty to her sickly mother. Late one evening, however, while her mother is asleep, Agnes slips outside in the midst of a violent thunderstorm to say goodbye to Robert one last time. In an utterly contrived and melodramatic climax, a stroke of lightning destroys the castle, killing Catharine Clifford and freeing Agnes to marry Robert.

A story that perhaps better exemplifies Gilman's appropriation of Hawthornesque themes, whether consciously or not, is one titled "Old Water."[18] While "Clifford's Tower" offers a baldly superficial imitation in its attempt to represent Hawthorne's New England landscape and character types, "Old Water" explores more intricately the complex Hawthornesque themes of monomania and obsession.

"Old Water" is a story in which the motifs of fantasy, obsession, and possession are intertwined. Although Gilman's didacticism remains intact, this story is somewhat unconventional in its denouement. Gilman centers the action around a prominent poet in pursuit of a beautiful young woman, who repels his attempts at seduction. But his quest for mastery of the woman, Ellen Osgood, compels him "madly, passionately, irresistibly" [sic] (128). Indeed, Gilman's poet, Pendexter, epitomizes Hawthorne's "daemonic" figure, described by Brodhead as one whose "attention fixes on a single object . . . and makes it into the sign of its obsession. . . . The Hawthornesque obsessive deforms reality, subjects it to a perverse pressure that distorts and violates its familiar contours; but through this deformation he discovers another state of things that is instantly known to be more deeply real, and that is not to be known otherwise than through his obsessive deformations" (Brodhead 35–36).

Pendexter's behavior exemplifies this obsessive process. When he meets Ellen for the first time, he is drawn to her beauty. "Her body is a poem!" he exclaims (122). As a poet, his transformation of Ellen's body into a poem—a product over which he customarily has creative control—immediately reduces her to an object, a trans-figuration that is further reinforced by his comparison of her to such mythological figures as Valkyr, Juno, and Atalanta. Indeed, his obsession with Ellen escalates to the point where he desires to mold her into the kind of mythical woman that he idealizes in his poetry. Ellen's recognition of the inherent superficiality in Pendexter's practice of writing poetry about "people who never existed anyhow" (126) only fuels her dislike for him. "What on earth does he want to make over those old legends for, anyway!" she complains to her mother (126).

This "conjunction of monomania and figure-making" (Brodhead 35), so often present in Hawthorne's characters, is reinvented in Gilman's Pendexter.[19] His obsession with Ellen intensifies as she continues to resist his advances. His original fantasies about her elegant beauty metamorphose into a brutal quest to possess both her body and soul. He conceals "the storm of passion which was growing within him; a passion of such *seething intensity* as would have alarmed that gentle soul exceedingly. . . . His heart was *hot and dark* within him. The longer he pursued and failed the *fiercer* was his desire for her" (127–28; emphasis added). The daemonic figure rages darker and fiercer as the object of his obsession continues to reject him.

Gilman's depiction of Ellen suggests her resistance to Pendexter is not only the result of simple incompatibility—clearly the two have little in common—but she also fears her own sexuality. Ellen has an irrational fear of water and dreams of "big beasts" that jump out at her (124). She becomes alarmed by Pendexter's "mighty strokes" when he paddles her canoe. "Not so hard!" she cries. "You are stronger than I" (126). And although "she did rather enjoy the well proportioned bulk of him," she "felt a real dislike for the heavy fell of black hair on his arms and hands." The beast of Ellen's dreams becomes an obvious metaphor for Pendexter, whose primordial animalistic impulses threaten to destroy her innocence.

But the real focus of the story is on Pendexter's deformation of reality. He convinces himself that he and Ellen were paired in another life and that it is their fate to be together again: " 'Ah' he cried. 'It is your fate! Our fate! We have lived through this before! We will die together if we cannot live together!' " (129). Thus he is aligned with the Hawthornesque obsessive, who through his distorted perception constructs another version of reality.

In the final scene, Ellen escapes a sexual attack by Pendexter, whose "blood [was] pounding in his veins, his voice shaken with the intensity of his emotions" (128). Pendexter continues his pursuit, and as Ellen attempts to flee, the two end up struggling on the edge of a cliff. Pendexter's literal and figurative descent is completed as the two plummet into the lake below.

The ending of the story is somewhat ambiguous. Gilman presents at least the possibility that Pendexter has been murdered by Ellen: she survives; he doesn't. " 'It's pretty lucky I could swim,' said Ellen, as she hurried home, 'and he couldn't.' " We never see what actually transpires in the water, however. In what appears as a postscript to the story, Ellen has escaped both an actual and a symbolic death at the hands of Pendexter. Gilman thus frees her protagonist, who in the final words of the story articulates the daemonic nature of Pendexter's obsession: "He must have been crazy!" she concludes (129).

Along with obsession, the depiction of the "fallen woman"—so sympathetically rendered in the character of Hawthorne's Hester Prynne—is also a common theme in Gilman's fiction and one that she treats with great compassion. Certainly Gilman could relate to Hawthorne's sensitive portrayal of Hester, a single mother condemned and ostracized by her community. Gilman was similarly persecuted when she relinquished custody of her nine-year-old daughter to her ex-husband, Walter Stetson, after accepting a job in a place that would be unsuitable for a child (*Living* 162). Publicly condemned for her actions and "violently slapped"[20] by a long-time acquaintance who objected to her lifestyle, Gilman, like Hester, was similarly branded—as an "unnatural mother." Also like Hester, however, Gilman relied on inner strength to survive the ordeal.

There is, in fact, a strong parallel between Hester's views about the "whole race of womanhood," and the philosophy that Gilman evolved. In chapter 13, "Another View of Hester," Hawthorne's progressive ideas about the ability of women to realize their potential and to transform the world are reflected in Hester's quiet musings, which she perceives as "such a hopeless task before her" (*TSL* 113). She considers the process through which an egalitarian world might be created:

> As a first step, the whole system of society is to be torn down, and built up anew. Then, the very nature of the opposite sex, or its long hereditary habit, which has become like nature, is to be essentially modified, before woman can be allowed to assume what seems a fair and suitable position. Finally, all other difficulties being obviated, woman cannot take advantage of these preliminary reforms until she herself shall have undergone a still mightier change; in which, perhaps, the ethereal essence, wherein she has her truest life, will be found to have evaporated. A woman never overcomes these problems by any exercise of thought. (*TSL* 113, ch. 13)

Indeed, as Gilman argued, women can overcome these problems only by action. Of course, she also saw the tearing down and rebuilding of society as the means by which egalitarian relationships between men and women might be established. But while Hester can intellectualize the process, she cannot act. Gilman, however, called upon women to take an active role in effecting progressive change, and she chastised those who remained complacent:

> Women ought to feel a glorious new pride in their sex, now that it is shown to be the main trunk of the tree of life. They ought to feel an unbounded hope and power in their ability to remake the race and to help manage it on better terms than ever before. And they ought also to burn with shame, deep scorching shame, at the pitiful limitations with which so many of them are still contented.

They have no longer the excuse of ignorance. They have no longer the excuse of helplessness. Our intelligent, educated American women who are not informed of their real duty in life—and doing it—have no real excuse.[21]

In many respects Gilman herself enacted the role of the "destined prophetess" about which Hester Prynne could only dream in vain. Gilman spent the better part of her life lecturing and writing about how the world might best "establish the whole relation between man and woman on a surer ground of mutual happiness" (*TSL* 177, ch. 24). Surely, she would have agreed with Hawthorne's declaration at the end of *The Scarlet Letter* that "the angel and the apostle of the coming revelation must be a woman" (177, ch. 24). But with the exception of her utopian novels, Gilman's fiction didn't look to the future, it didn't look to the past; it looked to the moment. "The immediate hope of the world is in women," she asserted. "Humanity 'groaneth and travaileth' for its mother. She'd better hurry," Gilman urged.[22]

Much of Nathaniel Hawthorne's fiction was beautifully rendered: it was powerful, passionate, and provocative. Charlotte Perkins Gilman could admire the eloquence, applaud the artistry, and even attempt to imitate the style. But her ultimate goal in writing fiction was not to entertain; she was less concerned with chronicling complex moral dilemmas than in educating her reader and demonstrating possibilities for effecting positive social change.[23]

Notes

1. Although Gilman also published under the names of Charlotte Anna Perkins and Charlotte Perkins Stetson at various points during her career, for the sake of consistency I have opted to refer to her only as Gilman.

2. Gilman, diary entry for 20 Aug. 1882. *The Diaries of Charlotte Perkins Gilman.* 2 vols. Edited by Denise D. Knight. Charlottesville: UP of Virginia, 1994, p. 140.

3. Gilman, *Impress* 3 Nov. 1894: 4.

4. The opening night performance was staged on 1 Jan. 1877. Gary Scharnhorst, ed., *The Critical Response to Nathaniel Hawthorne's "The Scarlet Letter"* (Westport, Conn.: Greenwood, 1992) xxv.

5. Gilman, diary entry for 25 Dec. 1883.

6. Qtd. in Gilman, *Forerunner* 1 (Dec. 1910): 33.

7. Amy Wellington, "Charlotte Perkins Gilman," *Women Have Told: Studies in the Feminist Tradition* (Boston: Little, Brown, 1930) 115–31, rpt. in Joanne Karpinski, ed., *Critical Essays on Charlotte Perkins Gilman* (New York: Hall, 1992) 67–72.

8. See Gary Scharnhorst's *Charlotte Perkins Gilman* (Boston: Twayne, 1985) for an overview of Gilman's social theories.

9. Gilman, *The Living of Charlotte Perkins Gilman* (1935; rpt. Madison: U of Wisconsin P, 1990) 308; hereafter cited in the text as *Living.*

10. Richard S. Brodhead, *The School of Hawthorne* (New York: Oxford UP, 1985) 65; hereafter cited in the text as Brodhead.

11. Gilman, *The Man-Made World; or, Our Androcentric Culture* (New York: Charlton, 1911) 102.

12. Gilman, "Coming Changes in Literature," *Forerunner* 6 (Sept. 1915): 230–36.

13. The undated quotation is from a folder in the Gilman Papers, Arthur and Elizabeth Schlesinger Library, Radcliffe College, titled "Thoughts & Figgerings." Gilman often wrote her thoughts, her objectives, and her long-term plans on odd scraps of paper which she collected and saved over the years.

14. Nathaniel Hawthorne, *The Scarlet Letter,* ed. Seymour Gross et al. 3rd ed. (New York: Norton, 1988) 177; hereafter cited in the text as *TSL.*

15. "Clifford's Tower" appeared in the 27 Oct. 1894 edition of the *Impress,* 4–5. It stands among Gilman's earliest fictional works. The majority of her fiction was written much later (between 1909 and 1916), when she was the writer, editor, and publisher of a monthly journal, the *Forerunner.*

16. Gilman, *Impress* 1 (6 Oct. 1894): 4.

17. Gilman, *Impress* 1 (3 Nov. 1894): 4.

18. Gilman, "Old Water," *Forerunner* 2 (Oct. 1911): 255–59, rpt. in Denise D. Knight, ed., *The Yellow Wall-Paper and Selected Stories of Charlotte Perkins Gilman* (Newark: U of Delaware P, 1994) 122–29; subsequent page references are to the reprint edition.

19. See also Nina Baym's description of obsession in Hawthorne's characters in "Thwarted Nature: Hawthorne and Feminism," *American Novelists Revisited: Essays in Feminist Criticism,* ed. Fritz Fleischman (Boston: Hall, 1982) 65–66.

20. Gilman reports being slapped by her old friend, Gussie Seuter, in a letter to Houghton Gilman dated 25 Dec. 1899, Gilman Papers, Schlesinger Library.

21. Gilman, *Forerunner* 7 (Dec. 1916): 327.

22. Gilman, *Forerunner* 7 (Dec. 1916): 327.

23. Space does not permit a fuller discussion of Gilman's fiction, which includes such forms as fictionalized autobiography, fantasy, science fiction, fables, adventures, satires, and Gothic horror stories. Gilman also wrote allegories and parables, numerous examples of which can be found in the reprint edition of the *Forerunner* (New York: Greenwood, 1968).

BOURGEOIS SEXUALITY AND THE GOTHIC PLOT IN WHARTON AND HAWTHORNE

Monika M. Elbert

The focus of this essay is on *The Scarlet Letter* and *Summer,* but other instances of Hawthornean influences on Wharton's depiction of gender and class can be found in *The House of Mirth, Ethan Frome, The Reef, The Custom of the Country, The Age of Innocence, Old New York,* and in Wharton's ghost stories.

Though critics are quick to point out superficial resemblances between two of Wharton's and Hawthorne's chief protagonists (the two Zenobias, the two Ethans),[1] they are not comfortable discussing the deeper legacy which Hawthorne left to Wharton. The latter is fascinated by the Gothic, "that peculiar category of the eerie which lies outside of the classic tradition" and which she perceives in the writing of "Scott, Hawthorne, and Poe" (*Writing of Fiction* 34). Certainly, Wharton's New England novels owe much to Hawthorne, as Wharton herself readily concedes in the oft-quoted passage which links her to the School of Hawthorne rather than to the school of women regionalists (Mary W. Freeman, Sarah Orne Jewett) who see New England through "rose-coloured spectacles" (*Backward Glance* 293). She complains about the New Englanders' negative reception of *Summer*: they "had for years sought the reflection of local life in the rose-and-lavender pages of their favourite authoresses—and had forgotten to look into Hawthorne's" (*Backward Glance* 294). Indeed, as writers, both Hawthorne and Wharton are rather elitist in wanting to separate themselves from the "mob of scribbling women."[2] Wharton allied herself with a male author, who was as ambivalent about his class status as she, and this class ambivalence is expressed in their development of a New England Gothic genre.

In their autobiographical sketches as well as in their fiction, both Hawthorne and Wharton use Gothic conventions to describe a burgeoning capitalist society with its attendant class fluctuations and tensions. A recent critic defines the Gothic as a genre which "has a great deal of relation to the undeniable growth . . . of a particular class and its concomitant anxieties" (Bernstein 165). Whereas he pinpoints rightful inheritance and the transference of property (when classes merge) as the dilemma of the Gothic, I perceive that for Hawthorne and Wharton this central Gothic issue is expressed through the image of woman's body as sexual commodity. Moreover, in the regulation of sexuality, both Hawthorne and Wharton are obsessed with replicating and reproducing, on a figurative level, good ancestral blood and, on a biological level, good hereditary genes. Puritan predestination is transformed into biological determinism, with sexual depravity or promiscuity as original sin becoming the cause for individual mutations or family aberrations.

Though Hawthorne declares in the introduction to *The Scarlet Letter* that he has cut himself off from the earlier intolerant Hathorne clan, the professional aristocracy of Puritan culture, he takes a strange pride in his lineage: "strong traits of their nature have intertwined themselves with mine" (10). And like a Gothic protagonist who seeks to atone for the sins of his intolerant fathers, he asserts, "I, the present writer, as their representative, hereby take shame upon myself for their sakes, and pray that any curse incurred by them . . . may be now and henceforth removed" (10). Significantly, Hawthorne describes the persecuting spirit of these forebears as acts specifically directed against women—against a Quaker woman and against martyred witches. It makes sense, too, that the *ghostly* figure of Surveyor Pue comes back to haunt him in order that he write/right the story of a woman who has been wronged, Hester Prynne. Hawthorne feels of two minds about Hester as he takes on his duty of being her biographer: "she gained from many people the reverence due to an angel, but *I should imagine,* was looked upon by others as *an intruder and a nuisance*" (32; emphasis mine). This view of Hester as "intruder and nuisance" is important in light of the narrative proper: for Hawthorne allies Hester with the disenfranchised members of society, those on the periphery, Native Americans, witches, sailors, widows, Quakers, antinomians, and bondservants. Historically speaking, the Puritan notion of depravity and original sin was secularized in the nineteenth century, so that "depraved nature" was associated "with the inferior social elements—notably, Negroes, Indians, Irish immigrants, the urban masses, and, in a crucially qualified sense, *women*" (Goshgarian 41; emphasis mine). Moreover, Hawthorne delineates Surveyor Pue's character as representing His Majesty and, with that, a bygone era and class, and "who was therefore illuminated by a ray of the splendor that shone so dazzlingly about the throne" (33). In contrast is "the hang-dog look of a republican official, who, as the servant of the people, feels himself less than the least, and below the lowest, of his masters" (33).

Though Hawthorne may be portraying the current type of bureaucratic workers in the Custom House, he also describes his own plight; as a dethroned civil servant, Hawthorne follows Surveyor Pue's injunction to write Hester's story: "do this, and the profit shall be all your own! You will shortly need it; for it is not in your days as it was in mine, when a man's office was a life-lease, and oftentimes an heirloom" (33).[3] Not only does this show Hawthorne's hankering for the olden days, when class flux and tensions were unheard of and job security was ensured. It also catapults him into the bourgeois dilemma of exploiting woman's body for public consumption—exposing Hester in the marketplace—and of exploring class anxieties and allegiances using woman as a battleground for these tensions. Moreover, to continue along the line of Gothic conventions, the persona that Hawthorne the narrator assumes is that of the decayed aristocracy who continue in the evil quest to oppress the selfsame people, whether it be the Hesters of *The Scarlet Letter* or the Maules of *The House of the Seven Gables,* they have exploited in the past. The family power and money are ill gotten, and now Hester's story will continue to bring the modern Hawthorne, the fallen aristocrat, a "profit." In embarking upon the capitalist money plot, Hawthorne is still implicated in making dirty money—at the expense of a fallen woman. Moreover, in an attempt to democratize and secularize the Puritan notion of original sin, Hawthorne has to make everyone wear the scarlet "A." From the narrator himself who affixes Hester's "A" to his chest, to the main protagonists in the drama, to the community members, and finally to the readers themselves, sexual sin becomes the great equalizer. As one critic points out, "Unable to overlook its inferiors' natural depravity, yet unwilling—given its democratic commitments—to deny that it shared a common humanity with them, the bourgeoisie had grudgingly to retain something *like* original sin even in its own conception of itself" (Goshgarian 43).

Wharton, too, tries to trace her genealogy in terms of the conflict between the middling and aristocratic classes; movement between classes entails overstepping or transgressing sexual boundaries. She talks about the early select colonial class, who established the traditions of this country: time transformed a "group of bourgeois colonials and their republican descendants into a sort of social aristocracy" (*Backward Glance* 5), and she guards her class status jealously. She counts herself among this fortunate group of Old New York, a group which, she nostalgically notes, is now dying out but whose memory she seeks to preserve—by listing the illustrious family members and forebears and asserting, "On both sides our colonial ancestry goes back for nearly three hundred years" (9). Most of her colonial forebears hailed from New York "where people seem from the outset to have been more interested in making money and acquiring property than in Predestination and witch-burning" (9). Though Wharton insists that her "ancestry . . . was purely middle-class," she believes that her "family belonged to the same group as this little aristocratic nucleus" (11). She takes pride in the fact that her relatives, on the paternal and maternal sides, all "belonged to the same prosperous class of merchants, bankers, and lawyers" who excluded retail dealers; "So little did the Revolution revolutionize a society at once middle-class and provincial that no retail dealer . . . was received in New York society until long after I was grown up" (11). Moreover, Wharton extols the virtues and integrity which her class exemplified and promoted, suggesting that the bourgeois must maintain appearances which the true aristocracy can dispose of: "In old-established and powerful societies originality of character is smiled at, and even encouraged to assert itself; but conformity is the bane of middle-class communities, and as far as I can recall, only two of my relations stepped out of the strait [*sic*] path of the usual" (23). One of these relatives, her cousin George Alfred, "vanished . . . out of society, out of respectability, out of the safe daylight world of 'nice people' and reputable doings" (23). Wharton explains how her mother took a perverse delight in mentioning the unspeakable cousin; "If my mother pronounced his name it was solely, I believe, out of malice, out of the child's naughty desire to evoke some nursery hobgoblin by muttering a dark incantation . . . and then darting way with affrighted backward looks to see if there is anything there" (24).

Just as Hawthorne gothicizes his authorial plot in reconstructing his ancestral past, so too does Wharton use the Gothic in explaining the dark spot of her lineage and as a way of entering the world of her novels. Wharton's curiosity, "But, Mamma, *what did he do?*" is finally assuaged by her mother's muttering, "Some woman" (*Backward Glance* 24). Wharton pursues the detective work of the Gothic writer: "George Alfred—and some woman! Who was she? From what depths had she fallen with him, to what depths dragged him down? For in those simple days it was always a case of 'the woman tempted me.' To her respectable sisters her culpability was as certain in advance as Predestination to the Calvinist" (24). Like Hawthorne, Wharton traces the myth of the fallen woman with Puritan metaphors, and finally she creates a fiction of it, a somber kind of Gothic:

> The vision of poor featureless unknown Alfred and his siren, lurking in some cranny of my imagination, hinted at regions perilous, dark and yet lit with mysterious fires, just outside the world of copy-book axioms, and the old obediences that were in my blood; and the hint was useful—for a novelist. (25)

Wharton's New England novel *Summer* is an analysis of such class disruption in its portrayal of a woman who is alternately perceived as fallen and empowered as seductress/siren. Moreover, Wharton, like Hawthorne, perceives the fall of upright family members in terms of woman's sexuality. And her achievement as a novelist will depend upon re-creating the story of "regions perilous," with woman as its victim (and selling point).

But it is more than just women's bodies for sale: sexuality becomes the concern and obsession of the family and community at large. Michel Foucault describes the construction of nineteenth-century sexuality in terms which ring peculiarly Gothic:

> [Society had] suddenly discovered the dreadful secret of what had always been hinted at and inculcated in it: the family, the keystone of alliance, was the germ of all the misfortunes of sex. . . . from the mid-nineteenth century onward, the family engaged in searching out the slightest traces of sexuality in its midst, wrenching from itself the most difficult confessions, soliciting an audience with everyone

who might know something about the matter, and opening itself unreservedly to endless examination. (III)

In a world in which "sexuality is linked to the economy" (Foucault 106), the "commerce" forbidden included crimes, if not sins, of adultery, incest, prostitution, and masturbation—the acts which would tear away at the fabric of the bourgeois family and hence need to be publicly avowed. The discourse of sexual repression led to full-fledged exposure in the middle-class novel. Thus, in Hawthorne's *Scarlet Letter,* Hester's and Dimmesdale's adultery as well as Dimmesdale's self-flagellation in the closet (which could be construed as masturbation) are the hallmarks of a Gothic travesty. Moreover, the community is never sure of Pearl's paternity—a manifestation of the secret fear of bourgeois thinking as well as the skeleton in the Gothic closet. In fact, if Hester's sexuality is perceived as monstrous, her offspring, Pearl, is seen as demonic. Chillingworth also participates in the drama of sin: he seems sexually perverse in establishing an almost incestuous relationship with a much younger Hester, a union which remains barren. It is no wonder that, when she can, Pearl escapes the bourgeois house of horrors by trying to reclaim her aristocratic birthright in Europe (one should recall that Hester's parents belonged to the dying aristocracy). Yet Pearl, ironically, is able to escape into an orderly, aristocratic past, through her marriage to an Old World gentleman, only through the help of new bourgeois money, the dirty money Chillingworth leaves behind as his legacy to Pearl; if she is not a lady at the end of the text, she certainly has the money to lure the fallen aristocracy.

Similarly, in *Summer,* Lawyer Royall tries to seduce his foster daughter when his barren wife dies. In fact, it seems a stunning irony that Charity's mother, described in such savage, primitive terms, can provide the barren middle-class family (with its icon the effete, dying mother), with a child who, through her sexuality, becomes more and more seductive to the upstanding citizen of North Dormer, Lawyer Royall. Charity's mother herself is perceived as a prostitute; in fact, Charity's entire clan of Mountain outlaws is seen in subhuman terms as copulating indiscriminately and incestuously. Though Charity is able to resist the incestuous relationship early on, she finally capitulates to marriage, as she finds herself single and pregnant with no option other than the impalatable one of abortion. But she sells her body as surely as does her friend Julia, another fallen woman, in order to ensure the welfare of her child. Marriage seems just another version of Charity's earlier licentious relationship with Lucius Harney as both arrangements are based on her obsession with consumerism. Harney, the architect from New York, is researching (ostensibly) the old "Colonial houses" of the area but, as a member of the privileged class, has easy access to the Mountain people's homes and women. He offers Charity the knickknacks and toys of civilization, whereas Royall offers her a stable financial future. Though the rich class can use her for sexual favors and then abandon her, Royall is willing to marry her and make her an "honest woman." Moreover, Charity knows her place in the "natural" order of class: Annabel Balch, the cultivated girl whom Charity perceives as her rival, is "if not the girl Harney ought to marry, at least the kind of girl it would be *natural* for him to marry" (220; emphasis mine). Charity can only move one step up the ladder by marrying Royall, the upholder of bourgeois values, as he expresses them in his official "Old Home Week" speech (cf. Dimmesdale's Election Sermon).

In both *The Scarlet Letter* and *Summer,* novels of seduction, love triangles are formed between two men vying for one woman: in either case, the more established but older and less sexual man (Chillingworth, Royall), the proponent of middle-class values and moderation, needs to compete with the younger, aspiring, ambitious young man (Dimmesdale, Harney), whose identity is shaped by his conquest of woman (Hester, Charity). Finally, it is not just a struggle for the woman but a competition between two stages of manhood; the older men jealously guard their possession of the young sexual woman, as it keeps them in control of the sexual market. Within this panorama of sexual indiscretions, there are the "hag" figures (creatures of men's imaginations) who would lead Hester and Charity away from the sanctioned middle-class role of mother. The "witch" Mistress Hibbins is constantly trying to kidnap Hester and make a convert of her in the forest, a fate Hester would have willingly submitted to, had the patriarchs in the Governor's mansion removed Pearl from her care/custody. Dr. Merkle, with her black hair, gypsy jewelry, and false teeth is the modern hag, who threatens to disrupt the bourgeois control of sexuality by offering the termination of pregnancy to Charity, civilization's foster child (and responsibility); in a most reprehensible manner, she robs young women of their dreams and of the little money (or love mementos) they've saved. To enter the game of sexuality outside the boundaries of bourgeois controls entails potential exploitation by those other deviants. The energies of both books go against the image of women having custody of their own bodies: in fact, Mistress Hibbins, the childless widow, and Dr. Merkle, the abortionist, are obstacles to the bourgeois order which would regulate women's reproductive, maternal capacities.

The deterioration and regeneration of the Gothic family and of society at large are Hawthorne's and Wharton's preoccupations in *The Scarlet Letter* and *Summer.* Heredity can be seen as, figuratively, the curse of the fathers. But it is also biological, in terms of evolutionary eugenics, and expresses the ambivalence Victorians felt toward sexuality—"that sex was an animalistic attribute which must be curbed and that sex was a sacred gift designed to produce superb children" (Aspiz 147). Wharton, for example, in writing about her conception of New England landscapes, explains that when she lived in Lenox

> the villages of Western Massachusetts were still grim places, morally and physically; insanity, incest, and slow mental and moral starvation were hidden away behind the paintless wooden house-fronts of the long village street, or in the isolated farm-houses on the neighboring hills. (*Backward Glance* 294)

Ironically, she maintains that she was an accurate observer of the "derelict mountain villages of New England," but it is only from her vantage point, from her privileged perspective at the Mount, her Lenox mansion. She even gets the story for the death and funeral of Charity's mother from hearing about a similar event from the rector, the virtuous intermediary between her class and the "outlaw" class of the Mountain: the rector is "fetched . . . by one of the mountain outlaws to read the Burial Service over a woman of evil reputation" (*Backward Glance* 294). The drunken family who await him and the woman of ill repute are enough to send the rector into a tailspin: he returns "with his eyes full of horror and his heart of anguish and pity" (294). This is the same stance that the bourgeois narrator of Wharton's *Summer* takes. Charity is embarrassed to admit her relationship to Liff Hyatt, the local idiot, with his blundering ways and with his "feverish hollows below the cheekbones and the pale yellow eyes of a harmless animal" (56). However, even more so, Wharton sides with the voice of civilization, as she allows Royall to speak for her. As she writes to Bernard Berenson, "I'm so particularly glad you like old man Royall. Of course, *he's* the book!" (*Letters* 4 Sept. 1917). Royall is able to bring Charity down from the Mountain and to civilize her through marriage, thus providing her child with a father. But his attitude toward her kin on the Mountain resounds through the book: "Why, the Mountain's a blot. . . . The scum up there ought to have been run in long ago. . . . They just herd together like the heathen" (*Summer* 71). But it is the sexuality of Charity's mother which he finds so repulsive and yet in Charity so tantalizing: "They ain't half human up there. I guess the mother's dead by now, with the life she was leading" (73). However, the incestuous breeders of the Mountain are not so different from Royall in the incestuous relationship he has with, first, Julia, a prostitute of Charity's age, and then with Charity herself: incest is a psychological phenomenon that transcends class. What Hawthorne hinted at in his Gothic plots— incest and inbreeding—become more than the figurative sins of the fathers in Wharton. According to Foucault, the late-nineteenth-century study of "perversion-heredity-degenerescence" (118) allowed for a new politics of procreativity and family control: if a family "were suspected—through lack of space, dubious proximity, a history of debauchery, antisocial 'primitiveness,' or degenerescence—of practicing incest" (129), the child could be handed over to a legal guardian. This is exactly how Charity's birthright and heritage are robbed by Royall, significantly the law maker of North Dormer, who claims the Mountain territory as his own—to be taken and then civilized.

Though Hawthorne only hints at the incestuous relationship between an old man, Chillingworth, and a young woman, Hester, he does spend much time debating who should get custody of Pearl, the spritelike child of the wilderness. In the protracted scene at the Governor's Hall, the leading officials of Boston decide Pearl's fate. Because they are convinced that Hester has not taught Pearl the proper catechism, they feel compelled to remove her, but the debate ends with Dimmesdale's sympathetic appeal for female nurturing. Though Hester gets the child, the men examine her progeny as crassly as they had eyed her in the first scaffold scene: the Reverend John Wilson, the religious spokesman, feels that "the little baggage hath witchcraft in her" (116), whereas Chillingworth, the voice of science, promotes hereditary theory as an explanation for the child's behavior: "Would it be beyond a philosopher's research ... to analyze that child's nature ... and to give a shrewd guess at the father?" (116). If Hawthorne obsesses about his own ancestry in the introduction to *The Scarlet Letter,* he worries about New England heritage and paternal lineage in the narrative itself. Speaking about the Puritan women, he warns about the degeneracy of subsequent generations of American women:

> Morally, as well as materially, there was a coarser fibre in those wives and maidens of old English birth and breeding, than in their fair descendants, separated from them by a series of six or seven generations; for, throughout that change of ancestry, every successive mother has transmitted to her child a fainter bloom, a more delicate and briefer beauty, and a slighter physical frame, if not a character of less force and solidity, than her own. (50)

This fear, if not of a demented offspring, then of a degenerate stock, was common to many Victorians, especially the reformers: "assuming that one's bodily condition reflected one's spiritual state, Victorian reformers often lamented a perceived physical decline among their contemporaries when compared to the supposedly superior condition of their ancestors; and they interpreted this falling off as a sign of moral decay" (Aspiz 144). The Hawthorne narrator also comments that if women are to change their "ethereal essence," they will need to change their "long hereditary habit, which has become like *nature*" (184; emphasis mine). It makes sense to such a traditionalist mind that, if Pearl is to avoid the fate of a deteriorating New England maiden, she needs to mate with someone from the Old World, to invigorate the family line. So Hawthorne sends her packing—back to the old homeland, where Hester's family, the erstwhile aristocracy, had fallen. It is a meeting of new and old as Pearl's money and her husband's good name promise to bring the classes together in much the same way that the Pyncheons and Maules of *The House of the Seven Gables* are reconciled. With proper monitoring and sanctioned mating, regeneration and class integrity could follow.

At the center of Hawthorne's and Wharton's New England Gothic is the exposure of fertile woman and of fecund nature as grotesque, dangerous, and treacherous. The scenes which are most horrible are not those which take place in the patriarchs' household, whether that be in the Governor's mansion (*Scarlet Letter*) or in Lawyer Royall's house (*Summer*). The real danger lies in the feminine landscape, which seems to be haunted by inexplicable ghostly visions and/or by a suffocating type of wilderness, which seems threatening to the established order. Thus Hester, in her seaside cottage on the periphery of civilization, is visited by dangerous thoughts, "such as dared to enter no other dwelling in New England; shadowy guests that would have been as perilous as demons to their entertainers, could they have been seen so much as knocking at her door" (183). The operative fear on Hawthorne's part, though, is that nature, as well as woman, will nourish as well as strangle and thus must be controlled. So, juxtaposed with the "wild rose" of the initial prison-door scene are various ugly and poisonous herbs, among them "burdock, pigweed, and apple-peru," which grow indiscriminately and which are linked to Chilling-worth's tampering with nature as he cross-breeds plants so that the monstrous growth results not just in "nightshade, dogwood, [and] henbane" but in "poisonous shrubs, of species hitherto unknown" (176). Hawthorne even describes nature as having deteriorated: the "luxuriant heap of moss" upon which Hester and Pearl sit and converse in the forest had been "at some epoch of the preceding century . . . a gigantic pine . . . with its roots and trunk in the darksome shade, and its head aloft in the upper atmosphere" (185–86). This process of decay is also Hawthorne's tech-nique for desexualizing an initially vibrant and passionate Hester. But Hester's sexuality is permissible only as long as it is allied with the maternal; the narrator conjures the picture of "Divine Maternity" (if only in contrast to the "sacred image of sinless motherhood") in order to feel in command of her sexuality; maternity becomes a safe outlet for her sexuality. In fact, Hester is continually desexed through the text so that she appears as shadowlike, cold, statuelike, and ghostlike once she loses her passion and gains in rationality; in fact, toward the end of the narrative, she glides "shadowlike" back into her New England cottage, a veritable ghost. Hester, neutered in the marketplace, does not wield much power in the man's world. In the forest, when Hester lets her hair down one last time with Dimmesdale, Pearl re-minds her to put her "A" and her cap back on—to remind her that, at heart, her identity is maternal and not sexual. And finally, when Hester begs Dimmesdale to say whether they will meet again in another realm, he tells her to "hush," reminding her that a woman out of sexual currency cannot strike a bargain with a man, even if he is on his way out! Hawthorne has made sex safe and uninteresting by spiritualiz-ing the body and by secularizing the spirit.

Similarly, Charity's sexuality, which is initially perceived as honest, wholesome, and in tune with nature, is transformed into the "blot" of the Mountain once she has had sexual relations with Harney. In fact, as a virgin, Charity is revealed as lolling about in the fields, "her face pressed to the earth and the warm currents of the grass running through her" (*Summer* 53). The flowers, trees, and meadows are described in a protracted swoonlike passage which has Charity feel in Whitmanesque sync with nature: "all were merged in a moist-earth smell that was like the breath of some huge sun-warmed animal" (54). However, nature appears increasingly more malev-olent as Charity's dangerous, lawless qualities (in Royall's eyes at least) of sexuality are revealed. Lucius Harney initiates her into the wild territory from which she descends as he has her accompany him on his visits to their old, dilapidated homes; among the swamp people, the kin to the disenfranchised Mountain people, the description of the morass of the garden reveals the family's moral degeneracy: "the garden was a poisonous tangle of nettles, burdocks, and tall swamp-weeds over which big blue-bottles hummed" (82). It is the same type of poisonous landscape which haunts Hawthorne's Hester. Similarly, the "little deserted house" of a "ghostly gray" color in the hills, which becomes Charity's refuge from North Dormer, is not exactly an idyllic Wordsworthian cottage: this hideaway in which she loses her innocence is described as run-down and wild. Nature has encroached upon civilization in a most Hawthornesque way:

> the path to the house was marked by rose-bushes run wild and hanging their small pale blossoms above the crowding grasses. Slender pilasters and an intricate fan-light framed the opening where the door had hung; and the door itself lay rotting in the grass, with an old apple-tree fallen across it. (166)

And if Harney can momentarily remove her from the "strict code" of North Dormer, the escape is finally illusory, and her sexual existence in the abandoned house is gothicized in relationship to her conventional existence in the town: Harney had "carried her away into a new world, in which, at stated hours, the ghost of her came back to perform certain customary acts, but all so thinly and insubstantially that she sometimes wondered that the people she went about among could see her" (182).[4]

Just as Hawthorne resolves the sexual tensions of his novel by first maternalizing Hester and then making her progressively more cold, less passionate, even ghostlike in the last scene, so too does Wharton civilize her Charity by making her insubstantial and ghostlike. In fact, Charity begins to lose "all spontaneity of feelings" and appears to be "passively awaiting a fate she could not avert" when Royall proposes to her (214). Moreover, civilization tries to recapture its hold of nature's child when Charity finds herself single and pregnant: she concludes morally that "In the established order of things as she knew them she saw no place for her individual adventure" (235). Whereas Julia is able to evade the clutches of North Dormer by taking charge of her body and having an abortion, Charity is forced to go the way of "poor Rose Cole," one of the many casualties of "village love-stories" who had "married 'to make things right'" (234). Finally, Wharton shows that the Mountain, the mystical, almost numinous landscape which Charity perceived as her final refuge, offers nothing but a horrible encounter with the deteriorating, dead mother. Throughout the text, Charity is seen gazing up at the Mountain, entertaining thoughts about how she would escape the sleepy town of North Dormer. The Mountain is seen idyllically as "bathed in waveless gold" of a sunset (182), illuminated by either a "fiery sunset" or the soft light of the stars (203), substantial and massive against the backdrop of a "rainy sky" (236). However, her ascent up the Gothic Mountain is a parody of the numinous in Gothic fiction: it is not the unity of spirit and body which takes place on the "sacred mountain"[5] but rather the depletion of the spirit, the despiritualization of the flesh. Though Charity's mother has been associated with the Mountain throughout the narrative, we now see in the most intense moment of horror the body of a dead woman, "who seemed to have fallen across her squalid bed in a drunken sleep, and to have been left lying where she fell, in her ragged disordered clothes" (248). The mother's face was "thin, yet swollen, with lips parted in a frozen gasp above the broken teeth. There was not sign in it of anything human; she lay there like a dead dog in a ditch" (250). In Charity's mind, and from the narrator's moralizing viewpoint, this was the price a woman paid for unbridled passion and reckless sexuality: a return to respectable bourgeois morality seems warranted.

Woman's body becomes, for the narrative voice in Hawthorne and Wharton, the locus of public scrutiny: her sexuality has been monitored and regularized, reproductive functions have been legitimized, and sensuality has been approved through maternal definition. Hawthorne translates the concept of the Puritan sin of sex into the nineteenth-century need for communal regularization: Hester's body and her letter "A" become public property (even her seaside cottage appears to be a public donation), just as Charity, Hester's literary descendant, is forced—through her sexual indiscretion—to live off the "charity" of civilization. According to Foucault, sex had become "a matter that required the social body as a whole, and virtually all of its individuals, to place themselves under surveillance" (116). Both Hawthorne and Wharton, who share the anxieties of bourgeois sexuality, depict the site of class confrontation as woman's body (Hester's, Charity's) outside the realm of public control—in an effort to expose the sexual obsessiveness and potential anarchy of the bourgeois family. As Foucault points out, it was in "the bourgeois or aristocratic family" and not in the working class that the surveillance of female sexuality developed, along with a compulsion to control procreative behavior and to define normal and pathological sexual practices (104–5). These realms of sexual restriction were especially important to Wharton and Hawthorne in their description of the "eerie" New England landscape which gave birth to Charity Royall in *Summer* and her precursor, Hester Prynne, in *The Scarlet Letter.*[6]

Notes

1. For brief discussions of similarities between Wharton's *Ethan Frome* and Hawthorne's *Blithedale Romance* and "Ethan Brand," see Goodman 74–75, 145; Waid 6–7, 90–94; and Wolff 156, 163–64. My reading differs from Emily M. Budick's recent reading of Hawthorne and Wharton, which focuses primarily on Hawthorne connections to Wharton's *House of Mirth*. Whereas Budick feels that Wharton's work "ignores the simple radicalism of Hawthorne's *Scarlet Letter*" (124), which refigures the family on "nonpatriarchal terms" (136), I show that Hawthorne and Wharton are equally hopeless in their portrayal of the status quo and in their depiction of desexualized women. Budick maintains that, unlike Hawthorne protagonists, Lily Bart is denied her motherhood "along with sexuality and marriage." If Budick had examined *Summer,* she would have realized that Wharton grants Charity mater-

nity but not the dangerous sexuality of the Mountain wilderness; similarly, Hawthorne allows Hester her motherhood but robs her of her sexuality (and marriage).

2. As Waid notes, "in her development as an artist it was more important for Wharton to distinguish herself from what Hawthorne called 'the damned mob of scribbling women' than from any of America's recognized male authors" (7).

3. For a recent assessment of Hawthorne's middle-class ties to Hester, see Gilmore 232–36, and for a thorough examination of class in Hawthorne's oeuvre, see Joel Pfister's study. Citing the feminist historian Joan Scott, Pfister perceives the construct of femininity as being used "ideologically to naturalize and therefore legitimize other social relations, such as class divisions and the unequal distribution of wealth and power" (135).

4. This trysting place in the woods is a parody of the good middle-class home of North Dormer and is similar, in terms of the lawlessness it represents, to Hester's cottage on the periphery of society, where Hester enjoys "a freedom of speculation," which Puritans "would have held to be a deadlier crime than that stigmatized by the scarlet letter" (Hawthorne 164). Charity's wilderness hideaway is also similar to the second story of the Custom House, a dangerous place where "ghosts might enter" (36), and which reflects Hawthorne's daring, illicit imagination.

5. Here I am using S. L. Varnado's Gothic definition of the numinous, as respect and love for the supernatural and wonderful (the sacred in nature, as well as in religion). Varnado shows how experiences on "the sacred mountain" connect "heaven and earth" (and spirit and body) and represent a spiritual high. To Charity, before she is dragged down by the reality of her mother's death, the Mountain is seen as a vision of supernatural beauty: "The Mountain was turning purple against a fiery sunset from which it seemed to be divided by a knife-edge of quivering light" (*Summer* 203); at the same time, it is personified, on a more earthly level, as a protective "shaggy shoulder" (202).

6. The sense of Gothic paralysis in Wharton's New England novels (*Ethan Frome* and *Summer*) and in her many ghost stories is very much akin to the sexual/Gothic dilemma found in Hawthorne's novels. But the houses do not have to be haunted in the New England, Hawthornesque tradition to reveal the oppressiveness of bourgeois mores. Lily Bart becomes as much a sellable, movable commodity in the many houses of *The House of Mirth* as does Charity or Hester, and the possibility of freedom in her encounter with Selden in the countryside early in the book parallels Charity's and Hester's fleeting moments of passion in nature. However, most of Wharton's houses of Old New York are like the houses of gloom which Hawthorne creates in the Pyncheon House of the Seven Gables, where the issue is the battle over old and new money but also the proprietary claim to the female protagonist, about whose sexuality the battle is often being waged. And the odd love triangles which emerge as a result of convention-bound relationships and marriages are as apparent in Hawthorne's *Blithedale Romance* as they are in Wharton's *Age of Innocence* or *The Custom of the Country*.

Though Judith Fryer does not concern herself directly with Hawthorne/Wharton parallels, she makes an interesting comparison: "The issues of social order and the wilderness of individual abandon that she [Wharton] explored in *The Custom of the Country, The Age of Innocence,* 'Beatrice Palmato,' the ghost stories and *A Backward Glance* are those Hawthorne had explored in *The Scarlet Letter*" (199). Another perceptive remark that a Wharton critic makes about Wharton's characters alone can also be applied to many of Hawthorne's characters: "This is the condition of many Wharton characters: unable to live in a new, freer world, finding the freedom somehow coarse and shallow or unsuitable, but unable to turn back to the old world, they hang in limbo" (French xxv).

Works Cited

Aspiz, Harold. "Sexuality and the Pseudo-Sciences." *Pseudo-Science and Society in 19th-Century America.* Ed. Arthur Wrobel. Lexington: UP of Kentucky, 1987. 144–65.

Bernstein, Stephen. "Form and Ideology in the Gothic Novel." *Essays in Literature* 18.2 (1991): 151–65.

Budick, Emily Miller. *Engendering Romance: Women Writers and the Hawthorne Tradition, 1850–1990.* New Haven: Yale UP, 1994.

Foucault, Michel. *The History of Sexuality: An Introduction.* Vol. 1. Trans. Robert Hurley. New York: Vintage, 1990.

French, Marilyn. Introduction. *Old New York.* By Edith Wharton. New York: Berkeley, 1981. v–xxix.

Fryer, Judith. *Felicitous Space: The Imaginative Structures of Edith Wharton and Willa Cather.* Chapel Hill: U of North Carolina P, 1986.

Gilmore, Michael T. "Hawthorne and the Making of the Middle Class." *Rethinking Class: Literary Studies and Social Formations.* Ed. Wai-Chee Dimock and Michael T. Gilmore. New York: Columbia UP, 1994. 215–38.

Goodman, Susan. *Edith Wharton's Women: Friends and Rivals.* Hanover, N.H.: UP of New England, 1990.

Goshgarian, G. M. *To Kiss the Chastening Rod: Domestic Fiction and Sexual Ideology in the American Renaissance.* Ithaca: Cornell UP, 1992.

Hawthorne, Nathaniel. *The Scarlet Letter.* Vol. 1 of the *Centenary Edition of the Works of Nathaniel Hawthorne.* Ed. William Charvat et al. Columbus: Ohio State UP, 1962.

Pfister, Joel. *The Production of Personal Life: Class, Gender, and the Psychological in Hawthorne's Fiction.* Stanford: Stanford UP, 1991.

Varnado, S. L. *Haunted Presence: The Numinous in Gothic Fiction.* Tuscaloosa: U of Alabama P, 1987.

Waid, Candace. *Edith Wharton's Letters from the Underworld: Fictions of Women and Writing.* Chapel Hill: U of North Carolina P, 1991.

Wharton, Edith. *A Backward Glance.* New York: Scribner, 1985.

——. *The Letters of Edith Wharton.* Ed. R. W. B. Lewis and Nancy Lewis. New York: Collier, 1988.

——. *Summer.* New York: Perennial, 1979.

——. *The Writing of Fiction.* New York: Scribner, 1925.

Wolff, Cynthia Griffin. *A Feast of Words: The Triumph of Edith Wharton.* New York: Oxford UP, 1977.

THE SCARLET LETTER AS PRE-TEXT FOR FLANNERY O'CONNOR'S "GOOD COUNTRY PEOPLE"

John Gatta

In addition to "Good Country People" and "Introduction to *A Memoir of Mary Ann*," Hawthornean influence can be traced in such O'Connor writings as "A Good Man Is Hard to Find," "A Late Encounter with the Enemy," "The Lame Shall Enter First," *Wise Blood*, and *The Violent Bear It Away.*

R esponding to an interviewer in 1960, Flannery O'Connor named Hawthorne alongside Dostoevsky as one of two favorite writers to whose work she returned "at regular intervals."[1] Her library holdings and allusions as essayist demonstrate her familiarity not only with the Hawthorne of the tales and full-length romances but also with the consul to Liverpool's reports on his life abroad. In addition, she was surprisingly well read in critical commentary about Hawthorne by figures like Henry James, Harry Levin, and Mark Van Doren. Her library inventory even includes a specially marked article on Hawthorne printed in *PMLA!* In her letters O'Connor described Hawthorne as "a very great writer" with whom she felt more kinship "than with any other American," going so far as to declare herself "one of his descendants."[2]

Such a line of ancestry would seem at first unlikely. Though Hawthorne died just one century before O'Connor in 1964, more than time divides the amorphously Protestant New Englander from the earnestly orthodox Roman Catholic woman from Georgia. Yet the temperamental and spiritual affinities between these two writers are striking. Both were regionalists of a sort, both preoccupied with themes of guilt, obsession, and the drama of salvation. They also shared a distaste for scientism and a suspicion of reforming optimism. As fictionalists, they were similarly disposed toward comic irony and the medium of semi-allegorical romance. Both excelled in the writing of short fiction, with O'Connor insisting that she wrote "tales in the sense Hawthorne wrote tales."[3] And both show an imaginative fascination with what might be called "abnormal psychology"—a rather lame term to encompass Hawthorne's fictional array of haunted Puritans, tormented artists, and mad scientists, or the freaks, misfits, and fanatical preacher-prophets that crowd the stories of O'Connor. Though neither writer admitted any lack of personal hope, each has been susceptible to charges of congenital gloom, of a Gothic overinvestment in the mysteries of human depravity.

Hawthorne's graphic portrayal of evil is indeed a logical point of entry into the larger question of his influence on O'Connor that has already engaged critics such as Thomas M. Walsh, Ronald Emerick, and Leon V. Driskell and Joan T. Brittain.[4] Thus, for an understated moral-thematic summary of Hawthorne's tale "Young Goodman Brown," one need look no further than the title of a celebrated O'Connor tale and story collection, "A Good Man Is Hard to Find." But within the broader sphere of moral psychology, it is the sense of a palpable, incarnational demonism that especially marks O'Connor as Hawthorne's progeny. One thinks most immediately, perhaps, of the satanic struggles faced by Goodman Brown, but a good deal of Hawthorne can serve as antecedent to O'Connor's self-described fictional project to reflect the agonistic "action of grace in territory largely held by the devil."[5] O'Connor explored this strange, horrific conjunction between demonism and divinity in tale after tale, including her final novella, *The Violent Bear It Away*. So any number of comparative textual readings are possible. But for purposes of illustrative comparison, I want to consider here the way in which *The Scarlet Letter* offers a kind of satanic pre-text for the spiritual confrontation O'Connor presents in her comically devastating tale of "Good Country People."

Although these two works hardly seem equivalent in their action or texture, both show the devil doing God's work despite his destructive designs. Both demonstrate also how intellectual pride and distortions of language can obscure the truths of the human heart. Each tale focuses its dramatic action in a central symbol: an embroidered letter, a wooden leg. Finally, there is a personal rather than purely textual dimension of Hawthorne's presence for O'Connor that deserves reflection. Identifying with the inner tension she perceived in Hawthorne between artistic detachment and the heart's engagement with humankind, O'Connor tried to work out her own literary response to this dilemma. Evidence of her reaction can be found in the nonfiction account she wrote of Mary Ann, a child-saint cared for in an Atlanta cancer home by the congregation of nuns that Rose Hawthorne had founded, as well as in her fictive portrayal of the Joy/Hulga character in "Good Country People."

Thanks to Arthur Kinney's published literary inventory, we know that O'Connor owned at least two copies of *The Scarlet Letter*.[6] But just what would have seized her in Hawthorne's best-known romance? To which of the characters would she respond most powerfully? Not the long-suffering Hester, I suspect, or Pearl but the God-haunted preacher Dimmesdale and the compulsive, apparently demonic Chillingworth. Moreover, if "Good Country People" is any indication, O'Connor would have been more intrigued by the undercurrents of *spiritual* seduction in Haw-thorne's story than by its related problem of sexuality. I refer here not only to the tortured psychology of temptation exposed by Dimmesdale during and just after the crucial forest scene with Hester but also to his intense involvement with Chillingworth.

Chillingworth, of course, plays the fiend in his relentless burrowings into Dimmesdale's soul. Hawthorne suggests that Chillingworth has, through his re-morseless ministrations as false physician in residence, "violated . . . the sanctity of a human heart."[7] In his culpable scrutiny he resembles George Rayber in *The Violent Bear It Away,* a character who "had secretly been making a study" of Mason Tar-water, "creeping into his soul by the back door" while living under the same roof. Chillingworth intensifies the torment that leads Dimmesdale toward self-inflicted violence in the form of his secret scourging. The gesture is as unmistakably O'Con-noresque as Hazel Motes's donning a barbed-wire vest, packing his shoes with broken glass, and blinding himself in the novella *Wise Blood.*

Yet in the process of tormenting his victim, Chillingworth at the same time reveals a mysterious, unholy kinship with the minister. It is precisely by breaking *down* Dimmesdale's psychic defenses that Chillingworth helps draw him finally *up* to the scaffold, to public confession, and thereby to whatever solace and integrity he is still capable of realizing in his broken condition. Despite himself, then, Chilling-worth leads Dimmesdale toward salvation—or at least toward what the minister, *perhaps* mistakenly, conceives to be his salvation and "triumphant ignominy." In the end he even thanks God for "sending yonder dark and terrible old man, to keep the torture always at red heat" (*Scarlet Letter* 257, 256).

That O'Connor was struck by the paradoxical nature of Chillingworth's interven-tion is indicated by her annotative reaction to a passage in Harry Levin's book *The Power of Blackness.* "If the minister cannot shrive himself," wrote Levin, "the physi-cian has a disease he cannot cure. Yet it is his concentrated malevolence, more than anything else, that implants the idea of confession in Dimmesdale's mind. Whether Chillingworth may be his double or else a demon, the spokesman for Dimmesdale's conscience or a devil's emissary—these are possibilities which are raised but scarcely probed." O'Connor not only lined this passage but wrote into the margin a telling reference to Chillingworth as the "devil doing the work of grace before."[8]

This reaction, though recorded a few years after her composition of "Good Country People,"[9] suggests a link between *The Scarlet Letter* and O'Connor's tale of a Bible salesman who bedevils an emotionally arrested woman with a doctorate in philosophy and a wooden leg. Chillingworth's counterpart in the later story is evidently the gaunt Bible salesman who, like Chillingworth, presents himself under an allegorical-sounding pseudonym. Manley Pointer, as he calls himself, first shows up at Mrs. Hopewell's home in the guise of a countrified innocent engaged in the "Chrustian [*sic*] service" of selling God's Word. But he is in fact an experienced con man. And he wants more than filthy lucre. Eager to demean his victims by fleecing them of cherished medical artifacts, he immediately spots Mrs. Hopewell's daughter as one of his own. Joy, as she was initially christened, had tried to rename and re-create herself as Hulga out of disdain for her mother's outlook. To spite her, Joy/Hulga now parades about the house in a cowboy-embossed, faded sweat shirt, visibly seething with resentment.

In her prideful immaturity, though, she fails to see how much her spiritual obtuseness actually resembles that of her mother. To achieve his destructive ends, Manley Pointer is able to prey more or less equivalently on the sentimental naivete of Mrs. Hopewell and the cynical nihilism of her Joy. After feigning amazement at Joy/Hulga's atheism, he allows her to dream she can seduce him out of his na-tural innocence through sex and tactical cynicism. Instead, Manley overpowers *her* through a craft of spiritual seduction amounting to a rape of the soul. So at the close of this bizarre tale, we see him running off with Joy/Hulga's artificial leg while she lies astonished and abandoned in a hayloft.

Just how is Manley Pointer able to hoodwink the worldly-wise Ph.D.? One way is through the distortions of language. So fully has this false purveyor of the scriptural Word mastered the evasions and distortions of language that both Joy/Hulga and her mother take him *at* his word that he is "just a country boy" who is "real simple."[10] In *The Scarlet Letter* one is similarly reminded of Dimmesdale's self-deceived and deceiving pulpit confessions, of the seductive rhetoric of corporate pride in his final Election Sermon, and of his eloquent opening speech charging Hester to "speak out the name" of one who knows his secret is safe. The degenera-tion of language into cliché assures Mrs. Hopewell that "good country people are the salt of the earth" even though the salt in its original biblical context refers to a regenerate rather than a "natural" species of humankind. This verbal mismatch crystallizes much of the story's subsequent action.

The seductive force of language also figures significantly in O'Connor's portrayal of Joy/Hulga. Compared to characters in *The Scarlet Letter*, she resembles Dimmes-dale more than Hester in her disposition toward intellectual self-deception. "In my economy," she tells Manley Pointer, "I'm saved and you are damned but I told you I didn't believe in God." And as for love, she insists "I don't have illusions. I'm one of those people who see *through* to nothing. . . . [S]ome of us have taken off our blindfolds and see that there's nothing to see. It's a kind of salvation." She is not just an atheist, then, but one who believes in nothing by way of spiritual or emotional realities. She defines herself negatively as one who "didn't like dogs or cats or birds or flowers or nature or nice young men" (286–88, 276).

O'Connor plainly intends to dramatize the vacuousness of Joy/Hulga's nihilistic rhetoric and philosophy. Nothing, it seems, shall come from nothing. Fixed in her rationalistic materialism, Joy/Hulga regards the world "with the look of someone who has achieved blindness by an act of will and means to keep it." Her real infirmity, then, has to do not with the leg she once lost in a hunting accident but with her "weak heart" which, as in the case of Dimmesdale, leads her to seek refuge from existential fear in her intellectual status and attainments. O'Connor develops this heart motif in a way that recalls Hawthorne's familiar opposition between head and heart. Joy/Hulga suffers more from a hardened heart, overruled by her "clear and detached" intellect, than from reliance on a wooden leg.

Manley Pointer draws out Joy/Hulga's latent evangelical impulse insofar as she lusts above all to convert him to her philosophic worldview, thereby confirming it for herself. In O'Connor's outlandish seduction scene, Joy/Hulga finds all her pride brought to naught. When she fulminates against the Bible salesman as just one more hypocritical Christian because of his shameful advances in the hayloft, he returns with blighting sarcasm: " 'I hope you don't think . . . that I believe in that crap! I may sell Bibles but I know which end is up. . . . And I'll tell you another thing, Hulga . . . you ain't so smart. I been believing in nothing ever since I was born' " (290–91).

There is yet some suggestion of potential gain or grace in this defeat. By reducing Joy/Hulga's nihilistic philosophy to nothing, Manley Pointer has unwittingly destroyed her false faith in self-sufficiency. Knocking away all her sustaining illusions, he has left her, if I may say so, without a leg to stand on. He has battered her heart, stirred her emotions, negated her negations, in a way that just might lead her toward conversion. For unlike Mrs. Freeman, Joy/Hulga discovers she has never been entirely free of susceptibility to the longings of the heart.[11]

But like *The Scarlet Letter,* "Good Country People" ends without a definitive clarification or revelation.[12] Pointer functions as both demon and savior, but as savior he only *points toward* Joy's salvation without yet effecting it. And as purely "Manley" savior he is no God-Man, despite Joy/Hulga's "losing her own life and finding it again, miraculously, in his." At one level we can indeed feel a quite human sympathy for this child of poverty and wrath whose father had been crushed by a tree. So also Hawthorne leads us to mourn Roger Chillingworth's transformation from "a pure and upright man" to a misshapen casualty of his own obsession. But Pointer's leechlike machinations, like those of Chillingworth, do reflect for O'Connor the devil's "work of grace" before salvation. Within this grotesque mystery, neither figure emerges as a truly autonomous agent in a Manichaean drama; both fulfill roles in a larger design Chillingworth finds shrouded in "dark necessity." As O'Connor hinted at times,[13] something of her own ironic disposition and intellectualism is embodied in Joy/Hulga. Perhaps only a writer who was herself afflicted with a crippling disease—in this case, disseminated lupus[14]—could get away with using her character's physical handicap to symbolize a crippling moral and spiritual defeat. Scornful of self-pity, O'Connor sought thereby to annihilate willful pride, expunging through Joy/Hulga some version of the self she feared to become.

This self-fictionalizing on O'Connor's part reflects at once a deliberate artistic detachment from egotism—a negative capability—and a form of deep emotional involvement. To enter the mystery of that paradox, we need to take account finally of O'Connor's 1960 "Introduction to *A Memoir of Mary Ann,*" with its tribute to Hawthorne's personal example and legacy. The child Mary Ann, afflicted with a facial tumor and a missing eye, presents from real life yet another physically defective character and is explicitly compared to Georgianna in Hawthorne's tale "The Birth-mark." Unlike Joy/Hulga, she becomes within her affliction a visible icon of divine love made perfect in death.

Yet the character from this sketch with whom O'Connor identifies most intensely is not Mary Ann but Nathaniel Hawthorne. She cites an episode recounted by Hawthorne in *Our Old Home* in which a "fastidious gentleman" encounters a diseased, wretched-looking child in a Liverpool workhouse. The child apparently wants to be held, but the gentleman is inhibited by "that habit of observation from an insulated standpoint which is said . . . to have the tendency of putting ice into the blood." After some internal struggle, however, the gentleman does take up the "loathsome" child in his arms; and thereby, concludes Hawthorne, he "effected more than he dreamed of toward his final salvation."[15]

Seized by the explicit reference to "salvation," O'Connor was intrigued to discover from the *English Notebooks* that the gentleman described was none other than Hawthorne himself. This "fastidious, skeptical New Englander who feared the ice in his blood" had effaced himself fictionally from the more public narrative. Yet for O'Connor his gesture of the heart was indeed a sign of salvation, a word she understood in a more orthodox Christian sense than Hawthorne may have intended. In the thematic substance of his writing Hawthorne had largely triumphed over the self-insulating, Hulga-like tendencies he indicted in himself. But for O'Connor, Hawthorne's greatest work—beyond all his writings—was his physical and spiritual coauthorship of Rose Hawthorne. In her, Nathaniel's charitable instinct and zeal for truth bore fruit; through her, he "gave what he did not have himself." O'Connor saw the loving witness of Mother Alphonsa's order toward patients of incurable cancer as the "tree sprung from Hawthorne's small act of Christlikeness," with Mary Ann as its flower.

In several respects, O'Connor's art shows itself to be yet another offshoot from the Hawthornean tree. But whereas Mother Alphonsa's gift was to embrace the leper in the modern world, O'Connor conceived her own literary-prophetic vocation as something different and probably inferior. Like Hawthorne, she would manage through her writing to expose, but rarely to heal, the grotesque deformities of humankind. " 'We go to the Father of Souls,' " she cited St. Cyril of Jerusalem as saying, " 'but it is necessary to pass by the dragon,' " and it is the "mysterious passage past him, or into his jaws, that stories of any depth will always be concerned to tell."[16] Within the earthly agon, then, demonism is apt to appear more vivid than grace. So when we reach the end of "Good Country People," we have to imagine that Manley Pointer, accompanied by the ghost of Ethan Brand, still roams the world seeking the ruin of souls.

Notes

1. Rosemary M. Magee, ed., *Conversations with Flannery O'Connor* (Jackson: U of Mississippi P, 1987) 47.

2. *Flannery O'Connor: The Habit of Being,* ed. Sally Fitzgerald (New York: Farrar, Straus, Giroux, 1979) 70, 457, 407.

3. Magee 98. O'Connor does end the sentence with a qualifier: "though I hope with less reliance on allegory."

4. Thomas M. Walsh, "The Devils of Hawthorne and Flannery O'Connor," *Xavier University Studies* 5 (1966): 117–22; Ronald Rine Emerick, *Romance, Allegory, Vision: The Influence of Hawthorne on Flannery O'Connor,* diss., U of Pittsburgh, 1975; Leon V. Driskell and John T. Brittain, *The Eternal Crossroads: The Art of Flannery O'Connor* (Lexington: UP of Kentucky, 1971) 16–23. Walsh's concerns come closest to anticipating mine.

5. O'Connor, *Mystery and Manners,* ed. Sally and Robert Fitzgerald (New York: Farrar, Straus, Giroux, 1961) 118.

6. Arthur F. Kinney, *Flannery O'Connor's Library: Resources of Being* (Athens: U of Georgia P, 1985) 156.

7. *The Scarlet Letter, The Centenary Edition of the Works of Nathaniel Hawthorne,* ed. William Charvat et al. (Columbus: Ohio State UP, 1962–) 1: 195.

8. Harry Levin, *The Power of Blackness: Hawthorne, Poe, Melville* (New York: Vintage-Random House, 1958); Kinney 121.

9. Composed and published in 1955, O'Connor's story predates Levin's book by three years.

10. *The Complete Stories of Flannery O'Connor* (New York: Farrar, Straus, Giroux, 1971) 278; hereafter cited in text by page number.

11. In *Flannery O'Connor: A Proper Scaring* (Wheaton, Ill.: Harold Shaw, 1988) 38, Jill P. Baumgaertner makes a good case that Joy/Hulga is indeed touched by some grace of feeling, if not by love, through her encounter with the Bible salesman.

12. I explore this issue further in "The Apocalyptic End of *The Scarlet Letter,*" *Texas Studies in Language and Literature* 32 (1990): 506–21.

13. O'Connor, *Habit of Being* 158, 170.

14. According to Robert Fitzgerald, O'Connor first acquired her aluminum crutches in 1955, the same year she wrote "Good Country People."

15. Cited from "Introduction to *A Memoir of Mary Ann*" in *Mystery and Manners* 217–18. For Rose Hawthorne's strong reaction to reading about this episode, see the remarks reprinted in the *Nathaniel Hawthorne Review* 12 (Spring 1986): 13–15.

16. "The Fiction Writer & His Country," *Mystery and Manners* 35.

"GHOSTS MIGHT ENTER HERE"

Franny Nudelman

For important discussions of Gothic fiction, see Teresa A.
Goddu's *Gothic America: Narrative, History, and Nation* (New
York: Columbia UP, 1997) and *American Gothic: New
Interventions in a National Narrative,* ed. Robert K. Martin and
Eric Savoy (Iowa City: University of Iowa Press, 1998). For an
illuminating contemporary instance of the pathologizing of
mother-daughter relationships, see Nancy Friday's *My Mother,
Myself: The Daughter's Search for Identity* (New York: Dell, 1977).

Rereading "The Custom-House," Nathaniel Hawthorne's introduction to *The
Scarlet Letter,* I am brought up short by these sentences:

> Ghosts might enter here, without affrighting us. It would be too much in keeping with
> the scene to excite surprise, were we to look about us and discover a form, beloved, but
> gone hence, now sitting quietly in a streak of this magic moonshine, with an aspect
> that would make us doubt whether it had returned from afar, or had never once stirred
> from our fireside.[1]

Hawthorne is sitting up late in his deserted parlor, hoping the moonlight will revive
his creative faculties, when he imagines his beloved appearing at his side. This return
is unspectacular, invoking none of the dread typically associated with Gothic images. Instead his description conveys a sense of quiet and uncomplicated satisfaction. Hawthorne expresses a powerful desire: our dead might return, and it would be
as if they had never left; the fact of separation and loss might be revealed as fancy, a
mistake. I find this desire, and its realization, tremendously moving. The intensity
of this response—I am moved to tears—provokes my curiosity: why does this passage
make such an impression?

I am tempted to explain my reaction in psychological terms. When I was nine my
grandfather died. He had raised me during my early childhood, and we were ex-

tremely close. Twenty-five years have passed, and I haven't stopped hoping that he will come back, at least for a visit. But feeling that I've already overstepped the bounds of literary critical decorum, I might hesitate to say more about my own particular history. I might instead notice that, to a reader familiar with Toni Morrison's novel *Beloved,* Hawthorne's description of the dead returning and his choice of the word "beloved" to evoke the pathos of this reappearance have peculiar resonance. Morrison's novel might be read as an extended meditation on Hawthorne's passing fancy. In the character of Beloved, Morrison gives body to Hawthorne's generic beloved. But this comparison would also provoke a degree of critical embarrassment as it indulges in the crudest sort of ahistorical homology: the word "beloved" appears in two novels, written 138 years apart.

And yet, even as I hesitate to take up the problem of my emotional response to this passage, I also hesitate to abandon the impulse that prompted me to begin this essay. My sense is that for many of us historical inquiry begins with responses as uncomplicated as mine. We are moved by a particular text. Perhaps immediately, certainly over time, we come to understand this response, this sense of recognition, as the product of our own peculiar life experience and of our reading history. We say "this speaks to me," and what we mean is: this reminds me of something I know. Generally, this recognition remains private. Although we take our own latenight inspiration from these associations, we do not tend to disclose them in our scholarly work.

While we are eager to interrogate psychological categories in our critical writing— asserting that "experience," "affect," "interiority" are historically constructed—we still shy away from analyzing our own emotional responses to texts as historical evidence. I want to take up the figure of the dead returning to life in both Hawthorne and Morrison as a way of thinking through our critical association with the past. How do we begin to complicate a notion of history which relegates our untutored readerly responses—intuitive, emotional, sometimes spiritual—to the category "ahistorical"? Because Morrison and Hawthorne are deeply interested in how narrative realizes the enduring influence of the dead, they can help us to reconsider how we render our own reading history.

Using Gothic conventions—ghosts and corpses in particular—to frame their novels, both authors describe history as an interaction between past event—concrete, factual, complete—and its narrative reconstruction in the present. Both novels originate, at least ostensibly, from a written account of a historical event. While Surveyor Pue's manuscript provides the framework for Hawthorne's tale, *Beloved* was inspired by a newspaper account of Margaret Garner, a runaway slave who killed her two-year-old daughter to prevent her from being captured and returned to slavery.[2] Hawthorne and Morrison describe themselves as historians: they do not make up stories—they inadvertently discover the written record of an event which captures their attention. For both authors, literary invention begins with a reader's encounter with historical documentation.

These primary documents, however, leave much unsaid; Morrison and Hawthorne must work to animate, and thus interpret, the information they have discovered. The challenge posed to the author by the defunct or cryptic historical document is literalized by the figure of the corpse. Hawthorne depicts his efforts to bring Hester Prynne's story back to life as an attempt to revivify dead bodies. Describing the documents he discovers in the Custom House attic as "the corpse of dead activity," he exerts his "fancy, sluggish with little use, to raise up from these dry bones an image of the old town's brighter aspect" (29). But these relics refuse his imaginative efforts; they "retained all the rigidity of dead corpses, and stared back at me with a fixed and ghastly grin of contemptuous defiance" (34). The inhabitants of Morrison's past prove far more compliant; she claims that her characters speak to her from beyond the grave. Translating the dead, Morrison attempts to put them, finally, to rest. She recounts feeling responsible "for the woman I'm calling Sethe, and for all of these people; these unburied, or at least unceremoniously buried people." She claims that "the fear of not properly, artistically, burying them is extraordinary."[3]

These authors, like their readers, are never free from the pressure exerted by the object of interpretation—the manuscript, letter, or corpse—which stands in, I believe, for the specificity of past experience. While each author figures efforts to reanimate the dead somewhat differently, they are both motivated, even obliged, to grant fullness and immediacy to these experiences. And they both acknowledge the necessary failure of their efforts: the title of each book is an epitaph that suggests the ultimate recalcitrance of dead matter. Presenting Hester Prynne's history to a contemporary readership, Hawthorne asserts that while he has taken some liberties, imagining "the motives and modes of passion that influenced the characters who figure in it," he has remained faithful to the letter in its broadest contours: "What I contend for," Hawthorne writes, "is the authenticity of outline" (33). And indeed the novel does conform to the shape of the letter: the book begins with the scarlet letter, its title, and concludes with the scarlet letter as it appears on Hester's tombstone. The novel's title, in retrospect, doubles as Hester's epitaph. Morrison's novel both begins and ends with an epitaph: *Beloved,* the novel's title, is the single word carved on the headstone of Sethe's baby daughter. Like *The Scarlet Letter,* Morrison's novel comes full circle: in the end it reiterates the seven letters—Beloved—from which it began, thus recapitulating the problem of Beloved's origin and identity that occupies the whole.[4]

The epitaph, which lays the dead to rest without adequately accounting for them, at once prompts and constrains these narratives. The strict inexpressiveness of the headstone, like the outline of letter "A," the cursory newspaper article, or the rigid corpse, presses both writer and reader to elaborate. We begin with nothing but the barest sign of, memorial to, the past: the name of one lost, the beloved, the token, a frayed letter they have left behind. And from this point of departure—our inadequate knowledge of the dead—narration, the act of recovery, itself always partial, begins. But in the end, as in the beginning, the most reliable indications of the past are the letters, strictly inexpressive, inscribed on a tombstone, the letters that speak a name, or a deed, and little more.

The circularity embedded in the structure of these narratives marks them as Gothic. The Gothic construes history, particularly family history, as repetitive, or haunted. Gothic conventions—curses, ghosts, haunted houses—make it clear that the past is never distinct from the present. The Gothic adamantly rejects history as linear or causal and is instead preoccupied with relations of resemblance and repetition which offer past and present as deeply intertwined if not identical. But even as it aspires to a conflation of historical epochs, the Gothic gestures toward a sort of historicity. The Gothic may seem ahistorical in that it asserts that everything that once happened is still happening. But in their concern with the epitaph, the original chronicle, these Gothic texts propose history as an author's return to, and consequent reconstruction of, the dead. Both authors locate history in the interpretation of dead letters, texts we can return to time and again. This vision of narrative and its relation to the past expresses a deep commitment if not to historical truth then to the project of historical interpretation.

Perhaps in response to the limitations of this model of historical knowledge—it denies certainty and closure—Hawthorne and Morrison apply their desire for an intimacy between generations and across centuries to the world of the familial present. While the sins of fathers—witch hunts and slavery—provoke these novels, it is the sins of mothers—adultery and infanticide—that preoccupy them. Both authors take up our relation to our collective past by asking after a mother's relation to her own criminal past as it is embodied by her unruly, otherworldly daughter.

In the wake of their crimes, and specifically in response to the scorn of their communities, both Hester and Sethe become hardened, seemingly insensible. Morrison describes Sethe as "The one who never looked away, who when a man got stomped to death by a mare right in front of Sawyer's restaurant did not look away; and when a sow began eating her own litter did not look away either."[5] Hawthorne dwells on the tendency of the letter to isolate Hester. Throughout, Hawthorne expresses the extremity of Hester's detachment by describing her as ghostly, or as dead. As a result of the scarlet letter, Hester stands "apart from mortal interests, yet close beside them, like a ghost that revisits the familiar fireside, and can no longer make itself seen or felt" (84). When Hester appears in public on Election Day, after having decided to leave the country with Dimmesdale, the crowd cannot discern her impending disobedience in her appearance. Hawthorne tells us that

> Her face . . . was like a mask; or rather, like the frozen calmness of a dead woman's features; owing this dreary resemblance to the fact that Hester was actually dead, in respect to any claim of sympathy, and had departed out of the world with which she still seemed to mingle. (226)

Hester's inscrutability, figured here in dramatic, indeed violent terms, is reminiscent of the Custom House corpses that refuse to be revitalized by Hawthorne's imagination.

But while the community may fail to animate Hester, thus allowing her to withdraw into an impenetrable privacy, her past deeds are kept alive in her daughter's form. Both novels are ghosted by daughters who bring the past, specifically their mothers' sins, back to life. In doing so, they judge and punish their mothers most effectively. Morrison describes Beloved's appearance in the novel in this way:

> I got to a point where in asking myself who could judge Sethe adequately, since I couldn't, and nobody else that knew her could, really, I felt the only person who could judge her would be the daughter she killed. And from there Beloved inserted herself into the text.[6]

In a peculiar twist on the Gothic convention of haunting, the protagonist's daughter effects the spirit of retribution in the world of the novel's present.

As both Hester and Dimmesdale inform the Puritan magistrates, it is Pearl, unlike the letter, that has the power to "keep [her] mother's soul alive" (114). They also make it clear that by keeping Hester alive Pearl punishes her. Hester claims that Pearl "is the scarlet letter, only capable of being loved, and so endowed with a million-fold the power of retribution for my sin" (113). Eliciting her mother's affections, Pearl mitigates against Hester's apathy; inflicting pain upon Hester, Pearl keeps her from the insensibility that Hawthorne, throughout the novel, associates with ghostliness and death.

Although Pearl embodies Hester's past, she does not recognize or understand the history she carries. She approaches the letter, which she so resembles, with an insistent curiosity, as if, as Hawthorne remarks on one occasion, "the one only thing for which she had been sent into the world was to make out its hidden import" (178). Pearl torments her mother by riveting her attention on the scarlet letter and insisting that Hester divulge its secret history. When Hester asks her if she understands the letter's meaning, Pearl turns the question back on her: "Mother, what does the scarlet letter mean?" (181). On another occasion Pearl responds to Hester's demand "Tell me, then, what thou art, and who sent thee hither?" by insisting "Tell me mother . . . It is thou that must tell me" (98). Like the reader of historical fictions, Pearl confronts a past she must labor to comprehend; pressing her mother for information, she works to elicit a satisfying account of her own origins.

Like Pearl, Beloved insists that Sethe narrate the past for her: " 'Tell me,' said Beloved, smiling a wide happy smile. 'Tell me your diamonds' " (58). Beloved's appetite for narrative, like her taste for sweets, is a desire Sethe believes she can satisfy. Morrison writes, "It became a way to feed her . . . Sethe learned the profound satisfaction Beloved got from storytelling" (58). While Sethe, unlike Hester, takes an unexpected pleasure in recounting her past, Beloved's hunger proves insatiable. As the novel proceeds, the seemingly "natural" interaction between mother and daughter takes a decidedly unnatural turn. Sethe takes pride in remembering that she was able to feed her daughter with her own breast milk after their long separation. But when Sethe recognizes Beloved as the daughter she has murdered, her desire to nourish Beloved becomes excessive. She gives every scrap of food in the house to Beloved, who grows big as her mother and sister get thinner and weaker. Beloved resembles an expecting mother, while Sethe, reduced, whines and complains like a child. As Denver realizes, violence lies at the far side of mother-daughter symbiosis. The reunion of Sethe and Beloved sets the stage for the reenactment rather than the resolution of Sethe's original act of violence: "little by little it dawned on Denver that if Sethe didn't wake up one morning and pick up a knife, Beloved might" (242).

While the mother's character is the focal point of these novels, a centrality emphasized by the preternatural daughter's own fixed and excessive gaze, the father is notably absent. While the mother is the site of judgment, the father is the site of loss and nostalgia. Morrison explains her decision to leave Beloved's father, Halle, out of the narrative: "Well, that's the carnage," she explains, "It can't be abstract. The loss of that man to his mother, to his wife, to his children, to his friends, is a serious loss and the reader has to feel it, you can't feel it if he's in there. He has to not be there."[7] Interestingly, this is a significant departure from the historical record; Margaret Garner's husband attempted to attack the slaveholder who had come to steal his family while she tried to kill their children. So, while the mother's violence, internal to the family, becomes the novel's focus, the father's violence, his attack on the slaveholder and, implicitly, on the institution of slavery, is left out.

Pearl, who badgers her mother for the story of her own origins, insists that her father take her hand in public. Pearl's desire for reconciliation is satisfied twice in the novel: once when mother, father, and daughter hold hands on the scaffold, and again when Dimmesdale at last claims Hester and Pearl in public. Their first reunion recalls Hawthorne's description of his moonlit parlor. The light is again "unaccustomed," with the power to transform the town's familiar landscape. And again this light sets the scene for the family's reunion. In this instance, however, the family is reunited not across time but in response to its own internal fragmentation. In "The Custom-House," Hawthorne articulates a desire for reconciliation which is structured vertically, between one generation and another, along the axis of inheritance. Returning to Salem, his ancestral home, Hawthorne confronts the figure of his "first ancestor" who he claims "still haunts me" (9). Unearthing Surveyor Pue's account of the persecution of Hester Prynne, Hawthorne obliquely confronts the transgressions of his forefathers. In the novel proper this desire for reconciliation gets played out in the family's reunion in the present. Joining hands on the scaffold, Hester, Dimmesdale, and Pearl stand "in the noon of that strange and solemn splendor, as if it were the light that is to reveal all secrets, and the daybreak that shall unite all who belong to one another" (154).

In *Beloved,* the arrival of a surrogate father allows, briefly, for the reconstitution of the family. Sethe and Denver make an unprecedented public appearance at the circus with Paul D. Sethe takes pleasure noticing that as the three of them walk to the circus and back they cast a shadow in which they appear to be holding hands. As in *The Scarlet Letter,* this moment of familial union proves ephemeral. Returning from the circus, Sethe finds Beloved, who will drive both Paul D and Denver away, waiting. And yet this image of father, mother, and daughter joining hands raises the reader's hopes that the family's reconciliation may remedy the violence and disloca- tion, slavery's legacy, which continue to plague Sethe's family.

As the problem of our relationship to a violent past is understood by way of the family's fragmentation, an enduring desire for reconciliation with the dead is an- swered by the possibility of family reunion. In order to depict historical violence and its recuperation, we need a fragmented family that can produce the daughter's sad frustration and satisfy, at least briefly, her desire for reconciliation. But one conse- quence of this displacement is that we may lose sight of the past events or circum- stances that produced this family or, more broadly, this idea of family: while a historical problem is initially charted onto the family, family dynamics, represented as weirdly self-generating and self-perpetuating, begin to take on a life of their own, thus absorbing the social dilemma and the historical desire that prompts these tales. This is particularly evident in *Beloved.* By the end of the novel, Morrison's examina- tion of enslavement and its aftermath has been largely displaced by the story of a symbiotic, cannibalizing relationship between mother and daughter.

I want to return full circle now to the problem of my own response to Haw- thorne's proposition that the beloved might return home. My response is largely nostalgic—born from my desire for reunion with a lost father, a desire at once personal and cultural that I have begun to investigate here. But this desire also speaks to my methodological dilemma: the relationship between the critic's affective response and her historical inquiry. Reading this passage, I respond to the notion that we might redeem a dead past through narrative. I respond to the possibility that historical narrative—both fictional and scholarly—is the product of a conversation not necessarily between the dead and the living but certainly between dead texts and living readers.

Some object that historicist literary critics tend to let associations between texts, potentially coincidental, stand in for history. If history is understood as linear, as the consequence of particular causes and their local effects, this objection is sound. But this critique, like the effort to authorize literary critical discussions of history by way of an appeal to accuracy, misses some part of what literary critics contribute to the study of history: a rich understanding of the very process of association, and methods for analyzing cross-historical responsiveness. What I find as a twentieth- century reader of nineteenth-century texts—correspondences between texts, or cor- respondences between the text and my own experience—is one sign of how history is borne out. If we construe history as a relationship between past and present, itself unstable, then our readings hold valuable information. As students of literature and history we tend to produce narratives which assume that the past is still in our reach, but somehow not within us. It seems to me that the objects we create may tell us every bit as much about this history as the objects we discover. I find a document, it impresses me, I take it up: this is where the story begins.

Notes

1. Nathaniel Hawthorne, *The Scarlet Letter,* vol. 1 of *The Centenary Edition of the Works of Nathaniel Hawthorne.* Ed. William Charvat et al. (Columbus: Ohio State UP, 1962) 36; hereafter cited in text by page number.

2. In Hawthorne's case, of course, this discovery is itself a fiction: Surveyor Pue's manuscript is Hawthorne's invention. While Morrison is determined to produce a narrative that approximates the lived experience of enslavement, Hawthorne is more thoroughly occupied with the problems of interpretation that confront the reader of history. His discovery of Surveyor Pue's account, like his discovery of the scarlet letter, does not work to authorize his account of the past but rather complicates the efforts of both writer and reader to fathom it.

3. Danielle Taylor-Guthrie, ed., *Conversations with Toni Morrison* (Jackson: UP of Mississippi, 1994) 209.

4. For an interesting discussion of the function of the epitaph in *Beloved* and *The Scarlet Letter* and, more generally, of the problem of family in *Beloved,* see Emily Budick's *Engendering Romance: Women Writers and the Hawthorne Tradition, 1850–1990* (New Haven: Yale UP, 1994) 183–218.

5. Toni Morrison, *Beloved* (New York: Penguin, 1987) 12; hereafter cited in text by page number.

6. Taylor-Guthrie 248.

7. Taylor-Guthrie 250.

APPENDIX

JANE SWISSHELM

"THE SCARLET LETTER"

THE SATURDAY VISITER,

28 SEPTEMBER 1850: 146

This appears to be *the* romance of the day, and is decidedly a curiosity. The author opens with a most humorous description of the Custom House at Salem, and its numerous officers, including himself, during his time of service, or rather leisure, in the establishment. While there employed in serving our mutual uncle Samuel, he spent a portion of his time burrowing amongst a pile of old manuscript which had accumulated in one of the unfinished rooms, and one day he found a roll in which he discovered a bit of old worm-eaten scarlet embroidery, which had once been in the form of the letter A. The manuscript was found to contain an outline history of this curious shred; and our author tells of his many futile endeavors to weave of this material a romance. When he was about giving up in despair, Gen. Taylor's election sealed his political death; he was released the task of doing nothing, and then comes the story. We incline to think much of the fame of the book was acquired by the introduction, which contains the most amusing portraits of persons still living, or recently dead, and many decided political hits. But the tale itself is unique, and told in a most masterly manner.

It opens with a description of the jail at Boston in the early times, its dingy walls and iron-barred portal, with the wild rose-bush which grew close by. On a bright morning a solemn and expectant crowd had assembled here, from whose looks and demeanor one might have expected an execution. Presently from a dingy doorway, the Beadle comes, leading forward a woman of commanding mein and surpassing beauty, clad in sombre gray, and on her bosom the letter A blazing in embroidery of scarlet and gold. In her arms she carried an infant of two months, which, upon seeing the crowd, she clasps so as to cover the badge upon her breast. Then, as if remembering the folly of covering one emblem of her disgrace with another, she set the child on one arm, and with a firm step proceeded to the pillory, which she ascended, and where she was secured in the usual position which prevented the hiding of the face. Here for many hours she sat bearing the reproving looks of the assembled throng and listening to lectures from the clergy and elders of the church, and exhortations to reveal the name of her partner in sin. This she refused, and the Rev. Arthur Dimmesdale, her pastor, a young man of great beauty and talent, and of commanding reputation for sanctity, is called upon to address her, which he does in a most impressive speech, begging her to name him who caused her fall, and thus aid him in coming to repentance—reminding her that as he was too weak to acknowledge his sin she would do him a great service by preventing his living in hypocrisy, &c. &c.—to all which she replies by a short and peremptory refusal to implicate any one. He turns away with an apostrophe to the constancy of women, which leads the reader to suspect he himself is the sinner thus screened; but of this the spectators never dream; none except one old man who has just arrived with an Indian, that comes to receive a ransom for him who has long been his prisoner. This old man, Hester Prynne, the heroine on the scaffold, sees and recognizes as her husband, a preacher whom she had preceded to the colony two years, and who had been thought dead. When she is released from the pillory and taken back to prison, the old man visits her in the character of physician, and endeavors to wring from her the name of her seducer. She is firm on this point, but finally promises under oath not to reveal their previous connection, but to permit him to live under an assumed name. He already suspected Rev. Dimmesdale, and in the character of physician and friend devoted his life to a most subtle and fiend-like vengeance. When Hester is released from prison she takes up her abode in a lonely cabin by the seaside, where she maintains herself and child by needlework. Her poetic imagination and inventive genius find outlet in her employment, and her embroidery becomes the fashion. Her child is a perfect incarnation of the spirit of beauty—a wild, fitful, impulsive little sprite, who is even in babyhood attracted by the blazing insignia on her mother's sombre dress. This becomes a bitter portion of Hester's punishment, and every fit of passion in little Pearl the author attributes to the circumstances of her birth—paints the child's fitful spirit as a mark of Divine displeasure, on account of the law broken by her parents. Whenever mother and child appear they are greeted by the Puritans, old and young, with cold and silent contempt, or hootings and epithets of infamy. If they appeared in church, all shrank from them, and the language of every one was, "Come not near me! I am holier than thou!" In no crowd did Hester stand in fear of being jostled. She was the moral leper whom no one dared to touch—the blazing emblem of the virtuous indignation of an entire community. Yet Hester went quietly on her way. Was any sick, or suffering in great distress, Hester was there to administer to every want. Even scorn and insults from those she aided did not drive her from their side while aid was wanted, but that time past she never recognized them more. Did gratitude prompt them to notice her kindly in public, she laid her finger to her scarlet letter—the emblem of her shame, and passed on in silence. So the years sped, and after a while she acquired the title of "our Hester," and many said the A upon her breast meant Able, she was so strong to assist and comfort. In the mean time poor Dimmesdale underwent most terrible penance from the serpent-cunning of his old tormentor—the lashings of conscience and the enthusiastic admiration of his parishioners. He becomes a monomaniac and one night at midnight and during a storm, he goes and mounts the pillory, there alone and unseen to undergo the ordeal Hester had passed. Here Hester and Pearl find him as they return from a death-bed. They go up and sit with him there, and the old doctor comes to witness the scene. This showed Hester the abject state to which her weak lover was reduced, and she resolves to free him from the fangs of the old serpent, the doctor. So she meets him in the forest and reveals the identity of the doctor and former husband— advises, urges him to fly to Europe, and offers to accompany him. A plan is fixed upon, and he falls into a state of fiendish excitement, which to us appears somewhat preposterous. He is strangely impelled to blaspheme and swear, indulge in brutal jests, and mock at every thing he believes to be sacred! In this frame of mind he composes a sermon to be preached on the occasion of the installation of a new governor. This sermon is a miracle and electrifies collected thousands. In the crowd without stands Hester, at the foot of the pillory, within sound of his voice, and surrounded by the circle of infamy which kept all from approaching within some yards. Here she learns their plan of flight has been discovered and frustrated by the old doctor, and stood in her despair when her lover came out of the church, tottering and pale, surrounded by admiring, almost worshipping thousands. When he sees Hester he approaches and asks her to aid him in ascending the scaffold. They and Pearl go up, and there to the electrified crowd he proclaims his guilt, and dies. The old doctor had now nothing to live for, and soon died, leaving Pearl heiress to a large fortune. Pearl's nature appears changed from the time of her father's death, and she becomes gentle, affectionate—comprehensible. She and her mother disappear for some years, and then Hester returns to the cabin alone. It is supposed from signs that Pearl is the wife of some nobleman in a foreign land, but Hester voluntarily returns, takes up her old badge of shame, lives and dies in the cabin by the sea side, and finally sleeps beside her lover.

When one has read the book the query is, "what did the author mean! What moral lesson did he want to inculcate? What philosophy did he mean to teach?"

If he meant to teach the sinfulness of Hester's sin—the great and divine obligation and sanctity of a legal marriage contract, and the monstrous depravity of a union sanctioned only by affection, his book is the most sublime failure of the age. Hester Prynne stands morally, as Saul did physically amongst his contemporaries, the head and shoulders taller than the tallest. She is the most glorious creation of fiction that has ever crossed our path. We never dreamed of any thing so sublime as the moral force and grandeur of her character. Scott's Jeanie Deans sinks into insignificance beside her. Jane Eyer is a chip floating with the current of popular opinion, while Hester rows her boat up from the brink of the Niagara, and lands at Buffalo as calm and self-possessed as ordinary people from a ride on the "raging canal." The Divines and Elders and Governors and Magistrates and honorably married dames of her day look like pasteboard puppets beside breathing men and women, when they come in contact with "their Hester." What one instinctively blames her for is, that she did not save her poor imbecile lover from the persecutions of the old sinner who was putting him to death by slow tortures. She should have protected Dimmesdale as well as kept his secret. It was not like herself to desert him, and leave him in the embrace of such a wily old serpent.

As for the author's lame attempts to make Pearl a punishment sent to her mother, we never saw a mother who would not be happy to be so punished—never knew a child who did not give fifty times the evidence of being sent in wrath. If any argument, pro or con, could be drawn from Pearl, she was surely a special evidence of the Divine approbation of the law which governed her birth. If such a little "jet of flame" as Pearl can be considered a sign of a broken law, we do wonder what Hawthorne thinks of the royal idiots whose existence testifies to the validity and legality of the pompous marriage rites of Queens and Empresses?

If Hawthorne really wants to teach the lesson, ostensibly written on the pages of his book, he had better try again. For our part if we knew there was such another woman as Hester Prynne in Boston now, we should travel all the way there to pay our respects, while the honorable characters of the book are such poor affairs it would scarce be worth while throwing a mud-ball at the best of them.

ADA CLARE

"THOUGHTS AND THINGS"

THE NEW YORK SATURDAY PRESS

10 MARCH 1860: 2

A new romance by Hawthorne is an epic-event in literature. Hawthorne is, with one exception, the best prose-writer in America. His language and the characters he creates bear a close resemblance to each other; they have a high nervous temperament and a vital color.

The "Marble Faun" is not equal in energy and dramatic vigor to most of his earlier works. The characters seem more faintly defined—probably from the fact that the narrative rambles loosely through a wide field of art-life. The scene is laid in the Halcyonland of story—Italy—which the author has wisely studied in reality, before attempting to weave it into fiction.

There is a double plot in this story; there are two women who are supposed to contrast with two great female types, and the two men created with the same view. Hilda, whom the author creates as the type of all that is soft and tender, of the dove-nature in woman—utterly falls short of his object. Her gentleness seems like affectation; her purity, a want of feeling; her angelic horror of sin, a ridiculous and impertinent exaggeration of her own virtues. Miriam, the stronger character in the story, is one day her dearest and most devoted friend, while the next she forbids her even to touch her dress, because the deeper-hearted woman has not been able to lie with her eyes. O fie! they slander us heartily, these men. This is no woman; 'tis a piece of pale Italian marble, that cheats us with a semblance of life. The truly angelic woman would be the last of her sex to cast off her best-loved friend, in such a scene as this book pictures. Crime is at times indistinct—its boundary lines intermingle often indistinguishably with those of necessity; but sorrow is never to be mistaken; grief clutches itself with an awful scientific certainty.

Miriam, the unangelic, is the more womanly and lovable of the two. Nothing could be more touching and beautiful than her love for Donatello. These two characters have caught a flow from the warm Italian sky, while the other two have still the dust of Salem on their hearts—a drop of that blood in their veins, which burned young women at the stake as witches.

The story is full of interesting details of Italian life and scenery; and the treatment of art-life in Rome will probably prove of vast interest to many.

[Clare then quotes from the scene where Donatello pushes the model from the parapet: *Centenary Edition of the Works of Nathaniel Hawthorne* 4: 172–74.]

MRS. H. B. STOWE FROM "HOW SHALL I LEARN TO WRITE?"

HEARTH AND HOME

16 JANUARY 1869: 56

We have presupposed, in our former article, that there is a great deal of ability for good writing lying dormant in the community. This is particularly the case among women.

It is our opinion that certain gifts of expression, and certain graces and faculties of style, belong more naturally to women than to men. As far as the two sexes study together in our normal and high schools, is it not a fact that the very best compositions come from the female pupils? Why is it, then, that the best writing is done by men? This is the reason: The education of women stops short at the very point where the boy's education really begins. At the age that the boy enters college for an arduous and mature course, the girl comes home and addresses herself to going into company; and the five or six years following, that her brother spends in severe intellectual drill, she fritters away in what is called society.

The result of all this is that women are deficient in the very first requisite of a good writer— namely, something to say that is worth saying.

A man who is educated to any purpose goes around a certain circle of human knowledge, and if he improves his advantages, gets thus a solid basis of ideas and opinions on which he can profitably and instructively build in after life; while a woman is spending the same five or six years in forgetting all that she learned during her school education.

But it is a fact that the experiences of woman in real life, in all that comes to her in her domestic capacity as mistress of a family, sister, daughter, wife, and mother, do furnish a class of subjects wherein a woman, trained to think wisely and justly, may find a great deal that is worth saying. She may have subject matter of peculiar weight and importance—subject matter which woman, and only woman, could possibly be able to present.

Let us suppose, then, a woman with something to say, about which she is truly and really in earnest. How is she to get the gift of expression?

The manner of saying things to make them vivid and clear and interesting, is a fine art. It is a thing that may be studied; it is a thing that *must* be practiced.

There is a great deal of writing, very charming, very acceptable, and much in demand, which consists simply in painting by means of words the simple and homely scenes of every-day life.

The most commonplace object, well represented in a painting, often commands an artist's price. In the same manner, the most commonplace object or scene, well painted by words, has an artistic value.

The greatest artist of this sort that we have ever had in America is Hawthorne. To every young writer, who wishes to study how to learn to use language so as to make every-day scenes and things picturesque and charming, we recommend a thorough and diligent reading study of his writings.

The sketch called "The Apple Dealer" is a specimen of what can be done by a thoughtful and careful study of apparently the most uninteresting subject in the world. A poor, stupid, commonplace old man is made the theme of one of his most wonderful pieces of writing.

Many have supposed that writing comes by fits and starts, and by dashes—by bursts and inspirations. But there is no good writing that has ever come without great labor, great study, and incessant practice.

The publication of *Passages from the American Note-Books of Nathaniel Hawthorne* has done a great service to all who wish to learn to write, in opening before their view all the processes by which the greatest American writer found that inimitable style, whose sheeny gloss and exquisite word-painting are so astonishing.

We can see in these books that he studied nature day by day; going out to study, as a painter goes out with pallet and brushes, only instead of pallet and brushes, he used the words of the English language.

The young writer can see in these note-books how in this daily process of walking, studying, and writing, he accumulated that wonderful store of imagery which is reflected in all he says.

It also illustrates what we say—that he excelled in writing because his love for it led him to practice it incessantly.

These note-books are but a small specimen of volumes after volumes filled with minute descriptions of all that he saw and did. Just as a gymnast becomes graceful by a constant use of his muscles, so Hawthorne, by a constant dealing with words and a constant daily habit of writing, acquired flexibility and versatility of style.

[Stowe then refers to specific pages and passages in Hawthorne's *American Notebooks* as examples of good writing, all of them involving entries that Hawthorne made during his time at Brook Farm.]

MRS. HUMPHRY WARD, PERSONAL LETTER TO JOSEPH H. CHOATE, 8 JUNE 1904

Stocks, Tring, England.
June 8, 1904

Dear Mr. Choate,

You have asked me to write you a few pages that, in the coming celebration at Salem of the hundredth anniversary of Nathaniel Hawthorne's birth, may be laid, with all the other tributes which the day will call forth, at the feet of Salem's famous son. It seems to me a great honour that you should have asked me to join in the homage of this anniversary; for the author of "The Scarlet Letter" has always filled a place of peculiar sacredness and delight in my literary memory. So that to express my feeling of admiration and gratitude is only to give a voice to something long since conceived, to shape into some kind of utterance that which for many years has been an emotion and a force. For when I look back to the books which most strongly influenced my own youth, I am aware of a love for certain writings of Hawthorne, a love most ardent, and tenacious, which succeeded a passion of the same kind for certain writings of Mr. Ruskin. In both cases the devotion was hardly rational; it did not spring from any reasoned or critical appreciation of the books, for it dates from years when I was quite incapable of anything of the kind. It was the result, I think, of a vague, inarticulate sense of an appealing beauty, and a beauty so closely mingled with magic and mystery that it haunted memory "like a passion." Some scenes from "The Scarlet Letter," and some pages from "The Stones of Venice," haunted me in this way. And I can still sharply remember how much this early impression depended upon Hawthorne's *austerity*, upon his deep-rooted

Puritanism, upon what has been often pointed to as "the sense of sin" in him. Many of the short stories, no less than "The Scarlet Letter," and long before I truly understood them, used to awaken in me a sort of aching and painful joy, which was partly sympathy and partly rebellion. Again and again I have read over the scene between Hester, the minister, and Pearl, in the wood, insisting with myself that it must end with the flight and freedom of these tortured beings, and hardly able—though always conscious of its shadowy approach—to bear the moment when hope departs and Pearl brings back the fatal letter. So in the last scene, one of the most poignantly beautiful in literature, when Hester hangs over the dying minister and says to him: "Shall we not meet again? Shall we not spend our immortal life together? surely, surely we have ransomed one another with all this woe! Thou lookest far into eternity with those bright dying eyes! Then tell me what thou seest?"—and the minister replies: "Hush, Hester, hush! . . . I fear! I fear!"—the awe and shudder of such a last denial of hope has always remained with me as one of the greatest things of imagination, deriving its power from that stern spiritual energy which is its ultimate source.

So, in later years, "Transformation," with a still more daring combination of the same elements—Romantic beauty with Puritan austerity—exercised a like effect, spoke with the same exquisitely mingled voice. Kenyon and Hilda, set against Miriam and Donatello,—they are themselves the symbols of Hawthorne's genius, or rather of the strangely varied strands of which it was woven. For above all, and before all, it seems to me, he was a Romantic—a romantic of the great time. He was born two years later than Victor Hugo; a year after the father of nineteenth-century Romanticism, Chateaubriand, had shown in the tale "Atala" the power of the Americans wilds to infuse new spells into the imagination of the Old World; and a year before the publication of "The Lay of the Last Minstrel." And whether at Salem or Boston, and long before his feet had trodden France or Italy, he shared to the full in the heritage of that generation, in its characteristic love of mystery and terror, which was also a passionate love of beauty; in its new perception of veiled and infinite horizons on the one hand, and in its sheer defiant delight, on the other, in the many-coloured detail, lovely or horrible, magnificent or grotesque, wherewith nature and man are always filling that small illuminated space amid the darkness, in which life revolves. How many instances might be given of the Romantic temper in Hawthorne!—the wonderful passage in the "House of the Seven Gables" where Phoebe, before her eyes perceive him, is conscious in the shadowed room of Clifford's return; the grim vengeance of Roger Chillingworth; the appearance in the Catacombs of Miriam's mysterious persecutor; that swift murder on the Tarpeian rock; Hilda's confession in St. Peter's:—not to speak of such things as "Malvin's Burial" or "The Ambitious Guest" or "Rappaccini's Daughter," each of them a Romantic masterpiece which may match with any other of a similar kind from the first or second generation of the European Romantics. Surprise, invention, mystery, an unfailing command, now of rich colour, now of things terrible or ironic, and now of a grace, half-toned and gentle as a spring day, combined with that story-teller's resource which is the gift of the gods alone:—these things we shall find in Hawthorne, just as we find them—some or all of them—in Hugo or Musset, in Gautier or Merimée.

But what a marvel of genius that it should be so! For while Victor Hugo's childhood and youth were passed first in Naples, then in Spain, and finally in the Paris of the Restoration, amid all that might fitly nourish the great poet who came to his own in 1830, Hawthorne's youth and early manhood, before the Brook Farm experience, were passed, as he himself tells us, in a country where there were "no shadows, no antiquity, no mystery, no picturesque and gloomy wrong, nor anything but a commonplace prosperity in broad and simple daylight,"— in a town and society, which had and could have nothing—or almost nothing—of those special incitements and provocations which, in the case of his European contemporaries, were always present. As to the books which may have influenced him, they do not seem to be easy to trace. But I remember a mention of Bürger's "Lenore" in the "Note-Books," which links him with Scott's beginnings; and a reference to a translation he was making of a tale by Tieck gives me particular pleasure, because it connects him with our great English Romantic, Emily Brontë, who was reading Tieck just about the same time. Naturally in the thirties and forties a man of fine literary capacity, commanding French and German, and associated with Emerson, Longfellow, and Margaret Fuller, must have read the European books of the moment, and must have been stirred by the European ideas and controversies then affecting his craft. And indeed the love of the past, the love of nature, curiosity, freedom, truth, daring,—all these Romantic traits are Hawthorne's.

But what makes him so remarkable, so perennially interesting, is that he is a New-England—a Puritan Romantic; a Romantic with "a sense of sin!" That is not how we shall any of us describe Victor Hugo, or George Sand, or Alfred de Musset! A French critic finds the inmost note and essence of Romanticism in that mad glorification of the "I," which in the wilder Romantics set all laws, aesthetic or moral, at defiance. M. Brunetière must be wrong! Hawthorne's genius is enough to prove it. For in his case the Romantic instinct finds its chief food in what seem to him at all times the majestic verities and sanctions of the moral life and those not the verities and sanctions of the individual conscience merely, as George Sand might have enforced them, but the plain matters of ordinary law and custom, as the plain man understands them. His attitude is the Pauline one, "the strength of sin is the law," and it is in the vengeance or the triumph of law that he is perpetually seeking and finding his noblest artistic effects. He moralises perpetually, and his danger of course is the didactic danger, wherein he differs from your other great Romantic, Edgar Allan Poe, whose danger is that of morbid excess and extravagance, as with so many European writers of the movement. But Hawthorne is saved, first by poetry, and then by his perpetual love of and interest in the common life. The preacher indeed is ultimately absorbed in the poet, and his final aim is not reform but beauty—the eternal immortalising aim of the artist. While for him, also, the spectacle of human character and human suffering is in itself so absorbing, that he is able to communicate his vision to us, just because his touch is so disinterested and true,—so free indeed from that preoccupation with the "I" which we are told to regard as typically Romantic. "He liked," it has been said, "to fraternize with plain people, to take them on their own terms, and put himself, if possible into their shoes." There indeed is the wide sympathy of the poet, the surest condition of abiding work. The "Note-books" are full of it. "The strange fellow in the bar-room—a sort of mock Methodist—a cattle drover," whose talk turned upon religion "while quaffing fourteen cups of tea"; "the man with a smart horse," who, when congratulated upon it, replies gaily that he "has a better at home"; the blacksmith, whose conversation has much "strong unlettered sense," imbued with "humour," than whom "I know no man who seems more like a man, more indescribably human,"—the surgeon dentist, the school teacher, the travelling actor, the dogs, the horses,—all parts and all figures and accessories of the human play, as he sees it, are equally delightful to him,—all enter into that heightened illuminated feeling whereof the fruit in literature is such a story as "The Seven Vagabonds," or such a novel as that which tells the story of the Pyncheons.

Thus, with Beauty haunting his path, "an hourly visitant," and all the intricacies of human character for subject, did Hawthorne shape himself, through the long years at Salem, and through the drudgeries of his Custom House post, into the ever-delightful artist he now appears to us,—an artist whose place grows larger and more certain as the days roll on, and, in the quiet of our after-judgment, he and the other great ones of his day rise to the honour which is duly theirs. "On the pure horizon far" we see his star shining beside its fellows, and we know it for one of those lights of poetry which live when other lights grow dim, let the years fleet as they may.

Forgive these too hasty thoughts. They are meant only as the dropping of a rose on your poet's grave—nothing more!

SELECTIVE BIBLIOGRAPHY

The "woman question" began coming sharply into focus with the publication of *The Scarlet Letter,* but it was a topic that Hawthorne had considered much earlier than 1850, the year his most celebrated romance appeared. He was weighing it, obviously, in "Mrs. Hutchinson" (1830) in which he digressed from his historical sketch of a rebelling freethinker among the Puritan settlers to comment, more than snidely, on women writers of his day, whom he called "ink-stained Amazons," fearing that their industrious pens would drive their male rivals from the literary field. But his concern was not solely commercial. How women fared in their relations as daughters, sweethearts, wives, and mothers caught his attention, perhaps nowhere more pointedly than in "The Birth-mark" and "Rappaccini's Daughter," both written after his marriage, the first appearing in 1843, the second in 1844. Here women are victims and suffer death because the men in their lives cannot accept them as they are. His presentation of Hester Prynne invited a more open discussion of the woman question, stirring a discussion that shows no sign of flagging even as the romance approaches a sesquicentennial celebration. Master of ambiguity that he is, Hawthorne is hard to pin down, appearing to some readers to present Hester as a challenge to patriarchal dominance, seeming to others to force Hester back into a role of domestic subservience. For a few critics, Hawthorne emerges as a champion of feminism while others see him as abiding by Victorian standards regarding the relations of men and women. Does he stand with his Hester and Zenobia, his Margaret Fuller–like advocate of women's rights in *The Blithedale Romance,* or with Priscilla of the same romance or Hilda of *The Marble Faun?* These questions have their sociopolitical ramifications and, as such, apply to society at large. They surely have relevance, also, to aspiring women writers, whether of Hawthorne's day or ours, for, as a revered master of fiction, Hawthorne assumed the role of mentor to an untold number of women who attempted to establish themselves as fiction writers.

The following selective bibliography offers both a means of tracing the debates that have gone on among Hawthorne readers regarding his take on the woman question and a jump-start to exploring how women writers responded to Hawthorne's mentoring. Our hope is that some scholar/critic will be stimulated to analyze and synthesize Hawthorne's reputation in the sociopolitical arena and his standing as a mentor to women writers.

Adams, Dena Wills. "Female Inheritors of Hawthorne's New England Literary Tradition." Diss. U of North Texas, 1994.

Baym, Nina. "Hawthorne's Women: The Tyranny of Social Myths." *Centennial Review* 15 (1971): 250–71.

——. "Nathaniel Hawthorne and His Mother: A Biographical Speculation." *American Literature* 54.1 (1982): 1–27.

——. "Thwarted Nature: Nathaniel Hawthorne as Feminist." *American Novelists Revisited: Essays in Feminist Criticism*. Ed. Fritz Fleischmann. Boston: Hall, 1982.

Blanchard, Paula. *Margaret Fuller: From Transcendentalism to Revolution*. New York: Delacorte, 1978.

Britton, Wesley. "The Puritan Past and Black Gothic: The Haunting of Toni Morrison's *Beloved* in Light of Hawthorne's *The House of the Seven Gables*." *Nathaniel Hawthorne Review* 21.2 (1995): 7–23.

Brown, Gillian. *Domestic Individualism: Imagining Self in Nineteenth-Century America*. Berkeley: U of California P, 1990.

Budick, Emily Miller. *Engendering Romance: Women Writers and the Hawthorne Tradition, 1850–1990*. New Haven: Yale UP, 1994.

——. "Hester's Skepticism, Hawthorne's Faith; or, What Does a Woman Doubt? Instituting the American Romance Tradition." *New Literary History* 22 (1991): 199–211.

Buell, Lawrence. *New England Literary Culture: From Revolution through Renaissance*. New York: Cambridge UP, 1986.

Cargill, Oscar. "Nemesis and Nathaniel Hawthorne." *PMLA* 52 (1937): 848–62.

Carton, Evan. "'A Daughter of Puritanism' and Her Old Master: Hawthorne, Una, and the Sexuality of Romance." *Daughters and Fathers*. Ed. Lynde Boose and Betty Flowers. Baltimore: Johns Hopkins UP, 1989.

——. "Paternal Guilt and Rebellious Daughters: Hawthorne, Una, and *The Marble Faun*." *Essex Institute Historical Collections* 125.1 (1989): 92–103.

Cary, Louis. "Margaret Fuller and Hawthorne's Zenobia: The Problem of Moral Accountability in Fictional Biography." *American Transcendental Quarterly* ns 4.1 (1990): 31–48.

Casson, Alan. "*The Scarlet Letter* and *Adam Bede*." *Victorian Newsletter* 20 (1961): 18–19.

Cather, Willa. "The Novel Demeuble." *Willa Cather on Writing*. New York: Knopf, 1949.

Coale, Samuel Chase. *In Hawthorne's Shadow: American Romance from Melville to Mailer*. Lexington: U of Kentucky P, 1985.

Conrad, Susan Phinney. *Perish the Thought: Intellectual Women in Romantic America, 1830–1860*. New York: Oxford UP, 1976.

Dahl, Curtis. "When the Deity Returns: *The Marble Faun* and *Romola*." *Studies in Honor of Robert Dunn Faner. Papers on Language and Literature* Supp. 2 (1969): 82–100.

Dauer, Dale M. *Feminist Dialogics: A Theory of Failed Community.* Albany: State U of New York P, 1988.

Delamotte, Eugenia C. *Perils of the Night: A Feminist Study of Nineteenth-Century Gothic.* New York: Oxford UP, 1990.

Desalvo, Louise. *Nathaniel Hawthorne.* Atlantic Highlands, N.J.: Humanities Press International, 1987.

Doubleday, Neal Frank. "Hawthorne's Hester and Feminism." *PMLA* 54 (1939): 825–28.

Eakin, Paul John. "Margaret Fuller, Hawthorne, James, and Sexual Politics." *South Atlantic Quarterly* 75 (1976): 323–38.

——. *The New England Girl: Cultural Ideals in Hawthorne, Stowe, Howells, and James.* Athens: U of Georgia P, 1976.

Elbert, Monica M. *Encoding the Letter "A": Gender and Authority in Hawthorne's Early Fiction.* Frankfurt am Main: Haig and Hershen, 1990.

Emerick, Ronald Rine. "Romance, Allegory, Vision: The Influence of Hawthorne on Fuller." Diss. U of Pittsburgh, 1975.

Erlich, Gloria. *Family Themes and Hawthorne's Fiction: The Tenacious Web.* New Brunswick, N.J.: Rutgers UP, 1984.

Fetterley, Judith. *The Resisting Reader: A Feminist Approach to American Literature.* Bloomington: Indiana UP, 1978.

Fleischner, Jennifer. "Female Eroticism, Confession, and Interpretation in Nathaniel Hawthorne." *Nineteenth-Century Fiction* 44.4 (1990): 514–33.

Fryer, Judith J. *The Faces of Eve: Women in the Nineteenth-Century American Novel.* New York: Oxford UP, 1976.

Fuller, Frederick T. "Hawthorne and Margaret Fuller Ossoli." *Literary World* 16 (1885): 11–15.

Gilbert, Katherine Elizabeth. "Nineteenth-Century Feminist: The Development of Hawthorne's Anti-Patriarchal Attitudes in His Life and Writings through 1850." Diss. U of South Carolina, 1996.

Gilbert, Sandra, and Susan Gubar. *The Madwoman in the Attic: The Woman Writer and the Nineteenth-Century Literary Imagination.* New Haven: Yale UP, 1979.

Gollin, Rita K. "Louisa May Alcott's 'Hawthorne.'" *Essex Institute Historical Collections* 118.1 (1982): 42–48.

Gura, Philip F. "Poe, Hawthorne, and One of the 'Scribbling Women.'" *Gettysburg Review* 6 (1993): 38–45.

Harris, Susan K. *19th-Century American Women's Novels: Interpretive Strategies.* New York: Cambridge UP, 1990.

Hawthorne, Julian. *Hawthorne and His Circle.* New York: Harper and Brothers, 1903.

——. *Nathaniel Hawthorne and His Wife.* Boston: Osgood, 1884.

——. "Such Is Paradise: The Story of Sophia and Nathaniel Hawthorne." *Century* 119 (1927): 157–69.

Hawthorne, Manning. "Nathaniel and Elizabeth Hawthorne, Editors." *Colophon* 3 (1939): 1–12.

Herbert, T. Walker, Jr. *Dearest Beloved: The Hawthornes and the Making of the Middle-Class Family.* Berkeley: U of California P, 1993.

———. "The Erotics of Purity: *The Marble Faun* and the Victorian Construction of Sexuality." *Representations* 36 (1991): 114–32.

———. "Nathaniel Hawthorne, Una Hawthorne, and *The Scarlet Letter:* Interactive Selfhoods and the Cultural Construct of Gender." *PMLA* 103.3 (1988): 285–97.

Herzog, Kristin. *Women, Ethnics, and Exotics: Images of Power in Nineteenth-Century American Fiction.* Knoxville: U of Tennessee P, 1983.

Houston, Neal Bryan. "Nathaniel Hawthorne and the Eternal Feminine." Diss. Texas Tech U, 1966.

Hurst, Nancy Luanne Jenkins. "Selected Literary Letters of Sophia Peabody Hawthorne." Diss. Ohio State U, 1992.

Jordan, Cynthia S. *Second Stories: The Politics of Language, Form, and Gender in Early American Fiction.* Chapel Hill: U of North Carolina P, 1989.

Kearns, Francis E. "Margaret Fuller as a Model for Hester Prynne." *Jahrbuch fur Amerikastudien* 10 (1965): 191–97.

Lenarcic, Faye Mertine. "The Emergence of the Passionate Woman in American Fiction." Diss. Syracuse U, 1985.

Leverenz, David. *Manhood and the American Renaissance.* Ithaca: Cornell UP, 1989.

———. "Mrs. Hawthorne's Headache: Reading *The Scarlet Letter.*" *Nineteenth-Century Fiction* 37.4 (1983): 552–75.

Lind, Sidney E. "Emily Dickinson's 'Further in Summer than the Birds' and Nathaniel Hawthorne's 'The Old Manse.'" *American Literature* 39 (1967): 163–69.

Lloyd-Smith, A. G. *Eve Tempted: Writing and Sexuality in Hawthorne's Fiction.* London: Croom Helm; Totowa, N.J.: Barnes and Noble, 1984.

Lombardi, Linda C. "Female Metaphysical Rebellion in the Works of George Eliot and Nathaniel Hawthorne." Diss. City U of New York, 1995.

MacMaster, Anne Cecilia. "Edith Wharton in the House of Hawthorne." Diss. U of Virginia, 1992.

McCall, Dan E. "'I Felt a Funeral in My Brain' and 'The Hollow of Three Hills.'" *New England Quarterly* 42 (1969): 432–35.

McKibben, Karan. "Hawthorne's Quarrel with Scribbling Women and Art." Diss. U of California, Riverside, 1985.

Marks, Margaret Louisa. "Flannery O'Connor's American Models: Her Work in Relation to that of Hawthorne, James, Faulkner, and West." Diss. Duke U, 1977.

Matheson, Terence J. "Feminism and Femininity in *The Blithedale Romance.*" *Nathaniel Hawthorne Journal* 1976.

Miller, Edwin Haviland. *Salem Is My Dwelling Place: A Life of Nathaniel Hawthorne.* Iowa City: U of Iowa P, 1991.

Mitchell, Thomas R. "Julian Hawthorne and the 'Scandal' of Margaret Fuller." *American Literary History* 7 (1995): 210–33.

———. "Veiling and Unveiling Hawthorne's Fuller Mystery." Diss. Texas A&M U, 1994.

Moore, Margaret B. "Elizabeth Manning Hawthorne: Nathaniel's Enigmatic Sister." *Nathaniel Hawthorne Review* 20 (1994): 1–9.

———. *The Salem World of Nathaniel Hawthorne.* Columbia: U of Missouri P, 1998.

Murphy, John J. "Willa Cather and Hawthorne: Significant Resemblances." *Renascence* 27 (1975): 161–75.

Norko, Julia M. "Hawthorne's Love Letters: The Threshold World of Sophia Peabody." *American Transcendental Quarterly* 7 (1993): 127–39.

Paglia, Camille. *Sexual Personae: Art and Decadence from Nefertiti to Emily Dickinson.* New York: Vintage, 1991.

Pearson, Norman Holmes. "Elizabeth Palmer Peabody on Hawthorne." *Essex Institute Historical Collections* 94 (1958): 256–76.

Person, Leland S., Jr. *Aesthetic Headaches: Women and a Masculine Poetics in Poe, Melville, and Hawthorne.* Athens: U of Georgia P, 1988.

——. "Hawthorne's Bliss of Paternity: Sophia's Absence from 'The Old Manse.'" *Studies in the Novel* 23.1 (1991): 46–59.

——. "Hawthorne's Love Letters: Writing and Relationships." *American Literature* 59.2 (1987): 211–27.

——. "Inscribing Paternity: Nathaniel Hawthorne as a Nineteenth-Century Father." *Studies in the American Renaissance.* Ed. Joel Myerson. Charlottesville: UP of Virginia, 1990.

Pfister, Joel. *The Production of Personal Life: Class, Gender, and the Psychological in Hawthorne's Fiction.* Stanford: Stanford UP, 1991.

Poelvoorde, Jeffrey J. "Women in the Novels of Nathaniel Hawthorne." *Interrelations: A Journal of Political Philosophy* 22 (1994): 65–89.

Pollock, Beth Ruby. "The Representation of Utopia: Hawthorne and the Female Medium." Diss. U of California, Berkeley, 1988.

Ponder, Melinda M. "Katharine Lee Bates: Hawthorne Critic and Scholar." *Nathaniel Hawthorne Review* 16.1 (1990): 6–11.

Prochnow, Herbert V. "Housekeeper to Genius." *Coronet* 27 (1949): 39.

Reynolds, David S. *Beneath the American Renaissance: The Subversive Imagination in the Age of Emerson and Melville.* New York: Knopf, 1988.

Ringler, Ellin J. "The Problem of Evil: A Correlative Study in the Novels of Nathaniel Hawthorne and George Eliot." Diss. U of Illinois, 1968.

Riss, Arthur. "The Figure a Person Makes: Racial Essentialism and the Liberal Aesthetics of Nathaniel Hawthorne and Harriet Beecher Stowe." Diss. U of California, Berkeley, 1994.

Roberts, Josephine R. "Sophia Hawthorne, Editor." *Saturday Review of Literature* 21 (1939): 9.

Rust, James D. "George Eliot and *The Blithedale Romance.*" *Boston Public Library Quarterly* 7 (1955): 207–15.

Scoville, Samuel, III. "The Domestic Motif in Hawthorne: A Study of the House, the Family, and the Home in Hawthorne's Works." Diss. Duke U, 1970.

See, Fred G. *Desire and Sign: Nineteenth-Century American Fiction.* Baton Rouge: Louisiana State UP, 1987.

Spitzer, Michael. "Hawthorne's Women: French Influences on the Life and Fiction of Nathaniel Hawthorne." Diss. New York U, 1974.

Stewart, Randall. "Editing the Notebooks: Selections from Mrs. Hawthorne's Letters to Mrs. Fields." *More Books* 20 (1945): 299–315.

——. "Mrs. Hawthorne's Quarrel with James T. Fields." *More Books* 21 (1946): 254–63.

——. "'Pestiferous Gail Hamilton,' James T. Fields, and the Hawthornes." *New England Quarterly* 17 (1944): 218–223.

Tharp, Louisa H. *The Peabody Sisters of Salem.* Boston: Little, Brown, 1950.

Tomc, Sandra M. " 'The Bombazine School': Feminine Writing in the Early 1850s Novels of Nathaniel Hawthorne and Harriet Beecher Stowe." Diss. U of Toronto, 1992.

Tompkins, Jane. *Sensational Designs: The Cultural Work of American Fiction, 1790–1860.* New York: Oxford UP, 1985.

Turner, Arlin. "A Note on Hawthorne's Revisions." *Modern Language Notes* 51 (1936): 416–29.

Valenti, Patricia Dunlavy. "Memories of Hawthorne: Rose Hawthorne Lathrop's Auto/Biography." *A-B AutoBiography Studies* 8 (1993): 1–15.

——. "Sophia Peabody Hawthorne: A Study of Artistic Influence." *Studies in the American Renaissance.* Ed. Joel Myerson. Charlottesville: UP of Virginia, 1990.

——. *To Myself a Stranger: A Biography of Rose Hawthorne Lathrop.* Baton Rouge: Louisiana State UP, 1991.

Waite, James J. "Nathaniel Hawthorne and the Feminism Ethos." *Journal of American Culture* 11.4 (1988): 23–33.

Walker, Nancy. "Of Hester and Offred." *The Disobedient Writer: Women and Narrative Tradition.* Austin: U of Texas P, 1995.

Wallace, James D. "Hawthorne and the Scribbling Women Reconsidered." *American Literature* 62 (1990): 201–22.

Wallace, Robert K. "A Probable Source for Dorothea and Casaubon: Hester and Chillingworth." *English Studies* 58 (1976): 23–25.

Walsh, Thomas F., Jr. "The Devils of Flannery O'Connor." *Xavier University Studies* 5 (1966): 117–22.

Warren, Austin. "Hawthorne, Margaret Fuller, and 'Nemesis.' " *PMLA* 54 (1939): 615–18.

Warren, Joyce W. *The American Narcissus: Individualism and Women in Nineteenth-Century Fiction.* New Brunswick, N.J.: Rutgers UP, 1984.

Wienk, Marilyn Dowd. "Hawthorne's Heroines and the Feminine Ideal: The Four Major Romances in the Context of Nineteenth-Century Women's Novels." Diss. State U of New York, Binghamton, 1989.

Woidet, Caroline M. "Talking Back to Schoolteacher: Morrison's Confrontation with Hawthorne in *Beloved.*" *Modern Fiction Studies* 39 (1993): 527–46.

CONTRIBUTORS

NINA BAYM, professor of English at the University of Illinois, is the author of many articles on Hawthorne, as well as *The Shape of Hawthorne's Career; The Scarlet Letter: A Reading;* and *Woman's Fiction: A Guide to Novels by and about Women in America, 1820–1870.*

CAROL MARIE BENSICK is the author of *La Nouvelle Beatrice: Renaissance and Romance in "Rappaccini's Daughter."*

MONIKA ELBERT, associate professor of English at Montclair State University is the author of *Encoding the Letter "A": Gender and Authority in Hawthorne's Early Fiction* and the associate editor of the *Nathaniel Hawthorne Review.*

JOHN GATTA is professor and head of the English department at the University of Connecticut. His essay on Hawthorne and Flannery O'Connor appeared originally in the *Nathaniel Hawthorne Review* and is reprinted here with permission.

RITA GOLLIN, distinguished Professor of English at State University College, Genesee, N.Y., is the author of *Nathaniel Hawthorne and the Truth of Dreams; Portraits of Nathaniel Hawthorne: An Iconography;* and many articles. She is the author with John L. Idol Jr. of *Prophetic Pictures: Nathaniel Hawthorne's Knowledge and Uses of the Visual Arts,* with the assistance of Sterling K. Eisiminger.

ELIZABETH GOODENOUGH, Visiting Professor of English at the University of Michigan, is coeditor of *Infant Tongues: The Voice of the Child in Literature*.

LUANNE JENKINS HURST, teacher of literature and composition at Clearwater Christian College, received her doctorate in English from Ohio State University, where she did a selected edition of Sophia Hawthorne letters for her dissertation.

JOHN L. IDOL JR., Alumni Professor Emeritus of English at Clemson University, is past editor of the *Nathaniel Hawthorne Review* and past president of the Hawthorne Society. He is the coauthor of *Prophetic Pictures: Nathaniel Hawthorne's Knowledge and Uses of the Visual Arts* and the compiler (with Buford Jones) of *Nathaniel Hawthorne: The Contemporary Reviews*.

CLAUDIA DURST JOHNSON, professor of English at the University of Alabama, is the author of *The Productive Tension in Hawthorne's Art* and compiler of *Understanding "The Scarlet Letter": A Student Casebook to Issues, Sources, and Historical Documents*. She serves as series editor for Greenwood Press's Literature in Context.

DAVID B. KESTERSON is professor of English at the University of North Texas. Cofounder of the Nathaniel Hawthorne Society and its first president, he served as editor of its newsletter. He also edited *Critical Essays on Hawthorne's "The Scarlet Letter."*

KAREN L. KILCUP is associate professor of American literature at the University of North Carolina at Greensboro. Editor of *Studies in American Humor,* she has numerous publications in nineteenth- and early-twentieth-century American literature. Her recent publications include " 'Ourself behind Ourself, Concealed—': The Homoerotics of Reading in *The Scarlet Letter*" and *Robert Frost and Feminine Literary Tradition* as well as *Nineteenth-Century American Women Writers: An Anthology* and *Nineteenth-Century American Women Writers: A Critical Reader*. Her forthcoming work includes the following collections: *Soft Canons: American Women Writers and the Masculine Tradition; Jewett and Her Contemporaries: Centennial Essays;* and *Early Native American Women Writers: An Anthology*.

DENISE D. KNIGHT is professor of American literature at the State University College of New York, Cortland. Her book publications include *Cotton Mather's Verse in English; The Yellow Wall-Paper and Selected Stories of Charlotte Perkins Gilman; The Diaries of Charlotte Perkins Gilman; The Later Poetry of Charlotte Perkins Gilman;* and *Charlotte Perkins Gilman: A Study of the Short Fiction*. Her articles have appeared in a variety of academic journals appropriate to American literature.

JANICE MILNER LASSETER is associate professor of English and department chair at Samford University. A specialist in nineteenth-century American literature, she is a member of the Hawthorne Society and a cofounder of the Hawthorne Discussion Circle at the South Atlantic Modern Language Association.

PATRICIA MARKS, professor of English at Valdosta State University, is the author of *Bicycles, Bangs, and Bloomers: The New Woman* and numerous articles. Her special interest is the novel in the Victorian era.

THOMAS R. MITCHELL is the author of *Hawthorne's Fuller Mystery*. His essays have appeared in *American Literary History, Studies in English Literature,* and *Studies in Short Fiction.* He is an associate professor at Texas A & M International University.

MARGARET B. MOORE, independent scholar, Athens, Ga., is the author of *The Salem World of Nathaniel Hawthorne.* She frequently presents papers on Hawthorne and other writers at professional conferences.

JOHN J. MURPHY, a teacher of American literature at Brigham Young University, edits the Willa Cather newsletter and serves on the editorial board of the *Willa Cather Scholarly Edition.* His recent *My Ántonia: The Road Home* is the only book-length study of that work. He edited *Critical Essays on Willa Cather* and *Willa Cather: Family, Community, and History.*

FRANNY NUDELMAN is assistant professor of English at the University of Virginia. She has published articles on Nathaniel Hawthorne, Harriet Jacobs, and Oprah Winfrey and is currently writing a book on violence, martyrdom, and Civil War culture.

MELISSA M. PENNELL, associate professor of English at the University of Massachusetts, Lowell, contributed an essay on Gertrude Atherton's "The Foghorn" to *Images of Persephone: Feminist Readings in Western Literature.*

MELINDA M. PONDER, associate professor of English and coordinator of women studies at Pine Manor College, has published on Hawthorne in the *Essex Institute Historical Collections,* on Katharine Lee Bates and Hawthorne in the *Nathaniel Hawthorne Review,* and is the author of *Hawthorne's Early Narrative Art.* She is currently at work on a literary biography of Bates.

GAYLE L. SMITH is associate professor of English, Pennsylvania State University at Washington Scranton. Her published pieces include studies of Emerson, Melville, and Whitman as well as others on Hawthorne and Jewett. Currently she is working on an interdisciplinary study involving nineteenth-century painting and literature.

PATRICIA D. VALENTI, associate professor of English at Pembroke State University, is a frequent contributor to the *Nathaniel Hawthorne Review* and the author of *To Myself a Stranger: A Biography of Rose Hawthorne Lathrop.* She is working presently on a biography of Sophia Peabody Hawthorne.

JAMES D. WALLACE, associate professor of English at Boston College, is the author of *Early Cooper and His Audience* and a number of articles on Cooper, Hawthorne, Louisa May Alcott, and other American writers.

INDEX